TRANSOCEANIC STUDIES
Ileana Rodríguez, Series Editor

For my poto mitan—
my maternal grandmother Ursula Hérard Scharoun,
my mother Denise Acacia Jean-Charles

and in loving memory of my paternal grandmother Anna Joseph Jean-Charles (1918–2007)

Conflict Bodies

The Politics of Rape Representation in the Francophone Imaginary

RÉGINE MICHELLE JEAN-CHARLES

THE OHIO STATE UNIVERSITY PRESS
COLUMBUS

Copyright © 2014 by The Ohio State University.
All rights reserved.

Library of Congress Cataloging-in-Publication Data
Jean-Charles, Régine Michelle.
Conflict bodies : the politics of rape representation in the francophone imaginary / Régine Michelle Jean-Charles.
   p. cm. — (Transoceanic studies)
Includes bibliographical references and index.
ISBN 978-0-8142-1246-2 (cloth : alk. paper) — ISBN 0-8142-1246-8 (cloth : alk. paper) — ISBN 978-0-8142-9349-2 (cd-rom) — ISBN 0-8142-9349-2 (cd-rom)
1. French literature—Foreign countries—History and criticism. 2. Rape in literature. 3. Violence in literature. 4. Politics and literature. 5. Haitian literature—History and criticism. 6. Guadeloupe literature (French)—History and criticism. 7. Rwandan literature (French)—History and criticism. 8. Congolese (Democratic Republic) literature (French)—History and criticism. I. Title. II. Series: Transoceanic studies.

PQ3809.J43 2014
843'.9099729—dc23
                    2013025855

Cover design by Janna Thompson-Chordas
Type set in Adobe Palatino

∞ The paper used in this publication meets the minimum requirements of the American National Standard for Information Sciences—Permanence of Paper for Printed Library Materials. ANSI Z39–1992.

9 8 7 6 5 4 3 2 1

CONTENTS

List of Illustrations — vii
Acknowledgments — ix

INTRODUCTION Can the Subaltern Survivor Speak? The Global Politics of Rape Discourses — 1

CHAPTER 1 "Bound to Violence?" A History of the Rape Trope in Francophone Studies — 17

CHAPTER 2 Rethinking Political Rape: Genealogies of Sexual Violence in Haiti — 57

CHAPTER 3 Islands Unbound: Beyond the Rape of the Land — 101

CHAPTER 4 Beneath Layers of Violence: Images of Rape and the Rwandan Genocide — 145

CHAPTER 5 Regarding the Pain of Congolese Women: Narrative Closure, Audience Affect, and Rape as a Tool of War — 205

EPILOGUE Not Just (Any) Body Can Be a Global Citizen: Rape and Human Rights Advocacy in the Twenty-First Century — 261

Notes — 273
Bibliography — 296
Index — 307

The abundance of real suffering tolerates no forgetting. This suffering demands the continued existence of art even as it prohibits it. It is now virtually in art alone that suffering can find its own voice, consolation, without immediately being betrayed by it.

—Theodor Adorno

ILLUSTRATIONS

FIGURE 1   Congolese women protesting. Photo credit: Gwenn Dubourthoumieu/AFP/Getty Images   4

FIGURE 2   *Little Crippled Haiti.* Photo credit: Edouard Duval-Carrié   105

FIGURE 3   "Dans une prison au Rwanda, Yolande Mukagasana, survivante du génocide, est devant Patrice qui avoue avoir tué cent personnes." Photo credit: Alain Kazinierakis, *Les blessures du silence*   183

FIGURE 4   Eugénie N from *Les blessures du silence.* Photo credit: Alain Kazinierakis, *Les blessures du silence*   190

FIGURE 5   Clémence and Agnès from *Les blessures du silence.* Photo credit: Alain Kazinierakis, *Les blessures du silence*   198

FIGURE 6   Victoire M. from *Les blessures du silence.* 37 ans, survivante du genocide au Rwanda. Bernadette N. 59 ans. Photo credit: Alain Kazinierakis, *Les blessures du silence*   199

FIGURE 7   *Ruined,* Josephine (Zainab Jah) dancing for soldiers. Photo credit: Kevin Berne/*Ruined,* La Jolla Playhouse   222

FIGURE 8   *Ruined,* Mama Nadi and Sophie (Tonye Patano and Carla Duren). Photo credit: Kevin Berne/*Ruined,* La Jolla Playhouse   226

FIGURE 9	*Ruined*, Salima's death. Photo credit: Kevin Berne/*Ruined*, La Jolla Playhouse	229
FIGURE 10	Les recluses in Greek chorus. Photo credit: Danièle Pierre, *Les recluses*, Théâtre Varia	233
FIGURE 11	Les recluses masked. Photo credit: Danièle Pierre, *Les recluses*, Théâtre Varia	235
FIGURE 12	*Les recluses,* projected images. Photo credit: Danièle Pierre, *Les recluses*, Théâtre Varia	243
FIGURE 13	Berrlyze attending school. Photo credit: Sherrlyn Borkgren, *Berrlyze's Story*	248
FIGURE 14	Girls fetching water. Photo credit: Sherrlyn Borkgren, *Berrlyze's Story*	249
FIGURE 15	A young rape survivor and her father weave through the local market in the DRC. Photo credit: Sherrlyn Borkgren, *Berrlyze's Story*	250

ACKNOWLEDGMENTS

THIS BOOK is first and foremost a product of God's grace. It is an important part of my prolonged meditation on how to " . . . remember those who are suffering, as though you yourselves were suffering" (Hebrews 13:3). Many have said that it takes a village for a book to be researched, written and published. I am blessed to have a vast village that spans cities, countries, and continents. It is a village made up of family, academic, cultural, intellectual, and spiritual relationships that feed, sustain and grow me—I am filled with gratitude for the provision of these different villages.

I began working on this project as a graduate student in the Department of Romance Languages and Literatures at Harvard University. I am so grateful to the members of my dissertation committee: Alice Jardine, Abiola Irele, and Odile Cazenave. Alice always pushed me to boldly claim my feminist space and the stakes of my intervention. Abiola came to Harvard at a key moment when those of us specializing in francophone literatures were in need of his intellectual breadth. Odile is a generous soul who continues to provide guidance as a literary critic, dynamic teacher, and example of commitment to the field. When I first began delve into the vast topic of violence Mary Beth Clack showed me how indispensible thorough and thoughtful librarians are. I am also grateful to Tom and Verena Conley who provided me with a village in Kirkland House where I benefited from their support both professionally and personally. When we formed Black Graduate Ministries (BGM) during my last year on campus it became another village, rooted in faith, that helped to usher me out of Harvard. Through BGM I was blessed to meet future lifelong friends in Ben and Lilly Piper.

I am incredibly thankful to many professors, mentors, and administrators at the University of Pennsylvania where I began my journey into the academy. I was first encouraged to become a scholar by Herman Beavers, Valarie Swain-Cade McCoullum, Pat Ravenell, and the late Susan Peterson-Pace under the auspices of the Mellon-Mays Mentoring Program. Lydie Moudileno brought me into the exciting field of francophone studies. By introducing me to black feminist theories, my mentor Farah Jasmine Griffin left an indelible mark that I will always cherish; it is from dear Dr. Farah that I first learned the importance of being an academic who engages both head and heart.

I am thankful to the Carter G. Woodson Institute for African and African American Studies at the University of Virginia where I had the privilege of being a postdoctoral fellow. At U. Va. Deborah McDowell offered important counsel at a critical moment in my career. Luann Williams, Robert Fatton and Cynthia Hoehler-Fatton made Charlottesville feel like home.

At Boston College this project transformed and matured significantly, and I am so grateful for my colleagues and friends who have been instrumental in the process. I was warmly welcomed into the Department of Romance Languages and Literatures where I learned the meaning of collegiality. I am especially grateful to Sarah Beckjord, Matilda Bruckner, Ourida Mostefai, Elisa Rhodes, and Laurie Shepard for their guidance and support. Ourida's commitment to junior faculty mentoring has benefited me tremendously over the years. I am also grateful to Franco Mormando, who served as chair when I was in the final stages of the book. Kevin Newmark has gone beyond the call of duty as a reliable mentor who is incredibly generous with time and resources. Many thanks to David Quigley and Larry McLaughlin, who provided financial support through generous subvention grants. Thank you so much to Larry Busenbark from BC's library who was always available (and incredibly quick!) to help with my research related inquires. I am especially thankful to Pat de Leeuw for her wisdom and support over the years.

I cannot say enough about the African and African Diaspora Studies Program: Shawn Copeland, Rhonda Frederick, Shawn McGuffey, Martin Summers, and Cynthia Young. It is an honor to be on this team of amazing thinkers. Cyn has taught me so much about navigating the academy, from her rigorous work ethic to her dazzling strategic mind. Rhonda is the perfect combination of senior colleague, beloved friend, attentive mentor, and big sister. Martin Summers's quiet brilliance, constant thoughtfulness, and wise counsel have meant so much to me. Shawn McGuffey has been a valuable interlocutor who understands what it means to work on sexual violence as not merely research, but as a deeper calling. I am also thankful to Zine Magubane, who was always available to discuss anything ranging from African feminisms to popular culture. I am grateful to my students at BC who have endured my lectures and ruminations on this difficult topic with curiosity and patience. Thank you to the students in my Black Feminisms and *Femmes francophones* classes for reminding me that cultivating a feminist classroom is an important part of eradicating a rape culture. Didem Alkan deserves special thanks for volunteering to proofread passages of the manuscript, as does my mentee Crystal Philippeaux, whose excitement about the project and concern for my wellbeing always warmed my heart.

I owe an intellectual debt and infinite gratitude to my magnificent writing group, the New England Black Scholars Collective: Aliyyah Abdur-Rahman, Sandy Alexandre, Nicole Aljoe, Alisa Braithwaite, Soyica Colbert, Stéphanie Larrieux, Monica Ndounou, and Sam Vasquez. NEBSC contributed enormously to my writing and thinking; this book bears their imprint in more ways than one. *Mesi anpil* to my *fanmi* in the Haitian Studies Association: Claudine Michel, Fabienne Doucet, Charlene Désir, Kyrah Daniels, Gina Ulysse, Marc Prou, Patrick Bellegarde-Smith, Nadège Clitandre, Mark Schuller, Carolle Charles, and others whose assiduous commitment to creating counter-discourses that embrace Haiti's complexity teach me and inspire me. Thank you to Charles Rowell for pulling me into the *Callaloo* collective, another dynamic village of scholars and creative writers that I am blessed to be a part of.

Research on this book could not have been completed without the prodigious financial and institutional support of several entities: I am thankful for the Mellon-Mays Undergraduate Fellowship, the Ford Foundation Predoctoral Fellowship, the Woodrow Wilson Foundation Junior Faculty Career Enhancement Fellowship. Throughout my time as a graduate student and as an assistant professor both MMUF and Ford provided a network of scholars who combine critical acumen with warmth and generosity—inclusion in this virtual village is an incredible gift that feeds my mind and spirit. During my junior faculty fellowship year, the Africana

Studies Department at Brown University offered intellectual camaraderie. I am so thankful to have had Carine Mardorossian as my Woodrow Wilson mentor; she read the first draft of my manuscript with painstaking care, and provided significant feedback that helped to make it more ambitious and rigorous.

At The Ohio State University Press, I am incredibly thankful to Sandy Crooms, whose interest in the project was enthusiastic even in the early stages. Many thanks to the anonymous reviewers whose suggestions brought important insight to my arguments. I am so thankful to my diligent editor Eugene O'Connor, to Kathryn Gucer for copyedits, and to Martin Boyne for help with the index.

In my village there are best friends, sisters, brothers, aunties, uncles, cousins, and co-mères who make me better. I am humbled that God has blessed me with my sisters in the spirit—Lilly Piper, Jody Rose and Valencia Miller. Lilly is the ultimate example of letting your light so brilliantly shine. Jody and Valencia faithfully prayed for every word, page, and chapter at each stage from proposal to proofs. The encouragement and unconditional friendship of these remarkable and prayerful women builds me up in more ways than I can count. I am thankful for my UPENN friends Traci Curry, Kaji Dousa, Carrie-Ann Pierce, Khalilah Lawson, Serena Poole, and Jasmine Sykes-Kunk who always cheered me on as I matured from a college student to PhD candidate and professor. Nicole Pritchard's sweet support in the form of baked goods, messages, and long chats pushed me through. My *co-mère/co-madre* Alex Mauristhene shared her heart, wit, and family with me. Both she and *frè mwen* Ernest Mauristhene were particularly helpful with childcare and pick up when I needed the time to write. I am thankful to Vanessa Perez-Rosario, my book completion buddy, for being a source of daily encouragement and camaraderie in the home stretch. Thank you to my Life Church family fanning my gifts into flame, understanding my heart, and encouraging me to ask God what my role is in ending a rape culture. I am so thankful for the gift that is Salamishah Tillet, who is without doubt the godmother of this book, not to mention a feminist scholar, sister, and activist of my dreams. My co-blogger and intellectual twin sister Nadève Ménard is a creative thinker and phenomenal person with whom I am honored to collaborate—thank you, Na, for your translation help and hard questions. I am fortunate to be a part of the A Long Walk Home family, a group of energetic and engaged people from board members, Girl/Friends youth leaders and staff, these people put the move in movement! I am especially thankful for our exquisitely visionary leader Scheherazade Tillet who lives to be the change that she wants to see in the world. Her art, activism, and passion are reflected in these pages. Sher and Salamishah sparked my determination to write a book about sexual violence. I am thankful to them and to all the survivors who have disclosed to me—not only those I have worked with over the years but also family, friends and students whose stories have helped me to actively question the binary between theory and practice. Rape survivors, and their stories constantly motivate me to go back and take up Barbara Christian's important question, "For whom are we doing what we are doing when we do literary criticism?" This book is for them too.

For providing me with constant love and encouragement, I am eternally grateful to my family, especially my parents, Roger and Denise Jean-Charles, and my *très chères soeurs* Ronise, Nadine and Melissa for their unwavering confidence in me and in my work. My many wonderful nieces and nephews have provided me with love and energy along the way since my first year of college. I am also thankful for all of my aunts, uncles, and cousins in the US, Belgium, and Haiti, especially Shasha, Tatie Marlene, and Tante Nicole. Three cousins in particular—Danielle Wells, Mirtha Lovius, and Géraldine Ainé—have been steadfast in their support and friendship. Through the Asare family I have received another set of parents, brothers, and sisters. I am thankful to Seth and Dorothy Asare for their unyielding prayers. Abena, Amma, Solomon, Amir, and Kerim—my bonus brothers and sisters to whom I am thankful for friendship and babysitting as well as razor sharp minds that keep me on my toes.

I am so grateful for my precious children Bediako Dessalines and Kwaku Toussaint, whose drumming, laughter, singing, hugs, questions, and kisses have filled my days with an unexpected joy. Dessalines learned to read while this book was being written and sweetly informed me of his plans to read it. Toussaint burst into the room where I was working one night just to thank me for "all I do," at the exact moment when I was struggling through a difficult chapter. Every day my sons refine my character, affirm my calling, show me God's face, and renew my hope.

Most of all thank you to my perfect husband, Ohene Kwaku Asare. You embody what Morrison describes in *Beloved:* "a friend of my mind . . . the pieces I am [you] gather them and give them back to me in all the right order." For interrogating my sentences, wiping my tears, celebrating my successes, being a true partner, reminding me to have faith in the face of failure, making my late nights hilarious, loving me lavishly, building me up, pushing me to do better, living life with faith, passion, grace and joy, manifesting agape: your love lifts me. Your emotional, physical, and spiritual presence in my life makes each day better.

PARTS OF chapters 2, 3 and 4 are partial revisions of earlier publications. I am grateful to the publishers for permission to reprint.

"'They Never Call it Rape:' Critical Reception and Representation of Sexual Violence in Marie Vieux-Chauvet's Colère," *The Journal of Haitian Studies* 12.2 (Fall 2006): 114–21.

"Terre et chair: Rape, Land, and the Body in Gisèle Pineau's *Macadam Dreams*," *Reclaiming Home, Remembering Motherhood, Rewriting History: African American and Afro-Caribbean Women's Literature in the Twentieth Century*, edited by Marie Drews and Verena Theile. Cambridge: Cambridge Scholars Press, 2009. 29–50.

"Beneath the Layers of Violence: Images of Rape in the Rwandan Genocide," *Local Violence, Global Media: Feminist Analyses of Gendered Representations*, edited by Lisa Cuklanz. New York: Peter Lang, 2009. 246–66.

INTRODUCTION

Can the Subaltern Survivor Speak?
The Global Politics of Rape Discourses

> On the basis of the un-gathered evidence of millions of women all over the continent . . . African women have not been passive recipients of abuse, as some authorities would have us believe. The evidence that is available suggests that they have found numerous ways of resisting the humiliations meted out to them, both individually and with the help of sympathetic friends and relatives.
> —Amina Mama[1]

> Feminist modes of 'reading' rape and its cultural inscriptions help identify and demystify the multiple manifestations, displacements, and transformations of what amounts to an insidious cultural myth. In the process, they show how feminist critique can challenge the representations that continue to hurt women.
> —Lynn Higgins and Brenda Silver[2]

ON OCTOBER 17, 2010, thousands of women in the Democratic Republic of the Congo (DRC) protested the mass rapes of women that have been going on for more than a decade in the eastern region.[3] The systematic use of rape has been a feature of the war since it began in 1996 and continues today at alarming rates.[4] Having just ended a week-long forum on peace, gender and development in the DRC, women marched, carrying signs with titles such as "Say no to sexual terrorism."[5] Together, these women, decrying the daily battles waged on Congolese women's bodies, having had enough of being caught in a war in which female bodies have been the enduring spoils, demanded international attention and outcry for their cause. The women sang and protested, marching through the streets of Bukavu, the capital of the south Kivu province.[6] Several thousand strong, they marched from Kadutu, Ibanda and Bagira, the three communes of the town, to converge at the Independence Square, intoning songs of protest—"we will continue marching as long as all women are not free."[7]

This protest scene demonstrates the central thesis of this book, that examining the way the so-called "subaltern speaks" about rape reveals narratives that destabilize key ideologies of violence and provides new frameworks for understanding sexual violence in a global age.[8] Put differently, foregrounding survivor narratives of rape that call into question the established dialectic of struggle between the colonizer and the colonized will yield new and necessary theorizations of violence that are more complex and complete than are previous ideologies. Looking at texts from Haiti, Guadeloupe, Rwanda and the Democratic Republic of the Congo, *Conflict Bodies: The Politics of Rape Representation in the Francophone Imaginary* examines novels, human rights reports, films, photography, documentaries, and drama that rework and re-imagine the way rape representations and rhetoric figure in epistemologies of violence. In bringing together this diverse body of texts and contexts, this inquiry stands to intervene in and unite several fields: francophone studies, transnational global feminisms, and rape cultural criticism. Understanding that conflict disproportionately affects women and girls, this book focuses attention on the ways the bodies, minds, lives, and experiences of women and girls are represented through different forms of cultural expression.

Reading such a contemporary manifestation of anti-rape activism as the example above, one is struck by the symbolic use of well-known ideas that circulate in today's climate of globalization—terrorism, freedom, human rights—each in the gendered, sexed, and politicized context of rape. Talk of terrorism, freedom, and human rights enters into the global imaginary by invoking the discursive and rhetorical frameworks surrounding sexual violence, and it requires close attention. The strategic deployment of the word "terrorism" signals the inaction of the international community in the face of issues that have received greater global attention, interest, activism, and policy.[9] The logic behind its use highlights the extreme nature of the violence against women, as well as the comparable lassitude about sexual violence given the post-9/11 "War on Terror," whose parameters do not include sexual terrorism. Allusions to terrorism in relation to sexual violence implicitly refer to and indict what has been left out of the "War on Terror," which, as feminist critics have observed, "is produced, constructed, and waged on highly gendered terrain."[10] In this way, the use of sexual terrorism displays the shortcomings of U.S.-dominated understandings of terrorism in the post-9/11 moment, calling our attention to raced, sexed, gendered, and Third World positionalities.

Similarly, what is sometimes lost in the cacophony of terrorism discourses is a stripped down idea of what constitutes human rights. The platitudinous chorus that women's rights are human rights often fails to account for the ways in which *black bodies* are configured, objectified, and emptied of their subjectivities in these rhetorically structured frames. These women's demonstration reminds us that a better understanding of human rights goes beyond the mere equivalence with women's rights to include attention to multiple locations, subjectivities, agency, and activism in relation to the violence that they are continually subject to *in both conflict and peacetime*. Global iterations of black feminism are uniquely positioned to interrogate the way human rights frameworks operate in the production of black female bodies that occupy the multiple locations as postcolonial subjects from Africa and the diaspora. This approach provides a critical methodology for understanding the way subjugated bodies self-assign meaning rather than always being caught in a field in which meaning is assigned to them. As a black feminist critic, I am especially interested in mapping out ways to view violence differently by focusing on rape and parsing out the multiplicities and duplicities of what representations of sexual violence could be telling us.

Finally, the evocation of "freedom," through the lyrics "we will continue marching [until] all women are free" is another important gesture that can be framed in the larger context of postcolonial independence Africa. The convocation on Independence Square doubly recalls continental freedom struggles of the past. We can understand this protest as one proclaiming the futility of independence while women's bodies remain yoked to repeated acts of violence. By inserting the end of violence against women as essential to freedom, they recast the notion put forth by the Ghanaian leader and Pan-African visionary Kwame Nkrumah, who stated during decolonization, "independence is meaningless unless it is linked up with the total liberation of the African continent."[11] National liberation that maintains the domination of women is futile, an example of what Edouard Glissant would call an *incomplete resistance*. Again, these Congolese women recast our understanding of African liberation by affirming that people cannot be free until women's bodies are not forced to endure intimate violence, whether by partners, family members, soldiers, or actors of the state. This

Figure 1. Congolese women protesting by Gwenn Dubourthoumieu/AFP/Getty Images

suggests that even when the armed conflict of what has been called "Africa's world war" ends, for freedom to be achieved, the quotidian forms of violence against women that take place in peacetime must also be put to an end.

This cry for freedom should be understood as a new variation on former movements against colonialism, apartheid, and neo-imperialism that have taken place throughout the region and on the entire continent. An anti-rape movement across parts of the eastern Congo offers a new type of space in which women decry and denounce the transformation of their bodies into battlegrounds. It is a protest narrative that positions African women as advocates, survivors, and agitators rather than only as victims and vessels of violation. These women deploy traditional protest methods and mobilize universally recognized political language to marshal support for their efforts to create a gender-specific antiviolence movement. The promise of the march and the breadth of these women's voices was one that had not yet been heard on such a large scale prior to this moment with regard to this particular conflict. These were not the passive female victims who had been subject to countless violations in "Africa's World War." These were not submissive receptacles of violence, left for dead on the side of the road. These were not brutalized and victimized women in need of a Western vehicle to make their voices audible. These were not abused and forgotten women trapped in the rape capital of the world. Yet while their activism contends with U.S. (neo-imperial) and Western (colonial) ideas about African women's subjugation, it also challenges the teleological construction of victims and survivors that characterizes the field of anti-rape advocacy.[12] These protesting women are a striking reminder of anthropologist Amina Mama's point of caution that "on the basis of the un-gathered evidence of millions of women all over the continent . . . African women have not been passive recipients of abuse, as some authorities would have us believe. The evidence that is available suggests that they have found numerous ways of resisting the humiliations meted out to them, both individually and with the help of sympathetic friends and relatives."[13] Demonstrating Mama's observation, this anti-rape protest locates Congolese women as acting subjects (rather than raped objects) who are central to the way we understand and analyze violence in the Congo.

In *Conflict Bodies*, I bring together diverse and (in most cases) underexplored forms of francophone cultural productions of rape representation to argue that not only does the "subaltern" "speak" about sexual violence, but that in so doing she participates in international dialogues about human rights, and she contributes to the construction of new circuits of power through discourses that are national and transnational, allegorical and material, colonial and post-independence. By opening with the example of Congolese women protesting against the widespread violation and pillaging of women's bodies in a country deemed "conflict zone," I begin the work of purposefully shifting the way we understand the discursive dynamics and politics of rape representation in Africa and the Caribbean. Throughout this study, rape victim-survivors become the focus of violence as subjects rather than as objects. They are active subjects ready to "call it rape," explicitly naming their experiences. Due to the recurring instantiation of violence as gendered, the body is an established site onto which histories of violence can be mapped. One of my central preoccupations is with the toll that rape takes on the body, both physically/materially and emotionally. How can these bodies develop into more than passive receptacles of violence and emerge as agents of discourse and transformation?[14]

Conflict Bodies intervenes in three areas that require attention and conjunction. The first is *francophone studies*, a field that is being revised, especially in the past several years since the appearance of the *Manifeste du 44: Pour une littérature francophone mondiale*. In this document, forty-four signatories, including Maryse Condé, Édouard Glissant, Koffi Kwahulé, and Gisèle Pineau (the latter two are writers featured in this study), declare, "la fin de la francophonie. Et naissance d'une littérature-monde en français [the end of *francophonie* and the beginning of world literatures written in French]."[15] Arguing that "le centre, n'est plus le centre [the center is no longer the center]," they announce a forthright cultural dismantling of the previously incontestable hold of the French empire over the world of arts and letters. In the *Manifeste*, described by scholars such as Kaiama Glover as "a controversial text, which has sustained at once vociferous praise and virulent condemnation," the authors demand a rejection of the francophone label and a revision of the field.[16] To them, "world literatures in French" offers a more complete, less imperial, and more nuanced descriptor better aligned with publication and production trends.

Their incisive intervention posits another direction for the widely interrogated, somewhat derided, and constantly reformulated label of "francophone studies." Take for example, Charles Forsdick's point in *Francophone Postcolonial Studies* that, "Use of the epithet—in phrases such as *littérature francophone* . . . referring to all literature written in French except that produced in France itself—suggests a neocolonial segregation and hierarchization of cultures that perpetuates the binary divides on which . . . colonialism depended on for its expansion and consolidation."[17] The problematic nature of the term *francophone*, and its even more troubling neo-imperial valences, inclines scholars of the field towards deeper reflection on the rubric itself. Indeed, as Forsdick reminds us, "the term francophone is in itself highly problematic, as it is used interchangeably in so many contexts—political, linguistic, cultural—that its precise meaning is unclear and elusive for many."[18] For this reason, the *Manifeste* appeals to me on a conceptual level, because it helps to foreground what Deborah Jenson calls "the transnational nature of *francophonie.*"[19]

Although this moment inaugurated by the *Manifeste* was largely symbolic, it should signal a difference in approaches to scholarship in francophone studies. By this, I mean that the *Manifeste* provides an opportunity to shift the way we understand the field not only in relation to the hexagon, but as a deeply dialogic and comparative field whose relationship to other areas of inquiry, both epistemological and geographic, should also be explored. By placing these texts in an interdisciplinary and multilingual conversation, *Conflict Bodies* begins to do this kind of work that challenges the boundaries of the field. As such, my work is in dialogue with and owes an intellectual debt to scholars working on francophone women writers from a feminist perspective, such as Françoise Lionnet, Renée Larrier, Tracey Sharpley-Whiting, and Omise'eke Natasha Tinsley among others.

The second main area of intervention is *transnational global feminisms*, a field that is dominated by Anglophone feminists working in South Asia and the Arab world, with less focus on Africa and the diaspora. As Inderpal Grewal and Caren Kaplan use the term, it "requires a feminist analysis that refuses to choose among economic, cultural and political concerns and foregrounds critical practices that link our understanding of postmodernity, global economic structures, problematics of nationalism, issues of race and imperialism, critiques of global feminism, and emergent patriarchies."[20] Transnational global feminist epistemologies are in constant negotiation of the local and the global, and foreground the interimbrication of race, gender, sexuality, nation, and ethnicity while maintaining and probing productive tensions among all of these. This project stages such an encounter by articulating some of the linkages between the representation of rape in both sovereign and non-sovereign spaces. Transnational feminist theory and praxis are essential for thinking about rape and representation because it provides "new ways to understand the prominent and often paradoxical nature of the claim of women's rights as human rights."[21] I am especially interested in exploring the implications of this theoretical model for women of Africa and the diaspora. To this end, my study builds on the work of black feminist thinkers such as Carole Boyce-Davies, Jacqui Alexander, and Patricia Hill-Collins. Black feminist epistemologies of standpoint theory are particularly helpful. Originally formulated by feminist philosopher Nancy Harstock, standpoint theory provides a Hegelian- and Marxist-based method for processing the truth claims of feminism. Expanding this framework, black feminists such as Collins subsequently used "the phrase 'Black women's standpoint' to emphasize the plurality of experiences within the overarching term 'standpoint,'" opening up a space for engaging representations from black women's points of view based on their multiple locations.[22] Though standpoint theory was a staple of second-wave feminist thought, it fell from prominence in the late nineties, and its significance has declined. I argue for renewed deployment of these methodological and epistemological arguments because, for the purposes of this study (which privileges victim-survivor subjectivity), standpoint theory lays the foundation for understanding how alternative perspectives on sexual violence broaden the contours of representations and analyses of colonial and postcolonial violence. Any analysis of sexual violence, in particular, demands an optic that acknowledges "that knowledge is situated and perspectival and that there are multiple standpoints from which knowledge is produced."[23] The texts gathered here call for an analysis such as this one because, as Aaronette White explains, "black feminist standpoint epistemology encompasses theoretical interpretations of black women's reality by those who live it."[24] Standpoint theory fundamentally provides an approach that processes knowledge from the perspective of marginalized groups and an understanding that this knowledge is nonetheless situated, alongside the recognition that this perspective makes a larger number of relations visible. I also hold that feminist standpoint theory, in its critique of relationships between power, material experience, and epistemology, as well as in its excavation of the effects of power relations on the production of knowledge, is an important precursor to transnational global feminisms.

Third, I intervene in the field of *rape cultural criticism*, an area of inquiry that has emerged in cultural studies over the past two decades but that has made only slight forays into analyzing sexual violence in Africa and the Caribbean.[25] Rape cultural criticism is concerned with the way the images, narratives, and rhetoric surrounding rape are historically, politically and socially informed. Because "the subject of rape and representation troubles the boundaries between literature, politics, law, popular culture, film studies and feminism," it helps weave a thread through multiple problematics.[26] At the same time, many of these analyses attempt to "disentangle the act of rape from the larger connotative web within which it operates."[27] I build on this approach, using black feminist and postcolonial theories and drawing from the area of rape crisis advocacy to interpret narrative logic, formal techniques, and rhetorical strategies deployed in stories and scenes of sexual violence. Examining violence in the postcolonial context means considering colonialism, slavery, war, dictatorship, genocide, and other types of conflict that have been waged in Africa and the diaspora. Thus, this book uses a comparative framework to traverse several contexts—from Haiti to the Democratic Republic of the Congo— and it travels through different types of texts: documentaries, novels, film, photography, and drama. Though the title of this manuscript is attendant to the way rape occurs in "conflict zones," it emphasizes *bodies* as operational material and psychological sites of conflict in order to acknowledge the way sexual violence occurs at astronomical rates in peacetime, as well as wartime. Put another way, the title *Conflict Bodies* foregrounds the way rape operates in quotidian life both inside and outside of conflict zones. Combining these three fields means opening space for a francophone iteration of transnational global black feminisms that is both multigenre and interdisciplinary.

My view is that (1) there is a dominant representation of violence in francophone studies in which rape is restricted or ignored and (2) rape is a generally undertheorized subject of critical inquiry.[28] What results from this is a script of violence, which (I argue) generates epistemic violence that both conscripts those who are subject to violence and restricts those who theorize violence. The phrase *script of violence* is a summation of the ways narratives of violence are culturally produced and socially informed and the ways they ascribe to dominant patterns. In reading the dominant narratives of violence from francophone cultural production and theory, my project illuminates the epistemic violence of colonialism and postcolonialism. One of my primary goals is to posit a counterdiscourse to theories of violence by beginning with rape representation. Rather than making only symbolic use of sexual violence, this counterdiscourse (1) foregrounds both the act of rape and what I refer to as its *paratext* (the context through which we understand rape and the other narrative, thematic or rhetorical signs that surround it) and (2) pays strict attention to the way violence is gendered and (3) privileges embodied subjectivity (female and male) as a mode for processing the occurrence of violence. Throughout, I formulate a system through which we can better understand the way the intricacies of sexual violence translate into texts, using each chapter to offer critical practices for representing and theorizing rape. Ultimately *Conflict Bodies* argues that the global incidence of sexual violence where one in three women will be raped in her lifetime, combined with the aggravated incidence of rape in so-called "conflict zones," require new theorizations and analyses of violence that account for rape. Thus, we need to analyze and understand rape not only as a weapon of war, a colonial heritage, a sign of political instability, or an example of what happens during natural disasters. We need also to critically examine the material, physical, psychological and social aspects of sexual violence.

Conflict Bodies takes on discussions of black sentience by painstakingly and sometimes painfully reading scenes of sexual violence. I borrow the term *black sentience* from Saidiya Hartman, whose articulation of the role of pain in the making of subjects offers one critical frame for my discussion of the way rape interferes in, intersects with, and intervenes in subject formation.[29] In the cultural production I explore, rape is represented differently but with attentive recognition of subjective, bodily, and traumatic experiences. My analyses of sexual violence foreground rape trauma syndrome as a theoretical lens for unpacking the politics of rape representation and elaborating its stakes in a global context. I also think through the limitations of prior theorizations of postcolonial violence and posit a new framework that, beginning with rape, attempts to account for some of the complicated ways that violence is sexed and gendered. The framework I am suggesting relies on rape trauma syndrome as a useful conceptual category for representation because it accounts for the physical (material), as well as the psychological *and* social, dimensions of sexual violence. In addition, the categories within rape trauma syndrome—the (1) impact, (2) acute, and (3) resolution stages—offer different ways for imagining the way the trauma of sexual violence comes forth in cultural production. I take these categories and shift their positions, sometimes blurring their lines, and at other times overlapping them, in order to offer a nonlinear or resolute approach to the scene of sexual violence whether on stage or on the page, in documentary film or photographic image.

The prominence of articulations of violence in Africa and the diaspora has long been related to slavery and colonialism. Yet, given the explicitly sexed and gendered manifestations of violence in today's global age, most of these theories fail to unpack the dynamics of sex and gender in the occurrence and representation of violence.[30] Although this project focuses on twentieth- and twenty-first-century works, my inquiry is motivated by theories and representations of violence from the 1800s through the present in order to explore the cultural significance of rape as a manifestation of epistemic violence that occurs in the subjective denial of "experience."[31] By beginning with a discussion of canonical francophone texts in the first chapter, the terrain I seek to map is one in which violence and its representation can be situated according to historic, social, and geopolitical currents that often begin with colonialism and slavery as a primary point of reference. Thus, the first chapter begins the work of subjecting rape to what feminist scholar Carine Mardorossian has described as "the kind of theoretical and genealogical scrutiny that other aspects of women's lives (the body, gender performativity, eating disorders, transgender politics, etc.) have occasioned [and which has been] remarkably absent from studies of sexual violence."[32] The subsequent chapters build upon this trajectory by using rape as a point of departure and by deploying the tools of rape cultural criticism in order to account for the politics of re-presenting and reading rape.

What are the stakes of beginning with rape in order to theorize violence? Rape, I argue, is a more effective way to understand violence because all acts of violation are gendered and structured according to power relations, regardless of the genders of perpetrator and victim. Whenever rape is re-presented, subjects may be revictimized, the violence may be pathologized, and binary terms may too strongly inform the way we perceive scenes of violation. Here I propose that rape is a core form of violence, a point that signals an overwhelmingly physical and material manifestation that is deeply psychological and emotional and is anchored in subject formation and negation. Figurations of sexual violence that attend to each of these dynamics re-order our understanding of scripts of intimate violence and expose their inherent limitations and paradoxes. The critical silence surrounding rape representation is another form of epistemic violence at issue here. Much of this book is informed by the rape crisis advocacy field, which has been discursively structured with attention to silences of different kinds, even as the subsequent chapters call into question these tropes of silence. Though I am conscious of the silence that looms over sexual violence, I am also skeptical about the way preoccupation with the idea of silence effaces work being done on the issue. To undercut this discourse of silence, I look for examples that suggest otherwise, as in the scene (at the beginning of this chapter) of Congolese women protesting. To continue to claim that there is only silence surrounding rape in the DRC is to ignore a broader history of women's activism.

The incommunicability of pain famously dissected by Elaine Scarry relates the expression of pain to subject formation. Subsequently black feminist scholars such as Saidiya Hartman and Christina Sharpe have attested to the different ways that "scenes of subjection" and "monstrous intimacies" call forth different issues that are historic, spectacular, and performative in the specific case of black bodies in pain.[33] This study is particularly indebted to the work of black feminists, such as Hartman and Sharpe, among others. Their considerations of black suffering bodies in relation to subjectivity foreground the ways that remembrance of scenes in which sex and violence intersect tend to objectify rather than acknowledge. Although Scarry pays ample attention to the intricacies of war and torture, she does not assess the role of gender violence, nor does she address torture of African and diasporic subjects. Notwithstanding this exclusion, her focus on the body has undeniable implications for gender violence, and when we accept the use of rape as a form of torture, several points in Scarry's work pertain to this study.[34] Her articulation of *pain* as "that which cannot be denied and that which cannot be confirmed" is crucial because of the dilemma faced by rape survivors in societies that either pathologically disbelieve or extraordinarily spectacularize their experiences of pain.[35] Likewise, when we consider, as Scarry points out, that "the person in pain is so bereft of speech," we are reminded of the traumatic silence that envelops and suppresses survivors.[36] This silence is given another dimension when added to the cultural silence in response to the phenomenon of gender violence in both a rhetorical and social context. However, using a transnational feminist theoretical approach to interrogate these silences, their rhetorical construction, and what they exclude from the view of whom, significantly unsettles the pervasiveness of silence as a totalizing corollary of sexual violence.

The current global statistics of sexual violence and the incorporation of rape into international human rights discourses make this a significant moment to conduct such an analysis. Recently established as fundamental to women's human rights, gender violence was first defined as a human rights violation in the 1990s. Nonetheless, stated efforts to emphasize the significance and the pervasiveness of violence against women have done nothing to diminish the frequency of rape all over the world—whether in the United States (where one in three women is raped), the DRC (where rape is a tool of war, mutilating scores of women), South Africa (where rape is being used to "correct" lesbianism), or Haiti (where peacekeeping forces like the United Nations Stabilization Mission in Haiti [MINUSTAH] are accused of rights violations, including the rape of women, girls, boys and men).[37] This work intentionally contributes to a public dialogue about sexual violence and exposes the limitations of human rights discourses, as well as established criticism of violence and representation, in order to challenge a global dialectic of violence.

My central literary concern is the way incidents of violence revolve around the scene of sexual violence—the way rape is structured and situated in relation to other forms of violence within the texts. I am especially interested in the way rape distills the possibility for dialogue about different aspects of violence. The body is a provocative site from which to consider rape in contexts where slavery, dictatorship, colonialism, and genocide provide a backdrop for scenes of violence. However, unlike the examples from the following chapter in which rape is elided, allegorized, or denied, I focus on the analysis of rape representation rather than situate it as a sign for/of different forms of violence. I lace theoretical strands that are black feminist and postcolonial, literary and historic, philosophical and empirical, African, African American and Caribbean, influenced by trauma studies and cultural studies in order to formulate a framework for understanding the fraught dynamics of rape representation in the francophone context. My understanding of sexual violence draws from studies in the fields of anthropology, ethics, philosophy, and sociology, as well as rape crisis intervention. *Conflict Bodies* is shaped by black feminist theory and feminist cultural criticism on rape, especially because my observations focus on the analysis of violence and because they are informed by gender and preoccupied with violations of the female body.[38]

This book begins with rape representation to see how we might challenge epistemic violence as an ideological subtext that informs cultural production. Ultimately my arguments build upon and push against prevailing discourses of violence to point carefully toward a future of alternative possibilities. The theorization of rape representation that I am calling for contains four key elements: (1) foregrounding of the physical and psychological dimensions of sexual violence, (2) positioning of the raped body, (3) problematizing violence in relation to a point of origin or primal scene, and (4) recognizing of the way the discursive presence of violence brings about tensions between reality and representation. Each chapter refigures the analogies that inscribe and inscript gendered violence, proposing a counterdiscourse to representations of violence by focusing on rape in diverse narrative forms, texts and contexts. Thus, each chapter of *Conflict Bodies* reconceptualizes a particular keyword that highlights the cultural limitations of metaphors that dominate the way rape has been imagined. The feminist narratives and theorizations take these keywords—colonial and postcolonial violence in chapter 1, political rape in chapter 2, rape of the land in chapter 3, genocidal rape and rape as a weapon of war in chapters 4 and 5, respectively—and make the case for centralizing the figure, bodies, and subjectivities of the characters they involve.

Chapter 1, "'Bound to Violence?' A History of the Rape Trope in Francophone Studies," provides a literary history of violence in francophone studies by interrogating examples that dominate the colonial and postcolonial eras. By considering the impact of colonial and postcolonial narratives of violence, the main objective of this chapter is to illustrate, through extensively drawn examples, the ways in which consideration of rape has been symbolically present but theoretically absent in francophone studies. I argue that gendered violence has often been obscured in favor of "broader" or "universal" forms of violence that occur in times of unrest (e.g., under dictatorial regimes). To explain this process, I think through the ways epistemic violence leads to a symbolic violence of exclusion against raped subjects. Chapter 1 critically engages other conceptual frameworks for the theorization of violence, ranging from Fanon's model for anticolonial violence; Glissant's explorations of trauma and violence; Hartman's discussion of rape, personhood, and consent, to Teresa de Lauretis' conceptualization of the violence, gender, and representation. As a whole, this chapter lays out a distinctly transnational and black feminist framework for thinking through the gendered dynamics of violence to uncover an ideological subtext that inscribes rape according to three dominant patterns that normalize, deny, and/or allegorize its occurrence.

Chapter 2, "Rethinking Political Rape: Genealogies of Sexual Violence in Haiti," examines how the idea of "political rape" figures in a nationalist framework. This chapter begins with the rape origin story as a central founding myth and then proceeds to chart an alternative, increasingly politicized understanding of rape representation that situates Marie Vieux-Chauvet's *Amour, colère, folie* (1968) as an urtext that informs subsequent figurations of sexual violence. The chapter argues that the tacit and overt denial of sexual violence seeps into rape representation, as well as into its critical reception. I identify the trilogy, which is set in 1939 post-occupation Haiti and during the Duvalier dictatorship (1957–1986), as one that moves against the impulse to "never call it rape." My reading of Vieux-Chauvet deliberately disturbs the culture of silence that surrounds rape in the text. I also explore how this culture of silence is metatextually present in how critics have approached scenes of rape in *Amour, colère, folie*. This chapter wrests the definition of *political rape* from state-related conflict in order to show that violence, though inexorably political, is not always a consequence of political events. The chapter then reflects on the ways contemporary representations of rape do and do not carry on this trajectory by looking at novels by Kettly Mars, Jaira Placide, and Edwidge Danticat, as well as human rights reports on sexual violence in the aftermath of the 2010 earthquake.

Chapter 3, "Undoing Island Rape Analogies: Beyond the Rape of the Land," challenges Caribbean postcolonial discourses by addressing the analogy of the female body as land, one of the most familiar tropes of

Caribbean and African literature. My reading of Gisèle Pineau's *L'espérance-macadam* (1996) is set against Antonio Benitez-Rojo's *The Repeating Island: The Caribbean from a Postmodern Perspective* (1996) and informed by Édouard Glissant's discussions of trauma, and depictions of rape in *La case du commandeur* (1980). I draw upon archival studies of sexual violence in Guadeloupe to argue that Pineau's construction of the cyclone parallel disrupts the traditional image of the postcolonial Caribbean landscape as a feminized space, offering a new conceptualization for the notion of *la terre violée* [the raped land]. Through an analysis of how sexual and natural violence are represented, I propose that foregrounding the female body and the psychological effects of rape trauma syndrome intentionally exploits the "woman as land" metaphor in order to insert nuanced feminist perspectives on violence. By analyzing the cultural significance of rape through archival material on sexual violence in Guadeloupe and placing Pineau's novel in the context of this work, I stage a dialogue between social scripts of rape and their cultural production, intentionally uniting material and symbolic realms.

Chapter 4, "Beneath Layers of Violence: Images of Rape and the Rwandan Genocide," takes on the prevalence of rape during the Rwandan genocide and considers its representations. In this chapter, I compare across genre and medium, juxtaposing the images linked to sexual violence in Yolande Mukagasana's collection of photographs *Les blessures du silence: témoignages du genocide au Rwanda* (2001), the book *L'ombre d'imana: Voyages jusqu'au bout du Rwanda* (2000) by Ivorian writer Véronique Tadjo, Boubacar Boris Diop's novel *Murambi: Le livre des ossements* (2000), and Haitian filmmaker Raoul Peck's *Sometimes in April* (2004) for examples of what is at stake in the portrayal of genocidal rape and the way different types of cultural production attempt to negotiate those stakes. I propose that Tadjo's use of form is a self-conscious attempt to reflect the complexity of genocide. Similarly, I read Diop, Mukagasana, and Peck's use of narrative voices—written, spoken, and visual—as critical endeavors to reframe retellings of the genocide. Throughout this chapter, I argue that in each of these texts, raped bodies go from being a familiar image of genocide to possessing specific, unique functions in which lies nascent subjectivity for the victim/survivor of genocidal rape.

Chapter 5, "Regarding the Pain of Congolese Women: Audience Affect, Narrative Closure, and Rape as a Tool of War," attempts to account for the far-reaching and ongoing effects of the Rwandan genocide by looking at works that focus on the current conflict in the Democratic Republic of the Congo (DRC). This chapter turns to the plays *Ruined* (2008) by Lynn

Nottage and *Les recluses* (2010) by Koffi Kwahulé to argue that the current international discourse or vocabulary of violence surrounding the DRC conflict is especially problematic when viewed through the lens of affect studies. Beginning with the documentary film *The Greatest Silence* by Lisa Jackson, I argue that sentimental and affective approaches discursively present in renderings of the DRC re-inscribe neo-imperial and neoliberal scripts of African subject erasure that date back to the colonial project. I then turn to the plays *Ruined* and *Les recluses* as alternatives that complicate rape representation in the DRC without overreliance on audience sentiment and intervention. The chapter also explores representation in relation to broader human rights discursive frameworks which routinely rely on spectacular representations of violence to make human rights claims. By closing in this way, I broaden the frame of analysis to offer an alternate, more global framework for the role of francophone studies in relation to a human rights project.

In this book, I elucidate ways to interlace the representation of rape with antiviolent, black feminist politics that re-imagine how human rights discourse could be attendant to its sexual and gender dynamics for black bodies on both sides of the Atlantic.[39] My central arguments revolve around the idea that, as Teresa de Lauretis has observed, "the representation of violence is inseparable from the notion of gender."[40] If de Lauretis' words can help to summarize an intention for this study, the subsequent chapters illuminate strategies that destabilize the use of rape as a signifier of singular meaning. Instead, this book provides the tools to theorize sexual violence, account for the dynamics of sex and gender, and scrutinize the politics of rape representation. *Conflict Bodies* delineates what happens when we really read, pay attention to, and analyze rape, not only as a way to understand and grapple with varying forms of violence that exist within African and Caribbean societies, but also as a constitutive phenomenon of violence in and of itself. Beneath this call for analysis is the same logic that we saw at work in the women's protests in Bukavu that opened this chapter: true freedom can reside only in recognition of women as human; as long as women's bodies are still subject to rape, understandings of violence and freedom and definitions of the human will continue to be compromised.

"Bound to Violence?"

A History of the Rape Trope in Francophone Studies

Appelons-les violences familières. Familières, parce qu'elles sont connues de tous et que personne n'ose les dénoncer comme étant des situations de violence. Familières aussi parce qu'elles sont historiques, sociales, ou économiques, que notre mémoire collective en est imprégnée, que nous ne pourrons jamais les oublier. Ces formes de violences ont, depuis des décennies, envahi le champ de la littérature.[1]

Let us call them familiar forms of violence. Familiar, because they are known to everyone and yet no one dares to denounce them as situations of violence. Familiar also because they are historic, social, or economic, that our collective memory is full of these, that we can never forget them. These forms of violence have, for decades, invaded the field of literature.
—Tanella Boni

In the time it takes you to read this sentence . . . someone will be raped. Somewhere a person is being violated. One person is forcing himself on another person and leaving a mark—a bruise, a scar from a cigarette burn, some torn tissue mixed with blood, some semen, perhaps none of these. In every case of rape, whether the mark is invisible or permanent, life or death, a mark remains: the memory of a violation—force without consent. . . . The mark may only be *an ineradicable memory.*[2]
—Catherine Clinton

Bound to Violence?

Bound to violence. This is how Yambo Oulouguem's 1969 novel *Le devoir de violence* had been translated for many years until the recent appearance of a new edition reissued in English as *The Duty of Violence*.[3] Although the original translation fails to convey the urgency suggested by the use of *devoir*, and is a less precise translation of the word, a problem that the new title corrects, the thought of being "bound to violence," is compelling for francophone studies. Bound to violence: we imagine bodies chained to violence that is unending and predetermined. Bound to violence: we slip uneasily, too quickly, into a problematic Conradian landscape of primordial violence imagining the primitive "heart of darkness." "Bound to violence" posits violence as the point of origin, whether it is historic, political, or social. Being bound to violence suggests that there is no recourse, no escape from the presence and existence of violence. Being bound to violence suggests an ineffable, immutable connection, impossible to uproot. Bound to violence suggests a primal, uncontrollable aspect of human nature that informs power relations. *Duty,* on the other hand, conveys obligation and perhaps choice. Duty evokes the fervor of colonial struggles for independence. The new title prompts us to dismantle the implicit meanings: "bound to commit violence," "bound to fall prey to violence," and "bound to be surrounded by violence." The possibilities are endless. Can an entire culture, an entire nation, an entire race be bound to violence? Who is bound to violence? Whom do they bind? Who are the victims of this violence? Who are the perpetrators? The title remains ambiguous in the face of these questions. The answers are ambivalent and discomforting.

An earlier work that Oulouguem perhaps echoes in his title is Frantz Fanon's *Les damnés de la terre/The Wretched of the Earth*, the landmark study on the subject of colonial and postcolonial violence written several years prior in 1961. The first chapter of *Les damnés* constructs the colonial subject as inextricably bound to violence. In some ways, Fanon's chapter "Concerning Violence" might be considered the genesis of Oulouguem's fictitious rendering of a community in which violence knows no bounds and "the cure for violence is violence itself."[4] *Les damnés* is a study of the decolonization process and its effects that advocates violence as an inevitable and necessary means for anticolonial ends. One of Fanon's major claims is that the last battle of independence will be the fight of the colonized against each other.[5] Despite what Tracey Sharpley-Whiting rightly describes as Fanon's "continued relevance for . . . contemporary black feminist literary and cultural studies," it is well known that aspects of his body of work call for more careful attention vis-à-vis the issue of sexual violence in particular and gender politics in general (161–62). His consistent equivalence of "the colonized" and "man" assure us that Fanon was referring to a violent struggle waged only between colonized men.[6] What happens, though, if only the "colonized" are *men*, and the "other" are *colonized women*? That is, when we turn our attention to the violence enacted upon women by their male compatriots, as well as by other women, what picture do we emerge with? How does the female body figure in this atmosphere of violence, this world turned upside down? Furthermore, what do these images of violation against women reveal about the phenomenon of violence? How does the duty of violence translate across sex and gender? What does it mean to be bound to violence when the violence in question is sexual?

The purpose of this first chapter is to raise critical questions about the gender dimensions of violence in order to propose a two-pronged framework for focusing on *le viol dans la violence*—the first four letters of the word *violence* in French that together translate into "rape." My analysis begins with four key figures in francophone studies—Frantz Fanon, Achille Mbembe, Mongo Beti, and Edouard Glissant—whose theorizations have guided critical work in the area and help to emblematize dominant threads of the discourse surrounding rape representation. From there, I proceed to track the figuration of sexual violence as a trope in francophone literary and cultural studies. I argue that embedded in the omnipresence of violence in francophone thought is a disabling discourse toward rape that ignores the bodily and subjective significance of violence and that ultimately reinscribes, or "engenders," patriarchal systems of violation. I take this argument further by proposing that in response to the disabling dominant discourse of violence, beginning with rape representation as a point of departure (rather than as a fleeting symbolic mention or metonym) can allow us to mark out a counterdiscourse. This counterdiscourse critically analyzes and accounts for the cultural significance of rape; parses its politics; and pores over the aesthetic, visual, and narrative conventions that characterize its representation. Such a counterdiscourse is carefully attendant to the ways "rape and its meaning . . . keep circulating in opposite directions."[7] Understanding that the reality of rape and its representation are in critical and productive tension with one another, this chapter attempts to examine and tease out those tensions. In order to explore and then challenge the cultural significance of rape in the context of francophone Africa and the Caribbean in this chapter, I examine the figure and the function of rape in a number of canonical texts and unpack their ideological subtexts. The examples here stand in stark contrast to many of the other examples throughout the book, because overall, I am interested in texts for which we can observe the conscious insertion of women into paradigms of violence to position them as subjects who can be victims and agents, critics and theorists of violence.

Of the authors named here, Frantz Fanon's views on violence are the most renowned; he is by far the most cited theorist of postcolonial violence. In *Les damnés de la terre*, he uses the example of the Algerian war for liberation (1954–1962) to posit that the process of total decolonization could occur only through violence. Fanon specifies violence as a trope of colonialism in its multiple stages: "la décolonisation est toujours un phénomène violent"/"decolonization is always a violent phenomenon."[8] Violence, he explains, is present at the genesis of the colonial endeavor: "Leur première confrontation s'est déroulée sous le signe de la violence et leur cohabitation—plus précisément l'exploitation du colonisé par le colon—s'est poursuivie à grand renfort de baïonnettes et de canons" (66)/"Their first encounter was marked by violence and their existence together—the exploitation of the native by the settler—was carried on by dint of a great array of bayonets and cannons" (36). Fanon argues that anticolonial struggle is necessarily imbued with violence, and he contends that native violence develops only in response to the colonizer's violence. He describes the colonizer as the one who "porte la violence dans les maisons et dans les cerveaux du colonisé" (69) ["[is] the bringer of violence into the home and the mind of the native"], suggesting that violence begins as a result of the colonial encounter (38).

Fanon's espousal of violence as liberation has been otherwise named as a quintessential act of what Nicole Waller terms "contradictory violence" because it is "violence understood by the perpetrators as a counter-violence opposing systems of brutal oppression . . . a violence of contradiction."[9] The violence he propagates is physical in the necessity for the colonized subject to take up arms and liberate himself. It is also psychological, as he refers to "cette violence atmosphérique"/"an atmosphere of violence" in which discourse plays a definitive role. His examples of "un vocabulaire colonial" ["a colonial vocabulary"] to describe the native's discourse calls attention to the psychological effects of rhetorical violence on the colonized subject (102/43). One of the main axes of Fanon's project endorses violence as an act of purging that is necessary for the re-creation of "man," society, and humanity. Because Fanon offered a framework for understanding violence in the context of colonial liberation, *Les damnés* was quickly established as an all-important study for unpacking postcolonial violence. However, many of Fanon's conclusions become deeply problematic when considered in relation to sexual violence. If, as Idelber Avelar puts it, "for the native the process of violently destroying colonialism is not a contingent, unimportant one but rather the very process through which s/he accedes to subjectivity," what are some ways to understand this relation between violence and subjectivity in the postcolonial context?[10] Of the books in his corpus, Fanon's *L'an V de la Révolution Algérienne/A Dying Colonialism* is singular for its treatment of questions related to sex and gender and the explicit analysis of how rape functions in the colonial project. "C'est ainsi que le viol de la femme algérienne dans un rêve d'Européen est toujours précédé de la déchirure du voile" (25). ["Thus the rape of the Algerian woman in the dream of a European is always preceded by a rending of the veil" (45).][11] Through detailed explanations of fantasies by French men, Fanon demonstrates the ways that sexual violence is tethered to the colonial enterprise especially because in these dreams he routinely encounters "le maximum de violence, possession, viol, quasi-meurtre" ["the maximum of violence, possession, rape and near-murder"] as recurring fantasies about Algerian women (25/46). These examples are consistent with Fanon's view of sexual violence in previous works in which rape is considered an outgrowth of the colonial project. Only in *L'an V de la Révolution* does Fanon give brief mention to the role and position of Algerian women in relation to this violence. Explaining that "la conduite de la femme n'est jamais d'adhésion ou d'acceptation, mais de prosternation" (25) ["the woman's conduct is never one of acceptance, but of abject humility" (45)], he assigns absolute passivity to the raped women in question.

Fanon's relative silence on violence against women has been challenged. As Anne Donadey asserts, "Francophone women writers have taken up issues of violence and written back to Fanon. Not only have they contended with colonial violence, they have also brought to the forefront a variety of other types of violence, particularly sexual and familial, which Fanon never thought of addressing."[12] Donadey's point is a reminder that women writers have never hesitated to explore and unveil gender-based violence in their works. In addition to their own renderings of violence in different forms of cultural production, they have also critiqued extant theories of violence, such as those proposed by Fanon.

Most recently, the Cameroonian Achille Mbembe has built upon Fanon and contributed to the discussion of postcolonial violence through his philosophical inquiry *On the Postcolony* (2001), a detailed study of the development of the postcolonial state and its contemporary legacies.[13] His argument relies heavily on the idea that "colonialism is a relation of power based on violence" and that the development of the colonial state as well as its current situation, are informed by violence.[14] His theorization of the postcolonial state suggests that both the colonial and postcolonial state are ineluctably bound to violence. Mbembe engages Fanon's theory of violence and decolonization, arguing that the current state of African regimes, what he calls their "decomposition" or "implosion," is indissociable from the violence meted out by colonial powers. Mbembe goes on to describe a state that was structured around and according to violence. Three forms in particular were integral to the pursuit and realization of the colonial project: (1) founding violence, (2) legitimating violence, and (3) maintaining violence. According to Achille Mbembe, what is today the "postcolony" is in many ways a result of the conjunction of these three forms of violence.[15]

Mbembe's neologism, *postcolony*, is informed by the lasting phenomenon of violence. He explains the term:

> "Postcolony" identifies a given historic trajectory—that of societies recently emerging from the experience of colonization and violence which the colonial relationship involves . . . the postcolony is also made up of a series of corporate institutions and political machinery that, once in place, constitute a distinctive regime of violence.[16]

The "regime of violence" delineated here is a legacy of colonialism, on the one hand, but it is also born out of processes of globalization and corporatization evident in the Global South. To this end, Mbembe goes on to describe how "as was clearly seen during the colonial period, the relations between violence, production of inequality, and accumulation are extraordinarily intricate and complicated. And there are no necessary causal links among these three variables."[17] His conclusions express the complexity of defining the origins and the continuation of violence in relation to the postcolony. In other words, determining the genesis of violence is unproductive because it is a multiheaded beast stretching forth from different directions, with different forces.

Prior to Mbembe, Mongo Beti also explored the topic of postindependence violence by beginning with the example of his native Cameroon, often thematizing the link between violence and historical struggle.[18] Rather than look at different examples of violence and corruption in his fiction, I want to turn to the nonfiction in which the use of rape as metonymy is the most apparent and helps to demonstrate the ways that rape is symbolically present but critically absent in theorizations of violence. The incendiary book *Main basse sur le Cameroun: Autopsie d'une décolonisation*

(1972) has been translated as *The Rape of Cameroon* for the ways that it explores the exploitation of Cameroon's resources and population. Like *Bound to Violence*, this book was considered controversial to the point of being banned in Cameroon and France. In his own republication of the book, Beti refers to the francophone African states as a "veritable laboratory of neo-colonial violence."[19] Like many of his contemporaries, Beti focuses on postcolonial violence and corruption in African states, as well as France's collusion in rampant government injustice. *Main basse* enumerates the crimes against humanity committed by Cameroonian president Ahmadou Ahidjo by focusing on the arrests of revolutionary leaders Mbanga Ouandié and Bishop Ndongmo, members of Cameroon's Communist party accused of plotting against the government. Following the process, Ouandié was sentenced to death and Ndongmo to life in prison. Beti is virulently critical of the complicit reaction of the French government, which was publicly displayed in an article in *Le Monde diplomatique*. Taking the letter as provocation, Beti decries postcolonial regimes responsible for violence, censure, and other human rights violations. The "rape of Cameroon" must be understood in at least two ways. It is the oppressive Ahidjo regime, as well as the maintenance of a neocolonial relationship of exploitation between France and Cameroon. Thus, the book recounts the effects of corruption and violence in Cameroon by indicting French and Cameroonian leaders; here the word *rape* is used only metaphorically. The designation links postcolonial corruption to colonial domination, with rape as a uniting signifier for each one.

The use of *rape* as metonym for racial oppression and injustice extends back historically and across the Atlantic geographically to slavery. The institution of slavery, with its systematized and ritualized violence against black bodies, provides one of the most harrowing contexts for the study of sexual violence. As an influential francophone Caribbean writer, Édouard Glissant's preoccupation with "the grief of slavery and its aftermath" is well known.[20] Within this body of work on slavery, Glissant has noted that the quotidian violation of African women's bodies, which begins during the transatlantic crossing, is an important mechanism used to enforce slavery's terror. " . . . là où les hommes déportés sont annihilés physiquement, la femme africaine subit la plus totale des agressions, qui est le viol quotidien et répété d'un équipage rendu dément par l'exercice de leur métier" [. . . where deported men were physically annihilated, the African woman experienced the most complete of aggressions, that is, the daily and repeated rape of a crew that had been made crazy in the practice of their trade] (297). Glissant's description establishes the rape of women as a more intense manifestation of violence that African slaves were forced to endure. At the same time, his reference partly obscures the power relations that structure sexual violence as he describes the perpetrators as having become crazed due to their work as slave traders. By subtly suggesting that psychosis, rather than power, undergirds these transatlantic rapes, Glissant impairs our understanding of how sexual violence operates in the context of slavery. The chaos of the slave ship, rather than the catastrophic and violence-riddled institution of slavery, is what leads the seamen to rape. Though on the one hand Glissant opines that women are the worst victims of the slave trade, his description of the seamen's mental state offers a logic of behavior that undermines the personhood of the raped women.

This impulse is somewhat corrected in Glissant's fourth novel, *La case du commandeur* (1981), which shows a more pronounced, sustained attention to rape. This novel, published in the same year as *Le discours antillais*, portrays Martinican families from Glissant's previous novel *Le quatrième siècle/The Fourth Century* (1962), spanning three generations stretching from the African continent to the Antilles. Here Glissant concerns himself with traumatic memory by focusing on the wounds of the Middle Passage, as well as the heritage of slavery. Here again the theme of insanity is linked to the violence of rape but in the different context of how it affects the victim-survivor in the form of the protagonist Marie Célat, affectionately named Mycea. In one passage, Glissant describes an anonymous woman, who is the victim of multiple rapes during the Middle Passage, and eventually gives birth to a child. "Une fleur soutint son corps et sa pensée pendant cette agonie. La dernière fleur qu'elle eut aperçue avant qu'on ne l'enfourne dans ce bateau . . . avant qu'on la jette dans le réduit aux ordres de vomi et de sel de mer où elle croupit le temps de ce qu'il fallait bien appeler le voyage. Et dès ces moments-là les marins la violèrent, jour après jour et nuit après nuit, ainsi que les deux femmes, l'unes contre l'autre" [A flower sustained her body and her thoughts during this agony. The last flower that she had glimpsed before she had been shoved into the boat . . . before they threw her into the ship's hold, filled with the scent of vomit and salt, where she wallowed throughout what should truly be called her 'trip.' And from that moment on, the sailors raped her, day after day, and night after night, as well as the two women, one up against the other"] (154). Rape was, without question, a definitive and central tool used to uphold the system of slavery. The systematic use of rape under slavery highlights the interimbrication of sex, race, and power as a necessity for maintaining the slave system.

But if, as Cilas Kemedjio proposes, "the history of collective withering of the Antilles forms the narrative thread of *La case du commandeur,*" then the explicit passage cited above and rape representation in general are almost irrelevant to this project.[21] *La case du commandeur* is stylistically structured around the articulation of a Caribbean collectivity expressed in the presence of the *nous.*"[22] The *nous* resonating throughout the novel is ultimately abandoned and considered untenable. Nowhere is this *nous* applicable to the scenes of gendered violence, suggesting that the issue of rape is not significant for collective preoccupation. In her study of the impact of this narrative voice, Dawn Fulton has argued that *La case du commandeur* fictionalizes the concept of the *roman du Nous,* which Glissant puts forth in *Le discours antillais.* On the one hand, *Le discours antillais* and *La case du commandeur* help frame how trauma—especially the legacy of slavery's unrelenting violence—emerges in francophone studies. At the same time, these examples demonstrate Doris Garraway's powerful argument in her study on the machinations of power, desire, and sexuality during slavery in the francophone Caribbean. In her examination of slavery as a system of sexual domination, Garraway explains that "the problem is that by setting aside issues of gender and sexuality, or by viewing them as mitigating factors in an otherwise brutal system of domination and subordination, these writers overlook the ways in which certain sexual practices contributed to and reinforced those power structures."[23] Though *La case du commandeur* helps provide context for the treatment of women under slavery and the use of rape as a tool of oppression, it does so more simply than do millennial novels written by women three decades later, such as Evelyne Trouillot's *Rosalie l'infâme* (2003) and Fabienne Kanor's *Humus* (2006), both of which deploy productive silence and first-person narrators as a way to narrativize rape. Kanor and Trouillot's treatment of the gendered oppression of slavery show how creative expression can successfully negotiate some of the troubling power dynamics Garraway points out in her study.

Given the allied brutalities of slavery and colonialism, violence figures as a preeminent theme in African and Caribbean cultural production; it is by no means a recent development.[24] Francophone cultural workers have a long-standing tradition of pursuing the relationship between violence and representation through their creative expression. The preoccupation with violence is contextual in the struggles for independence from colonialism and slavery; it is a referent to their origins in the upheaval of slavery; and it is a problem or a theoretical approach to a world where the residual effects of slavery, colonialism, and imperialism remain. Furthermore, postcolonial and contemporary conflicts in the forms of civil war, dictatorship, genocide, and *coups d'état* require reflection on the nexus of violence and representation. We can identify in these works a set of distinct, yet overlapping techniques in which the view of violence alternates between something that is (1) glorified and romanticized, (2) described as an originary force, (3) conceived as a means for unveiling injustice, or (4) measured according to language. In all the overdetermined attention to violence, where do we see *"le viol dans la violence"*? How does rape figure into this hyperdiscourse of violence? How is rape present in the francophone African and Caribbean contexts? How can we, instead of focusing so narrowly on these contexts, begin to think intercontextually about sexual violence? To address these questions, my goal for the remainder of this chapter is to offer a comprehensive—though certainly not exhaustive—overview of how rape and rape representation are present and absent in francophone Caribbean and African literatures and artistic production.

Variations on a Trope: Representing Rape in Francophone Studies

We can turn first to Haiti, celebrated for its historic "firsts." Among the narratives of the Haitian Revolution is a "rape origin story" that indicts colonial violence in order to advance a nationalist project. The story presents a rape metaphor in the example of Sor Rose, a slave who is raped by her French master and literally gives birth to the Haitian nation.[25] Whether she is raped by Frenchmen or by a fellow Black slave is unclear in the story. The point is supposed to be that "the origins of everyone is common," as Timoléon Brutus points out in his history of Haiti.[26] As I discuss in the following chapter, here the routine rape of slave women serves an allegorical purpose, not for displaying the violence of the French as one might expect, but to promote the notion of *métissage culturel* or *créolisation* as an integral element of Haitian culture. A related example of rape in the Haitian cultural imaginary is that of Anacaona, the Arawak queen violated and murdered by the Spanish during their rapacious conquests.[27] Anacaona's story was first captured in the play *Anacaona, Reine martyre* by Saint Arnaud Numa in 1960, then again in Jean Metellus' play *Anacaona, Fleur d'Or* (1986). Later on, Haitian-American writer Edwidge Danticat creates another version of the Taino queen in her young adult novel *Anacaona: Golden Flower, Haiti, 1490* (2005). The circulation of these stories in Haitian cultural memory establish that rape plays a role alongside other forms of violence in the creation of nation and national identity, and that women's bodies are understood to be territories of colonial conquest.

After the Revolution, violence seemed to punctuate Haitian politics with alarming regularity: presidents were killed mysteriously, *coups d'état* toppled governments, and popular uprisings erupted.[28] During the early twentieth century, the first (1915–1934) U.S. occupation inflicted damage on the development of the Haitian state. In the Caco rebellions, marines massacred Haitian insurgents in the southern city of Cayes and elsewhere.[29] Twenty years after the departure of the United States, the Duvalier dictatorship renewed the meaning of terror during a regime responsible for torture, death, and sexual violence on a larger scale than had ever been witnessed in recent history. In Raoul Peck's award-winning film *L'homme sur les quais* (1993), scenes of rape frame the film's opening and conclusion. After opening with the voice of one of Papa Doc's infamous speeches, followed by the classic song "Twa fey," the film maintains a terrifying silence throughout. Sarah's first words set the stage for what she is about to behold: "C'était au début des années soixantes, j'avais huit ans et le monde s'ouvrait déjà sur un désastre."[30] [It was at the beginning of the sixties, I was eight years old, and the world was already opening on a disaster.] These words are concretized as she walks onto the balcony to witness her godfather Sorel being beaten and raped. This scene images sexual brutality to denote the unparalleled violence of the Duvalier regime. Second, in one of the film's final scenes, the young protagonist runs in the field with her friend, celebrating the joy and innocence of childhood impeded by the terror of the regime. She is attacked by "the man by the shore," who (the film suggests) attempts to rape her. The rape signifies the ability of violence to mar innocence in a way that parallels the regime's destruction of lives under Duvalier. The symbology of rape continuously references and symbolizes state- or government-related terror in obvious, if fleeting, ways.

Discourses surrounding sexual violence peaked again in the 1990s after what was Haiti's greatest triumph in many years—the first successful democratic election—followed by a 1991 coup that overthrew Jean-Bertrand Aristide seven months after his inauguration. From 1991 to 1994, a repressive military junta ruled with unabashed violence and impunity. To quell Aristide supporters, the operation *machin enfènal* was set in motion: death squads flourished, the most notorious of which was the Revolutionary Front for the Progress of Haiti (FRAPH).[31] Aristide was restored to power in 1994, but ten years later, more violence resulted in the end of his presidency.[32] During this time, gender-based violence in general and rape in particular occurred at astonishing rates. These examples show that Haiti, where, as Michael Dash explains, "the dilemma as to the role of literature in the face of political violence is as old as the republic itself," offers a salient portrait of how the history of violence overlaps with its representation, as well as where rape fits into this larger narrative.[33] Today, in the post–earthquake-ravaged cities such as Port-au-Prince and Léogane, the reports of rape in displacement tent cities has caused discourses of rape to recirculate with renewed vigor. These narratives often recall that natural disasters have aggravated effects on women and children. The present situation also reveals how the tropes of resilience and survival and the problem of foreign intervention are informed by the same scripts that have been associated with different types of violence over the years.[34]

Rape is subtextually present in Joseph Zobel's Antillean classic *La rue Cases-Nègres/Black Shack Alley* (1950). In this autobiographical novel, Zobel traces how history and violence are inscribed onto daily life despite the abolition of slavery. He recounts the childhood of José Hassan, who lives with his grandmother, Man Tine, in Martinique during the 1920s and 1930s. José follows the path of many of francophone literature's masculine protagonists, moving from the village *case,* and small local school, to a more prestigious school in the urban center, Fort-de-France. His trajectory adopts a familiar progression that usually ends in the Parisian *métropole*. In *La rue Cases-Nègres*, which is principally a story about the legacy of the past upon the present, Zobel makes symbolic use of violence against women. In general, references to violence against women are fleeting. Zobel focuses more on the structural violence of racism and class stratification in order to indicate that for the descendants of slaves in Martinique, the end of slavery brings little change. The grandmother in *La rue Cases-Nègres* represents the essentialized maternal strength of Antillean womanhood. Man Tine is cast as an idealized version of a woman who sacrifices for her grandson's well-being, education, and success. Without her, the novel's hero would not have been able to escape the postslavery, poverty-ridden, racially segregated life of *La rue Cases-Nègres.* Because of her, he accesses education and can realize a life better than what his enslaved ancestors had been forced to endure. Man Tine exemplifies what Anne McClintock calls a "gendered division of labor . . . summed up in the colonial gospel of the family and the presiding icon of the mother of the nation."[35] Man Tine's character, raped by an overseer during her adolescence, provides insight into treatment of sexual violence. Her rape cursorily references the violation as an atrocity of slavery, serving as "reminder of the sexual helplessness of the female slave, who was forced to be a breeding machine for the plantation."[36] The use of rape as a metaphor for slavery is a narrative strategy that figures in cultural production throughout the diaspora. As a synecdoche for the brutality of slavery, the rape foregrounds the historic trauma of slavery and symbolizes Martinique's powerlessness in relation to the French. In this instance, the weathered grandmother represents a dispossessed land struggling to repair the damage to its legacy. Reparation, however, can be realized only through the mobility and the success of the male protagonist. If rape hampers the survivor's mobility, it is redeemed through the male character's success. This depiction of rape in Zobel's text is a passing point of reference within the project to denounce slavery and the social injustice that follows its abolition. Zobel focuses more on the structural violence of racism and class stratification to indicate that for the descendants of slaves in Martinique, the end of slavery brings little change.

Also known for his translations between image and print, the novelist turned filmmaker, Senegalese Ousmane Sembene, laid bare the negative toll of colonial violence on West Africans. One early example of rape representation in his oeuvre includes *Ô pays mon beau peuple!* (1957).[37] In this novel, Sembene presents Oumar Faye, who struggles to come to terms with the violence around him.[38] Through the eyes of his protagonist, Sembene explores the themes of interracial marriage, "return to the native land," and tradition versus modernity as evident between generations. Each of these themes unfolds in a colonial space: the French-occupied region of Casamance. Oumar speaks scathingly about the attitude of European colonizers that he encountered in France.[39] Like the *tirailleurs sénégalais* described in Senghor's poems and Sembene's film *Le camp de Thiaroye* (1988), Oumar Faye is embittered but emboldened by his experience fighting alongside the French during the war.[40] Resistance is a dominant theme in the novel— Faye meets a violent death because of his Communist-ideology-influenced attempts to wrest Casamance from the colonial power.

A striking reference to sexual violence in the *Ô pays mon beau peuple!* makes use of the threat of rape as a referent for racialized colonial relations. This example involves the protagonist Oumar Faye's French wife Isabelle who is attacked by members of the French guard.[41] Here we see one of the standard functions of rape narratives in which rape becomes a way to punish women for transgressions against racist ideologies. This attempted rape is intended to enact a form of punishment upon Isabelle for choosing an African husband and thus betraying her race. It also serves as a punishment to her husband for his political activism and for the transgression of having a French wife. The implications must be viewed in terms of the taboo against interracial marriage during the time in which the novel is set.

Violence punishes both parties responsible for sullying French womanhood with African blood through miscegenation. A familiar pattern of gender violence surfaces in this incident: at first Isabelle is ashamed to tell her husband, and she fears that she might ignite his anger. His forcefulness—as he violently pushes her to share with him—shows that she was correct in her hesitation, although she nonetheless discloses what happens. But unlike other male characters for whom the threat of rape for the women in their lives triggers a hypermasculinized reaction of militant action or a quest for vengeance, a textual interpretation reveals that for Oumar, what happens to his wife is negligible. Rather than address the attempted rape, Oumar's reaction is to explain to her that he cannot leave Senegal, regardless of any imminent danger. The lack of recognition of her vulnerability as a potential victim of violence is obscured by his nationalist quest to liberate Casamance. He tells Isabelle how his experience in the war led to a form of *prise de conscience*, as he realized:

> J'ai compris que nous sommes sans patrie, des apatrides. Quand les autres disent "nos colonies" que pouvons-nous dire, nous? [. . .] Mais moi, où trouverai-je ma dignité d'homme? Où dois-je la conquérir, si ce n'est pas dans le pays qui m'a vu naître?[42]

> I understood that we are without a nation, we are nationless. When others say "our colonies" what can we say, us? . . . But me, where will I find my dignity as a man? Where can I conquer it, if it is not in this country that saw my birth . . . ?[43]

Faye's speech demonstrates a psychological link between past violence (what he had to do as a soldier for the war); current colonial domination; and the urge to revolt, which burden his psyche. His words also perform the masculinization of nationalist discourse ("my dignity as a man") and the implicit feminization of the land ("land that saw my birth"). The rhetorical erasure of what happened to Isabelle engenders violence in the formal elements of the text.[44] There is a racial subtext legible in this interaction—as a white woman, Isabelle's rape would not generate the same type of nationalist politics as that of a Senegalese woman. Ultimately, Isabelle's experience is reduced to what it evokes for her husband. The example of Oumar and Isabelle highlights one of the most acceptable ways for rape to figure as a story involving women related to the male protagonist, who in turn wrestles with the consequences and implications of sexual violence.

Sembene's films supplement his vision of female subjectivity, especially in the later half of his career with the cycle of films that begins with

Faat Kiné (2001). In one of the most troubling scenes in *Moolaadé* (2004), the female protagonist bites down on her finger to temper the excruciating pain of intercourse with her husband. Her jaws clench around her pinky finger, causing the skin to break and rupture, and blood oozes onto her sheets. She attempts to temper the pain of sexual intercourse due to having had her clitoris cut and her vagina sewn back together in the ritual practice of female circumcision. The scene calls attention to the body in three distinct ways: first, the act of intercourse is framed as one that results in no pleasure for the woman; second, a reminder of the unmitigating pain of genital cutting as one to which women are continuously subjected; and third, with flashes of emphasis on another body part (in this case the finger) to shift her attention away from the pain, which refocuses the audience on it. The pain Argo Collé inflicts on herself in this moment is measured against the pain of her husband's physical entry into her body and the pain that young girls from the village are routinely subject to. Although this is not a rape scene per se, it is an important moment in which pain, sex, female embodiment, and violence collide to structure the protagonist's experience.

During the 1960s struggles for independence, there was a simultaneous intellectual explosion in the form of fiction and nonfiction engaging the subject of violence from a perspective that advocated its use. This chapter began with a consideration of the various implications in the title of Yambo Ouologuem's *Le devoir de violence*, which captures a colonial past, present, and future. Ouologuem boldly depicts a universe in which violence persists as a defining element across multiple generations. By tracing the story of the Saif dynasty from the eighteenth through the twentieth centuries, Ouologuem intended to chart the precolonial origins of violence. His goal was to refute the notion that European arrival on African soil was uniquely responsible for spirals of violence. In order to do so, he shows that African tradition and power were actually founded on and through violence. Here, Ouologuem can be situated in opposition to writers like Leopold Sédar Senghor due to his project to deromanticize the African past by revealing violence, corruption, and debauchery to the extreme. In the literary universe he creates, violence is inescapable, and brutally excessive. From the outset, there is an outpouring of violence in the form of multiple rapes, mass suicide, and killings.

> Non loin des corps de la horde des enfants égorgés, on comptait dix-sept foetus expulsés par les viscères béants de mères en agonie, violées sous les regards de tous, par leurs époux, qui se donnaient ensuite, écrasés de honte, la mort.[45]

> Not far from the bodies of countless slaughtered children, seventeen fetuses were counted, expelled from the gaping entrails of their mothers in death agony. Under the eyes of all, those women had been raped by their husbands, who then, overpowered by shame, had killed themselves.[46]

In this scene, located in the first few pages of the novel, the husbands rape their wives and then commit suicide out of guilt and shame. This strategy of narrating the effects of violence against women by focusing on men's reactions is one of the major ways in which the subjective experience of violation is overshadowed. Ouologuem often signals that violence constitutes part of tradition, depicting gratuitous violence as characteristic of African rule and an indicator of the inherently violent nature of power. Perhaps among the first francophone writers to advance a sustained representation of violence by Africans unto other Africans, Ouologuem presented a new trajectory for the discourse of violence.[47] By undoing the notion of a romantic African past, *Le devoir* introduces another stage in the writing of violence which uncovers its precolonial sources, a stage in which the treatment of sexual violence operates as a tangential sign of deviance.

When Ivorian writer Ahmadou Kourouma published *Les soleils des indépendances/The Suns of Independence* (1970), he too took on the project of revealing formerly concealed patterns of violence.[48] Like Ouologuem, Kourouma turned his critique toward African leadership by indicting the violence of postcolonial African governments. Kourouma and Ouologuem represent two points on a similar plane that reveals indigenous violence and moves away from positing the colonial origins of violence: Ouologuem shows that violence preceded colonialism, and Kourouma shows that violence followed colonialism. For Kourouma, the novel is also part political satire, inspired by events in his life when he was a victim of state corruption. The protagonist, Fama, a member of the aristocracy, represents a disillusioned people whose hopes were actually stymied by the arrival of independence. The postindependence state in *Les soleils* contains several types of violence, and throughout the novel various aspects of the society act in concert to highlight an atmosphere of extreme violence. Kourouma's project in *Les soleils* is twofold: he performs violence to the French language through the use of his language, Malinké, and he lays bare the violence and corruption of the postindependent regimes in Africa.[49] The critical discourse surrounding the novel has dealt extensively with the disruptive use of language as a flagrant example of what has been referred to as *la langue violée*.[50]

Les soleils also contains one of the most prominent representations of rape in francophone African literature in the example of Salimata, who is traumatized by her memories of sexual violence. She was first raped by a religious leader after the female circumcision ritual, and later on her first husband attempts to rape her when she could not sleep with him. After she is raped by a religious leader, the community believes his version of the story. This effectively silences the survivor, reflecting the way power relations inform the problem of sexual violence. To the members of the community, a man with such spiritual authority could not be capable of rape. Yet the memory of this violation haunts Salimata; remembering her childhood experience, she thinks to herself, "Le viol! Dans le sang et les douleurs de l'excision elle a été mordue par les feux du fer chauffé au rouge et du piment"/"Rape! Amidst the blood and pain of excision, something had seared her like a fiery pepper, like red-hot iron."[51] Salimata's experience shows that rape is a form of violence that is usually unspoken, that society denies, and does not challenge. This is especially true in the scene on her marriage bed with her first husband Baffi, when the elder women of the village collude with her first husband's attempt to violate her: "les matrones accoururent et la maîtrisèrent et il a désiré forcer et violer"/"the matrons rushed to hold her down and he tried to force and rape her."[52] But on the other hand, the case of Salimata emphasizes the male protagonist's experience, because he is viewed as the one who saves her from her previous life of violence. Her second husband, Fama the protagonist, is positioned as a savior who rescues her from the threat of rape; in this example, the rape of Salimata is significant only for what it can tell us about the couple and, more importantly, the male protagonist. Finally, Salimata's reaction to her rape suggests that running away is the only way to escape sexual violence. Although Kourouma attempts to present rape with more attention to its implications for Salimata, ultimately he fails by framing her experience in relation to Fama.

The theme of violence in Africa exemplified in *Le devoir de violence* and *Les soleils des indépendances* became even more common as writers witnessed the unfurling of dictatorships and state-sponsored violence that descended after independence. The corpus of Congolese writer Sony Labou Tansi demonstrates ostensible concern with state violence. Of course Tansi's representation of violence must also be considered in the context of his overt political activity, indicating again the way representation is often informed by the "reality" of violence in the francophone context.[53] Because Tansi is one of francophone Africa's most acclaimed novelists and playwrights, his representations of the way gender and sexuality play out in the use of violence are important for this study. As Dominic Thomas notes, "Sexuality, cruelty and violence are everywhere in Sony Labou Tansi's vision of the postcolony, and his treatment of the theme is considerably more forceful than that of his literary peers."[54]

One noteworthy example of this forceful tendency is *La vie et demie/Life and a Half* (1979), a novel set in the fictitious African country of Katamalanasie. Tansi proffers a portrait of the postcolonial state in which violence takes on several forms—psychological, physical, sexual, structural, and linguistic. Material violence done unto the body is glaringly present through scenes of torture and murder written in stirring detail. Martial (whose name bears a proximity to "material" that should not go unnoticed) is an official for the Providential Guide who repeatedly abuses his adult daughter to the point that "Il va sans dire que Chaidana avait les joues défoncées par les gifles répétées de son père . . . " / "[it] goes without saying that Chaidana had swollen cheeks due to the repeated slaps of her father."[55] In the scene excerpted below, Martial again resorts to sexual violence so as to punish his daughter's political involvement:

> Martial entra dans une telle colère avec qu'il battit sa fille comme une bête et coucha avec elle, sans doute pour lui donner une gifle intérieure. A la fin de l'acte, Martial battit de nouveau sa fille qu'il laissa pour morte. Il cracha sur elle avant de partir.[56]

> Martial entered into such a fit of rage that he beat his daughter as though she was a beast and then slept with her, no doubt in order to administer an internal slap. After the act, Martial beat his daughter again and left her for dead. He spat on her before leaving.

Here the father's use of sexual violence punctuates physical violation as a gender specific form of punishment. Literally, to punish her more deeply, he uses violent penetration through rape, further intensified by the fact of incest. The daughter, Chaidana, is the same character who prostitutes herself for nationalist causes. Rather than focus on this sexual relationship as one of domination, Tansi uses the character's identity as a woman to forge a disturbing link between gender, nationalist pursuit, and sexuality in order to allude to Chaidana's empowerment.[57] In Tansi's work, rape serves as another example of the endemic violence of postcolonial regimes of corruption.[58] *La vie et demie* illustrates the way the twentieth century was in many ways regulated by violence evident in problems brought on by dictatorship, military regime, civil war, and genocide.

Taken together, the examples traced here highlight the fact that revealing or exposing violence consistently surfaces as a principal concern across a variety of genres, cultures, and contexts in francophone Africa and the Caribbean. A core part of that unveiling is the underlying premise that instances and patterns of violence must be revealed. This is what Antonio Benitez-Rojo has named the preponderance to *revelar violencia*. Often the expository act of writing violence as a theme is meant to uncover what is patently concealed. The need for exposure is dictated by the silent refusal, throughout the dominant literature, of accurate portraits of violence. This refusal can be read as epistemic violence, creating a gulf where the representation of violence should be, and transforming the representation of violence into a violence of representation. The point where epistemic and physical violence converge also interpellates subject positioning and visibility in relation to violence. As Hartman establishes in *Scenes of Subjection*, the spectacle of violence too often assumes a white liberal spectator and subject. Similarly, what we see in these texts is that the spectacle of violence and the occurrence of rape require the centrality of a male subject in order to receive analysis and interpretation. Rape matters for what it means for the male subject. Subject displacement, then, comes to play an operative role in the machinations of rape representation.

Francophone Women Writers and Tropes of Sexual Violence

Alongside, in between, and against these dominant narratives, francophone women writers have also deployed the rape trope to serve various functions in their works. In contrast with the examples listed in the first part of this chapter, a number of texts by women writers reposition rape victim-survivors as female subjects whose personhood is foregrounded and often privileged. In 1969, Thérèse Kuoh Moukoury published *Rencontres essentielles* and became the first African woman to write a novel in French. Although Mayotte Capécia's *Je suis Martiniquaise* appeared in 1948, Caribbean women writers started publishing more novels in French—Simone Schwarz-Bart's *Pluie et vent sur Télumée Miracle* (1972) and Maryse Condé's *Hérémakhonon* (1976)—only in the late 1970s and early 1980s. Having gained momentum from these precursor texts, in the 1990s, francophone women's writing rose to prominence.[59] These works openly challenged masculinist traditions, or, as Brinda Mehta observes, an ostensible concern with "filling in the gaps in Caribbean discourse by inserting their feminist voices contesting non-representations, silencing and intellectual chauvinism."[60] Likewise, this literature also introduced different configurations of the rape trope. Francophone Caribbean writers Simone Schwarz-Bart, Maryse Condé, Paulette Poujol-Oriol and Evelyne Trouillot, as well as African authors Aminata Sow Fall, Calixthe Beyala, Fama Diagne Sène and Ken Bugul, are among those who have rendered rape with complexity and care, attempting to come to terms with the difficult issues posed by rape representation. These representations of sexual violence begin to lay the groundwork for cultural workers whose constructions move beyond the deployment of rape as a symbol of "universal" violence against formerly enslaved and colonized people and instead examine sexual violence as an indicator of the power relations of gender and sexuality. As Marie Chantal Kalisa has pointed out, francophone women writers bring new perspectives to the representation of violence that has dominated the tradition. Likewise, Odile Cazenave notes a marked difference in the treatment of violence by African and Caribbean writers. She posits that for francophone Caribbean women writers, "the constant presence of violence in the narratives associated with sexual abuses, rape, and incest, can be read as a long metaphor for the initial violence forced onto Caribbean women. Through a writing of a violent sexuality . . . [these] novelists are reconstructing colonial history."[61] Focusing on rape is one way to begin making note of how these differences play out in cultural expression.

In *Pluie et vent sur Télumée Miracle*, Schwarz-Bart delineates that "ce que signifie...être une femme sur la terre" [what it means . . . to be a woman on earth] is to be confronted by multiple forms of oppression. The novel, deeply steeped in Créole oral traditions, inaugurated a wave of *écriture féminine* that was anchored in the specificity of the Guadeloupean context.[62] *Pluie et vent* is widely regarded as a canonical example of francophone women's writing and has been lauded for its attention to fundamental concepts such as matrilineal genealogies, subjectivity, intersubjectivity, and history-memory, each one carefully delineated from the perspective of a female subject positioning.[63] Schwarz-Bart's rendering of Télumée's life prefigures many subsequent texts by francophone women of Caribbean and African descent. As an important precursor of Caribbean women's writing and francophone women's literature, *Pluie et vent* offers a contemplative condemnation of the historical, structural, and domestic violence that shapes black women's lives.

Most notably, Schwarz-Bart demonstrated the sources of this violence, which was perpetrated not only by white men but also by other compatriots. The example of Télumée's relationship with her abusive husband Élie illustrates how the intersections of race, class, and gender form a negative nexus of power that frames the protagonist's experience. Interestingly, Schwarz-Bart successfully complicates the gender politics of how we understand violence against women by noting the way Télumée's grandmother Reine Sans Nom encourages her to remain in that relationship, regardless of the ongoing violence. Despite this consideration of gender violence in the form of domestic abuse, the rape trope appears in a familiar pattern when Monsieur Desaragne attempts to assault the protagonist. The passage is described in detail: "à ma grande surprise M. Desaragne entra tranquillement, referma la porte derrière lui, s'adossant à la cloison. [. . .] Puis venant à moi il posa ses mains sous ma jupe, marmotta d'une voix nasillarde . . . 'on dirait que tu es sans culottes, ma fille.'"/[To my great surprise Monsieur Desaragne walked calmly in, shut the door behind him, and leaned against the wall. [. . .] Then he came over to me and put his hands up my skirt, muttering 'No pants, eh?][64] Explaining his desire for Télumée, M. Desaragne says to her, "écoute, j'ai besoin d'une petite négresse qui chante dans la vie plus vive qu'un éclair, j'ai besoin d'une petite négresse si noire que bleue, c'est ce que j'aime./[Listen, I need a little singing Negress more lively than lightning, a little blue-black Negress. That's just what I like."[65] For Télumée, this incident is not a passing preoccupation, but rather is informed by her locations of identity as a poor, black, Guadeloupean woman. Yet she is able to threaten him and thwart her employer's advances. Processing what happens to her, she thinks, "Le combat avec M. Desaragne était loin, et je n'y avais pas vu ma victoire de négresse, ni ma victoire de femme. C'était seulement un des petits courants qui feraient frémir mon eau avant que je noie dans l'océan./The struggle with Monsieur Desaragne was a thing of the past, and I hadn't realized the victory I'd won, as a Negress and as a woman. It was just one of the little currents that would ripple my waters before I was drowned in the sea."[66] Eventually it will be clear that the drowning to which she refers is her demise and the physical abuse at the hands of Elie. As a result the conclusion she reaches here establishes a link between the sexual assault of her white male employer and the domestic abuse at the hands of her black partner.

Ultimately, *Pluie et vent* casts black women's oppression in terms of resistance and resilience, highlighting the remarkable ways in which the Lougandour women in general and Télumée in particular endure and surmount the multiple forms of suffering in their lives. Télumée's use of folklore and memories passed down through her matrilineal genealogy acts as what Ronnie Scharfman has called the "key to the defense against the alienation by the Symbolic."⁶⁷ The scenes of gender-based violence in the novel operate not as allegories but as informative aspects of life central to the protagonist's personhood.

Maryse Condé, whose first novel, *Hérémakhonon,* was published four years after *Pluie et vent,* also devotes a significant portion of her work to representing sexual violence both as a major theme and a casual reference. Given the fact that, as Dash writes, "sexuality has always been a subversive force in Maryse Condé's work," she serves as an important model for how sexual violence figures in francophone Caribbean literature.⁶⁸ In *Moi, Tituba, Sorcière . . . noire de Salem* (1986), she uses the rape origin story as a point of departure for the novel. In the protagonist's opening monologue, we learn that "Abéna, ma mère, un marin anglais la viola sur le pont du Christ the King, un jour de 16** alors que le navire faisait voile vers la Barbade. C'est de cette agression que je suis née. De cet acte de haine et de mépris."/["Abena, my mother, was raped by an English sailor on the deck of Christ the King one day in the year 16** while the ship was sailing for Barbados. I was born from this act of aggression. From this act of hatred and contempt"].⁶⁹ Condé identifies rape as "aggression" inflected with "hatred and contempt," immediately foreclosing interpretations of sexual violence that mitigate the act's inherent violence. Here Condé uses sexual violations to illuminate a life of trauma that subsequently unfolds for the protagonist. Locating this fact of birth as a result of rape as central to the narrative demonstrates the ways that sexual violation can inform the elaboration of the female subject in a meaningful way, even when this original act of rape is not the focus of the novel.

A marked preoccupation with history evident in Condé's oeuvre results in frequent representations of colonial and postcolonial violence in a way that critiques the phallogocentrism of her male peers. To this end, Condé's first novel, *Hérémakhonon,* displays what Susan Andrade has described as "the obsession with history and sexuality [that] solicits a psychoanalytic interpretation of the two as naturally overlapping."⁷⁰ Indeed, Condé brings increasing texture and nuance to her representations of rape: *Célanire coucoupé* (2000) is a novel of speculative fiction infused with descriptions of sexuality, violence and power. There are references to rape in Célanire's relationship with her stepfather, and another character murders the man who raped and abused her. In *Histoire de la femme cannibale* (2005), the protagonist discovers her dead husband's proclivity for sexually abusing his male students demanding sexual favors in return for academic guidance. These examples indicate an evolution of how and the extent to which sexual violence figures in Condé's oeuvre.

In the African context, the theme of violence animates many of the novels of Calixthe Beyala—the self-proclaimed Afro-Parisian writer of Cameroonian descent, and arguably one of the most well-known and prolific women of African descent who write in French. Early on in her corpus, acts of violence such as rape, domestic violence, family abuse, and self-mutilation operate as guiding leitmotifs. In particular, her third novel, *Tu t'appelleras Tanga* (1988), features a protagonist who comes from a generation of rape survivors, as both her mother and grandmother were raped. In fact, Tanga's entire life is structured around her trauma from these events. She explains her current situation as a prisoner in terms of her father's violation, even though the event occurred years ago. She writes, "Ainsi que l'homme mon père, qui plus tard, non content d'amener ses maîtresses chez nous, de les tripoter sous l'oeil dégoûté de ma mère m'écartèlera les jambes au printemps de mes douze ans . . . cet homme, mon père qui m'engrossera et empoisonnera l'enfant, notre enfant, son petit-fils, cet homme ne s'apercevra jamais de ma souffrance et pourtant cette souffrance a duré jusqu'au jour de sa mort, jusqu'au jour de ma mort" ["And so it was that the man my father who, not content to bring his mistresses home, to fiddle with them under my mother's disgusted gaze, would later rip me apart in the budding of my twelfth year. And so it was that this man my father—who made me pregnant and poisoned the child, our child, his grandson—this man never noticed my suffering, and yet it lasted until he died, until the day of my own death"].[71] Likewise, gender violence plays a prominent role in the daily lives of the protagonists of *C'est le soleil qui m'a brûlée* (1987) and *Assèze l'africaine* (1994). Beyala's erotic novel, *Femme nue, femme noire* (2003), departs from this previous view by taking a libertine approach to sexual encounters that are informed by and rooted in violence. *Amours sauvages* (1999) details an environment fraught with violence, pain, and trauma in the Parisian banlieue. In this novel, the threat of rape is graphically described as "trouer l'utérus." There is a clear evolution in these portrayals of sexual violence through Beyala's recent novel, *Le roman de Pauline* (2010), in which the teenaged protagonist is raped by her stepfather yet is determined to take control of her own sexuality. In Beyala's novels, gender violence in general and rape specifically are used to delineate women's condition in postcolonial societies both on the African continent and in the French metropole. The forms of violence to which these women are subject constitute essential aspects of their identity and subjectivity. Sexual violence becomes a way of elucidating black women's personhood, as it informs the creation of their narratives and the texture of their personal stories. Beyala is an exemplar of how rape can function as more than as a sign of something else or in a symbolic mode. Rather, her texts illustrate the possibilities of personhood with which rape representations intersect.

Ken Bugul's vibrant corpus offers other examples of how women writers can rewrite dominant scripts of sexual violence in their works. While her autobiographical novel *Le baobab fou* (1983) is rife with scenes that point to the gender dynamics that undergird sex and violence, I want to turn to Bugul's fiction which powerfully visits these themes as well. In *La folie et la mort* (2000) Fatou Ngouye and Mom Dioum eventually die due to the different forms of gendered oppression they face. There is also an implicit intertextual link between Kourouma's Salimata and Bugul's Fatou. Like Salimata, she is a multiple rape victim-survivor and her violation is perpetrated by a police chief and a priest. Rape, the novel reminds us, is considered to be a lesser form of violence, a fact illustrated by the police chief who decides to rape Fatou rather than kill her. Like many of the postindependence novels, *La folie et la mort* establishes a link between corrupt government regimes and acts of violence. Yet here, the female characters who are subject to this violence do no operate only as symbols of the regime. Their stories are given wider significance and narrative authority in the novel at large, serving as an important example of how the conflation of sexual and political violence need not result in subject erasure.

Like Beyala and Bugul, Monique Ilboudo, Werewere Liking, and, more recently, Bessora have written at the intersections of sex and violence, offering texts in which sexual ideologies collide with violence to impact the evolution of the protagonist in definitive ways. In an attempt to offer as comprehensive a portrayal of the rape trope as possible, I have spent time considering how sexual violence figures in the works of canonical francophone texts. According to Jean-Marie Volet, the new generation of writers entered into the millennium portraying violence with unprecedented rigor and vigor: "the issue of violence and survival in hostile environments seems to gain momentum while the soothing virtue of human interaction becomes a kind of last refuge in the face of extreme economic hardship, domestic violence, the collapse of social values, and war."[72] He uses both francophone and Anglophone writers to show that, "violence is everywhere in African women's writing of the late nineties."[73]

Twenty-first-century novels extend this tradition. Haitian writer Evelyne Trouillot's novel *Rosalie l'infâme* is an important example that presents the machinations of race, gender, sex, and power at work during slavery in 1750 Saint-Domingue. Less than halfway through Trouillot's Haitian neo-slave narrative, the protagonist recounts:

"C'est encore Man Augustine qui me serra dans ses bras, quelques mois après, quand je lui arrivai de la grande case, les jambes triées de sang et de liquide gluant, les yeux humides et la bouche tremblante. 'Le maître ou Monsieur Raoul?' demanda-t-elle simplement. 'Monsieur Raoul,' balbutiai-je en essayant de chasser l'empreinte des mains blanches au fond de moi. 'Je l'ai mordu au bras,' ajoutai-je en crachant avec dégoût . . . 'Tu es une femme Arada, tu le resteras, les doigts de l'homme blanc ne peuvent t'enlever la marque de ta race. Elle est dans le blanc de tes yeux et tu mourras avec comme ta grande-tante Brigitte, comme ta grand-mère Charlotte, comme ta mère.' 'Et comme toi Man Augustine.' 'Oui, comme moi.'"

"It was again Man Augustine who held me in her arms, a few months later when I got to her in the large shack, legs streaked with blood and sticky liquid, moist eyes and trembling lips. 'Master or Mr. Raoul?' She simply asked. 'Monsieur Raoul,' I stammered, trying to chase the imprint of white hands inside me. 'I bit him on the arm,' I added, spitting in disgust. . . . 'You are an Arada woman, you will remain one, the fingers of the white man cannot take the mark of your people away from you. It's in the white of your eyes and you will die with it . . . like your great-aunt Brigitte, like your grandmother Charlotte, like your mother.' 'And like you Man Augustine.' 'Yes, like me.'"[74]

This passage is significant for the way it does not mention the details of Lisette's experience. Because of the prevalence of rape in Saint-Domingue, Man Augustine knows what her goddaughter has suffered before the young woman even shares it. Trouillot conveys the frequency of scenes of sexual violence by not explaining exactly what happened. In telling only parts of the story, Lisette leaves in what is important to her: (her resistance) that she bit Monsieur Raoul on the arm. As the entire novel indicates, Trouillot points out the ways in which female slaves were able to engage in small acts of resistance, whether through infanticide, refusing to have children, or (in this case) doing violence to their perpetrators. Finally, Man Augustine powerfully reframes Lisette's experience by recalling her identity *(tu es une femme Arada, tu le resteras, les doigts de l'homme blanc ne peuvent t'enlever la marque de ta race)* and by affirming that her identity is not located in this traumatic experience, but rather in her heritage and belonging to a matrilineal genealogy. Lisette's acceptance of her words and addition of Man Augustine to the equation emphasizes that not only has she understood the older woman's teaching, but she adds her own wisdom and interpretation to it. This gesture by Lisette powerfully underscores the successful transmission of a matrilineal legacy. Trouillot's novel also exemplifies Haitian feminist Carolle Charles' important point that, "Haitian women cannot be reduced to their experiences as rape victims," but that their subjectivities are composed of multiple factors that include responding to, resisting, and being oppressed by sexual violence. This stance helps negotiate a more complex personhood in which women are fixed as neither victims nor survivors but move fluidly between the two. These examples are an important reminder of how women writers such as Trouillot, Condé, Beyala, and Schwarz-Bart among many others have been instrumental in the development of a black francophone feminist tradition in which the rape trope is deployed for diverse ends.[75]

Vocabularies of Violence: Normalizing, Denying, and Analogizing Rape

The examples mapped on these pages are but fragments in the representation of violence in the francophone cultural imaginary. In no way do they constitute a complete list, but they are helpful signposts for tracing a history for discourses of violence in which there is a clear rhetoric of rape that operates almost exclusively at the symbolic level.[76] The texts mentioned here point to the frequency with which writers have boisterously take on ideologies of violence, at times with an unbridled belligerence of their own, advocating violence. Both their theories and fictions have informed the response to, function of, analysis of, and understanding of the problematics of violence in francophone literature and culture. My interpretation of how rape figures is ostensibly concerned with literal, visual, or symbolic representations. These examples contribute to the circulation of what we can name as an ideological subtext of violence: an implicit framework that designates the parameters of violence, as well as its interpretation. The subtext (unequivocally discernible yet never explicitly named) achieves more than a dominant representation, or even a master narrative that perpetuates violence with flourishing strokes of the pen. The subtext produces its own form of epistemic violence. Given the symbolic work that rape is made to do in these examples, examining the ideological subtext is my attempt to understand the operations of this symbology, as well as the gender and sexual politics that undergird them. Together these examples also point to an established rhetoric of rape. This rhetoric of rape shows how "transposed into discourse, rape turns into a rhetorical device, an insistent figure for other social, political and economic concerns and conflicts."[77] By asking that we look more closely at how and why rape is constructed in the extant discourses of violence, my readings of these scenes foreground what is at stake for the violated bodies in this rhetoric of violence.

Because gender is "a primary field within which or by means of which power is articulated," any analysis of gender violence is inextricably bound to questions of power.[78] Before turning to the ways sexual violation has been critically interrogated in rape cultural criticism (where the question of power has received ample and at times controversial attention), let us contemplate the ways violence and power intersect. As the examples from the francophone texts show, violence is often linked with colonial rule, imperial authority, and autocratic governments. In the succinct manifesto *On Violence,* Hannah Arendt contests the link between violence and power.[79] Attempting to disrupt the equivalence of violence and power, Arendt argues that "violence can destroy power ... but what can never grow out of it [violence] is power."[80] This approach is limited because it focuses primarily on the perpetrator of violence in order to propagate nonviolence. We can push Arendt's point further by focusing on the subjective experience of violence, that is, what the destruction of power means for the victim.[81] Looking closely at the moment when power and violence overlap accounts for the subjective experience of the victim/survivor of violence, for whom violence can in fact lead to greater forms of subjective recognition.

The tenuous nature of subjectivity and autonomy in the context of both slavery and colonialism largely depended on the use of violence, which (as it destroyed power) was integral to allowing these systems to thrive. As Saidiya Hartman observes, historically violence has been used to deny Black sentience and humanity through the disavowal of subjectivity.[82] One of the primary ways in which this occurs is through the scene of violence itself, which locates its significance in the spectator's affective understanding of that violence rather than in the body that is violated in the process. This dynamic results in the objectification of the subject of violence, effectively erasing *subjecthood* when *subjection* occurs. Hartman's conclusions are especially instructive for how she links the study of power to notions of spectacle and performance. Violence has the power to reshape the world for an individual, to force people into submission and obedience, and to make them feel pain; thus, it undeniably weighs upon subjective experience. In these contexts when we think about violence in terms of subjectivity, it *is* a viable form of power, contrary to what Arendt argued. Accepting violence as a way of maintaining power takes into account the way physical and mental force undermines subjectivity, leaving fewer options for the subject. This is the reason violence is often used to apply coercive force, as is clear in different manifestations of abuse (whether they are in the context of slavery, gender violation, torture, etc.) that serve to discipline, punish, and oppress. Because "the first aim of violence is to block the victim from any relationship to [their] own pleasure not mediated by violence," it emerges as an ostensible point of reference for subjective understanding.[83] We can understand the "blockage" as a form of power that subsequently shifts the subject's perception of the world around her or him.

This could be interpreted as a Foucauldian-influenced understanding of power, especially when he argues that "power is everywhere not because it embraces everything but because it comes from everywhere" in at least two ways.[84] I am concerned with cultural production that exhibits the destructive effects of violence upon the victim but also identifies ways that these subjects can be empowered. I also view power as fluid—power is not eternally inaccessible when violence is present. When viewed as a technology of power, violence has the ability to *suppress and augment* subjectivity.[85] On one hand, the victim can be dominated, but on the other hand, the experience of violence highlights the reality of a victim's subjectivity. Rather than focus exclusively on the victimization endured as a result of sexual violence, I am interested in the construction of narratives in which characters feel, survive, and succeed despite systems of domination that work against them. Power and domination are interwoven concerns in the dynamics of sexual violence, and together they help to elaborate how sexed and gendered bodies emerge as sites of oppression, but also the way subjects reconstitute their bodily selves to move beyond violence.

Based on historic moments, violence has been portrayed differently in cultural production; however, when we search for the ideological subtext, certain patterns in their representations reappear across periods. These patterns convey several related concepts and categorize violence according to "exterior" or "interior" modes—two overlapping spheres that are partially contained within each other and that are therefore not binary. In fact, these categories are exhaustingly postmodern in their nonbinary nature. When violence happens from the "exterior," it reveals the injustice of past or current violence that was done unto the subject by an outside (nonindigenous) force. These representations often organize around the experiences of slavery, colonialism, and/or neo-imperialism. In the francophone Caribbean, Odile Ferly reminds us, "the association between history and rape is a leitmotiv of Caribbean postcolonial writing: many counterhistories have qualified the colonization process as a rape of the islands together with their indigenous and subsequently transplanted inhabitants."[86] Also common within this sphere is the view that violence dominates the period after colonial independence *only because* it was originally introduced by the colonizer/slave-owner/occupant who—whether in their kidnapping of Africans to conduct the slave trade or through their imperial expansion of territory or their present-day exploitation in the age of globalization— can be deemed responsible for its proliferation. Within this exterior mode, violence can also be subdivided temporally and understood for past, present, or future implications. Sembene Ousmane exhibits the effects of colonial rule on quotidian life, and Zobel portrays the violent heritage of slavery long after its abolition. As these shifts in time occur, the idea that violence has an exterior, nonindigenous source remains constant.

The "interior" sphere is equally dedicated to exposure, but more so in terms of the violence that occurs from within the group. Here the view is that violence is organic in origin. This type can also be framed in terms of historic moments. According to Ouologuem, violence pre-dates colonization by several centuries. Many of the writers who attempt to unveil the occurrence of violence from an "internal" standpoint nonetheless locate the origins of violence in moments of European contact, indicating that the two directions are not opposite because they can be simultaneously present. In this light, Tansi's *La vie et demie* denounces totalitarian governments and acknowledges the legacy of colonial rule as a contributing factor to their proliferation. Mbembe's *On the Postcolony* is especially thought-provoking in this regard because his theory of the postcolony offers that both interior and exterior forces are present, interdependent, and instrumental in violence that is currently unfolding on the African continent. These directions indicate that whether they orient their texts in terms of the "external" or "internal" causes of violence, many francophone cultural workers are noticeably concerned with thinking about violence in relation to a point of origin and in terms of exposure. Yet, the exposure of violence is incomplete without a consideration of its gender and sexual dynamics, which do not seem to be pursued in either sphere.

In contrast to the different ways that violence functions across the canon of francophone cultural production, figurations of rape seem tellingly static therein. Whereas the violated (and invariably female) body is constantly present as a frame of reference for imagining rape, it is rarely invested with embodied and subjective significance. Whether the text orients itself to focus on interior or exterior violence, the treatment of rape perpetuates another form of epistemic violence as it routinely ignores subjective and bodily knowledge. Representations within the ideological subtext alternate between normalizing, allegorizing, denying, and altogether ignoring sexual violence. What happens here is an entanglement well captured by Sharon Stockton when she explains, "inducted into the symbolic through language, the subject is constituted as a function of discourse and inhabits a world similarly composed."[87] As rape operates only on this symbolic level, violated bodies and the subjectivities to which they are linked become abstractions. For example, Ouologuem's *Le devoir de violence* makes a case for pre-existing, precolonial, or "native" violence in order to challenge the purported origins of violence. A feminist reading of this text undermines its revolutionary nature because the treatment of violence against women in *Le devoir* subscribes to old patterns in every way.[88] As Eileen Julien observes, in the novel,

> Sexual violence and rape become near transparent signs of something else . . . sexual violence in these texts is elucidated, if we read carefully, by the context of political violence. Rape, these texts suggest, is not an aberration, not a singularly sick act, nor an individual problem in an otherwise healthy society.[89]

Here rape functions as metonymy, becoming the "transparent sign for something else," and it is directly linked with the political context, which informs the occurrence of sexual violence. Viewing sexual violence as a natural byproduct of the colonial legacy of violence *normalizes* its proliferation after decolonization and makes it indistinguishable from other manifestations of violence. Violence is ultimately regarded as a vestige of colonialism and slavery, those political and historical machinations that forever altered the Caribbean islands and the African countries. Just as this history cannot be undone, violence becomes an omnipresent element of these worlds effectively transforming them into societies that are "bound to violence."

Another prominent feature of this ideological subtext is that gender difference as a subjective experience is *denied* within the context of violence. In other words subjective experience is passed over in favor of a distanced discourse of sexual violence. Although the female subject's experience of violence on an individual level is rarely represented, the male experience in relation to violence against women is portrayed in great detail (e.g., Fanon, Ouologuem). Pain in this context becomes both political and personal, but the male subject is the person for whom it matters. This contributes to the silencing of the subjective gendered experience of violence because instances of rape are created not to disclose the painful experience of the woman, but for the psychological effects of *her rape* on her male family member (husband, father, son, or brother). Or, to put it in the words of Sabine Sielke, "rape remains a matter between men."[90] A manifestation of this practice that denies the "situated knowledge" of female subjects is apparent in the work of Fanon: sensitivity to rape arises when the reader learns that the colonizer rapes the wife of the colonized.[91] Implicitly, because women are typically understood to play less of a role in the revolutionary process, their experiences of violence are insignificant in a subjective register.[92] In the societies of colonial and imperial rule, where the rape of black women was the legal right of the colonialist/slave owner, violations against women were further instigation for resistance. As objects of oppression, women exist only as victims of rapes perpetrated by the slave/colonial master. Their violations motivate retaliatory forms of violence. A noticeable dialectic of ownership also follows from this logic: black women are raped because they belong to white slave/imperial masters. And black men, incensed by the ownership of what (according to patriarchal order) should be rightfully theirs, express violence against colonial men or, at times, seek to enact similar violence against colonial women.

This is precisely what we see at work in *Les damnés de la terre* when Fanon presents the example of an Algerian revolutionary whose wife is raped by French authorities as a form of punishment. There is also the often-cited example of *Peau noire, masques blancs*, in which Fanon makes plain the masculine impulse to protect women from being sexually assaulted by the European man in his disturbing interpretation of Mayotte Capécia's *Je suis martiniquaise*.[93] Fanon's reading of Capécia's text effectively robs the black female subject of capacity for desire by attributing relations with white men as a sign of alienation. However, sexual violence is sanctioned when the colonized longs to sleep with the colonizer's wife; here revenge for the injustice of colonialism is projected onto the white female body. This type of ideological praxis also makes it difficult to estimate what the consequences are for women when violence is made use of and, moreover, makes it difficult to grasp the complexity and the breadth of varying forms of violence. Instead, rape becomes accepted and even integral to the decolonization process rather than becoming something to be analyzed, critiqued, and theorized, like the violence of the colonizer against the colonized and that of the colonized against "*himself.*" Although different forms of violence are intentionally subject to scrutiny, rape seems impervious to sustained analysis. Here, rather than accepting this lack of attention to (or denial of) the subjective experience, I am concerned with what happens when we pay attention to and critically interpret what is happening to the body and to subjecthood in scenes of sexual violence.

The ideological subtext also engenders another form of violence by casting the female body in a *metaphoric or symbolic role* in the representation of rape. This allegorization of the female body often operates in service of a national project. As Françoise Lionnet has forcefully argued:

> Nationalist rhetoric often aligns women with a vocabulary of home and motherland that simultaneously dispossesses them of their individuality and physical autonomy while using their faces and bodies as representative icons of an idealized collective identity.[94]

First we saw that women are deprived subject positioning, and their rape is significant only for the way it affects the men around them. Now we see that they also emerge as symbols and icons for national identity. Similarly, the vocabulary of sexual violence used to channel the image of the nation disembodies and objectifies women. Violence against women, when it is condemned, is denounced because women are symbolic sites of nationalism. This process is especially clear when rape is used as a term to designate violations beyond the body, operating singularly as metaphor and metonymy.[95]

Of course, the continued redeployment and production of rape as a metaphor is certainly not particular to francophone Africa and the Caribbean; in works ranging from the Bible to Greek mythology to the African American literary canon, rape is deployed to signify cultural norms. As Sandy Alexandre has cogently argued, "the use of . . . imagery to discuss sexual violence committed against women's bodies is certainly not new, especially since the impulse to conflate female imagery into the natural landscape has long been a literary trope."[96] Within the francophone imaginary, rape metaphors proliferate through images such as *la langue violée* (the raped language); *la terre violée* (the raped land); and *la femme violée* (the raped woman). This gendered vocabulary of violence issues analogies that place the traumatic impact of rape on the margins. Sexual violence is evoked to justify retaliatory violence, once again placing the focus on the male subject's position and gaze. One of the most recognizable forms of this practice is in the trope of the land as a gendered female body. Conceptualizing the land as a feminized space invaded by a white male perpetrator offers little room to consider violence against the female body outside of the nation-as-woman configuration, which I consider in depth in Chapter 3. When women figure as more than symbols, in both nonfiction and fiction, they usually are the hapless victims of violence. They are the Awas and Tambiras of Ouologuem's *Le devoir de violence,* women who do not have ownership over their narratives of rape. In the case of Awa's violation, she is used as a bartering chip at the service of Saif, and the rape serves as punishment for her and her husband. The model of white masculine domination over a feminized landscape relegates gender violence to another nationalist cause, a reason for wrath against slavery and colonization rather than as a violation against women. Each of these forms of erasure—normalizing, denying, and analogizing—illuminates the lack of theorization and analysis in relation to the violation of the female body in the context of discourses of violence.

Ultimately, this ideological subtext re-inscribes violence, giving rise to epistemic violence that relegates the position of the raped subject to a subordinate role that is less significant than that which the rape is supposed to signify. This practice engenders violence by relativizing and denying the subjective experience of rape, allegorizing the female body to limit gender violence to a symbolic realm, normalizing the fact of gender violence by positing its origins, or simply ignoring the occurrence of gender violence. By framing the examples of works cited in this chapter according to the ideological subtext, I intend to begin mapping the ways sexual violence has been embraced as a topic and as a theme in francophone studies. However, few extensive interpretations and analyses of rape exist within this body of work. Given this superfluous production of thought on postcolonial violence, the "longstanding connection between rhetorics of gender and rhetorics of colonialism" and the ways that rape brings together the concepts of sex, gender, and power, it is alarming (though not unsurprising) that more consideration has not been given to examining the way the rhetoric of rape fits into extant cultural narratives of violence.[97]

Rape Cultural Criticism and the Politics of Representation

There are two ways in which the aforementioned lack of analysis surrounding sexual violence becomes significant for this project. Though I am interested in the frequency with which rape appears as a metaphor or symbol, I am especially moved by the lack of critical attention given to sexual violence, especially in the face of its hypersignification. As Carine Mardorossian explains in "Towards a New Feminist Criticism of Rape," this paucity of sustained analysis also occurs in feminist texts, for in many ways "sexual violence has become the taboo subject of feminist theory today."[98] What does it mean to turn away from the taboo and use *rape* as the principal term of textual analysis?

To do so is to begin with questions: how does one represent sexual violence? What is the relationship between rape and its representation? Indeed, as Toby Siebers puts it, "the link between representation and violence always involves a strange twist. Paradoxically, representation *contains* violence. Representation and violence limit each other."[99] How does rape extend or limit this definition of the relationship between violence and representation? My central concern is the ways incidents of violence revolve around the scene of sexual violence substantively rather than symbolically and the ways rape is structured and situated in cultural work. In many ways, these are not texts that pivot around the representation of sexual violence. However, by reading them as such, I hope to disrupt the lack of attention to rape and to draw attention to how analyzing sexual violence can lead to theoretical innovations. Unlike the earlier examples from this chapter in which rape is elided, allegorized, or denied, I foreground the analysis of rape representation. Of course, sexual violations against the female body are not the only forms that exist in the texts that I examine. However, in their marked recurrence, they can be interpreted as a sign, a code whose unlocking expands and extends understandings of violence.

In rape cultural criticism, sexual violence has been scrutinized for its cultural construction: critics and theorists interrogate the description and function of scenes of rape, extrapolating from them the implicit cultural significances and developing insight about the ways sexual violence operates within various categories. Twenty years ago, Helen Higgins and Brenda Silver were among the first to approach rape as an area of scholarly inquiry, with the publication of *Rape and Representation*. Though they were not the first to write about the social and cultural aspects of rape representation, they were the first to deeply engage the semiotics of sexual violence in an explicitly feminist- and humanities-oriented intervention. Their preoccupation with reading rape is especially helpful here; Higgins and Silver explain that in this process,

> one crucial step taken by feminist literary critics . . . has been to trace the ways in which women (artists or characters) 'represent' themselves. . . . This entails discerning where or how they break through discourses that have circumscribed their perceptions of the causes and the nature of sexual violation. . . . But the act of rereading rape involves more than listening to silences; it requires restoring rape to the literal, to the body: restoring, that is, the violence—the physical sexual violation.[100]

The editors call for poetics that creatively restore material violence in order to avoid eclipsing the violent experience of rape, and they demand that we rethink and re-examine the project of representation overall. The literal portrait of violation is essential to such a framework, but it is not without its difficulties. The example of rape in many ways underscores the failure of cultural production to fully convey an act that is at once corporeal, emotional, physical, and intensely traumatic. Rape resists representation. Rape and its meaning often function, as Sabine Sielke explains, in opposition to one another. When depicting rape, there are numerous points to consider: How is rape described in the text? Which rhetorical strategies are deployed to tell the stories of survivors/victims? How do survivors/victims react to their violations, and what are the short- and long-term effects of the assaults? Within each of these broad categories, there are more specific questions to address: Does the author portray the rape in detail? Is it explicit or implicit? Is the survivor story told in the first or third person? How is the memory of the rape approached? How does the author elaborate rape trauma syndrome? What becomes of the violated body? How does cultural production reflect, challenge or attempt to dismantle some of the basic premises of a global rape culture?

My use of the term *rape culture* echoes the definition offered in *Transforming a Rape Culture*:

> [It is] a complex of beliefs that encourages male aggression and supports violence against women. It is a society where violence is seen as sexy and sexuality as violence. In a rape culture women perceive a continuum of threatened violence that ranges from sexual remarks to touching to rape itself. A rape culture condones physical and emotional terrorism against women as the norm. In a rape culture both women and men assume that sexual violence is a fact of life.[101]

To think about the representation of violence in relation to a "rape culture" that is a *global phenomenon* is to espouse a feminist understanding of violence against women as a cultural and social reality. By conjoining the idea of a "rape culture" with "silence," I intend to emphasize the ways in which neither the prevalence of rape nor the representation of rape have been consistently noticed, read, analyzed, or theorized in the francophone context. The idea of a rape culture has been deemed controversial and contested by scholars such as Sielke, who questions the use of the term and its overinvestment in narratives of victimization. Despite this critique, establishing that there is in fact a culture of silence in relation to rape helps to demonstrate the urgency of a work such as this one. By interrogating the ways rape generates meanings that then circulate in the creation of rape scripts, we can begin to look for more productive modes of rape representation. As Higgins explains,

> The cultural meaning of rape is rooted in a symbiosis of racism and sexism that has tolerated the acting out of male aggression against women and, in particular, black women. An important part of the task of deconstructing the consciousness of rape is revealing the linkages between the social [and the] cultural mechanisms that empower violence against both racial groups and women and insure the fragmentation of marginalized and oppressed groups to consolidate the power of the patriarchy.[102]

Some of the linkages between social and cultural mechanisms that we have already seen at work in this chapter are intertwined with histories of the Global South that include slavery, colonialism and imperialism. Perhaps the hold that rape narratives have over these contexts is related to ways in which slavery and colonialism still haunt the cultural imaginary. These histories explain why rape emerges as an important cultural signifier for the oppressor, whether it is the slave or colonial master. At the core of this symbology, the black women signified in these representations of rape become an "absent center around which colonial and postcolonial discourses about rape turn."[103] By positing rape as a paradigmatic form of violence, rather than as a corollary manifestation of violence, this book reworks some of the basic taxonomies of violence that underanalyze rape.

Repenser la violence

The twenty-first century has already had formidable episodes of violence that seem to engulf the entire world in its interpretation and analysis. Beyond the looming specter of 9/11, the genocide in Darfur, and the war in the Democratic Republic of the Congo, these massacres give shape to a landscape in which critical attention to violence in the media and in the academy is historically informed. Two important journals in the francophone field help to make this point. In 2002, *Notre librairie: Revue des littératures du sud* published an edition titled *Penser la violence,* and in 2005, *Research in African Literatures* (RAL) had a volume featuring articles on "Political Violence," many of which focused on the Rwandan genocide. By way of conclusion, I want to turn to the *Notre Librairie* example as one that can properly attest to the tenor of discourses of violence within the francophone field.

On the pages of *Penser la violence,* we find a lengthy exegesis on Frantz Fanon and his role in shaping the theoretical framework of violence; mentions of genocide, including an article devoted to the Rwanda; and a section on "littérature de la violence" followed by "violence de la littérature"—an important distinction that divides the matter between thematics and semiotics. Bernard Mouralis rightly critiques Fanon and Sartre for neglecting the cultural dimension of violence, and Daniel Delas identifies "le chien" as a discernible leitmotif in texts about the Rwandan genocide.[104] Rarely in this collection is violence "thought" of in relation to women. The gendered aspect of violence (which is just as prevalent) occupies virtually no position within this issue. With a few exceptions, gender is an unnamed category in the analysis of violence. At times the different authors cursorily mention women writers, such as Nadine Bari and Calixthe Beyala (who is singled out for attention regarding her scathing use of language).[105] However, in the same article mentioning Beyala, there is a return to the notion of *la langue violée,* this time identified as a subversive action done unto the French language—inserting indigenous languages throughout the French in a piercing motion of violation. According to this interpretation, once again, rape serves a rhetorical or symbolic function.

Only two articles of the *Notre librairie* issue stand out for their inclusion of women: Véronique Bonnet's and Tanella Boni's. Véronique Bonnet thoroughly considers violence against women in a segment of her article on violence and cities, acknowledging that

> La violence subie par les femmes est un autre invariant de l'écriture des villes africaines: silence du viol (on frôle ici le pléonasme). . . . En ce sens l'opposition masculine/féminine reste une catégorie opératoire pour appréhender la violence urbaine.[106]
>
> The violence that women are subject to is another invariant of writing from African cities: the silence of rape (one can brush past the pleonasm). . . . In this sense the masculine/feminine opposition remains an operative category to apprehend urban violence.

Bonnet's reference to the silence of rape as a pleonasm, however, somewhat undercuts the politicization of gender violence. The use of pleonasm suggests that silence in response to rape has been thoroughly addressed or even adequately thrown into question, although in reality the silence remains deafeningly uncontested. Ivorian writer Tanella Boni, whose thoughtful designation of "familiar violence" is the epigraph for this chapter, alludes to the rape of women by using skin color. "La couleur de la peau constitue un autre témoignage de la rencontre souvent violente du maître blanc et l'esclave noire." ["Skin color constitutes another testimony to the often violent encounter between the white master and the black slave."][107] Through this innocuous example, Boni deploys the dominant image of the slave woman raped by the slave master but foregrounds female subjectivity by including the word *souvent* to suggest the possibility that some (albeit few) of these sexual interactions could be consensual. By echoing Monique Ilboudo's use of skin color as an example of rape, she further acknowledges innovative techniques that women have used to write about rape without falling prey to problematic rhetoric.[108]

Otherwise, *Penser la violence* maintains silence in the same way that many francophone texts mentioned earlier in this chapter do. Given the stated goals of *Notre librairie* to propose "[q]uelques angles d'attaque pour penser une violence souvent flagrante mais aussi complexe" [several angles of attack to think about violence that is often flagrant and also complex], these omissions are especially disturbing.[109] Each time the inclusion of women as victims, perpetrators, writers, or theorists of violence is but a footnote. Their inclusion is a mere afterthought within the broader field of inquiry (with the exception of Bonnet and Boni). I use the example of *Notre Librairie* to illustrate that the interface of violence and gender was overlooked as a locus for detailed analysis, and that women writers issue challenges to this view by inserting gender violence in ways that are both explicit (Bonnet) and implicit (Boni).

The presence of violence and its representation have been habitually recognized in the context of francophone African and Caribbean writing. Within the African tradition, the past experience of colonization and the present political situations inform the ways violence is represented.[110]

> Reconnaissons d'abord que la violence dans la littérature africaine de langue française est aussi ancienne que celle-ci, et qu'elle apparaît alors dans les compositions écrites comme la description de violences traditionnelles véhiculées par la mémoire collective.[111]

> Let us first recognize that violence in African literature written in French is also as old as the literature itself, and that it appeared in those days in the

written compositions as the description of traditional violence propelled forward by collective memory.

Likewise, violence has been acknowledged as integral in francophone Caribbean literature because of the institution of slavery. In the case of Martinique, Guadeloupe, and Haiti, slavery and its abolition were all entrenched in violence, so much so that we can read the violence that has since unfolded in terms of this heritage.

> La présence dans la littérature antillaise d'une thématique de la violence très marquée est l'une des conséquences de l'histoire d'innombrables violences qui constitue l'histoire même de la Caraïbe depuis l'époque de sa conquête et de sa colonisation par les Européens.
>
> The presence in Antillean literature of a well-marked thematic of violence is one of the consequences of the history of countless forms of violence that constitute the very history of the Caribbean since the time of its conquest and its colonization by Europeans.[112]

The intertwined relationship between history and violence repeatedly explains the presence of the latter in cultural production, yet the kinds of violence present are systematically uninterrogated. Examinations of these Black Atlantic literatures have framed the phenomenon in terms of its historical legacy, as well as its current manifestations and reality. Slavery and colonialism are violent historical traumas—this has been one of the main explanations for why violence is ubiquitous and virtually omnipresent in the Caribbean and Africa. There are historic and cultural reasons why violence is such a prevalent theme; similarly, there are cultural and historical reasons why rape is not a prevalent theme.

Le viol dans la violence

The French word for rape, *"le viol"* can be read as the excised version of the word *"la violence."* In French, the feminine noun becomes masculine when it designates the violation of women. Or perhaps the feminine noun becomes neutered because the masculine form is also the understood "universal," prompting us to read *le viol* as a sweeping manifestation of *la violence*, the masculine and the feminine collapsing into one.[113] Another way to think about this relationship is evinced in the embedded presence of *viol* within *violence*, so that *le viol* is the beginning of *la violence*. At the least, the language suggests that *viol* and *violence* are interdependent.

Yet, in all of the theory, history, and criticism that comprise francophone studies, this slippage of meaning, this erasure of sex difference in the context of violence, or the ways in which the masculine and the feminine encode our understanding of *le viol* and *la violence* have rarely been pursued. Although the difference here is a linguistic question of grammatical designation, and *viol* is ostensibly a form of *violence* (thus contained within it), this difference offers a compelling point of departure for an investigation of the rhetoric surrounding and the representation of violence in francophone studies through the lens of sex and gender. An etymological consideration of the word *violence* can extract from it the word *viol* in order to move toward an analysis of the intertwined nature of rape and violence. I locate the theoretical underpinnings of this project within the embedded containment of *viol* in *violence*, or the eclipsing of *violence* to create *viol* (a linguistic feat that seeks to obscure the presence of *-ence*, or the *violence* in *viol*). Based on these analyses of various texts in different forms and genres, I will continuously return to the uncomfortable relationship between *viol* and *violence*, a dynamic that, I argue, calls us to understand the prevalence of each in the presence or absence of the other. This practice, this act of gendering violence, offers a new way of thinking about what it means to represent rape in the francophone context.

2
Rethinking Political Rape
Genealogies of Sexual Violence in Haiti

> . . . To think about Haitian women solely in terms of the most popular forms of visual representation is to contribute to her marginalization in a society which already forcefully and violently occludes her full participation in the workings of a country to which she loses her sweat and blood on a daily basis.[1]
>
> —Myriam Chancy

> Women's stories of sexual abuse are often subordinated to larger political narratives of the nation-state, and this is especially true of Haiti, where the nation's political upheavals, poverty, and refugees overwhelm the global imagination.[2]
>
> —Donette Francis

ONE OF THE central founding myths about the genesis of the Haitian people is a story of intimate violation that is set in motion with the rape of Sor Rose. Telling a version of this tale and citing Haitian historian Timoléon Brutus, Colin Dayan explains that:

> The legend of Sor Rose or Sister Rose is a story of origins that depends for its force on rape. In this story, the Haitian nation began in the loins of a black woman. The ancestress must be ravished for the state to be born. . . . The legend of Sor Rose, like that of the land of Haiti . . . begins with a

woman "brutally fertilized" as [the Haitian historian] Brutus puts it, "by a slave in heat or a drunken white, a criminal escaped from Cayenne [the French colonial prison]; or a degenerate from feudal nobility in quest of riches throughout the continent."[3]

This gendered history emblematizes the way rape operates as a national symbol in service of a national myth consolidated around the violation of women. It stages a primal scene of violence that focuses on rape as a sign whose signification relates to the creation of the nation. Here the experience of sexual violence is endowed with national significance that glosses over the individual (invariably a woman) who has been the victim of such violations. In fact, the three possibilities for who may have raped her (a slave in heat, a drunken white, or a degenerate from feudal nobility) tell us more about the perpetrators' identity than about the victim's. As Dayan observes in the quote above, the story "depends on her violation," and "the cosmology begins with rape," with little consideration for or attention to what becomes of this violated body during and after the rape. Sor Rose's tale is an origin story that requires rape to occur for it to function. It is a narrative of necessary violation through which the woman's rape gives birth to the nation. In this configuration of origins, the Haitian people would not exist without rape. As such, the tale of Sor Rose stands as one of the earliest examples of the way the rape metaphor takes shape in the Haitian imaginary.

Yet there is far more that the story leaves out. Who was Sor Rose? What do we know about her other than the fact that she was raped? What did her "brutal fertilization" actually entail? What were the details of this violation? We know that its results produce the Haitian people, but what about the violent events that precede this birth? Beginning with Sor Rose to chart a genealogy or social history of sexual violence in Haiti displays how easily stories of rape are weaved into national narratives. What happens when we explore the details of Sor Rose's rape as a way to chart different, feminist genealogies of sexual violence in Haiti? In what follows, I use the example of Sor Rose's literary namesake, the protagonist Rose Normil in the second novella of Marie Vieux-Chauvet's *Amour, colère, folie* (1968)/*Love, Anger, Madness* (trans. 2009), as a point of departure for examining the social history of sexual violence in Haiti and exploring its discursive and cultural legacies.

I open this chapter with Sor Rose to begin making historical sense of the way rape functions as a sign for something else in the Haitian cultural imaginary. The story of Sor Rose extends to Chauvet's character because the representation of sexual violence in the novella has often been interpreted as the sign of the Duvalier regime. *Amour, colère, folie* has been critically identified as a text about violence, and in some instances even qualified as a "violent text."[4] The critical discourse surrounding the book has invariably named violence as a dominant trope of the trilogy, and suggested that this violence is evinced in its formal elements as well as in terms of the thematic content.[5] Thematically, the violence it explores is the notorious dictatorship—the reign of the father François "Papa Doc" Duvalier, succeeded by the son Jean-Claude "Baby Doc" Duvalier, an ever-present topic of Haitian literature.

Amidst the memories imprinted on the Haitian consciousness since 1957, the Duvalier regime (1957–1986) figures as prominently and as persistently as the violence it waged on Haitians for nearly thirty years. The images *of* and images *during* Duvalier have left indelible marks on the Haitian landscape, imaginary, popular consciousness, and cultural production. Although these traumatic marks for eternal life left by the "President-for-life" are routinely reproduced throughout Haitian literature, Chauvet's trilogy represents the first time that the Duvalier regime is rendered in such explicit and unabashed detail.[6] Its publication marks the earliest official "dictator novel" that attempts to capture the contours of *la terreur*.[7] Notwithstanding the consistent discussion of violence as a principal axis of *Amour, colère, folie*, there are instances of sexual violation in the trilogy that literary critics, Haitian and Haitianist scholars, and reviewers have approached with more reticence, thus creating a critical silence that mirrors societal and cultural responses to rape. Particularly, the depiction of the violence that Rose Normil—the heroine of the second novella—is subject to has rarely been identified as multiple acts of rape.

This chapter re-reads Rose's violation as a way to begin charting an alternative genealogy of rape representation that foregrounds acts of rape for what they do to the victim/survivor rather than what they mean for the nation. I am particularly concerned with the way a "rape culture of silence" gets transmitted discursively, and the ways contemporary Haitian writers follow the legacy of Marie Vieux-Chauvet, straining against the limits of these silences and prompting us to re-imagine, re-theorize, and prioritize sexual violence. Through close readings of Rose's rape, the circumstances surrounding it, and her family's reactions, I argue that sexual violation is not intended to be a sign of national or political violence but rather that it deliberately disturbs the culture of silence obscuring rape. Thus, I deploy methodologies that analyze *Colère* as a trenchant critique of the politics of sexual violence in Haiti. Throughout this chapter, I challenge the relationship between rape and politics, arguing that despite the fact that in *Amour, colère, folie* several female characters are subject to sexual violence by state actors, the trilogy is encoded with a recognition that gender violence is not only enmeshed in political instability, but rather that it is a social phenomenon that is always taking place. Ultimately my readings expose the ways the violence waged against women knows bounds that are limitless, and that violence, while inexorably political, is not always a consequence of (state) politics. From a methodological perspective, to do this, I read around the context of the Duvalier regime in *Amour, colère, folie* to speculate about what else the text tells us about sexual violence, as well as what it *does not* tell us. Put another way, this chapter reflects on what happens when, rather than focusing on the context of conflict, we focus on the material, psychological and bodily significance of sexual violence for the individual subject. What happens, when instead of considering Sor Rose's rape only as the birth of a nation, we consider the details—the material conditions, the presence of rape trauma syndrome, and the looks imposed by others?

Situating Vieux-Chauvet's triptych as foundational to an alternative Haitian genealogy of rape representation, the second part of this chapter moves on to contemporary Haitian novels that also illuminate ways of reconceptualizing sexual violence. The examples to draw from are numerous: Margaret Papillon's *La marginale* (1987) focuses on an upper-middle-class young woman who is raped during the carnival celebrations. Sophie Caco, the protagonist of Edwidge Danticat's *Breath, Eyes, Memory* (1994), is the product of rape; her mother was assaulted in the cane fields by an unknown perpetrator. Later on, Sophie is sexually abused by her mother. Gary Victor's *Le diable dans un thé à la citronnelle* (2000) begins with the scene of a young girl being raped. Guitèle Jeudy Rahill's *Violated* (2001) reminds us that sexual violence occurs in a number of different ways, with different perpetrators and different victims. In the novella the examples of rape range from young boys who are violated by U.S. marines during the Occupation, to young women caught in unequal relationships in which they are forced to give sex in return for security, as well as characters caught up in the family trauma if incest and sexual abuse. Josèphe, Myriam Chancy's protagonist in *The Scorpion's Claw* (2003), spends the duration of the novel draped in silences that are the result of sexual trauma. In *Rosalie l'infâme* (2003), Evelyne Trouillot unveils the sexual machinations of the slave era through references to rape on the plantation and in the Middle Passage. Jaira Placide's *Fresh Girl* (2004) presents a young protagonist struggling to heal despite the trauma of rape. Most recently, Kettly Mars' *Saisons sauvages* (2010) completely reforms our understanding of the sexual politics of the Duvalier regime and further unravels the dynamics of rape Chauvet begins to summon in *Colère*. To examine contemporary figurations of the politics of sexual violence in Haiti, I turn briefly to examples from Danticat's *The Dew Breaker* (2004) and Placide's *Fresh Girl* (2002) before devoting sustained analysis to Kettly Mars' *Saisons sauvages*. Throughout this chapter, to both complement and complicate my readings of rape representation, I also turn to nonfiction texts, such as historic and journalistic accounts of the Duvalier regime, and human rights reports about rape in Haiti based in different time periods, ranging from the post-coup period of 1994 to the post-earthquake investigative report from the Institute for Justice and Democracy in Haiti entitled *Our Bodies Are Still Trembling* (2011) and *Beyond Shock* (2013) a recent report on rape that works assiduously to undo post-earthquake rape myths. By incorporating these various texts of rape in grounded social contexts, I purposefully destabilize the dichotomy between reality and representation as a way to challenge the creation of rape scripts. Looking at the symbolic and material realms together, better equips us to rethink and reform the ideologies that seek to contain us. Focusing on literature and cultural production as a way to shift our understanding of rape narratives means reading and re-reading to unearth keys that unlock codes about sexual violence that persist in the Haitian imaginary.

The works I look at after Chauvet—Mars, Danticat, and Placide—re-politicize rape by shifting the emphasis from the context of rape to the embodied and subjective experiences of female rape survivors, despite the fact that for each story, political conflict is integral to the setting. The narrative logic of each novel as I interpret it here undermines the direct link to political unrest; only by theorizing these texts in a different way do we begin to lay hold of the way the women's bodies and the sexual politics at play are more important than are the conflicts that serve as their background. My methodology also draws on studies from various disciplines about rape in Haiti, to examine the way representations of sexual violation can challenge the oppressive gender dynamics of nationalist discourses. The limitations of the nationalist framework are exposed through critical tensions, often exhibited in terms of the silence and voice that surround sexual violence and the trauma that follows it. Brinda Mehta has observed that "while Haitian women writers stress the urgency of claiming and redefining history through a feminist lens in order to contest their erasure in nationally ratified commemorations and patriarchal scripts, it is also important to highlight the ways in which trauma codifies its own subjective text as another way of reading history," reminding us of the important role that trauma plays in fictive and historic texts.[8] The interplay of silence and voice, of seeing and being seen, helps to highlight the ways rape underscores the failure of cultural work in conveying an act that is simultaneously corporeal, emotional, physical, and intensely traumatic. Moreover, these discursive moments of intervention point to the way society has failed to interrogate gendered forms of violence and thus comment on the politics of rape representation. Before turning directly to these readings, the following section draws from the insights of rape cultural criticism to initiate a discussion that grapples with the various meanings of rape in Haiti and the different political inflections at play when we try to understand sexual violence in this context.

Given the positive correlation between political instability and sexual violence—numerous studies indicate that an increase in sexual violence is endemic to the heightening of political violence—it becomes particularly necessary to interrogate the context out of which these representations emerge.[9] This is important in Haiti, where the increase of sexual violence has repeatedly been linked to political violence. Whether during slavery until 1804, under the United States' occupation (1915–1934), during the Duvalier regime (1957–1986), or in the period of *dechoukaj* following the first coup that unseated Aristide (1991–1994), the occurrence of sexual violence has been framed in relation to specific historic and political upheavals. In contrast, the sustained portraits of rape, as I examine them here purposefully focus our attention on gendered violence that has often been silenced in favor of emphasizing the broader manifestations of violence (the violence of slavery, dictatorship, occupation, etc.). The construction and the codification of these narratives demonstrate the way the representation of sexual violence can challenge a rape culture of silence.

The Politics of Rape in Haiti

To speak of a rape culture in relation to Haiti is not a novel idea. As Ismène Zarifis writes, "a popular belief in Haiti . . . is that rape against women is not a serious crime. Instead, these human rights violations are too often viewed as an accepted part of social behavior."[10] One of the tacit contributions upholding this belief is the way rape becomes contextualized in terms of political conflict. Rape can be associated with criminality only when it is an element of dictatorship, occupation, coups, or other forms of institutionalized lawlessness during which the entire body politic is subject to widespread violence. But doing so displaces the significance of rape's sexual politics. Moreover, framing sexual violence in the context of political unrest diminishes the role that rape plays in the production of a specifically and socially-recognizable female body. Foregrounding the context of rape leaves the violated body in the background in a way that reifies cultural silences surrounding sexual violence. To begin the work of questioning the way we understand conflict, I am intentionally shifting the emphasis from the *context* of the conflict in which rape occurs to the *subjects* of rape in conflict, particularly to consider the physical and material consequences of violence for individualized bodies rather than for a body politic.

Any discussion of what it means to re-politicize rape will become slippery, and my discussion is perhaps purposefully slippery. I understand and am critically aware that some might find counterintuitive the notion that re-politicizing rape means extricating it from the context of "political unrest." However, being that this is part of my larger project to theorize rape in ways that are not always apparent, obvious, or even clear; this type of language, though unwieldy, is nonetheless necessary. We can perceive the intersection of rape and politics in two main ways. First, there is rape that occurs during periods of political instability or in the context of government or state-sponsored violence. The second links politics to power relations, sexual dynamics and social institutions at play in both the reality and representation of rape.

A brief history of several critical moments of conflict helps to highlight what I mean by the first, and more conventional, understanding of rape and politics. It would be difficult to conduct a detailed social history of rape in Haiti, but for the purposes of this book, I want to draw attention to five historical moments that help inform the way rape is understood. From a historical perspective, the problem of rape can go as far back as precolonial times and the development of the nation. As Mimi Sheller explains, "Women had no place in this construction of the nation and its moral destiny, except as mothers of warriors and symbols of the nation itself, which was envisaged as the great 'mother' of the people whom male citizens must venerate and protect."[11] This focus on veneration and protection is at play in rape discourses: the instances in which rape is decried are primarily related to forces of invasion and violation coming from the outside. During the first U.S. occupation (1915–34), Haitian women were raped by marines at a time when human rights abuses were generally ongoing despite the professed aims of military intervention.[12] These narratives of sexual violence are highlighted at the expense of other accounts of rape that were also ongoing during this historical period. As Donette Francis observes in her thoughtful study on the sexual politics of citizenship, the rape of Haitian women by the Cacos is a less well known and less well studied occurrence of violence in Haiti—"the complete story of the Cacos exposes the reluctance of nationalist narratives to disclose that these native insurgents also raped women of the very nation they were assembled to protect."[13] This offers another example for the way the occurrence and incidence of sexual violence is obscured in favor of a nationalist narrative that steadfastly limits rape to an act involving the colonial, imperial or occupying power as the perpetrators of Haitian women.

Twenty years after the occupation, under the Duvalierist state, rape was often used as punishment for political dissidence, or simply as a recreational activity for Tonton Macoutes. In *Haiti: State against Nation*, Michel-Rolph Trouillot asserts, "the Duvalierist preference for the sexual 'conquest' of females associated with the political opposition, from torture-rape to acquaintance rape and marriage infused the politicization of gender with violence."[14] One of the earliest documented examples of Duvalier's use of violence as a means of control was the gang rape of journalist Yvonne Hakim-Rimpel in January 1958, one year after the beginning of his presidency.[15] Yvonne Hakim-Rimpel was one of the founding members of the *Ligue féminine d'action sociale* [League of Feminine Social Action], as well as one of the main editors of the organization's journal, *La Voix des femmes*, and later on the founder of the journal *Escale*. In *Papa Doc et les Tons Tons Macoutes*, Diedrich and Burt describe the incident in detail:

> . . . une demi-douzaine d'hommes armés s'introduisent par effraction chez Mme Yvonne Hakim-Rimpel, une journaliste de l'opposition. . . . Ayant abandonné les enfants sur le trottoir ils s'éloignent en emmenant la mère avec eux. On retrouvera cette dernière le jour suivant sur une route peu fréquentée près de Pétionville. A demi inconsciente, dépouillée de la plus grande partie de ses vêtements, c'est dans un état critique qu'elle est dirigée immédiatement vers l'hôpital.[16]

> . . . a half-dozen armed men fractiously introduce themselves into the home of Ms. Hakim-Rimpel, a journalist from the opposition. . . . Having abandoned the children on the sidewalk, they went further away, taking the mother with them. She was found the following day on a road not often frequented near Pétionville. Half unconscious, stripped naked of most of her clothes, it was in that critical condition that she was immediately brought to the hospital.

The description makes no mention of the rape and directly links the attack to Hakim-Rimpel's political activity as a journalist. After the incident, the vocal journalist, feminist and supporter of Duvalier-contender Déjoie stopped writing and abandoned all forms of advocacy, having been literally silenced by the regime's violence. Likewise, the League of Feminine Social Action curtailed its political activities after launching a campaign demanding investigation of the incident, to no avail. Whereas scholars such as Michel-Rolph Trouillot and Carolle Charles have emphasized that the rape of women for political reasons became a problem for the first time under Duvalier, in charting a social history of rape in Haiti, my view is that rape under Duvalier was not a new phenomenon; it only took on a different tone that had all too familiar undertones.[17]

In her analysis of gender relations and feminism in Haiti from 1980 to 1990, Haitian feminist scholar Carolle Charles argues that the rape of women was widespread and intertwined with the political system. She refers to this process as "the gendering of state violence under Duvalier" and explains:

> In a country where the ideology of women's weakness was strong, the regime's indiscriminate use of violence against women and children was also a negation of the previous paternalist discourse of the state and a violation of the cultural codes of Haitian patriarchy. Women began to be detained, tortured, exiled, raped, and executed.[18]

At the same time, the significance of violence against women was continuously undermined by a national narrative that overdetermined the terms of political violence. Noting this phenomenon, Donette Francis extends Charles's point, observing that:

> Under the Duvalier regime, women emerged as a specific category subject to surveillance, discipline and punishment, and in many ways the state succeeded as the women's movement went underground and did not visibly reemerge until the 1980s. Yet, their narratives of sexual violation were rendered invisible as the state exercised its power to obscure violations against women by dismissing their testimonies as nonsensical and inconsequential to the political life of Haitian society.[19]

Viewed in this way, Hakim-Rimpel's story becomes the sign of "political sexual violence," and, as in the case for Sor Rose, we find that it is difficult to ascertain the details of that story, to discover more about her and so many others like her. The story of Hakim-Rimpel signifies another first, an example of rape being used to keep a woman in submission to a national project and a story that would be passed down for generations as a sign of the regime's oppression.

Another defining moment in the evolution of the concept of political rapes takes place several years after the revolts that resulted in the end of the Duvalier regime, when a military coup unseated the first democratically elected president, Jean-Bertrand Aristide, in 1991. The period following the coup gave rise to the operation *machin enfènal*, set in motion to quell the activities of Aristide supporters. Death squads flourished throughout the country, the most notorious being the Revolutionary Front for the Progress of Haiti (FRAPH), a group widely responsible for the routine violation of women's bodies.[20] Again, under this military junta, the incidence of rape swelled, and female supporters of Aristide were constantly subject to violence. During such politically tense periods, women's bodies are under siege, along with the body politic. The language surrounding the *dechoukaj* offers a particularly clear example of this practice. Again Charles explains that in 1991, "the military intervention resulted in state-inflicted and state-sanctioned human and civil rights abuses, including political assassination, detention, massacres, torture of prisoners, and disappearances . . . women were also subject to other forms of political violence, in particular, rape."[21] Likewise, in the groundbreaking collection of Haitian women's voices, *Walking on Fire: Haitian Women's Stories of Resistance and Survival*, feminist journalist-activist Beverly Bell links the incidence of rape to the *dechoukaj* period crackdown of violence against women activists from the peasant and rural classes.

Without denying the alarming rise of sexual violence in these specifically political contexts, it is helpful to ask a different set of questions by picking up where feminist scholars like Charles and Bell have left off. What gets left out of conversations about political rapes? How is gender-based violence acknowledged outside of these contexts? What is at stake when rape is merely relegated to seasons of political conflict? Although these studies achieve an important task in naming rape and advancing the movement to end sexual violence, they also perpetuate the notion that rape takes place mainly because of political instability. The corresponding suggestion could be that rape is used as a weapon to stabilize the nation when not at war and to destabilize it during political conflict. It is political only when it is the result of national and international conflicts. As a final example from international human rights advocacy, the report "Haiti: Curbing Sexual Violence at a Time of Political Turmoil" reads:

Sexual violence in Haiti does not only affect the marginalized population. A study shows that seven out of ten women in Haiti have been victims of violence, and that 37 per cent of those cases were sexual violence. During the political and social unrest that has been ongoing since 2003, the rate of sexual violence increased several-fold.[22]

Although the report begins by observing that sexual violence affects more than the "marginalized population," it focuses primarily on times of social and political turmoil and attaches the core of analysis to these moments. This study also fails to address the accusations of rapes perpetrated by members of MINUSTAH during the same period in question. Listening to this silence, we can note the irony that a "stabilizing force" would also be responsible for rapes, in a dynamic similar to the U.S. marines raping Haitian women during the occupation. The relationship between rape and conflict is further unsettled by the fact that supposedly "stabilizing" forces are also raping and creating more victims. A renewal of reported rapes occurred during the second administration of President René Préval and under the leadership of the United Nations Stabilization Mission in Haiti (MINUSTAH).[23]

Today's context also compounds our perception of rape in Haiti when we consider the aftermath of the earthquake that devastated Port-au-Prince, Leogane, Petit Goave and Jacmel on January 12, 2010. The proliferation of tent cities throughout these regions has also been linked to an increase in sexual violence.[24] Creating a genealogy of rape in Haiti and tracing the way it operates discursively requires that we also pay attention to the way rape narratives are being constructed and interrogated in post-earthquake Haiti. In light of Francis's point that "dominant narrative forms have failed to tell Haitian women's stories of violation," how do the most recent statistics surrounding the earthquake destabilize prevailing discourses that surround sexual violence?[25] To understand this phenomenon, it is essential to turn to a variety of texts because the archive is still being formed. To this end, I turn to two human rights reports about sexual violence in postearthquake Haiti: *Our Bodies Are Still Trembling: Haitian Women's Fight against Rape* and *Beyond Shock: Charting the Landscape of Sexual Violence in Post-earthquake Haiti*.

There have been numerous print accounts featuring stories of women who have been raped in the tent cities that now populate Port-au-Prince. Skimming some of these headlines, the same discursive figuration of violence relating to conflict is apparent: "Rape flourishes in the rubble of Haitian earthquake," and "Post-quake chaos fuels rape in Haiti." These titles tell us through language what the numbers of women being raped verifies—their bodies bear the brunt of conflict. A report by Amnesty International declares that "Haitian women are more at risk of sexual violence because of the breakdown of law and order and the spread of flimsy camps after last January's earthquake," shoring up the statistically proven idea that natural catastrophes exacerbate sexual violence.[26] Feminist scholars such as Gina Ulysse and journalists such as Beverly Bell have been instrumental in foregrounding the voices and experiences of Haitian women living in vulnerability under the flimsy tarmac cover of the tent cities, offering an important counterpoint to the dominant narrative.

The title of the human rights report, *Our Bodies Are Still Trembling: Haitian Women's Fight against Rape,* implicitly erects a parallel between the land that shook under the magnitude of the 7.0 earthquake and the bodies that shudder in its aftermath. But the signifier is not emptied of the sign, given how carefully the report foregrounds Haitian women's testimonials of rape, as well as their organized responses. Despite the fact that rapes are usually grossly underreported, the testimonials included illustrate that victim/survivors are speaking subjects and are not mute or muted objects of political rapes. From the beginning, the report establishes that "having no other options, Haitian grassroots women's groups have resorted to taking charge of their own security."[27] These groups' sustained efforts to address the needs of survivors, and to include individuals who seek justice for their rapes by attempting to report to authorities also disrupts the notion of survivors confined to silence; rather, the silence in question belongs to a broader cultural tendency that ignores narratives of rape. Although the efforts are in vain, given the government's established "lack of political will and capacity to respond," it is important to note that many of the victim/survivors present have sought justice in this particular way.[28] In fact, in many ways the study points to new directions for politicizing rape by arguing that "when states fail to bring perpetrators to justice, they implicitly condone such violence, giving rise to impunity that facilitates further abuses and *normalizes* GBV [gender-based violence]."[29] The logic that follows from this point does not relate sexual violence to the context or the political situation; instead it carefully addresses the way the normalization of rape occurs and helps to maintain a rape culture. By directly naming the larger context of sexual violence, this study avoids the pitfalls that only associate rape with moments of political unrest or instability. The examples from *Our Bodies Are Still Trembling* underscore the important ways in which Haitian women are contributing to their own liberation through speaking, testifying and organizing. This is an especially meaningful gesture, given the widely circulated notion that in the Global South women require Western vehicles to enable and activate their liberation. It is an effort that addresses the politics of rape representation and brings us to the second consideration integral to my conception of rape and politics: to name sexual violence as a facet of gender oppression and politics no matter the situation surrounding its occurrence.

Beyond Shock also marks a significant departure from the established rhetoric of rape surrounding the problem and proliferation of sexual violence in the aftermath of the 2010 earthquake. The comprehensive report, forthcoming as a book, makes an important intervention because it not only provides an overview of the problem but also highlights the different responses to sexual violence from different perspectives. This last point is essential because it considers the role of state and extra-governmental actors, local and community activists, victim-survivors, their loved ones and advocates, and every day individuals who are working to combat rape. This approach effectively dismantles a number of rape myths regarding agency and advocacy. It is also an attempt to extricate the rhetoric of postearthquake rape from an overdetermined narrative of devastation and ruin. As the authors state in the introduction, *Beyond Shock* "offers hope for the future while revealing a very difficult situation in the present."[30] Another critical aspect of *Beyond Shock* is the determination to offer a counternarrative to the pervasive rape scripts that emerged after the earthquake. Some of the major findings directly contradict sensationalized media reports about rampant rapes in tent cities. For example, *Beyond Shock* offers that, "Post-quake reports show more rapes are committed by persons known or familiar to the victim, often neighbors and friends. A minority involve gang rapes by masked attackers." This finding challenges 2010 media reports of "stranger rape" by escaped criminals.[31] Findings such as these demonstrate that general facts about rape can still remain applicable in the context of crisis.

The language throughout *Beyond Shock* reveals a consistent effort to undercut the spectacular element of rape rhetoric in postearthquake Haiti. Even the title—which can be read as a directive to move past the spectacle of rape—establishes this effort. To this end, with its focus on the holistic approach to recovery, the study also shifts attention away from the problem of rape to the strategies that victim-survivors engage to move beyond it. In this way the book establishes individual subjectivities and personhood as crucial and constitutive sites for the production of knowledge about sexual violence. Both *Our Bodies Are Still Trembling* and *Beyond Shock* present a new kind of human rights report on the subject of sexual violence that while it acknowledges the relationship between rape and conflict, does not delimit its occurrence to those circumstances. Together these reports demonstrate that social and political conditions shape how rape is framed and mediated. These dynamics can also be understood as taking into account the politics of rape.[32]

To understand that, regardless of its context, all sexual violence is relevant to politics and power in different registers takes politics to mean more than government- and state-related power. It is also to recognize rape as an institutionalized practice. This idea, the need to distinguish between the different definitions of *political*, is more readily understandable in French. *Le politique* refers to government- and state-related dynamics, policies and so forth (on the one hand). On the other hand, *la politique* refers to the principles reflecting a certain sphere, or theory, related to power in society.[33] Most studies about sexual violence in Haiti have focused on *le politique*, moments of political unrest as their context and thus fail to account for *la politique*, the gender politics of rape, by foregrounding the incidence of sexual assault as related to government activities and upheaval and not as a daily reality. To repoliticize rape is to account for and focus on the latter. In this context, repoliticizing rape means bringing this second sense of politics into rape representation, even at the cost of the conflict-related context.

Amour, colère, folie: An Urtext of Violence

Identifying *Amour, colère, folie* as an urtext of violence is to name not only the centrality of violence to the narrative's unfolding, but also to identify this work's significance in the context of *la terreur* with how precisely it captured the fear and brutality of the era. *Amour, colère, folie* helps us to think through the politics of portraying violence under the dictatorship as specifically sexualized and gendered.[34] As Elizabeth Walcott-Hackshaw points out, "there are few Caribbean women writers who have explored the inner workings of terror like Marie Chauvet . . . [the] triptych is destabilizing, haunting, and unsettling because of the works' penetrating, 'bare-all' portrayal of brutal atrocities."[35] Walcott-Hackshaw goes on to examine the violence in the lives and on the bodies of Claire, the protagonist of *Amour*, and Rose in *Colère*, although even she does not name what happens to Rose as an act of rape. As Myriam Chancy recalls in *Framing Silence: Revolutionary Novels by Haitian Women*, although during the 1990s rape was increasingly used as a weapon of violence against women, Chauvet's work serves as a reminder that this was not a new practice.[36] Feminist writers and

Haitian women have been particularly instrumental in foregrounding the way *Amour, colère, folie* "documented the effects of the Duvalier regime upon women's lives and very bodies."[37]

Much has been written about Vieux-Chauvet's daring use of sexuality, her creation of a violent universe in the novel, the scandal surrounding the publication of her book, and her subsequent exile. However, relatively few authors have explored the mechanics of how she deploys rape representation. Nor has there been focused attention to the way sexual violence actually functions throughout the book. It seems that (1) these paratextual aspects of *Amour, colère, folie* have occluded the critical discussions of the book itself or (2) when the text is analyzed, rape is subsumed into a larger category of violence under Duvalier. This marked reluctance to "read rape," as it functions in *Amour, colère, folie* underscores prevailing attitudes toward sexual violence. The collective failure to "call it rape" is related to the myriad issues surrounding *Amour, colère, folie*. The critical discourse on *Amour, colère, folie* has been fraught with questions that (although they bring together the themes of gender oppression, violence, sexual disclosure, and political unrest) rarely devote prolonged analysis to the representation of rape.

Held as a sex slave, Rose Normil, the only daughter of the bourgeois family at the center of *Colère*, is raped regularly for an entire month. Her perpetrator, never named, is referred to only as *le gorille* due to his gorilla-like features. This choice to not name the perpetrator helps foreground Rose's experience. She becomes a victim of violence after her family's lands are gradually taken away by the *hommes en uniforme noir* (the men in black), who represent Duvalier's Tontons Macoutes. *Colère* relates the story of the seizure of the land by the regime and the ostensible results: destabilization throughout the Normil family, futile attempts to barter for the land's return, and repeated violation and gradual deterioration of Rose's body. Understanding what happens to Rose while she undergoes thirty days of sexual exploitation is first contextualized in terms of the system of terror and the culture of fear that reigned under Duvalier.[38] The temptation here is to simply to associate the acts of violence with the dictatorial regime, an impulse that is not incorrect. But to do so and end the analysis there overlooks Chauvet's inscripted critique of a pre-existing culture of silence that obscures and ignores violence against women. Symbolically, Rose's predicament can be understood as the surrender of the female body to the dictatorial regime, or as the use of gendered violence as a tool to mitigate other forms of violence. The latter attempts to invert the relationship of sexual violence by offering the body within terms of consent. It also suggests that sexual violence is a less painful and better alternative to other forms of violence.

On the one hand, Rose is an example of the way seizure by the state also extends to the female body. Rose's rape is linked to the political context of Duvalier—to a period of intensified state violence, one in which rape is a prominent form of abuse against Haitian citizens. Still, focusing on the paratext, the acts of rape, and what happens to the Rose afterwards demonstrates that this is also about a society in which sexual violence is met with the same formulaic responses and drawn according to reductive patterns. My readings reveal how Vieux-Chauvet manages to repoliticize rape in a way that attends to its gender politics, by focusing on the rape culture of silence that is especially present in Rose's death at the end of the novella. What Rose endures, her family's reaction, and her own deteriorating physique display the consequences of rape on the mind and on the body. Whereas previous scholars have closely associated Rose's act as one of martyrdom, I want to suggest instead that the narrative logic of *Colère* actually demands that we identify Rose's predicament as rape, torture, and sexual imprisonment because of the conditions under which she "agrees" and the circumstances of each encounter.

Rose's sexual imprisonment illustrates what happens when rape is accepted, ignored, and obscured by other forms of violence. Representing the details of the ordeal from Rose's perspective in an entire chapter attaches another dimension to this story of sexual violence because it offers insight into the violated woman's actual experience. This insight is crucial—it frames violence in terms of the ways it affects the survivor, whereas previously in *Colère*, the aftermath of the occupation of the lands and Rose's situation are viewed only in relation to others. We can read this use of narrative devices as the author's simultaneous repetition and revision of tradition: she contextualizes rape in terms of political terror, yet she highlights violated women's subjective experiences of rape. She also mirrors societal reactions to survivors of sexual violence through the character of Paul, Rose's brother, and other family members.

The only chapter describing the sexual violence in detail opens with the use of a first-person narrator signaling that for the first time, Rose tells her own story of sexual trauma. In almost every other chapter of *Colère*, Rose is being spoken about, reflected upon, or looked at by others. Her brother repeatedly judgmentally assesses her and obsesses over her appearance. Her father is ashamed, as he contemplates his own complicity in the act. Her youngest brother disdainfully comments that she smells. Her mother follows her with guilt, not believing yet never asking her daughter to speak for herself. Before the sexual torture begins, two characters, referred to as "the gorilla" and "the lawyer," stare at Rose lustfully, making her uncomfortable in her skin with their objectifying gazes. "Il tourna lentement vers elle et elle eut l'impression désagréable que sous ses énormes lunettes son regard la déshabiller." [He slowly turned his head toward her, and she had the unpleasant impression that he was undressing her behind his glasses.][39] Now, for the first time, as though in response to all of these devouring gazes and appraisals by others, Rose tells her story through her eyes. That this moment arrives only after the other perspectives in the novella—although each one invariably reflects on what unfolds during this particular scene—underscores the importance of how voice functions in this moment. Rose is literally positioned at the end of others' opinions. We can read this in two ways: either the other family members precede her because they are more important, or allowing her to speak last highlights her ability to speak for herself despite the cacophony of other voices. The second option understands Rose's narrative as a counterpoint to how others view her. The latter reading undermines the idea of a silent survivor who does not understand, reflect on, or speak what happens to her. The produced effect is that we learn the details of the sexual violence based on Rose's experience, from her perspective, in a move that restores her voice.

In the first paragraphs, the reader witnesses a transaction occurring—Rose is being taken in exchange for the return of the land. Her body will negotiate the family's territory back into their hands. When she is deposited in the lawyer's office, he asks, "Marché conclu?" ["We have a deal?"] and the man in uniform replies with "Marché conclu" ["We have a deal"] (251/243). *Marché conclu*, the original French for "we have a deal," emphasizes the mercantile nature of the transaction, making it a veritable business arrangement. Like two businessmen closing a deal, they have little regard for what they are exchanging (Rose's body) and are consumed only by thoughts of its symbolic function. The exchange of Rose's body for the land in this scene references the ways women's bodies circulate in the global political economy in a way that is largely exploitative. This dynamic exemplifies Kamala Kempadoo's forceful argument that "sexuality in the Caribbean has been and continues to be material for the reproduction of the workforce, family and nation as well as for boosting national economies."[40] Viewed in this way, the transactional beginnings of Rose's sexual torture call forth a tradition of sexual exploitation of female bodies for the benefit of family gains that is not unique to Haiti. This example highlights my central argument, that re-reading scenes of sexual violence in today's globalized age demonstrates exactly how rape representation participates in and helps construct new circuits of power and discourses that are national and transnational, allegorical and material.

Although she claims to know what awaits her, Rose is unprepared for what happens next: "J'avais été prévenue par l'avocat et je savais ce qui m'attendait. Je commençai donc à me déshabiller et lorsque je fus moitié nue, l'homme en uniforme me tira vivement par le bras pour m'entraîner derrière le paravent. [The lawyer had spoken to me beforehand and I knew what to expect. I began taking off my clothes and once I was half-naked, the man in uniform pulled me sharply by the arm to drag me behind the screen]" (251/243). Her surprise accents the brutality of the situation and emphasizes the questionable nature of her consent. Rose is then given strict instructions: "Tu ne te débattras pas, tu ne crieras pas . . . parce que si tu le fais, tu t'en repentiras" (251)." "You're not going to struggle, you're not going to cry out . . . because if you do, you'll be sorry" (243). That he must "arrach[er] [ses] derniers vêtements" (251) "[tear] off whatever garments [she] had left," reminds us that Rose was only half-naked (243). She had not entirely succumbed to the plans that had been made for her; in fact, the removal of her clothes, soon punctuated by her refusal to obey, make the possibility of her complicity all the less tenable. This passage shows from the start that we cannot frame what happens to Rose as her "entry into a pact" or her "agreement" as it has been previously labeled—it is an incident of sexual violence.

The scene is delayed when Rose refuses *le gorille*'s instructions: "Je refusai d'obéir, alors il me jeta sur le divan" (251) ["I refused to obey so he threw me on the sofa"] (244). This moment of refusal is fundamental to our understanding of what happens: Rose does not go in eagerly or willingly; she ventures to find recourse, even if she is naked and seems to already be in a position that seals her fate. I want to emphasize this moment because it definitively characterizes what happens to Rose as rape. Because she explicitly attempts to resist, because she has refused the advances by not obeying after she is explicitly told that disobedience could result in death, she has tried to create another option for herself. She achieves a measure of resistance and refusal, without which her reactions would have to be read much differently.

Her resistance cements our understanding of this scene as one of coerced sexual activity rather than a consensual, compromising act of martyrdom, as it has been critically interpreted.[41] One of the most glaring examples of how this discourse situates Rose in terms of her violation can be found in the novel's back matter: "Rose, moderne Antigone, est prête à se sacrifier pour que sa famille récupère une terre spoliée . . . elle va tenter le diable./[Rose, a modern Antigone, is prepared to sacrifice herself so that her family can gain back the ruined land . . . she goes to tempt the devil.]"[42] Comparing her with Antigone suggests that she commits an act of bravery for the good of her people. *Colère*'s characters have also deemed Rose's actions as a choice—her brother labels her a whore, and her father is ashamed that she has lost her honor. In each instance, the family members, with the noticeable exception of Rose's mother, react as though Rose makes a choice willingly, happily, or at least indifferently. According to them, she stoically chooses her path as a martyr. By blaming Rose for her actions, these characters repeat society's reaction to rape. The short sentence that tells us of her refusal indicates that Rose longs to be the author of her own destiny, one that will not include violence. It also suggests that Rose is conflicted about her situation. She has made herself vulnerable in a literal sense by disrobing, yet she is still not willing to do all that she is told. Ultimately, Rose's initial refusal disturbs our ability to read her as a martyr. Although Vieux-Chauvet does not explicitly use the word *rape*, she has written the scene as one of rape, which is evidenced when we disassemble the various parts of the encounter, as I have done here.

Looking constitutes as much a part of Rose's torture as do touching and penetration. With each look, Rose experiences her body outside of herself as she watches the deformed hand glide over her. She is as horrified by the hand as she is by the fact that it is touching her. This contemplation of Rose's body acts as a break in the narrative—for a moment, all is still as he does not instruct, lecture, or rape her. "De longues minutes, il resta ainsi à me contempler et je vis son horrible main s'approcher de mon corps et le toucher légèrement avec une intolérable et malsaine curiosité" (252) ["He stared at me like this for some time, and then I saw his horrible hand approach my body and touch it ever so lightly with a kind of unbearable, sick curiosity" (244)]. When Rose moves outside of her body, she too participates in the spectacle of torture—she watches herself, an act that intensifies her pain. After this belabored account of the scene, *le gorille* finally enters Rose: "Il s'enfonça en moi d'un coup terrible, brutal et, aussitôt il râla de plaisir. Je mordis mon poing, de souffrance et de dégoût. Il se releva" (252). ["He rammed himself into me in one rough and terrible thrust, and immediately groaned with pleasure. I bit my fist in pain and disgust. He got back up" (244).] The brevity of the moment does not undercut the suffering, so excruciating that Rose violently bites into her own flesh to take away from the other intimate violence she experiences. This self-inflicted violence is intended to distract her from the pain, all the while conveying to the reader just how much pain there is. The juxtaposition of the gorilla's pleasure and Rose's pain reaffirms the dynamics of sexual violence because it emphasizes the pleasure of one at the expense of another.

The ordeal described is the first in a series of scenes that relay endless forms of sexual torture that involve the spectacle of looking, the brutality of touching, and the sadistic reenactment of ritual fantasy. For thirty days, Rose is subject to different forms of sexual cruelty. To highlight the duration and intensity, Vieux-Chauvet enfolds multiple days of torture into one condensed period, a single narrative, a single chapter. This use of temporality dramatizes the sexual terror for its intolerable length, just as the isolation of Rose's narrative voice in the chapter mirrors her isolation and alienation from the Normil family. This text of rape, then, makes use of narrative voice, character perspective, and temporality to represent what happens to Rose. These strategies allow us to identify it positively when we read it through a feminist theoretical lens. Feminist critic Rajeswari Sunder Rajan has contended elsewhere that "feminist texts of rape must also engage in textual strategies to counter narrative determinism. Such negotiations are achieved by and result in alternative structures of narrative. One means to this end is the structural location [and duration] of the rape incident."[43] Extended temporality is a key element in scenes of rape, because it accents the experience of the rape survivor, for whom sexual violence stretches time into eternity—causing the violated person to lose perception of time during the rape. Rather than shorten the length of the incident in order to spare the reader from too explicit contact with sexual violence, the prolonging of the scene and its graphic nature align the text with the survivor.

Forced to live with the pain of sexual violation each day, Rose's body becomes an instrument of torture. The pain is compounded because it is a repeated occurrence—each day her body becomes both a site and an instrument of violence. In Rose's case, the judgment cast upon her by her family is similar to the disbelief that challenges the experience of survivors. When we consider, as Scarry points out, that "the person in pain is so bereft of speech," we are reminded of the repression of survivor's voices, as well as the culture of silence that envelops sexual violence.[44] These conditions imbue Rose's predicament with another troubling layer. At no point does Rose share her pain with anyone; she suffers alone in silence. However, her pain is visible because, like for Dora Soubiran, a character who is violated in *Amour*, the damage is so extreme. Only the reader knows that for Rose, "J'avais si mal que je pouvais à peine marcher" ["It hurt so much I could barely walk"] (252/245). She utters this pain only in undecipherable cries: "il se jeta sur moi si brutalement que je criai" ["he threw himself on me so brutally that I cried out"] (252/244).

What does examining Rose's situation as an act of rape tell us about a rape culture? Through the character of Rose's brother, Paul, we can record some of the most common reactions to rape. His example highlights how often in stories of sexual violation "the woman's newly recognized identity—which may be more properly described as her function in an economy of sexual propriety and property—becomes an emotional war-cry and prelude to the virtual disappearance of the concerns of the woman herself."[45] Considered in this light, there is an implicit critique of patriarchy in Paul's reactions to Rose's sexual imprisonment. The narrative sequence encourages a reading of his reaction and the event in relation to one another because Paul's obsessive observations of his sister and his desire to avenge her honor precede the chapter disclosing the details of the rape. Reading what happens to Rose after we read of Paul's obsessive outrage (which easily qualifies him as the most angry character in *Colère*) makes the reader less sympathetic, and to a certain degree wary of this character.

The narrative logics of Paul's monologue reveal more about the social context of sexual violence and offer a kind of social script for how rape and rape victim-survivors are treated. Three main thoughts circulate in Paul's interior monologue: (1) anger that his sister is violated, (2) shame that she "chooses" her plight because of how it reflects on the family, and (3) a desire to avenge her violation through retaliatory violence. His anger does not result in sympathy or compassion for Rose; he is mostly concerned with the way her actions reflect on him, on their relationship as brother and sister, and on the entire family. Paul's most dominant urge to kill *le gorille* is an inclination toward violence that can be read, on the one hand, as a desire to be the savior of his family. It can also be read as a need to repay what he perceives as the sullying of his sister, which he feels is also an affront to him. As Marie-José N'Zengou-Tayo elucidates in her article about the role of women in Haitian society: "rape also functions as punishment for . . . the victim's male relatives."[46] Both his reactions reflect investment in patriarchy; he cannot accept the view that his sister took responsibility on the family's behalf. Although his mother tries to convince him that "[Rose] a osé affronter ces bêtes féroces pour toi, pour nous, et nous lui jetterions l'opprobre à la face" he can only respond with, "Je le tuerai! Je le tuerai!" (225). "[Rose] dared to confront these wild beasts for your sake, for our sake, and should we scorn her for it?" [. . .]

"I'll kill him! I'll kill him," his blind desire to exact his revenge through killing (218). He is especially ashamed that their surrounding community is aware of what he refers to as his sister's sexual pact and concerned about how they will react.

This fear of society's judgment upon the family displays the ways in which "traditional attitudes towards female sexuality and virginity makes rape a traumatic experience for the survivor by further alienating her from potential sources of support like family."[47] Paul's view of sexuality and virginity informs his incessant drive toward violence, so his concern emphasizes the societal norms according to which female sexuality reflects on the family. "Alors, maintenant l'histoire de Rose, tout le monde la connaît.... Putain! Sale putain! Mais c'est lui que je tuerai. Tant pis pour ce qui arriverait de suite. Je vais le guetter patiemment et je le tuerai" (237). "So that means Rose's story, everyone knows it.... Whore! Dirty whore! ... But he's the one I'm going to kill. Who cares what happens after that. I'll find him and I'll kill him" (229–30). His desire to kill is rooted in his selfish needs; this fact becomes clear when he thinks to himself, "Elle est taboue. Grâce au gorille. La putain taboue. Je le tuerai et puis je mourrai. Je ne pense pas aux autres. Mon acte entraînera notre perte à tous, je le sais" (240). "She's taboo. Thanks to the gorilla. An off-limits whore. I will kill him and then I will die. I'm not thinking of the others. My act will spell disaster for all of us, I know that" (232). Later on he orchestrates his plan to kill *le gorille* and to also end his sister's life: " ... Il me faut la supprimer pour moi, pour elle, pour nous" (282). "I need to finish her off, for my sake, for her sake, for us" (275). The progression from "my sake," then to "her sake," and finally to "our sake" reflects the order of importance in his mind: Paul places himself at the beginning of this progression. The desire to even kill his own sister follows the same logic as an honor killing—because she has been defiled, the best recourse for her and for the family, is for her to die. The men in black also contextualize Rose's violation in terms of Paul when they say, "Nous lui avons pris ses terres et sa sœur" (273)/"We took his land and his sister" (265). To them and to her brother, Rose represents the spoils of conflict, irrevocably broken and sullied because of the violence waged on her body.

The most coherent element of Paul's interior monologue is his desire to kill those responsible for defiling Rose. This urge punctuates seemingly unrelated sentences. Even his loving thoughts of his relationship with Rose and what they used to share inevitably turn toward killing her perpetrator:

Entre sa sœur et lui il y avait à peine un an de différence et dès l'enfance ils avaient été amis. "Ma sœur! Ma sœur!" répétait-il en lui-même. Et un goût amer lui envahissait la bouche. "Rose Normil! La belle Rose Normil! la sœur de Paul, vous ne la connaissez pas?" avait-on coutume de dire. Et il souriait avec fierté. "Je vais le tuer!" se dit-il encore, et il s'imagina enfonçant jusqu'à la garde un énorme couteau dans le dos du petit homme aux mains de gorille. (225)

There was barely a year's difference between him and his sister and they had been friends since childhood. "My sister! My sister!" he kept repeating to himself, as a bitter taste filled his mouth. "Rose Normil! The lovely Rose Normil. Paul's sister, don't you know her?" people used to say. And he would smile with pride: "I am going to kill him," he said again, and imagined an enormous knife sticking out of the back of the little man with gorilla hands as he thrust it in to the hilt. (218)

Here his determination to kill punctuates seemingly unrelated sentences. The need for revenge is predicated upon an understanding of his sister's honor that he hopes to restore, and a feeling that his family has been blemished because of her sexual acts. Paul's rage leads to revolt—Rose's personal trauma catapults him into political action, or violence as a means of resistance. He becomes politicized only because of the events in Rose's life; the sexually gendered nature of what his sister goes through foments his rage and inspires his action.

Paul's focus on how he has been injured by the perpetrators of Rose's rape is similar to what we find in the final chapter of Fanon's *Les damnés de la terre*, entitled "Guerre colonial et troubles mentaux" [Colonial War and Mental Disorders]. Fanon examines mental disorders that surface during the Algerian war for national liberation in order to demonstrate the pathology of the colonial. His observations take the form of over a dozen case studies, all of which display the interplay of psychology and violence. For our purposes "Guerre colonial et troubles mentaux" is useful because Vieux-Chauvet dramatizes what Fanon exposes, although she does so in the different context of state-sponsored violence. Also, Fanon's work recalls the ways gendered violence is contextualized in francophone literature through several examples of raped women whose ordeal is analyzed only for how it alters the men around them. In the comparison I draw here, the example within the family is the case of an Algerian couple's experience with torture during the war. Fanon focuses on the husband who has become impotent as a result of his wife's rape:

> Quand j'ai appris qu'elle avait été violée par des Français, j'ai d'abord ressenti de la colère contre ces salauds. . . . Et plusieurs semaines après je me suis rendu compte qu'elle avait été violée parce qu'on me recherchait. En fait, c'est pour la punir de son silence qu'elle fut violée. . . . Ce n'était donc pas un simple viol, par désoeuvrement ou par sadisme comme j'ai eu l'occasion d'en voir dans les douars, c'était le viol d'une femme têtue, qui acceptait tout au lieu de rendre son mari. *Et ce mari, c'était moi.* . . . *C'était à cause de moi qu'elle était déshonorée.* . . . Mais cette chose, est-ce qu'on peut l'oublier? Et était-elle obligée de me mettre au courant de tout cela? (308–9, 310; my emphasis)

> When I heard that she'd been raped by the French, I first of all felt angry with the swine. . . . And then a few weeks later I came to realize that they'd raped her *because they were looking for me.* In fact, it was to punish her for keeping silence that she'd been violated. That wasn't a simple rape, for want of something better to do, or for sadistic reasons like those I've had occasion to see in the villages. It was the rape of an obstinate woman, who was ready to put up with everything rather than sell her husband. . . . And the husband in question *it was me.* . . . *It was because of me that she had been dishonored.* . . . But that thing—how can you forget a thing like that? And why did she have to tell me about it at all? (259)

The former prisoner processes the rape according to the way it affects him. First he feels angry, then guilty. Eventually both feelings subside, and he feels ashamed of the woman, thereby indirectly placing the blame on her. Similarly, Paul is able to see the repercussions of Rose's violation only in terms of the way they affect him and drive his impulse toward violence.

Paul's ostensible concern with Rose's physical appearance recasts her in the role of object. Here again what matters to him is neither the traumatic effect of sexual violence nor its material manifestations, but rather its social implications. He worries about the deterioration of her flesh and her honor, that is, the effects on the entire family, and not her emotional and mental state. The incessant comments about her degenerating physique are excessive when we look to the redundant vocabulary that conveys his thoughts. Three times he remarks how skinny his sister has become. "Rose s'absente tous les soirs depuis dix jours. *Elle est maigre,* tellement maigre et personne ne s'en inquiète" (239; my emphasis). ["Rose has been out every night for the last ten days. *She's gotten thin,* and no one is concerned" (231)]. When Paul first makes this observation, he positions himself as the only family member who cares about Rose. As the torture sessions progress, and Rose is subject to more days with the gorilla, Paul continues to watch her. Again, his focus is on her body's outward appearance: "*Maigre. Tellement maigre. Je vais le tuer*" ["*Skin and bones. So gaunt.* I'll kill him" (248/231)] showing that there is a direct link between Paul's awareness of his sister's physical state and his desire to avenge her. In the English translation the use of "skin and bones" emphasizes Paul's view of her body; Paul seems literally obsessed with her flesh.

In his preoccupation with the way Rose looks, Paul shows that he cares more about what his sister's body represents than about what her body actually undergoes. In the final pages of *Colère* when he looks at his sister, Paul "avait l'impression qu'elle [Rose] luttait avec une horrible fatigue et que d'un moment à l'autre elle allait s'effondrer devant lui, maigre et disloquée" ["felt as if she were fighting off some sort of terrible exhaustion and that at any moment she would collapse before him, flimsy and disjointed like a puppet" (293/285)]. Whereas before Rose's form was a sign of her beauty, for Paul it transforms into a sign that her body is dwindling away as she is being devoured by *le gorille*, another symbol of the brutal regime. In comparison with the comments he makes about her physical state, Paul pays little attention to his sister's psychological, or inner experience.[48] He is not concerned about the psychological toll of the violation or what it means for Rose as a living subject. Rather than offer her the comforts of sharing to help her heal from the trauma, Paul resorts to anger, judgment and blame, each of which reflect the brokenness of their familial bond and his investment in society's patriarchal order.

Ironically, given his professed desire to protect her body from harm, and to repay the violence that she was subject to, Paul contributes to Rose's pain by physically assaulting her. "J'ai bondi sur elle et je l'ai frappée au visage" (without regret) after going to confront her (249). "I grabbed her and struck her in the face" (242). This act does not undermine his tendency toward protection; rather it re-inscribes his participation in the patriarchal cycle, according to which he has ownership over his sister's body. Within this system, Paul is responsible for what happens to her because, as he believes, "c'est le rôle d'un frère de veiller sur sa sœur" (247). "It's a brother's job to look after his sister" (239). He recognizes this link between his sister's body and the land taken away from the family, and he feels robbed of both. His objectification and abuse are informed by a relationship in which Rose's body is compared with the land and must be viewed within terms of ownership. This is particularly evident when we consider that, as Kali Tal points out in her discussion of the language of sexual abuse and trauma, "rape was originally conceived of as a crime against property—

women were presumed to belong to particular men (fathers, brothers, husbands) . . . and the loss of face [was] suffered by the owner who could not protect . . . his property."[49] Paul's reaction highlights the problematics within the metaphor of Rose's body as the Normil land that is prolonged throughout *Colère*. The land is slowly taken away from the family piece by piece, just as Rose deteriorates little by little, as though her body is literally decomposing. The comparable emphasis on the land's value suggests that women's bodies are of less value. Indeed this slippage reveals what N'Zengou-Tayo has named the "fusion/confusion between nature and women" that is always to their detriment.[50]

Sexual, physical, emotional, mental and institutional violence are glaringly present in *Amour, colère, folie*. Marie Vieux-Chauvet foregrounds the dynamics of sexual violence and deploys discursive methods that "politicize" rape by pointing to society's failure to interrogate it. In these scenes of sexual violation, Vieux-Chauvet stretches the frames of imprisonment. She does more than unveil the violent treatment of women under Duvalier; she shows how it intersects with oppression by the constellation of women's multiple locations. She reveals the psychological undoing of women who are surrounded by and subject to violence, and she frames it from a female perspective, showing how their experiences are met with silence. This point is further emphasized with the novella's conclusion, which finds Rose dead, unbeknownst to her family. Paul discovers his sister's death only the following morning. The implication here is clear: despite the parallel between Rose and the land, the family clearly valorizes the latter more than it does the former. They notice as soon as the land is under attack, but when the daughter dies, no one notices until the following day. This ending emblematizes the devaluation of the female body that is suggested throughout the entire story—Rose's value is linked to her ability to serve as a pawn in times of political conflict. Beyond this context, it has no intrinsic value, to the point that her death would go undetected by the Normil family. The family name, Normil, in its proximity to "normal" in both the original French and in the English translation, further inculpates society by suggesting that it would be normal for violence against and death of women to go unnoticed in any family.

By reframing sexual violence through Rose's perspective, unveiling and critiquing the cultural silence in response to rape, we can observe a society in which naming rape is virtually impossible due to political circumstances, as well as traditional values. The book also challenges readers, writers, and (inevitably) society to reframe accepted terms of violence that occur privately and publicly. My re-reading of rape in *Colère* shows that

Marie Vieux-Chauve has created a protagonist who is a victim of rape, not (as others have claimed intratextually and extratextually) a martyr for her family. The importance of *Amour, colère, folie* is that it shows the process by which societal forces refuse to name *rape*. The legacy of *Amour, colère, folie* as I have read it here is that it repoliticizes rape by drawing our attention to the discursive silences that enclose sexual violence while it simultaneously thwarts efforts to maintain such silence.

Repoliticizing Rape in Contemporary Haitian Novels: Danticat, Placide, and Mars

In contemporary Haitian literature, the theme of sexual violence resonates with even louder signals than does the ambiguous torture of Dora Soubiran in *Amour* or the sexual coercion of Rose Normil in *Colère*. Three contemporary novels help us map the course of representation of sexual violence.[51] Edwidge Danticat's *The Dew Breaker* (2004), Jaira Placide's *Fresh Girl* (2002), and Kettly Mars' *Saisons sauvages* (2010) undertake different approaches that I read as repoliticizing rape. I am again interested in reading for the way these authors call attention to the political context in which the sexual violence unfolds, but still emphasize the psychological and material ramifications of violence on female bodies.

Edwidge Danticat was instrumental in the republication and first English translation of *Amour, colère, folie* in 2009. Regarding Chauvet as an antecedent to Danticat, we find the same attention to violence and the female body often rendered in graphic detail. When we consider Danticat's esteem for *Amour, colère, folie*, the triple incantation of her debut novel, *Breath, Eyes, Memory*, can be read as an interpellation of Vieux-Chauvet. Thematically these works of fiction are similar in their focus on the inscription of violence upon the bodies of women. Yet the structural similarity ends here; whereas Chauvet's text is in three movements that express psychic experiences devolving into madness, Danticat's novel focuses on an exchange largely concerned with the project of memory and trauma. Nonetheless, the juxtaposition of these works reveals that the silences that Vieux-Chauvet implies discursively are featured more prominently in Danticat's novel. *Breath, Eyes, Memory* opens with a pre-existing narrative of rape already at the forefront of the novel. Martine, the protagonist's mother, was raped at the age of sixteen while she walked in the cane fields. Her unknown perpetrator was a Tonton Macoute, one of Duvalier's notorious henchman. Still, the sexual violence most prevalent in *Breath, Eyes,*

Memory is not the mother's violation, nor the production of her daughter who is the result of this violation, but the cycles of violence created by women themselves. A crucial issue in this novel is the concept of "testing," a practice that Danticat invents to depict the traumatic and cyclical nature of violence. *Breath, Eyes, Memory* is particularly instrumental in revealing the way women, regardless of class, are subject to different forms of sexual violence that is also socially encoded through practices observed by men *and* women.

Whereas the forms of sexual violence in *Breath, Eyes, Memory* have received much critical attention, far less analysis has been devoted to the incidents of sexual violence in *The Dew Breaker*, Danticat's fourth book, published in 2004.[52] *The Dew Breaker* is written at the intersection of the short story and novel genres; instead it adopts the short story cycle form, with individually named chapters, each concerning different protagonists. Danticat deliberately connects, weaves, and then imbricates stories with one another. The result of these calibrations further complicates even the simplest relationships. The book tells the story of a former Tonton Macoute—from a division known as the *choukèt lawoze*, dew breakers—living in New York among many of his former victims and family members, whose interwoven lives illustrate the longstanding and overlapping national trauma, even years later in the diaspora. The story begins with Ka's story about her art and her father and ends with the father's story bearing the same name as the book's title. Ka's world is disrupted when her father plunges one of her original sculptures into the bottom of a pond. This rash act of drowning the sculpture can be compared with the father's previous life, where rash and unwarranted action manifested itself in extreme ways. Under these circumstances, the father confesses to his beloved daughter, "Your father was not the prey, he was the hunter"; in this context, the other stories of his victims and family members can rise to the surface.[53] By ending again with the actual dew breaker's narrative, Danticat creates a cyclical motion that at once speaks to the repetitious cycles of violence and the enduring effects of traumatic memory.

A look at *The Dew Breaker's* female victims displays Danticat's preoccupation with telling the stories of Haitian women's encounters with sexual violence:

This is Rézia's story. When she was a girl, *her parents couldn't afford to keep her,* so they sent her to *live with an aunt who ran a brothel.* They lived in three rooms behind the brothel and that's where Rézia spent most of her time. One night when she was sleeping, a uniformed man walked in. She dug herself into the bed, but it did no good, so she passed out. *"I can always make myself faint when I'm afraid,"* Rézia says, fanning the smoke from the pots away from her face. "When I woke up in the morning, my panties were gone. *My aunt and I never spoke about it. But on her deathbed she asked for my forgiveness.* She said this man threatened to put her in prison if she didn't let him have me that night. (173; my emphasis)

I want to focus here on several points about the telling of Rézia's story, as well as the actual story itself. To begin with "this is Rézia's story" accentuates the creation, telling and transmission of the narrative by the victimized subject. Although Rézia does not tell the story herself, the fact that she tells it positions her as an active subject. This enunciatory act shows that Rézia did not fall into muted silence after being sexually violated; she not only literally "moves on," migrating to the United States, where she meets the story's protagonist, she does so figuratively, sharing her story with others in the diaspora.

That Rézia is "sent to live with an aunt," because her parents cannot afford her, highlights the way Haiti's geopolitical context has gendered consequences. The economic situation affects and essentially determines her fate. Had Rézia's parents been able to afford her, the story may have ended differently. Rézia is sent way because she is a girl and, as such, is less valuable to the family. Here gender and class oppression combine to decide Rézia's fate. Furthermore, when we consider the aunt's occupation as a brothel owner, a nonessential aspect of the story, we are reminded of the sexual economic transactions that govern gender relations in some Caribbean islands.[54] One wonders if even the unidentified "uniformed man" who walks into Rézia's room and rapes her is initially there as a customer in the brothel. He clearly represents the Duvalier regime through his uniform, but the location (just behind the brothel) of the violence reveals another possibility. At the very least, the writing here subtly implies the ways violence against women becomes institutionalized through codified practices that are not necessarily related to the political climate.

Reading further along in the passage, we learn that Rézia "can make herself faint when she is afraid," though it is unclear if this is something she learned to do in response to being sexually violated. If it is, the practice fits the clinical terms for a version of disassociation, during which the victim splits off or blacks out. Making this comment in the present to her new friends suggests that Rézia still carries the trauma of her rape. Her casual mention also marks this ability as a facet of everyday life. We can read the act of fainting as a protective measure enlisted by the victim since she "can always" do it "when [she] is afraid." Finally, the last few sentences also evoke the culture of silence that surrounds sexual violence because neither Rézia nor her aunt ever spoke about the incident. The reader understands that this is not only because of the conditions of fear regulating life under the regime, but also because stories of rape remain largely unspoken and untold. In the last sentence the aunt finally explains that her reason for allowing the rape was ostensibly political, "this man threatened to put her in prison if she did not let him have me that night." Rézia's reaction and situation associate the act of violence with the multiple locations of identity (e.g., race, class, gender and ethnicity) contributing to her individuated subjectivity.

This re-imagined deployment of the rape trope is also evident in Danticat's nonfiction. Her well-known essay, "We Are Ugly, But We Are Here" (1996), concludes with an example of sexual violence that transcends the metaphoric use of rape. Describing a rape survivor that she knows personally, Danticat relates the following:

> I know women who, when the soldiers came to their homes in Haiti, would tell their daughters to lie still and play dead. I once met a woman whose sister was shot in her pregnant stomach because she was wearing a t-shirt with an "anti-military image." I know a mother who was arrested and beaten for working with a pro-democracy group. Her body remains laced with scars where the soldiers put out their cigarettes on her flesh. At night, this woman still smells the ashes of the cigarette butts that were stuffed lit inside her nostrils. In the same jail cell, she watched as paramilitary "attachés" raped her fourteen-year-old daughter at gunpoint. Then mother and daughter took a tiny boat to the United States, the mother had no idea that her daughter was pregnant. Nor did she know that the child had gotten the HIV virus from one of the paramilitary men who had raped her. The grandchild, the offspring of the rape, was named Anacaona, after the queen, because that family of women is from the same region where Anacaona was murdered. The infant Anacaona has a face that no longer shows any trace of indigenous blood; however, her story echoes back to the first flow of blood on a land that has seen much more than its share.[55]

I quote Danticat's essay at length because it offers a telling example of the way rape narratives can be referenced and reconstituted in a meaningful way. The subject's remaking in the aftermath of rape takes place here at two levels. First, Danticat tells the woman's story and positions it as central to the narratives of violence that emerge in the fraught period of Haitian history that followed the coup unseating Aristide. Second, that the offspring of rape is named Anacaona is one more recuperative effort to reclaim a history of violation linked with political conflict. Even more, the act of reclaiming this bloody history, and of recalling its specifically sexed and gendered elements through the figure of Anacaona, also recalls the ways rape has historically functioned as metonymy in discourses of violence. Entering into this dialectic of historic and political violence, Danticat revises the tradition by inserting and reformulating the rape narrative from an alternative perspective.

In *Fresh Girl*, Jaira Placide's protagonist, fourteen-year-old Mardi Desravines, struggles with the repressed trauma of rape suffered during the military junta of the 1990s. Although this novel is a work of young adult fiction, it is noteworthy as an example that thwarts convention in its representation of rape. Like Chauvet and Danticat, Placide sets her character's violation in a moment of ubiquitous political instability when the rape of women was rampant. At one point, the young protagonist asks her uncle, "'Monnonk, why don't you ever talk about the camps in Guantanamo?' 'The same reason you never talked about what happened to you' he snaps."[56] In this exchange, Mardi's personal trauma of rape is associated with the oppression of Haitians occurring in the diaspora. The uncle's harsh answer and Mardi's hurt reaction echoes the facile way that rape is compared with political situations such as detainment.

Later on, the comparison of Mardi's experience with others' experiences is more appropriately signified in her observations of what goes on at the clinic she attends for therapy:

> I am listening to tape number three of six tapes from the clinic. It's about sexual violence and abuse and all that sort of thing. I hear girls and women crying and telling their sad stories. Once a week I go to this class now where I meet people like that, people like me. I don't say a word when I'm there. I just listen. (198)

By inserting Mardi into a larger dialogue about healing from the sexual trauma, Placide forges a link between survivors' experiences in different contexts. The reminder here is that rape takes place in contexts that are not overtly connected to government or institutional realities, and that these experiences (despite the difference in situations) can have similar traumatic effects. Throughout *Fresh Girl*, Mardi remains silent about her experience with rape. She is represented as a troubled adolescent who misbehaves with her family, suffers from nightmares, and performs self-mutilating acts to obliterate the traumatic memories that course within her. Placide's portrait of Mardi's actions coincides with the well-researched and documented accounts of children who survive sexual assault.[57] The project to repoliticize rape takes on several forms in *Fresh Girl*. Because the author delivers the posttraumatic effects of sexual violence in meticulous detail, she renders a protagonist who struggles to disclose what happened to her and name it as rape, and finally she shows that sexual assault straddles the public and the private realms.

Toward the end of *Fresh Girl*, when Mardi's rape is finally revealed to her family and the muted trauma that informs the entire novel develops into a pronounced encounter with sexual violence; Placide pushes her politicization of rape into another register. After Mardi discloses her own assault, her aunt shares that she too was the victim of sexual violence at the hands of her grandfather, and "no one believed [her] either (200)." In a single and sudden narrative turn, Placide manages to invoke, challenge, and undercut a culture in which rape is denied through silence or through relegation to times of political unrest. Through this example, my goal is to illustrate the way the politicization of rape can occur explicitly in overt terms. Whereas the previous examples from Chauvet and Danticat necessitated reading beyond the political background to focus on the raped body in question, Placide offers a character who clearly states what is present as a subtext in earlier works: rape happens during conflict and in peacetime, the perpetrators can be soldiers, militiamen, friends, or family members.

I NOW TURN to a final, longer analysis of Kettly Mars' *Saisons sauvages*. It may be the most provocative novel to consider in terms of Chauvet's legacy because it can be read in its entirety as a revision of *Colère*. *Saisons sauvages* tells the story of protagonist Nirvah Leroy, whose husband Daniel has been jailed by the dictatorship for his suspected dissident activities. The novel opens with Nirvah walking into a government office in order to inquire about her husband's release. As a result of this meeting, Nirvah encounters Raoul Vincent, one of Duvalier's ministers, and subsequently enters into a sexual relationship with him in exchange for her husband's safety and information about his case. Raoul becomes a part of the Leroy household and eventually engages in sexual relationships with Nirvah and Daniel's teenage daughter Marie, as well as a sexually suggestive and intimate relationship with their son Nicholas. The circulation of women's bodies as commodities in the political economy is again present here. However, unlike Rose, Nirvah is the negotiator of her exchange. *Saisons sauvages* helps to think through how the interpretation of sexual violence as "martyrdom," which we saw in *Colère* is especially problematic in the face of power relations under Duvalier.

Focusing on the intertextual relationship between *Amour, colère, folie* and *Saisons sauvages* demonstrates the way Mars' novel renegotiates the relationship between political rape and the victim-survivor's situated knowledge by foregrounding Nirvah's interior monologue, introducing the fraught poetics of erotic desire, and problematizing the different categories in the occurrence of rape. By exploring the sexual dynamics of the regime and the way the use of sex as a weapon manifested itself across age and gender, *Saisons sauvages* extends the project of *Colère*, redefining it in twenty-first-century terms. In a plotline reminiscent of what happens to Rose Normil in *Colère*, Nirvah is blackmailed by Raoul and enters into an ongoing sexual relationship so as to secure her husband's protection. As the protagonist puts it, "Avec le Secrétaire d'État [Raoul] ce sera donnant donnant. La vie de Daniel contre la jouissance de mon corps" [With the Secretary of State Raoul it will be giving for giving. Daniel's life for the pleasure of my body].[58] Here the opposition in question, *vie* (life) against *jouissance* (pleasure), foreshadows the erotics that will take center stage later in the novel. Nirvah clearly articulates the arrangement with Raoul, along with its terms, stakes and implications. We are less apt to see her as passive because so much of the novel is devoted to exploring her thought processes and reactions to her relationship with Raoul. In a way that goes far beyond what we were able to witness with Rose, with Nirvah we see that the protagonist's mental agony and emotional vexation are a virtually omnipresent interior monologue. She lays out two clear cut options, saying, "Coucher ou pas avec Raoul Vincent *n'est pas un choix innocent* pour moi. C'est une urgence et je dois décider de son opportunité pour ma survie et celle des enfants" [To sleep or not sleep with Raoul Vincent *is not an innocent choice* for me. It is an emergency and I have to take this opportunity for my survival and that of my children] (107). The language suggests the need for explanation, disclosing a point that constantly weaves through *Saisons sauvages:* Nirvah's incessant need to explain her situation. Writing that this is "not an innocent choice" renders explicit what Rose leaves implied. The logic through which Rose was branded a martyr and spoken of as making a choice is unraveled for Nirvah. In the latter's case her constant commentary sustained throughout the text throws into question any possible presuppositions that could have been made.

Locating Nirvah's interior monologue as a device to frame her dilemma brings to light the implications of her relationship with Raoul. As she appraises the details of this sexual relationship, she grapples internally with what it means. For Nirvah, what begins initially as an exchange based on rape is informed by her thoughts of desperation, guilt, shame, disgust, and outrage. Both desperation and resignation are evident through sentences that seem to attempt to justify the way she came to be in this situation. "Il me reste très peu d'armes pour lutter. Je n'ai que ma peau, mon corps, mon sexe" [I have very few remaining arms with which to fight. I have nothing but my skin, my body, my sex] (108). Here the body becomes a literal instrument of battle, caught in a field of power dynamics in which the female protagonist has no authority, no agency. Later on she goes so far as to describe herself as submissive, and making a decision that is ultimately beyond her control, given her husband's imprisonment. "Cet homme devra me dire qu'il veut me posséder, dans ma maison qui est celle de Daniel, alors que mon mari emprisonné au Fort-Dimanche est à sa merci. . . . *Je me soumets à son désir*, que j'accepte la profanation de mon foyer sachante que c'est le prix à payer pour sauver Daniel" [This man should tell me that he wants to possess me, in my house, which is also Daniel's, while my husband is imprisoned at Fort Dimanche to his mercy. . . . *I submit myself to his desire*. I accept this profanity in my home, knowing that it is the price to pay for saving Daniel] (130; my emphasis). In this description, it becomes clear that Nirvah suffers from guilt and shame even though she imagines her body having a transactional function directly related to the political context. In another testimonial-like passage, Nirvah confesses:

> C'est vrai que je suis lâche, j'aurais pu me battre, refuser, crier au scandale. Mais j'aurais été seule, tout à fait seule. Seule face à la peur. . . . Je ne suis pas la seule dans cette situation mais . . . Je ne trouve aucun soulagement ni de satisfaction à savoir que d'autres connaissent un sort pareil au mien. C'est moi qu'il s'agit. C'est moi qui deviens folle certains jours. C'est moi qui dois fermer mes yeux, ma peau, mes oreilles à la condamnation de l'opinion. C'est moi qui ouvre mes jambes et ma bouche au plaisir du Secrétaire d'État, un plaisir qui devient plus exigeant, plus vorace avec les jours et les semaines qui passent. (154–55)

> I know that I am a coward, I could have fought back, refused, screamed about this scandal. But I would have been alone, completely alone. Alone in the face of fear . . . I am not the only one in this situation . . . but I find no comfort or satisfaction in knowing that others are experiencing the

same outcome as I am. It is about me. I am the one who is becoming insane on certain days. I am the one who must close my eyes, my skin, my ears to condemnation and public opinion. I am the one who opens my legs and my mouth to the Secretary of State's pleasure, a pleasure that is becoming more demanding, more voracious with each passing day and week.

I cite this passage at length because it introduces several points essential to understanding the confluence of sexual violence, the political context, and its traumatic effects. First through language, Nirvah passionately decries her situation, using the past conditional tense, stating that she should have done something. Describing her hesitation as related to being "seule" (alone), Nirvah's explanation seems untenable because in her present condition she appears to be even more alone. The evocation of others' experiences shows that Nirvah fully recognizes that her predicament is indicative of the political situation, yet for her, this matters little. Her body is glaringly present here through the eyes, skin, legs and ears. Together these aspects of her body become a part of the sexual subjection and bear the brunt of societal perception and judgment. She is overwhelmingly concerned about bodily and psychic harm she must endure—her ostensible focus on her embodied experience rather than the conflict points to the ramifications of rape for an individual and not for its metonymic function. Contrary to the remarks about Rose that placed what she experienced only in relation to her brother Paul, these sentences foreground Nirvah's "moi"—her self. "*C'est moi* . . . " she repeats four times. That this is the same number of people in her family allows us to further associate what happens to her in the context of the family, although the emphasis is clearly on her. The repetition of '*c'est moi*' situates her experience over Daniel's, Marie's and Nicholas's. Nirvah's assessments of her situation position her as an active participant in what unfolds, an aspect of her experience that is further underlined when she becomes an active and desiring sexual subject.

Nirvah's desire and her role as a sexual subject become evident when her pleasure is made explicit in *Saisons sauvages*. Marie sees an inherent contradiction between her mother's pleasure and her victimization: "qu'elle ne vienne pas prendre son petit air de martyr après. Une fois j'ai regardé par le trou de la serrure. Ils font l'amour tout le temps . . . Je sais ce qu'ils font [But she better not put on airs as though she is a martyr afterwards. Once I looked at them through the keyhole. They make love all the time . . . I know what they are doing]" (160). Marie's observation provides another perspective on these sexual dynamics. To Marie, from the outside looking in, pleasure is a constituitive element of their sex acts. By including this assessment by the daughter, Mars offers a different angle on Nirvah's situation. For Marie, seeing her mother and Raoul in the throes of pleasure inculpates Nirvah. Pleasure is an important part of the way the younger girl processes her mother's relationship with the man who will eventually rape her as well. Through this depiction, the reader must also understand Nirvah's entry into the situation as more than a victim, or (as Marie puts it) as a martyr. This critical moment of pleasure confounds readings of Nirvah as the ultimate victim. Instead we can see Nirvah as engaging in a transgressively erotic act—transgressive not only because it is a betrayal of her husband, but also because it begins with violation and ends in pleasure. Rather than being in control of her body and her pleasure, Nirvah is bound by it. Later on, when Marie states that "j'ai compris que je pouvais le contrôler avec mon corps" [I understood that I could control him with my body], these dynamics are thrown into greater confusion (175). Is the young girl's use of her body to control Raoul the same as her mother's? Does the use of her body have the same connotation without the pleasure? Is Nirvah's pleasure a way to exact control over her perpetrator-lover? Does this pleasure actually render her complicit or powerful? The role of the erotic here must be understood in terms of the sexual dynamics of power and control. By blurring the line between victim and survivor and by placing pleasure alongside violation, Mars approaches one of the most controversial issues in the representation of sexual violence. She illuminates the shades of gray that could be present under the obscure cover of the regime. Here, rape functions as a way to recalibrate our understanding of the machinations of sex, power, desire, and victimization.

Yet the novel makes it clear that Nirvah's lucid understanding of her situation does not diminish the disturbing nature of the scenes of sexual violence. In other words, the context of the rape, or even the fact that Nirvah could derive pleasure from the sex, does nothing to obviate its brutal impact. In one scene after Nirvah's first night with Raoul, she has the typical reaction of a rape victim-survivor going through the impact phase of rape trauma, longing to wash herself of the guilt and shame:

> Me laver. Me laver longuement et profondément, me défaire de cette souillure qui n'est pas seulement dans ma chair mais aussi dans mon âme. Laisser couler une eau claire et neuve sur l'impuissance et la rage de mes mains. Nettoyer ma mémoire des gestes, des odeurs et des bruits de la nuit qui ne me quittent pas. *Me laver de ce plaisir arraché de force à mon corps.* (141; my emphasis)

> To wash myself. To wash myself for a long time and deeply, to undo this dirtiness that was not only in my skin but also in my soul. To let a clear and new water flow over my impotence and the rage in my hands. To cleanse the memory of these gestures, the odors, and the noises of the night that will not leave me. *To wash myself of the pleasure ripped by force from my body.*

Like the passage describing Rose's observations while she is being raped, this passage underscores the traumatic and violent nature of what Nirvah experiences. No reading of this passage can alter its unambiguous casting of Nirvah as a victim of sexual trauma. Her desire to wash herself clean of the act extends as deeply as her soul, which she also longs to purify. The references to water and washing recall tropes of rape trauma syndrome: the survivor's desire to wash herself clean of the act. The purifying shower or cleansing bath is finally made available to Nirvah through the help of Solange, the *mambo* next door who uses vaudou to help Nirvah through her trauma. As such, the desire to clean and rid herself of the memory, the sex, and the shame is literally answered in the form of her neighbor and takes on a spiritual tenor. The need for washing is pivotal in narratives of rape that focus on victimization. Likewise, the final two sentences intimate rape as an intense bodily act that invades every sense (gestures, odors, noises) that *will not leave* her precisely because she is traumatized. In this passage, the poetics of sexual violence are intricately laced with the effects of rape trauma syndrome to indicate its physical and psychic toll on the body. Furthermore, it is important to note that despite having control over what she feels sexually and having some measure of erotic agency, Nirvah still feels victimized, reminding us of a controversial point that pleasure can still take place in the context of being a victim. The physical response to rape does not invalidate its violence. Here Mars effectively renegotiates the fraught relationship between victimhood and agency in the context of sexual violence.

This account of Nirvah's relationship to her own body, as well as to her predicament, becomes increasingly thorny as she begins to take pleasure in her relationship with Raoul, develops feelings for him and experiences erotic pleasure as she had never been able to before. To this end, Mars attends to the various entanglements at play in the nexus of power, violence, sexuality and pleasure. If, as Odile Cazenave has pointed out, "the writing of sexuality in Francophone Caribbean women writers' novels is strikingly steeped in violence"; then here Mars offers an added complication related to *plaisir*.⁵⁹ Nirvah then can be controversially viewed as an example of what Kempadoo describes as the "sexualized Caribbean bodies [that are] self-actualizing and transformative . . . sexual agents . . . that shape and are shaped by larger political and economic forces, social structures and institutions, and relations of gender, ethnicity, and race."⁶⁰ That Nirvah can take pleasure in the sexual acts as they evolve from rape to consensual intercourse challenges the boundaries that entrench political rape, as well as theorizations of rape in general. Here, ambiguity is linked to sexual pleasure rather than to the violence itself in a way that openly challenges some of the restrictions for the way rape is traditionally imagined. But this ambiguity functions differently than what we saw in *Colère* because it is rendered explicit, elaborated in greater detail, and meticulously attentive to the victim-survivor's situated knowledge of her experience.

One theorization of this dynamic could entail using Omise'eke Natasha Tinsley's recuperative reading of Glissant's theory of opacity. Discussing "why opacity might necessarily be theorized as an Afro-Atlantic strategy for negotiating not only race and ethnicity but also sexuality and gender," Tinsley offers the shades of gray in representations of sexuality as potentially self-defining, creative, and liberatory.⁶¹ Incorporating the protagonist's pleasure into the text shifts the understanding of political rape in important ways that are troubling and that upset the static relationship between victim and survivor. Dissolving the boundary between victimization and agency rests on sexual pleasure as an organizing principle. This portrayal of sexual dynamics develops from an incident of sexual violence to a consensual and pleasurable relationship that, though it began as a violent encounter, has evolved into a different type of liaison. This new relationship is no less informed by power, but now it incorporates consideration of erotic pleasure and desire, controversial topics to introduce in representations of rape. Given the victim-blaming ethos that characterizes dominant discourses of sexual violence, advocates against and theorists of sexual violence have treated sexual pleasure gingerly, for fear of re-inscribing circuits of power that problematically render survivors complicit in their rapes. This situation demonstrates the double bind of rape trauma syndrome because pleasure brings on blame, as does passivity. By bringing pleasure into this dynamic, Mars activates a discourse of agency that is not necessarily in opposition to victimization—again, that Nirvah begins to enjoy the relationship does not diminish the terms under which it began nor does it exculpate Raoul as a rapist. Examining Nirvah's new relationship to Raoul illustrates the way *Saisons sauvages* is a book that "rather than merely describes a reality, causes us to question the terms through which reality is made intelligible," exactly what Carine Mardorossian calls for in more rigorous theorizations of rape.[62]

Like Chauvet, Mars illustrates how violence against women should be viewed differently in the context of the regime, though not for the reasons traditionally argued. In setting the context for the type of violence taking place under Duvalier, early in *Saisons sauvages*, Mars mentions what happens to Yvonne Hakim-Rimpel, conjoining history and fiction in a manner consistent with the dictator novel genre. This is the first scene of violence in the book, "Une terreur sans précédent dans notre culture politique, établie dès la genèse de la présidence de Duvalier. Yvonne Hakim-Rimpel a payé de son corps cette nouvelle violence. Une femme brisée qui se terre aujourd'hui dans le silence pour protéger de ses proches" [An unprecedented terror has established itself in our political culture since the genesis of Duvalier's presidency. Yvonne Hakim-Rimpel paid with her body for this new violence. She is a broken woman who is quieted in silence today in order to protect her loved ones] (53). The details here position Hakim-Rimpel as a victim of the regime and then relate the traumatic effects on the body (broken, quieted, silence) of the once-animated feminist activist. Inserting Hakim-Rimpel into the narrative evokes one of the earliest most well-known instances of a woman being violated by the regime, as mentioned in the first section of this chapter. Reading about Hakim-Rimpel in the context of Nirvah's story brings to mind the different forms of gender violence under Duvalier.

The reference multiplies the possibilities for how women become subject to state terror. At the beginning of the novel, Nirvah thinks to herself, "Cette attente délibérée et calculée définit clairement le scénario. . . . Son pouvoir peut me sauver ou me détruire. Je suis dans la pire situation où peut se trouver un citoyen du pays" [This deliberate and calculated attempt clearly defines the scenario . . . His power can save me or destroy me. I am in the worst situation that a citizen of the country can find themselves in] (53). The use of power to violate women is clearly calculated and deliberate. Casting her situation in these particularly stark terms, "*je suis dans la pire situation où peut se trouver un citoyen du pays,*" is directly bound to gender, almost as though to comparatively quantify sexual torture and sexual imprisonment as greater than imprisonment. Nirvah, not Daniel, the book seems to suggest, is the "real victim" of the dictatorship. The use of the masculine, and not feminine, version of citizen is used once again linking sexual violence to an act that compromises humanity and human rights, regardless of gender and context.

Nirvah's relationship with Raoul literally opens the door of the Leroy home to Raoul, allowing him entry into the family. He then has enough access to sexually prey upon and exploit her children, Marie and Nicholas. Yet, as though to avoid casting the blame on Nirvah for this situation, Mars supplies clues about Raoul's behavior before he makes advances toward the children. Mars describes Raoul in the beginning of the novel as the type of man who "gardait une collection de mouchoirs tachés de sang de jeunes vierges qu'il dépucelait en les violant" [kept a collection of handkerchiefs stained with blood of all the young virgins he defiled by raping] (22). This characterization foreshadows the relations he will have with Marie and Nicholas. The language of violence and vulgarity infuse Raoul's sexuality with underlying deviant behavior. While this information is given to the reader, Nirvah is unaware of his sexual history. That Mars repeatedly describes him as a rapist throughout the novel can be read as a way to challenge any arguments to exonerate or absolve him. Raoul's pleasure and joy from raping is noted in unequivocal terms when we learn of "la joie sombre qu'il trouvait dans la possession de corps inconnus qu'il violait" [the somber joy he found in the possession of unknown bodies that he raped] (79). When we consider that his proclivity for sexual violence predates his role in the government, it is possible to effectively disassociate rape from the political context. The power he gains through his role in *la terreur* does not define his appetite for rape; it merely gives him more access to potential victims.

Like her mother, Marie's relationship with Raoul is launched through an act of rape when he lunges on her unexpectedly one afternoon. She recounts what happens in the first person:

> Je couche avec Raoul depuis mes quinze ans. C'est arrivé un jour où je gardais le lit à cause de la grippe. Raoul est passé à la maison par hasard.... Il est entré dans ma chambre prendre mes nouvelles ... trente secondes après il revenait en tombe dans la pièce, les yeux fous, les mains en feu. Il se jetté sur moi comme une brute. Je me suis débattue, je l'ai repoussé des ongles et des dents. Nous nous sommes battus sans un mot, sans une plainte. Il soufflait comme un boeuf. De la salive dégoulinait de son menton. Il m'a giflé à deux reprises, ma tête bourdonnait autant qu'une touche, j'ai pris pour la première fois du sang dans ma bouche. Il a eu raison de moi, j'ai fini par céder, mes forces ne tenaient plus. Il m'a fait mal et j'ai saigné. Après je suis restée prostrée, incapable de bouger. Avec son mouchoir blanc, il a essuyé le sang et la bave qui coulait d'entre mes jambes et l'a remis dans sa poche. (172–73)

> I have been sleeping with Raoul since the age of fifteen. It happened one day when I was staying in bed due to a cold. Raoul passed by the house randomly.... He entered into my room to see how I was doing ... thirty seconds after he came back into the room as though in a tomb his eyes crazy, his hands on fire. He threw himself on me like a brute. I fought back, I pushed him with my nails and my teeth. We fought like that without a word, without a complaint. He was breathing like an ox. Saliva was running down his chin. He slapped me two times, my head bounding up and down like a piano key, and for the first time I got blood in my mouth. He was right about me though, I finally ceded to him, my forces could no longer hold. He hurt me and I bled. After I remained prostrate, unable to move. With his white handkerchief, he wiped the blood and the drool that streamed between my legs and put it back in his pocket.

This narrative turn gives further meaning to the sexual dynamics of state terror, inviting questions about how and why rape gets normalized and accepted within certain categories. More specifically, the inclusion of Marie and Nicholas into Raoul's web of sexual exploitation highlights the ways the rape of women can be deemed as less significant than the rape of men and minors. Marie's matter-of-fact disclosure *"je couche avec Raoul depuis mes quinze ans"* comes as a shock to the reader, contrasting the simplicity of the phrase. Going on to describe the way the event came about, we follow Marie's logic, unprepared for the scene of rape that follows. The reader, like Marie, is caught off guard, disarmed by the brutality that ensues. As such, the passage aligns with Marie's perspective, representing the entire scene of violation in detail, then continuing to relay the way she subsequently suffers from rape trauma syndrome. Marie experiences the same guilt and shame that her mother has expressed in her own relations with Raoul. Marie's example thus underscores her reactions to sexual trauma, rather than to the political situation. In other words the link between Nirvah and Marie's responses is to be found in the violent nature of the first act and the lasting effects of rape trauma, not in the context of the Duvalier regime.

The resemblance between the intimate violence that ensnares both mother and daughter further underscores the power dynamics of sexual violence when read in parallel with Raoul's and Nicholas's relationship. Contrary to what happens with Nirvah and Marie, Raoul's relationship with Nicholas begins with an intimate bond of mentorship. Whereas Raoul violently rapes the woman and the girl in the first sexual act, with Nicholas, he orchestrates a romantic and seemingly tender interaction that is preceded by intense pursuit. "Le Secrétaire de l'État se déshabilla et avec des gestes d'une infinie tendresse aida Nicholas à retirer ses vêtements" (195). [The Secretary of State got undressed and with gestures of extreme tenderness helped Nicholas remove his clothes]. Unlike the first scenes of sexual encounter with Nirvah and Marie, this scene is tender, careful, and even amorous. The writing at once reflects Raoul's entrenched misogyny and conveys the extent to which something else is at work in the sexual dynamics of power. In this example of statutory rape that involves the same gender, no script of violence exists; by using a different type of poetics, the writing forcefully acknowledges silenced narratives in discourses of rape. Invoking the Greek tradition allows Raoul to place his sexualization and fetishization of the young boy in a different light. "Dans la bonne tradition des fils de nobles familles grecques . . . son mentor allait aujourd'hui lui faire connaître de ses mains paternelles l'extase sublime" [In the proper tradition of noble Greek families . . . his mentor would today make known to him a sublime ecstasy from his own paternal hands] (195). But it also shows the extent to which the idea of political rapes (1) are specifically gendered and (2) allow perpetrators of sexual violence to see their practice as justifiable. Whereas with Nirvah and Marie, he sees their bodies as rightful spoils of *la terreur*, with Nicholas, he elaborates a narrative from Greek tradition to justify his behavior. This lens is also turned back onto the reader for its social significance: would Nicholas be considered a martyr? Would he be analyzed as complicit in these acts of sexual exploitation? The answer is a resounding no, which means that there is a range of acceptability that determines the confines of the notion of political rape.

By further exploring the consequences of Nirvah's "choice" and its noxious ramifications for the entire Leroy family through the sexualization of both children, Mars taps into another aspect of the discursively structured, socially-informed silences surrounding sexual violence. In *Colère*, Rose's rape was quickly normalized as an act of violence linked to the regime. On the other hand, in *Saisons sauvages*, Mars perverts the "normal" political rape of Nirvah by adding the underaged Marie and the underaged and male Nicholas to the equation. Using behavior well established as sexually deviant to provoke further outrage should give us analytical pause. There is the troubling implication here that the rape of women in the context of a state under siege is normal, common, accepted even, but raping young girls and boys is unequivocally deviant. Through these incidents of violence, Mars creates a continuum that critiques socially acceptable rape scripts. By placing these three instances of sexual violence together (though each is written in different terms), Mars draws our attention to rape as a deviant behavior. Framing rape as a deviant sexual act extracts it from the context of the dictatorial regime.

Saisons sauvages takes up where Vieux-Chauvet left off in *Colère*, which provided a powerful model of how the violence of *la terreur* was sexualized and gendered in a way that consistently attacked women's bodies. Mars goes far beyond Chauvet by exploding these dynamics and causing the reader to sort through the scattered debris of their consequences. *Saisons sauvages*' intertextual relationship to *Amour, colère, folie* invites us to revisit the gendered and sexual dynamics of the Duvalier regime in an unsettling way that proposes no resolutions and that renders the reader complicit for participation in social scripts of rape. Taken this way, *Saisons sauvages* opens up a space for creating rape representations that are no less attendant to its politics—its multiple sexual, sexed and gendered implications.

Conclusion: When the Details Are No Longer Too Much

Sharing her story of sexual violence with her daughter in the novel *Breath, Eyes, Memory*, Martine tells Sophie, "the details are too much, but it happened something like this. A man grabbed me from the side of the road, pulled me into a cane field, and put you in my body."[63] The vague terms that Martine uses recount her rape gloss over the material and bodily signs of violence. Because of trauma, re-creating the rape beyond implicit details amounts to reliving her violation. Martine does not realize that uncovering some of these details could help restore and reconcile her relationship with her daughter. My readings in this chapter have intently examined the details in scenes of sexual violence, probing the sights, sounds, and feelings of the raped subject in order to suggest that focusing on the details of "political" rape re-orders the way we understand its politics. By focusing on the details—the position of the body, the force of entry into the body, and the victim/survivor's perspective before and after, I have explored what scenes of violation are able to reveal about societal scripts of violence. In so doing, I demonstrate the way the poetics of rape representation help navigate its politics.

In Haiti, where the presence of so-called political rapes has proliferated in key historical moments of conflict, the reading practices offered here render rape legible for the way it functions in epistemologies of violence. By this, I mean that considering how the body is represented in "political rapes" and what more is at work materially, psychologically, and socially becomes a way to challenge the hegemony of these discourses of violence that are more concerned with nationalist and anti-imperialist agendas than with bodies raped. In their attentiveness to these bodies, my readings offer ways to engage rape as more than a symbol. These practices deploy the imagination as a site through which to transform a rape culture. Narratives of sexual violence like the ones written by Vieux-Chauvet, Mars, Danticat, and Placide participate in transforming a rape culture of silence by acknowledging the context of political conflict and then positioning it as a paratext, as what surrounds the scene of sexual violence rather than what informs, explains, and excuses it. By prominently figuring and repositioning rape, these representations go beyond the problem of political rapes to foreground the politics of rape, placing the bodies subject to sexual violence at the center of its occurrence.

3

Islands Unbound

Beyond the Rape of the Land

> Depuis longtemps, je voulais parler de l'inceste, du viol, mais je ne savais jamais comment m'y prendre. Or, en '89 j'ai vécu, comme tous les guadeloupéens, Hugo. . . . Et quand j'ai découvert la Guadeloupe au petit matin, j'ai vu une île dévastée, dénudée, comme violée par la force du vent. Ce cyclone m'a permis de faire un parallèle entre la violence des hommes et celle de la nature et j'ai enfin pu écrire sur l'inceste.[1]
>
> For a long time, I wanted to talk about incest, about rape, but I never knew how to do so. Then, in '89 I lived through, like all of Guadeloupeans, Hugo. I spent nights frightened by the noises, barricading and holding the door. And when I discovered Guadeloupe the next morning at dawn, I saw an island devastated, stripped, as though it was raped by the wind. This cyclone allowed me to make a parallel between the violence of man and that of nature and finally I was able to write about incest.
>
> —Gisèle Pineau

THE EPIGRAPH of this chapter comes from an interview conducted with Guadeloupean writer Gisèle Pineau in which she shares that she longed to write about incest and rape, but that she lacked the language to represent sexual violation, until the passing of Hurricane Hugo over Guadeloupe in 1989. Of course, in this part of the Caribbean, which Raphaël Confiant designates as *bassin des ouragans* [hurricane basin], these storms are a part of quotidian life.[2] The hurricane, with all of the destruction and trauma left in its wake, provided Pineau with a vocabulary that had previously eluded her. In Hurricane Hugo, she found a discursive mode through which she could initiate a literary discussion about rape, incest, and other forms of gendered violence. Throughout Pineau's novel, the use of the hurricane as a vehicle for metaphorizing sexual violence functions in stark contrast to the way metaphors of rape, or of the imagined violations of a feminized land, typically operate. Instead, *L'espérance-macadam/Macadam Dreams* (1995) adopts and dismantles rape-of-the-land metaphors by placing the destruction of the hurricane-ravaged land and the violated body side by side as a way to stretch beyond the symbolic use of sexual violence and to draw attention to the limitations of meaningless metaphors.

L'espérance-macadam is a searing portrait of physical, sexual, emotional, verbal and psychological violence that exposes the routine violations of women who are abused but who, despite this violence, somehow manage to realize miraculous dreams of hope. The novel presents women as the most common targets of violence; their experiences form its core and are the reason for the surprisingly optimistic title. Pineau (1) takes on the complexities of gendered violence through a description of natural violence[3] by exploring the toll that natural catastrophe can take on the land and (2) draws a parallel with the effects of sexual violence on the female body. This parallel associates the passing of the hurricane with the act of rape, a comparison that can function only if the land itself is imagined as a raped and victimized female body.[4]

This chapter explores *L'espérance-macadam* as a prolonged reflection on the point at which the violence of nature (in the form of the tropical cyclone) intersects with gendered violence—rape of, rage against, abuse and murder of women. I argue that the elaboration of the cyclone parallel focuses our attention on the female body in a way that disrupts the traditional image of the Caribbean landscape as a feminized space. More traditional representations tended toward objectification and usually disregarded women's bodily experiences of rape. I demonstrate how Pineau places the body *back into* the notion of a raped land (*la terre violée*) and affirms female subjectivity by providing the testimonies/narratives of survivors and victims of violence, disclosing the profundity of sexual trauma through diverse techniques, and narrating the novel primarily through the eyes of a female protagonist. My readings indicate that her use of the cyclone image is a deliberate exposure of rape that emphasizes the female body and foregrounds the perspective of victim-survivors of incest. Taken together, these strategies offer a new conceptualization for the way we understand the relationship between the female body, rape, and the land.

A superficial reading of the novel may leave us with the cyclone and gendered violence parallel, whereby the rape of the female body is comparable to the rape of the land. However, I propose that a much more complex project is at work, which constitutes the foundation of *L'espérance-macadam*. By focusing on rape representation in the form of incest, my goal here is not to take on the symbolic meanings of the incest trope, as other black feminist literary and cultural critics have done in important interventions that take on rape metaphors.[5] Most recently in the francophone context, Odile Ferly proposes that "the motif of incest in particular may be a literary device to signal the alienation of Antillean men . . . caused by the (neo) colonial status of the region."[6] What interests me here, is not the incest trope as a symbol of something else, but rather the power of incest in shaping subjectivity and its bodily implications. Even more, I am invested in the particular trauma of incest, for as Elizabeth Barnes puts it, "the literary study of incest sharpens our awareness of trauma as a social and cultural, as well as personal, experience."[7]

From a methodological perspective, two main points of reference undergird my analyses in this chapter. First, there is the relationship between the material body and subjectivity: the ability to act, speak, think, see and move as a subject rather than as an object, which was so evident in the previous chapter about Rose's rape in *Amour, colère, folie* and Nirvah's destruction in *Saisons sauvages*.[8] My understanding of the way Pineau's representation relies on the bodily experience of women in order to enhance their subjectivity and self-actualization echoes feminist philosopher Ann J. Cahill's exploration of rape as an "embodied experience." In *Rethinking Rape*, Cahill provides a theory based neither on rape as an act of power nor on sex as an act of violence—the two schools of thought argued by U.S. American feminists Susan Brownmiller and Catharine MacKinnon, respectively. Instead, she analyzes rape as "an embodied experience . . . by emphasizing the significance and nature of embodiment while refusing any determinate model of the body itself."[9] As Cahill makes clear, understanding rape in terms of its bodily significance does not mitigate thinking through its political implications. In fact, she implores that we must

> . . . understand rape as an act charged with political and bodily meanings, as a threat to the possibility of the bodily integrity of women, and therefore a threat to her status as a person.[10]

Her argument invokes a range of feminist theorists of the body (from Judith Butler to Elizabeth Grosz), as she outlines the major axes of her discussion to "locate the problem of the body as central to feminism's struggle with the problems of subjectivity and inclusion."[11] Feminist theory effectively highlights the way Pineau undercuts the tradition of *la terre violée* through her attentiveness to the female body and meticulous elaboration of the female subject.[12] Pineau's use of the cyclone metaphor allows her to emphasize the significance and the nature of what a physical body undergoes in the act of rape.

This brings us to the second point of reference I engage in this chapter: traditional formulations of (1) the land and landscape as generally both feminine and female in Caribbean literature and culture and particularly and (2) the woman as violated or raped land. The union of the Caribbean landscape and the female body has a long and vexed history in cultural production. As Omise'eke Natasha Tinsley points out, "if anything in the archipelago has been constantly, systematically transformed, exploited, contested, and subverted as the colonial intervention called Caribbean womanhood, it is the colonial invention called Caribbean landscape," an observation that is only compounded when the two are united.[13] Various imaginings of the land as a feminized and female topos violated by a colonial oppressor remind us of the enduring nature of this particular trope as well as its specifically Caribbean inflected meanings. Usually the allegorization of the female body is in service of a national project aiming to expose colonial, postcolonial and neocolonial violence and uses rape as an expedient metaphor to relay the depths of violation.

The example of Zobel's *La rue Cases-Nègres* from the first chapter of this book exemplifies the way rape becomes a sign for oppression from slavery. Zobel is among the many Caribbean writers have repeatedly substituted brutalities endured by the flesh of Caribbean women as a way to explore the violation of the land at the hand of a colonial oppression. Commenting on this dynamic, Emilia Ippolito observes in *Caribbean Women Writers: Identity and Gender* that "intimate narratives remain firmly within the broader postcolonial framework in that they prove to be as much explorations of national and political, as of personal concerns."[14] Taking Ippolito's point further, I argue that intimate narratives more often signal national and political concerns rather than personal ones. These rape metaphors denote colonial domination, a shorthand for violations considered "more universal" than the specific example of sexual violence. To this end Brinda Mehta has also argued that "the feminization and subsequent colonization of the land through sexualized tropes of male power have further confirmed the overdetermined link between the feminine and nature found in idyllic images of tropical paradises, virgin rainforests, sandy white beaches, and lush flora

Figure 2. *Little Crippled Haiti*. Photo Credit: Edouard Duval-Carrié

and fauna."[15] In the long catalogue of metaphors of landscape, significations of rape are also pre-eminent. Figurations of the landscape intervene in Caribbean corporeal, cultural, and national scripts, revealing the different ways in which the land is considered to be both sexed and gendered. They are visually apparent in art (see fig. 2), paid homage to in poetry, sung about in music, and referenced in nonfiction. Here, I am interested in the way Pineau reclaims the rape-of-the-land metaphor by filling its emptiness with survivor subjectivity. Whereas Marie Chantal Kalisa has argued that "Pineau superimposes images of Caribbean landscapes that have been threatened and destroyed repeatedly by history and frequent hurricanes over revelations of intimate violence," my argument examines the ways that

Pineau decenters the violated land in order to draw attention to the violated female subject, repositioning her in an allegory in which she was once object in order to make her subject.[16] The following two examples help highlight the problematics of the woman-as-land metaphor as this configuration relates to rape.

The Caribbean Landscape as Violated Woman

Figurations of the land as a violated woman offer insight into the way rape metaphors function in the Caribbean imaginary; after all, as Elizabeth Walcott-Hackshaw also observes, "writers from Ronsard to Roumain have engaged in gendered metaphorical readings of land and the woman."[17] Bringing together the woman and the land serves a wide range of functions, whether it is a way to invoke beauty, suggest the need for submission (who can forget Roumain's Manuel in *Gouverneurs de la rosée* explaining that "la terre est comme une bonne femme à force de la maltraiter, elle se révolte" [the land is like a good woman, when you mistreat her, she revolts]?), or simply as a vehicle for objectification.[18] Caribbean landscapes have been represented as feminine topos as early as the colonial invasion; the ways in which gender and sexuality discursively regulate imaginings of the land are also apparent in postcolonial cultural production and scholarship. I want to pause here to consider the example from one of the most critically acclaimed and referenced tomes of Caribbean Studies, Antonio Benítez-Rojo's *The Repeating Island: The Caribbean and the Postmodern Perspective*, which surveys the evolution of Caribbean discourses, relating them to myth making, performance, and cultural epistemologies. In his attention to the production of Caribbean discourses, Benítez-Rojo surveys a range of texts, forthrightly engaging and seeking to unsettle the dominant myths that "repeat" throughout Caribbean literature, culture and history. The examples offered in *The Repeating Island* intersect problematically with the way rape is represented in discourses of violence.

Committed to undoing the dominant mythologies of Caribbean postcolonial discourses, Benítez-Rojo focuses on two concepts central to this chapter: landscape and violence. The two intersect forcefully early on when he describes the Atlantic as "the painfully delivered child of the Caribbean, whose vagina was stretched between continental clamps . . . all of Europe pulling on the forceps to help at the birth of the Atlantic," from a symbolic perspective.[19] I will turn to examine this example in greater detail shortly, but first I want to consider a moment later in *The Repeating Island*, where the author devotes sustained attention to an analysis of the way violence operates in the construction of a Caribbean imaginary. Pinpointing the centrality of violence in the Caribbean imaginary, in his discussion of Derek Walcott, Benítez-Rojo asks,

> What is the problem that, according to Walcott, remains constant in the Caribbean? Violence, sheer violence, historic violence. It does not matter whether the theme is 'War and Rebellion' or any other: in the end its ultimate meaning will be violence, whether this is called discovery, conquest, slavery, or colonialism.[20]

Benítez-Rojo's reading of Walcott's play *Drums and Colours* rightfully critiques the ways in which the drama reinforces "a system of binary oppositions that conform the discoverer with the discovered, the conqueror with the conquered, the colonizer with the colonized, the master with the slave; in sum, the violence of power with the counter-violence of the subjugated."[21] This is a critique that can also be extended to renderings of the land as a violated female body in its commitment to reproducing some of the essential ingredients of colonial dynamics. Gender relations fall neatly into this binaristic system, staging a male and a female placed on opposite ends of the spectrum, female as victim and male as protector or violator depending on race.

Violence can be identified as an insistent thread that is visible throughout *The Repeating Island*, even if Benítez-Rojo refers to it only a handful of times. The book suggests that violence undergirds social and cultural aspects of the Caribbean in different ways that are evident in tradition, folklore and cultural practices. For example, regarding race, he writes, "in the Caribbean, skin color denotes neither a minority nor a majority; it represents much more: the color imposed by the violence of conquest and colonization, and especially by the plantation system."[22] Thus, as we see with the examples from the first chapter on the use of rape narratives in francophone studies, there is a propensity for locating violence in relation to a colonial point of origin. For his explicit exploration of violence, Benítez-Rojo devotes analysis to "an entire field of allusion, *scarcely explored in literary criticism* which speaks of sackings and kidnappings, of burning and booty, of buried treasure and secret maps, of the terrible black flag and duels to the death," on the topic of piracy.[23] My preoccupation here lies in the way Benítez-Rojo calls attention to the discursive silences produced in relation to certain literary themes that pivot around acts of violence. He goes onto argue that, "it has been impossible to effect a complete elimination of the violence that lies deep in the marrow of this *or any other Caribbean historical theme.* If someone had to define, at once, the meta-archipelago's historical novel and its folk narrative, using just two words, these would be, unquestionably: *revelar* (to reveal and re-veil in Spanish) *violencia.*"[24] I am particularly taken by this quote for how effectively it states one of the main arguments of the present study: that in revealing violence, both colonial and postcolonial writers re-veil sexual violence. In other words, the abiding desire to unveil violence simultaneously veils another type of violence.

Based on this formula, we might ask further: could the same be written of figures of comparison such as the feminization of the land that Benítez-Rojo stages in his introduction? Would it also be impossible to effect the complete elimination of the material violence that lies deep in the marrow of images of violated female bodies? Though he recognizes the ways that both history and culture are intertwined with violence, Benítez-Rojo does little to contemplate the way the preoccupation with violence also results in its rescripting and re-inscription. Combined with his inattention to gender, this aspect of *The Repeating Island* helps to reinforce rape as one of the pernicious blind spots of Caribbean scholars writing about violence, even when they carefully delineate the pervasiveness of violence as a theme, the particularities of sexual violence fall away. Benítez-Rojo is careful to note that "it also happens in real life," productively associating histories and social realities of violence to their cultural production.[25] His examination of the link between folklore and local Caribbean literatures presents several ways of thinking about the violence of the Caribbean as an inevitable, though infrequently analyzed, aspect of culture.

Nowhere is the function of the woman as violated land more apparent than in the early pages of the book, where Benítez-Rojo explicitly suggests that the history of the Caribbean can be imagined in terms of sexual violation. In these opening pages of *The Repeating Island,* he presents a long metaphor of the Caribbean as a raped woman:

> The Atlantic is the Atlantic (with all its port cities) because it was once *engendered by the copulation of Europe*—that *insatiable solar bull*—with the Caribbean archipelago; the Atlantic is today the Atlantic (navel of capitalism) because Europe in its mercantile laboratory conceived the project of *inseminating the Caribbean womb with the blood of Africa;* the Atlantic is today the Atlantic (NATO, World Bank, New York Stock Exchange, European Economic Community etc) because *it was the painfully delivered child* of the Caribbean, *whose vagina was stretched between continental*

clamps . . . all of Europe pulling on the forceps to help at the birth of the Atlantic.[26]

Drawing upon the image of a violated maternal figure embodied (or disembodied) by the landscape, Benítez-Rojo's ubiquitous passage has been frequently critiqued and deconstructed by Caribbean feminists. The feminization of the land is strategically necessary to facilitate the creation of his pan-Caribbean analogy, which conflates the landscape of the Atlantic, and (by extension) the Caribbean, with a violated female body. His elaboration of this metaphor encapsulates the accepted discourse on the interplay between gendered bodies, rape, history, and the land. The female body becomes a symbolic site that has endured the brunt of slavery; beyond this, analyses of violated women are virtually absent. Rape operates here as one of the main ways that the daily violence is referenced. At the same time, gender difference is somehow rendered invisible in this example because the woman stands in as a simplified signifier for the nation. When representation relegates the female body to an emblematic mode to convey national oppression, any understanding of rape remains at the symbolic level. In this dynamic, there is an implicit and unchallenged designation of the female slave body as property: rape is authorized because the women are the legal property of the slave owners.

The violation of female slaves serves as a reminder to male slaves that nothing belongs to them, not even their domestic partners, which, according to the order of patriarchy, should be the case. This logic underscores the impotence of male slaves, consistent in the critiques of slavery citing the emasculation of black men. Of course, rape was originally understood as a crime of property because women's bodies were understood legally as belonging to their fathers or husbands. The idea that black women were unrapeable originates from their status as property, but was secured by the circulation of images that branded them as hypersexual. In fact, "rape of the enslaved was routinely, violently justified by natural histories' equations between Africans and beasts in heat . . . [and the] uncontrollable sexuality of black women."[27] Within the context of this particularly colonial grammar, "dehumanization enables physical violence, justifying the systematized rape and sex work deployed or required by slave owners."[28] Given the violent order of the plantocracy, sexual violence becomes fundamental to maintaining its function and ensuring the oppression, domination, and dehumanization of enslaved women and men. Notwithstanding these sexual dynamics, many representations of rape discursively ignore female subjectivity; instead, sexual violence becomes an issue of exchange and power dynamics among black and white men. Furthermore, the example above highlights that the function of metaphors of violence are repeatedly sexed and gendered even if those sex- and gender-related machinations are left uninterrogated.

The historicization of the relationship between the land, slavery, and the female body often occurs along these lines, casting the experience of sexual violence only as the threat it poses to black masculinity. In an insightful analysis of Benítez-Rojo's use of the female body for the purposes of his metaphorical project, Tinsley critiques the way that "sexual violence and painful reproduction are simultaneously abstracted and reinscribed in regional imaginations; projected onto the water by which Caribbean women arrived in the archipelago, they conceive a disturbing image that spreads women's metaphoric legs in unsettling ways."[29] The example from *The Repeating Island* uses the metaphor of the woman as raped land as a way to conjure the quotidian violence of the Caribbean without challenging its gender-specific imbrications. This imagining of the violated female body ends, as Tinsley points out, with her legs straddling and objectifying her all at once.

Similar equivocations of women's bodies and Caribbean topos exist in the francophone context. On the one hand, in the francophone imaginary the confrontation with history, gendered or otherwise, is cast as intranslatable and incommunicable, inevitably linked to trauma. Mireille Rosello has designated it as a space where "l'Histoire se heurte à l'intraduisible et où tout changement politique et économique est presque impossible à décrire" [History is fraught with the untranslatable where all political and economic change is almost impossible to describe].[30] This is the same logic Glissant elaborates in his examination of traumatic history in *Le discours antillais* (1981). As one of the most rigorous explorations of Caribbean societies as "post-traumatic cultures," *Le discours antillais* explores how language and history are fundamental products of trauma. In particular Glissant's preoccupation with the role of the Middle Passage and its indelible imprint on the Caribbean necessarily grapples with trauma's legacy. For Glissant this trauma—one that included the quotidian exposure to sexual violence as *La case du commandeur* makes clear—is inextricable from history and culture. Indeed, the "tortured geography" that Glissant concerns himself with has significant implications for the "fusion/confusion" of women's bodies with the land. Glissant's constant invocation of ancestors whose collective pain is inscribed onto their bodies, engraved in memory, and passed down through generations emphasizes the role of slavery's traumatic past in Caribbean identity formation. As shapers of history, Glissant reminds us, trauma and catastrophe critically form, inform, and reform identity. When we consider the specificity of gender-based violence, this point further highlights the need to consider the relationship between female subjectivity and rape of the land metaphors.

Reclaiming the Land and The Body: Feminist Renderings of the Woman as Land

Feminist scholars have been especially invested in interrogating the facile union of the Caribbean landscape and women's violated bodies in both their critical and creative work. These writers issue challenges to the feminization of the land through their cultural work and scholarship, often by invoking and then dismantling it. In an attempt to negotiate the symbolism of the female body as land in a more meaningful way, feminist cultural workers find ways to effectively reclaim these contested tropes. Staging the island as female, these writers indicate, can serve multiple functions that are not always at the cost of female subject formation. By "[forcing] the reader to reexamine how the image of the woman and her body has been used and accepted as part of our Western literary imagination" and suggesting alternative ways to make use of the trope, cultural work can re-imagine the possibilities for one of the most frequently invoked conceptualizations of violence against women.[31] Beyond the literary examples, the feminist scholarship of those working on the Caribbean and attempting to destabilize oversimplified and uninterrogated iterations of the land as feminine topos helps to frame the arguments in this chapter. In her provocative study on love and eroticism between Caribbean women, Omise'eke Natasha Tinsley observes that "metaphors of landscape and sexuality have long proven central to Caribbean women's poetics of erotic decolonization . . . not as rarified tropes, but as everyday praxes of black feminism."[32] Tinsley's astute observations about women's use of landscape metaphors to elaborate a distinctly feminist iteration of one of the longest-standing tropes of Caribbean literature serves as a salient reminder that figures of comparison can be used productively rather than divisively. By engaging and then excavating these tropes, black feminist Caribbean writers tread on contested terrain, re-imagining and reclaiming the land in a way that does not elide their violations, effectively "revising the theoretical landscape."[33] In other words, by taking on the rape of the land trope and reproducing it with revision that attends to agency, subjectivity, and voice, feminist writers offer an alternative way for imagining the relationship between rape, the body, and the land in the Caribbean context.

Similarly, Shona Jackson convincingly argues that, "to identify woman with land so entirely, at particular historical moments, regardless of cultural belief, is to instantiate a relational subjection where each referent's place validates, explains, or codifies the other's."[34] Put differently, this dynamic undergirds the patriarchal power operations according to which women have less significance in nation-building unless they are operating in a submissive, symbolic role. A symbolic system that relies on the violated woman to represent the dominated land calls into question claims that female subjects can make on national belonging and, ultimately, citizenship. Through readings of authors' oversimplified collapse of the land into its women, Jackson critiques scholars who fail to interrogate "what it means to establish a metaphoric link between two substantively different types of 'rapes.'"[35] Similarly, as we will see below, in *L'espérance-macadam,* Pineau actively interrogates what it means by using the metaphor of two different types of rape in an effort to substantiate their disturbing, inherent and glaring contradictions.

Also, focusing on the francophone context, Pascale Naudillon cites the different ways that bodies are linked to acts of violence. She writes, "L'acte sexuel est bien souvent synonyme de viol. Viol fondateur commis par l'équipage des négriers chez Marie-Célie Agnant, viol du père ou viol commis par un géniteur anonyme chez Gisèle Pineau, le corps des femmes est d'abord objet de violence, source de souffrance." [The sexual act is often synonymous with rape. Founding rape committed by the slaveship crew in Marie-Celie Agnant's work, rape of the father or rape by an anonymous parent in (the work of) Gisèle Pineau, female bodies are first the object of violence, a source of suffering.][36] The metaphor that Naudillon refers to is that of sexual relations generally standing in for rape, rather than rape as a symbol of something else. Her focus on the female body urges a return to embodiment and recalls the ways in which Caribbean women's bodies have been subject to multiple oppressions and violations that are present both materially and physically, as is evidenced through cultural production.

Likewise, Sandra Duvivier intentionally exploits the female body as land trope in her study of Caribbean women writers for whom "'*Kom se kawo tèm'*" [My body is my piece of land].[37] In her use of this Kreyol expression, Duvivier opens a perspective on the way women/land symbology might function differently when women are seen as subjects in charge of their own sexuality rather than as objects. Duvivier's focus on agency uses this point to argue that "unlike larger Haitian discourse's patriarchal constructions of women's bodies, which place the benefits of women's sexuality at the hands of men, poor and working-class Haitian women's definitions allow for female agency and capitalizing off of their own bodies."[38] Her analysis centers specifically on the intersections of race, class, sexuality and gender in the Caribbean context as a way to map sexual economies in Haiti and Jamaica differently. These interventions help us understand that the purpose of critiquing woman/land poetics is not to say that these metaphors should not be deployed. Instead, I suggest that the metaphors could be engaged in more complicated ways that consider the critical tensions that arise in their deployment. The above-named feminist scholarship by Tinsley, Jackson, Naudillon, and Duvivier help frame my reading of *L'espérance-macadam* as a novel whose redeployment of the "woman as brutalized land" metaphor categorically re-imagines epistemologies of violence in the Caribbean context, offering a new way to track the figuration of rape in these narratives.

We can situate Gisèle Pineau in this cadre exploiting the woman as land metaphor in service of an alternative, feminist project that is more attentive to the inner workings of subjectivity. Like those cited above, Pineau uses metaphorically and symbolically rich language to reclaim the Caribbean landscape and reveal the flesh that it signifies. Using the notion of the woman violated like a piece of land, Pineau recuperates the image with a difference that calls the reader to scrutinize the mechanics of subject formation at work in the use of metaphors and metonymy that render women's bodies only as symbolic sites. This revision of the ubiquitous trope complicates our understanding of the way rape figures into extant discourses of violence. Focusing on the toll that sexual violence takes on the brutalized body, Pineau addresses the gendering of the landscape and illuminates its limitations as well as its possibilities. The problem with the rape of the land metaphors, the novel demonstrates, is not the easy use of symbology to represent national concerns, but it is what these metaphors leave unspoken. The silences, margins, and gaps produce a system of signification in which the politics and materiality of rape become irrelevant, secondary to the elaboration of a national project. In contrast with these silences, Pineau offers an unequivocal portrait of violation juxtaposed with a muted representation in which the use of metaphor evinces the presence of a repressed sexual trauma.

Though some have referred to Pineau as a female writer within the Créolité movement, I offer instead that Pineau's graphic depictions of violence are not related to the school that has critiqued the absence of sexuality in francophone Caribbean texts, but rather a function of a more emboldened sexual poetics alongside a determination to render rape.[39] As Maryse Condé has argued, Pineau's work in general and *Chair Piment* (2002) in particular go well beyond the Créolité call for the thematic use of sexuality in francophone Caribbean literatures. She explains that for Pineau, "Sex, which made a discreet appearance in French-speaking Caribbean literature, especially in the novels by Raphael Confiant, no longer appears in a playful, even obscene, mode. Suddenly, it is thrust under the spotlight and operates as a fact of individual, subjective liberation of the characters."[40] Rather than relying on nationalist longing and linguistic models of identity, writers such as Pineau focus on writing the body, revising regional histories and proposing multivoiced narratives. By taking on sexuality, Pineau explodes its dominant narratives and challenges the presuppositions that accompany its representation.[41]

Tellingly, the effort to endow the woman as land metaphor with fuller dimension is not exclusive to *L'espérance-macadam* or even to Pineau's fiction in general; the author has revisited the topic in both her interviews and her scholarship to the point that we can identify a marked preoccupation with unpacking the power and sexual dynamics at work in sexual violation. In her nonfiction work, Pineau openly identifies the existence of an established dialectic that genders the Caribbean landscape because of its sustained violations:

> Tout part de *l'histoire de l'île*. On y revient toujours à cette histoire. Celle d'une terre qui a été *violée comme un corps de femme*, comme celui des femmes qui ont été amenées captives. . . . *Cette histoire il faut la transcender, aller au-delà, et c'est possible.* (my emphasis)

> Everything departs from the *history of the island*. We always return to this history. That of a land that was *raped like the body of a woman*, like the women who were brought there as captives. . . . *We must transcend this history, to move beyond it is indeed possible.*[42]

Pineau's explicit use of the woman as land trope in the context of slavery is unequivocal as she describes "a land that was raped like the body of a woman." Yet her analogy does not end there. She reminds the reader that the symbol is one based on a historical reality that involves real flesh and bones by invoking "the women who were brought there as captives." The sexual vulnerability of enslaved women travelling across the Atlantic is again one of the most common ways that figurations of rape enter into the Black Atlantic imaginary. As an indicator of the sexual machinations the plantocracy's oppression, the figure of the raped slave woman helps to highlight systems of domination. Rape becomes a feature of slavery even before the journey across the Atlantic is complete, because even in the treacherous Middle Passage, "females were often packed onto ships unchained, a state that left them more vulnerable to systematic rapes."[43] Upon arrival on the plantations, again, women were subject to routine violation, a representation that Zobel's *La rue Cases-Nègres* renders explicit through the example of Man Tine.

Noting the conjunction of history, land, and gendered violence, Pineau calls for representations that move beyond this dialectic. In *Femmes des Antilles: Traces et voix, cent cinquante ans après l'abolition de l'esclavage*, this attention is further evident as she delves into the history of the ways that slavery's violence was gendered and attempts to give voice to the ways in which women suffered under slavery. She explains the plight of the slave woman for whom

> Sa chair, son sexe, l'ont parfois couchée auprès de son bourreau. Elle a été, sitôt jetée sur le bateau négrier, convoitée par les matelots, abusée sexuellement. Elle a enfanté les premiers mulâtres, chabins, quarterons. . . . Elle a prêté le sein à des nourrissons blancs, ses futurs maîtres. . . . Elle a été, selon le Code Noir, propriété du maître blanc avant d'être la femme d'un homme de sa race et de sa condition. . . . Ce livre raconte des histoires des êtres bannis de l'humanité. . . . Les femmes n'ont guère eu l'occasion d'exprimer tout cela.[44]

> Her flesh, her sex, often made her have to sleep with her oppressor. As soon as she was dropped onto the slave ships, she was coveted by the sailors and sexually abused. She gave birth to the first mulattoes, chabins, quadroons. . . . She lent her breast to nursing white babies, her future masters. . . . She was, according to the Code Noir, the property of the white master before being the wife of a man of her own race and condition. . . . This book tells the stories of beings banished from humanity. . . . Women have barely had the chance to express all of this.

Throughout *Traces et voix* Pineau approaches the subject of sexual violation in the context of slavery, making plain the different ways in which rape figures as a gender-specific form of oppression that helps maintain the slave system. The citations above help us see the ways in which

Pineau's preoccupation with rape as a thematic was manifestly informed by a commitment to understanding sexual violence as a constitutive element of subject formation. In the analyses that follow, I situate *L'espérance-macadam* as a work of fiction deeply engaged with the stakes of representing rape and mining the possibilities on the margins of epistemologies of violence. Overall Pineau's fiction has evinced a steady trajectory of investment in rendering violence against women. As Françoise Naudillon points out, "De *L'exil selon Julia* [1996] à *Chair piment* [2002], les héroïnes de Gisèle Pineau sont confrontées aux douleurs de la chair" [From *L'exil selon Julia* to *Chair piment*, Gisèle Pineau's heroines are confronted by the pains of the flesh].[45] In the novel *L'âme pretée aux oiseaux* (2001), a teenage girl gives birth to the protagonist, Marie who is the product of rape and incest. *Chair piment* presents a protagonist, Mina, who embodies her sexuality boldly, fully, and obsessively. In this novel, sexuality is vividly and violently present through explicit language. Mina's desire for sex is described in violent terms; she longs for "un sexe d'homme planté dans son ventre comme un couteau" [a man's sex to be planted into her stomach like a knife].[46] The jarring collision of sex and violence in *Chair Piment* disturbs the reader as it prompts greater reflection on the way trauma can be psychically present though physically manifested. In the protagonist's many trysts lies the haunting presence of a secret family trauma. Pineau links the trauma of the past and the protagonist's pleasure of the present by making her sister's ghost appear to her with each sexual encounter. "C'était toujours après la jouissance que Rosalia faisait son apparition, visite fugace. Rosalia remontée de ses ténèbres le 11 septembre 1998, jour anniversaire des vingts ans de l'incendie dans lequel elle avait péri.... Visage brulé étonné. Peau grillée. Chemise de nuit en Nylon fondue dans ses chairs ... " [It was always after the orgasm that Rosalia made her appearance, a fleeting visit. Rosalia raised from the shadows of September 11, 1998, the twentieth anniversary of the fire in which she died.... Her face burned and astonished. Her skin burned. Her nylon nightgown melted into her flesh.] (13). By linking the hot flesh of Mina's sexual pleasure to the burnt flesh of her dead sister, Pineau draws a disturbing parallel between pleasure and pain. The graphic nature of the scenes of sex and violence draw the reader into Mina's complicated life of intimacy and trauma.

The trope of incest also present in *Chair Piment* functions as relevant to the development of the entire plot, yet not driving the narrative in the ways we see almost a decade prior in the main novel under consideration here. Based on these examples, after long years of being unable to write about sexual violence, *L'espérance-macadam* not only appears to inaugurate the author's treatment of rape and incest, but these tropes are subsequently pursued to some degree in many of her novels.

Where the Land Meets Flesh: Natural and Sexual Violence Intersect in Gisèle Pineau's *L'espérance-macadam*

L'espérance-macadam can be read as a book length-effort to endow the rape-of-the-land metaphor with fuller dimensions of female subjectivity, extending beyond more patriarchal imaginings of the woman as raped land. Pineau effectively mines the metaphor in order to reveal the limitations and complications that spring from it. Taking on violated landscape poetics allows the author to write about rape in a purposeful way that is carefully attentive to trauma, healing, and subject formation. The representation of rape is never intended to serve as a symbol of colonial domination; rather it serves to further materialize and highlight the far-reaching, devastating effects of sexual violence. It is enough, the book seems to suggest, to think about rape as rape rather than as a sign of something else. Furthermore the silences that surround incest are also meant to indicate a societal indictment of how sexual violence is treated in Guadeloupe. This approach locates rape as creatively and critically generative in and of itself, rather than as only a convenient figure for colonial and postcolonial narratives of violence. The ostensible focus on the dialectics of trauma, pain and healing as an integral part of narratives of sexual violence points to what had been previously excluded from the island rape analogies that populate Caribbean literature.

Set in Savane-Mulet, a village of Guadeloupe's Basse Terre region, *L'espérance-macadam* relates the experience of the almost-seventy-year-old Éliette Florentine during the days leading up to Hurricane Hugo. As the hurricane approaches, Éliette reflects on the different forms of violence that have overwhelmed her community. She also interacts with her young neighbor Angela, whose encounter with incest triggers the traumatic memories of the older woman's past. Whereas the novel appears to focus on the hurricane and its rapacious destruction of the land, the central narratives are concerned with iterations of violence that are natural, physical, and social. The novel introduces a cast of characters, most of whom have been affected by violence in some area of their lives. In fact, we might even go so far as to argue that every character in the novel is either a victim, secondary victim, perpetrator or witness of violence; some manifestation of violence has touched each of their lives.

Natural violence appears to wage itself onto the protagonist Éliette's body from a young age; she is eight years old when she lives through the 1928 Okeechobee hurricane, the first storm in the novel. However, *L'espérance-macadam* reveals only at the end of the novel that the first trauma sustained by the protagonist was not the experience of living through the storm but rather the experience of being raped by her father. Even though the conflation of the father and the violent storm is not apparent until the end of the novel, for the purposes of this analysis, it is important to foreground Éliette's rape as the first trauma she endures during her childhood. Incest informs our ability to understand the way Pineau constructs the parallel between natural violence and sexual violence, although she does not make this explicit until the conclusion. This technique evinces a parallel with the occurrence of sexual violence in general and incest in particular, which is often kept a secret, muted or suppressed in the memories of those who experience it. The narrative logic echoes the societal implications because, like the subject of sexual violence, society's refusal to name, recognize and believe rape adds to the dialectics of silence that enshroud its occurrence. As such, *L'espérance-macadam* mirrors and performs the trauma of sexual violence by suppressing then gradually revealing the memory of rape. It is the literal manifestation of what Benítez-Rojo called the Caribbean project to "revelar violencia," slowly unveiling the depths of a repressed trauma (215). However, in the example of Pineau's novel, the initial veiling serves an intentional purpose to facilitate its eventual unveiling.

Before continuing, here it is important to think about the limitations of structuring an entire novel on the notion that natural violence can effectively elucidate the trauma of sexual violence. That is, what are the dangers of equating the occurrence of natural violence with gendered violence? In my view, there are two important points at which the use of the cyclone metaphor can be problematized. First, by turning to the role of the female body, we note that the metaphor could re-inscribe the objectified dynamic of woman-as-land that we noted in the beginning of this chapter. In the cyclone parallel, the female body must be understood as the land. This introduces the possibility that the woman is objectified if rape is noted as a form of violence separate from how it affects specific female bodies. The second point at which we can interrogate the use of the hurricane to represent rape is in the uneasy affiliation between nature and violence. That is to say, the ways in which the parallel could suggest that man's violence is inherently natural or disturbingly unnatural. This view is potentially problematic, because it could ultimately serve as an excuse or a justification for violence against women and could pathologize the black male rapists of the novel.[47]

The landscape poetics throughout *L'espérance-macadam* rely heavily upon the processes of naming the hurricanes, which helps to conjure the breadth of sexual violence. Pineau designates the status of the 1928 Okeechobee hurricane as another active character by capitalizing references to it so that it becomes "Cyclone" and, alternately, "the Beast."[48] Of course, the appellation of hurricanes with proper names is an established international environmental practice, but instead of referring to the Okeechobee hurricane as Hurricane San Felipe, the name that it was originally assigned on the official record, the author uses "the Beast," thereby indicating the horrific attributes of the storm. Conversely, in the case of Hurricane Hugo, which is also known as "the Beast," Pineau often uses its proper name to set it apart from the 1928 cyclone. This practice destabilizes the equivalence of natural and sexual violence, diminishing the significance for the former. On the one hand, Pineau constructs a parallel between the hurricanes of 1928 and 1986, yet, on the other hand, by referring to the former exclusively as "the Beast," which also stands for the Éliette's rape and her rapist, she renders the latter as a more relentless type of violation. Textually, the image of the Beast alternates between designating the natural violence of the storms, referring to the sexual violence of the rapists, and the rapists themselves. The resulting effect is that "the Beast" Éliette knows through her mother becomes like the one that Angela sees in her father each time he sexually abuses her.

As a survivor of sexual trauma whose memory is repressed, Éliette illustrates the way that "what returns to haunt the victim is not only the reality of the violent event but also the reality of the way that its violence [is] *not yet . . . fully known.*"[49] To convey the piecing together of the original trauma of sexual violence and the subsequent repression of its memory, Pineau relies on textual fragmentation to highlight memories that must be put back together for healing from trauma to occur:

> À cause du Cyclone de 1928, tellement mauvais qu'il lui avait fait perdre la parole pendant trois ans pleins, l'avait blessée à la tête et au ventre, l'avait dépossédée de toute foi en elle-même. . . . Elle ne savait plus que trembler, sa bouche battant une peur phénoménale. . . . Le Cyclone l'avait rendue ainsi, lâche, indifférente, faible et molle. Elle avait gardé quelques rares souvenirs des événements. . . . (124–25)

> With the cyclone of 1928, so bad she'd been unable to speak for three full years, it had wounded her in the head and the belly, had dispossessed her of all faith in herself. All she could do was tremble, her teeth chattering out phenomenal fear. . . . The cyclone had made her like this, cowardly,

indifferent, weak, and inactive. She still had a few scattered memories of the events that took place. (88)

"Scattered memories" here reinforces the dismemberment of memory as a definitive experience, as well as the significance of the repressed sexual trauma. These traumatic wounds on Éliette's body have a dual origin: the tragic memory of the hurricane and the muted past of sexual violation lurking within her. The quote above also emphasizes the ways that rape becomes *"an ineradicable memory"* even when it is a repressed trauma. Despite the psychic repression that overcomes the rape survivor's mind, the memory is tethered to her and is eventually unearthed. At this point in the novel, the latter memory is dormant, but a re-reading of the text reveals its methodical awakening through the cyclone image.

The storm's negative ramifications on Éliette's body are threefold: the loss of her voice, the fracturing of her body, and a deleterious branding of her mind and sense of self. Like the act of rape, the combination of these physical effects compromises her subjectivity and agency, allowing us to understand her rape as "a sexually specific act that destroys (if only temporarily) the intersubjective, embodied agency and therefore personhood of a woman."[50] The emphasis on what her body undergoes highlights rape as a physical act of violation, a characteristic that is not frequently noted when the violated woman is collapsed into a metaphor of the dominated land. *L'espérance-macadam* charts Éliette's journey to recover her female identity, her loss is temporary (albeit long); by the end of the novel, she reformulates her self as a subject, and she begins to rebuild her life. Éliette's example also affirms the physical and psychological effects of sexual violence without privileging one over the other, creating an opening that allows us to consider rape in more complex terms rather than along the purview of oppositional binaries.

To this end, Éliette's literal embodiment of the land destroyed by the hurricane occurs in two registers. "Cyclone" first takes from her the power of speech, leaving her voiceless. The inability to speak poses a challenge to the recreation of narrative because Éliette cannot name the effects of the powerful storm on her; instead, she must rely on the words of others to do so. She is physically unable to break, stop, undo, or challenge the silence. Instead, silence encloses her like a dense cloud throughout the book. Like her body, her memory is traumatically fragmented; she has no ownership over the memories of "the Beast" and is thus forced to reconstruct what her mother remembered:

Non, en vérité, Élliete ne se souvenait de rien. C'était sa manman qui lui racontait toujours la nuit le Cyclone avait chaviré et pilé la Guadeloupe. Elle criait ce cauchemar: Le Passage de la Bête. Et, pour mieux embobiner l'histoire dans la mémoire d'Éliette, elle ne cessait de faire défiler le souvenir de la blessure à la tête et au ventre, le sang dans les draps, la grosse poutre tombée qui avait manqué fendre Éliette en deux parts, le vent entrant méchant, bourrant, calottant. (125)

No, the truth is, Éliette didn't remember a thing. It was her mama who had told her about the night when Guadeloupe had capsized in the cyclone and had been smashed to bits. She called that nightmare the Passage of the Beast. And to better burn the story into Éliette's mind, she was constantly rehashing the memory of head and belly wound, the bloodstained sheets, the big beam that fell and nearly cut Éliette in two, the cruel wind penetrating, buffeting, lashing. (88)

Here the generational transmission of memory causes Éliette to associate her mother Séraphine with "the Passage of the Beast." The experience of trauma is mediated through the mother. As Éliette sifts through secondhand memories, she cannot be sure whether this was the way the storm was as she lived it, or if the experience was reshaped, having been filtered through her mother's words. This uncertainty creates distance between her and her trauma. Also, because "the Passage of the Beast" is so indistinguishable from the memory of her mother, the entire mother–daughter relationship is defined by violence, allowing us to evaluate "the Passage of the Beast" as the "Passage of Memory" from one generation to the next. Coming into her own identity throughout the course of the novel, Éliette will eventually fully occupy her own subjectivity by remembering details despite the distortion and persistence of forces that throw her in the direction of forgetting and misremembering. At the same time, looking at Éliette as a nonspeaking subject effectively challenges the ways that breaking silence operates as an overdetermined vehicle for healing from sexual violence.

The significance of her own personhood is accentuated here because whereas "breaking the silence" acts as a mandate for survivors, demanding that they tell their stories of pain, what becomes necessary for Éliette is to realize and acknowledge the rape for her own self rather than for the performative act of speaking to rupture silence. Thus, the urgency of speaking circles back to the protagonist herself rather than focusing on fulfilling the public's need for education and awareness. What matters here is her relationship to her own enunciation rather than the act of speaking in order to educate others. The need for recognition that tropes of silence and voice often invoke is replaced by self-actualization and personhood. These aspects of the protagonist's character indicate that instead of being irrevocably trapped in the discourses of signs and images, the violated female subject is more fully elaborated and constituted. She is offered greater attention to the vicissitudes of the way rape affects her.

"The Beast is My Papa": Angela's Rape and the Expository Act of Writing Sexual Violence

The novel's "beasts"—though one superhuman and one the result of human behavior—resemble one another. The comparison presents several points at which sexual violence is related to the hurricane's violence: both chart a relentless course, pursue their victims voraciously, and leave indelible marks upon survivors. Similarities between the act of rape and the passing of the hurricane are especially pronounced when we turn to the most graphic and sustained exposition of violence in *L'espérance-macadam:* the explicit scenes when Angela is sexually abused by her father, Rosan. Rosan's violent, incestuous encounters with Angela are consistently related in the same language that evokes "Cyclone." Rosan's abuse of his daughter begins as molestation when she is less than ten years old; as she grows older, he goes from fondling to eventually raping her. Pineau provides details in lengthy passages, beginning with this one:

> Enragé, il cherchait un butin, lui écarta les cuisses comme pour la *déchirer*. Elle poussa un râle qui ne l'arrêta pas. *Il écrasa* sa bouche. Sentant qu'il enfonçait un fer dans sa petite coucoune bien boutonnée, elle voulut le repousser loin de son ventre qui s'ouvrait. Elle voulait crier encore une fois, mais elle avait perdu la parole. Elle voulait se débattre aussi, mais la bête l'avait déjà forcée l'entré, saccagé, embouti. Était déjà en elle. Au plus profond de ses entrailles. (215; my emphasis)

> Crazed, in search of some secret booty, he spread her legs as if *to tear* her apart. He *smashed* in her mouth. When she felt that he was *jamming a* rod into her little well-knit *coucoune*, she wanted to push him away, far from her belly that was splitting open. She wanted to cry out again, but she'd lost her voice. She wanted to struggle too, but *the beast* had already forced

open the gate, staved it in, pillaged. Was already inside of her. Deep in her entrails. (154; my emphasis)

This passage does not obscure the severity of the violence—it is both physical and psychological—as the girl struggles to understand what is taking place inside of her. Rosan is described as a wild, monstrous creature; animalistic words express his behavior, and, by the end of the episode, he mutates into "the beast." Thus the reader is exposed to the process through which "man" becomes "beast" in the act of rape. Angela is silenced and paralyzed by her father's actions. He becomes a part of her body that she will feel deep from within, just like the trauma that follows her after she leaves home. The rhetoric of the cyclone is adopted to describe rape through the use of terms such as "tear," "smash," "jam," "beast," "forced," and "pillage"—words that draw our attention to the physical nature, the bodily experience, of what Angela goes through.[51]

Within this dialectic of natural and sexual violence, Pineau repeatedly makes use of explicitly graphic actions as she constructs parallels between the two. I would like to focus on three in particular: ripping apart, penetrating, and burning, for the ways they give fuller meaning to the act of rape. First, Angela experiences a "splitting" or is being ripped open by her father in the scene of the initial assault. During the storm, Éliette, as we learn toward the end of the novel, is also "ripped open." Initially, this is the literal bodily ripping caused by the rafter that supposedly falls on her during the 1928 Okeechobee hurricane (though eventually this, too, is revealed as the ripping open of rape). Second, the land is literally ripped open and torn apart as the hurricane ravages it: "Une poutre m'était tombée dessus, m'avait presque traversée. J'ai eu le ventre ouvert à ce que disait ma manman. Le Cyclone, elle l'appelait toujours Le Passage de la Bête, comme si, véritablement, une bête m'était passée dessus" (216) ["A rafter fell on me [Éliette], almost went right through me. My belly was ripped open according to what my mama said. She always called the Cyclone the Passage of the Beast, as if a beast had actually passed over me" (154)]. Later Anoncia also reflects on "Éliette déchirée, sauvée et recousue par la femme Éthéna . . . " (293) ["Éliette ripped open, rescued, and sewn back together by the Ethéna woman" (209–10)]. By contrast, for Angela, the images are evoked during her rape, as we saw in the use of "jamming" in the passage cited above. With regard to the land, the same vocabulary of tearing something apart is used to describe what happens in the course of the hurricane: "Et puis, il y eut un terrible chuintement, déchirure de chair et fracas d'os, comme si la terre s'ouvrait en deux pour laisser entrer le fer du Cyclone" (295) ["Then there was a tremendous ripping sound, flesh tearing and bones breaking, as if the earth were splitting open to let the blade of the Cyclone in" (211)]. These references emphasize the physically wrenching nature of what happens in the act of sexual violence. Rendering this scene with such meticulous attention to the details of violation further destabilizes the island rape analogy at work in *L'espérance-macadam* as it calls attention to the body beneath the symbol. These examples help us think about how naming the act of sexual violence is different from actually rendering rape in explicit detail. Whereas naming serves a function that is highly performative, providing detail focuses more on the body of the violated subject. With such graphic scenes being depicted, it is difficult to imagine a neutral reference to the rape of the land. The stakes, as these scenes of rape demonstrate, are high, and the pain—both physical and psychological—is intense.

Along with these instances of ripping, tearing, or splitting open, there is a penetrating object responsible for the damage caused through natural and sexual violence. This object overwhelms the passages in its prominence and pursuit. Angela refers to the object that penetrates her by giving it different names. The movement from one object to the next takes us through the stages of Angela's violation as she is repeatedly molested and raped. Rosan's hand "pierces her body," then he "[jams] a rod into her." The literal puncturing of the body is the result of violent penetration, and the naming of the object discloses the rape. In Éliette's case, rape is also revealed in relation to the penetrating object. Her experience is finally disclosed when she identifies the rafter as bearing her father's imprint: "C'était mon papa, hein, marraine? J'ai vu son visage taillé dans le bois [. . .] j'ai vu la poutre et son visage taillé dedans (297) ["He was my papa, wasn't he Godmother? I saw his face carved in the wood . . . I saw the rafter with his face carved in it" (213)]. The original penetrating object is etched with the human face of Éliette's perpetrator-father. Again, emphasis on the violent penetration focuses attention on what the female body undergoes during the physical act of rape. Rape is rendered in its embodied significance, not merely as a symbolic form of violation that relates principally to structural violence. Phallic imagery here serves to emphasize what happens in the act of rape without any use of symbolic referents. Reading this scene of sexual violence clarifies the different stages and effects of rape without reducing their significance in the broader cultural context. The context we see here becomes less significant than what the physical embodied subject experiences in the act of violation. This strategy marks out a rhetorical space in which rape can become representable, undoing the established notion that rape resists representation. There are ways, Pineau's portrait of violation suggests, to navigate the slippery edges of representation with steadfast focus on the multivaried effects of sexual violence.

The third image in the mirrored descriptions of rape and the hurricanes is fire and/or burning to evoke the sensations felt by victims of assault. Over and over, Angela is left with the sensation of being burnt:

> La bête fouillait en elle, *brûlante. Du feu,* oui. Il y avait du feu entre ses cuisses. . . . *Du feu! Du feu,* Seigneur partout du feu! Dans sa petite coucounne violentée, dans son ventre, dans toutes les veines de son corps, jusqu'à sa tête qu'elle sentait *brûler toute entière comme savane en Carême.* (215; my emphasis)

> The *beast* was rooting around inside of her, burning. Yes, *fire.* There was a *fire burning* in between her legs. . . . *Fire!* . . . *Fire,* Lord, everywhere! In her little ravaged coucoune, in her belly, in all the veins in her body, all he way up to her head that *she could feel was completely ablaze, like the savanna in dry season.* (154; my emphasis)

In this passage, mention of the land reinforces bodily experience. Here, Angela's own words associate her with the land, using the latter as a symbol to vehicle understanding of sexual violation rather than the inverse relationship, which we see at work in the novels of Zobel and others. When Éliette thinks, "the same hot iron had branded them both," it can refer to the penetrating and raping phallus that pierces Angela and her mother, as well as to Éliette and Séraphine. Through these examples, we witness the tropical cyclone operating as a material manifestation of several aspects of rape: it is at once the rapist, the body's experience, and the trauma of survivors of rape and their loved ones. The interconnectedness of these three images carries the reader through the physical stages of rape—as the female body is split open, penetrated, and branded. Representation of rape is thus achieved by highlighting the physical properties of sexual violence and revolves around the bodily reception of that violence.

Focusing on the material and physical properties of sexual violence is one of the main ways that Pineau explodes the woman as violated landscape metaphor. Her poetics give rise to a strategy that questions the established dialectic by obligating the reader to carefully contemplate the act, the costs, and the aftermath of rape. Giving meaning to the metaphor and substance to the symbol, Pineau calls into question the facility with which "the rape of the land" in conjured in the Caribbean imaginary, as though to say: these are the costs of using rape metaphors; this is what we are really saying when we use the symbol of rape in such a way. By doing so, she forthrightly engages the politics of rape representation, offering rhetorical strategies and narrative devices that move beyond metonymy and metaphor and allow us to think through figurations of sexual violence from another vantage point.

In addition to describing the material effects of sexual violence, efforts to protect and elaborate Angela's subjectivity are evident through representational strategies that allow the reader to imagine her agency and self-actualization despite the rape. By narrating the rape entirely from Angela's perspective, the author privileges her character's point of view. Although the narrative is told from the third person, we enter into Angela's mind, and her eyes offer the primary gaze in each passage. Such a use of the gaze dynamically incorporates female subjectivity. In the context of Antillean literature Sam Haigh has written that, "the gaze is a locus of power: it is directed from a powerful subject to a less powerful object, and the assertion of the black [female] gaze is necessarily an act of resistance."[52] Haigh's observations establish Angela's vantage point as empowering and as the protagonist's refusal to be objectified. The gaze becomes a way of affording some type of agency to the violated subject and dissolving the lines of the victim category in which she finds herself. Through her gaze we also witness another form of resistance as she finds a coping mechanism to deal with the rape:

> Alors, Angela referma ses doigts sur les montants de la couche. Elle ne lutta plus. Ouvrit davantage les jambes. Et puis, serra les dents au moment où le feu se rallumait entre ses cuisses [. . .]. Ne pas crier. Juste baisser les paupières comme une morte dans son cercueil. (224)

> So then Angela closed her fingers around the bars of her headboard. Stopped fighting. Opened her legs more. And then clenched her teeth when the fire started burning again between her legs [. . .] Don't scream. Just close your eyelids like a corpse in a coffin. (159–60)

The use of disassociation as a technique made use of by rape survivors is one that further demonstrates Pineau's investment in the use of rape representation as a way to engage the trauma it leaves in its wake. As her disassociation indicates, Angela experiences many of the feelings typically associated with victims of sexual violence: shame, fear, and guilt. Her reactions reveal the manifold emotions that can accompany rape trauma syndrome. With the first rape, "la peur descendit sur son âme" (214) ["fear fell upon her soul" (152)]. Despite moments of agency and power, the depiction of her rape demonstrates a confluence of a wide spectrum of emotions. Ashamed, she tries to find an excuse for Rosan's behavior. She literally attempts to "lui trouver une autre excuse . . . se figurait parfois que son papa était possédé par un esprit et qu'il ne connaissait rien des agissements de ce demon qui usurpait son envelope pour l'abuser, elle" (212) ["find an excuse for him . . . sometimes [imagining] that an evil spirit had taken possession of her papa and that he had no idea how the demon used his fleshly envelope to abuse her" (151)]. She also feels guilty, as though she, not her father, has betrayed the family through acts of sexual violation.

> Quand *la bête* arracha sa culotte, Angela voulut appeler sa manman, mais une voix la cria Judas, alors elle garda le crie dans sa gorge. Non, c'était pas son papa. Elle ferma les yeux pour ne pas le voir. Le diable avait pouvoir de prendre n'importe quelle forme. Elle le savait. Non, c'était pas son papa. (214)

> When *the beast* tore her panties off, Angela wanted to call her mama, but a voice called her Judas, so she kept the call locked in her throat. No it wasn't her papa. She closed her eyes to keep from seeing him. The devil had the power of taking on any form. She knew that. No, it wasn't her papa. (153)

With each episode of incest, Angela invariably goes through several stages of emotions, from fear to desperation and submission. Telling herself that her abuser is not her father is a way to survive the betrayal of incest. The focus on her affective response as well as her pain foreground the different levels at which the trauma of rape occurs. Again, this catalogue of emotions functions as a way to fill out the contours of sexual violence in a more substantial way. Moving from one feeling to the next, Angela even passes from the material world into an imagined alternate universe, aided by her mother's fictions. From this exterior, invented space, she contemplates what is happening to her internally:

> Elle se mit à pleurer tandis qu'il la serrait plus fort, enflait en elle, cherchait à gagner plus loin encore dans les sentes de son corps, l'étreignait, gémissait. Alors, elle pleura des petites larmes de sang, qu'on aurait pu confondre avec des larmes ordinaires, transparentes et salées. Mais, c'était

bien du sang. Des petites larmes de mort, puisqu'elle allait mourir cette nuit-là dans sa chambre, c'était sûr. Comment aurait-il pu en être autrement. . . . Des pleurs sans paroles, pour pas faire de la peine à son papa, à sa manman Rosette. Il la tenait par les deux pommes de ses fesses, la serrant de force tout contre lui, pour que la bête entre jusqu'à la garde, *l'entaille et la pourfende. Elle était pleine de cette bête longue qu'elle ne pouvait vomir ni arracher.* . . . Des petites larmes de sang de mort. Pleurs sans paroles versés dessus ce *feu*. (215–16; my emphasis)

She began to cry as he held her tighter, swelled within her, sought to push still further along the paths of her flesh, gripped her, groaned. Then she wept small tears of blood that one might have mistaken for ordinary, transparent salt tears. But it was really blood. Little tears of death, since she would surely die that night in her room. How could it be otherwise. . . . Wordless weeping, so as not to hurt her papa, her mama Rosette. He was clutching the two buns of her buttocks, smashing forcefully against him so that the *beast* could go in all the way up to the hilt, *slice* and *rend* her. *She was filled with the long beast that she could neither vomit nor turn away from.* . . . Little tears of blood and death. Wordless tears shed over that *fire*. (154; my emphasis)

The passage features emotions ranging from fearful sadness (exemplified through her crying) to the nightmarish possibility that her tears might be blood pouring down her face. The reference to crying tears of blood can be read as an implicit Messianic reference that requires careful analysis as the reader places Angela's rape in the context of sacrifice. This understanding follows her logic of sacrifice and suffering for the sake of the family. Inherent in these variegated emotions lies one of the fundamental elements of sexual violence: that it presents a panoply of different emotions that vary in intensity and duration, that are socially constructed, and that can even appear to be contradictory. Relating these affective permutations tells a story about rape that attempts to capture its different facets, rather than assign a fixed meaning to the experience of sexual violence for a single individual.

Despite her inability to physically dislodge the traumatic remnants of her father's violent assault from herself, Angela accesses a tiny repository of power within herself in the act of renaming him a "beast." From this position, she accords her own significance to the experience of violation. Although she has lost control, she recovers an element of power by renaming and reframing Rosan. By naming and identifying her perpetrator, by assigning an identity to him, she participates in an act of recognition that leads to her own self-recognition. In naming the beast, Angela interpellates both the novel's author and protagonist, making use of a vocabulary of sexual violation that functions metatextually, referencing both the survivors in the book and the book's main rhetorical strategy for representing rape. Additionally, naming him "the beast" serves as another tie that sutures the perpetrator of sexual violence to the phenomenon of natural violence. The politics of recognition is differently imbricated here because, like Éliette, Angela's act of recognition is directed toward herself. She is not in need of any vehicle to help her articulate the pain of her experience. As the most rigorously detailed incident of rape in *L'espérance-macadam*, the scenes of Angela's violation present a model of representation, reaction, and resistance to sexual violence. Her case vividly demonstrates the way bodily experience is rendered palpable through the metaphor of the violent storm.

In these scenes of father–daughter incest, the cyclone metaphor operates as an illustration of the depths of trauma, demonstrating that reactions to assault are deeply psychological, as well as material and physical. Studies on sexual violence indicate that the victim-survivors of rape trauma syndrome go through a "retriggering phase," during which smell can be a source of anxiety caused by the assault.[53] For the novel's characters, assault is so powerful that it actually has an identifiable scent and the trauma extends secondarily to those around them. When Rosette comes to Éliette to discuss her daughter's abuse by the father, Éliette smells the trauma that rape has left on the family, and the smell triggers her memory.

> Elle [Rosette] sentait. Et son odeur emplissait la chambre, flottait sur les mots qui évoquaient le passé. . . . Puanteur qui disait la honte malpropre, dénonçait la souillire, *l'odeur-charogne du viol*, l'horreur putride, les affres pestilentes du remords, la décomposition. (271; my emphasis)

> She [Rosette] smelled. And her odor filled the room, lingered in the words that brought up the past. . . . Stench that stated the filthy shame, revealed the stain, *the carrion smell of rape*, the putrescent horror, the pestilential depths of remorse, decomposition. (194; my emphasis)

The first lines of this passage are among the strongest words of the entire novel—the only instance where the actual word "rape" is explicitly stated. Rosette's scent is so potent that it "fills" the entire room. Rape is represented as a stench, stain, and pestilent. Together, these words designate the saturating nature of sexual violence and elevate it to an action that goes beyond the act of penetration, indicating its social context. Trauma left in the wake of abuse is the enduring effect of sexual violence. Pineau reminds us that it is also immeasurable, through the use of the words "depth," "carrion," "horror," and "decomposition," each of which expresses unending or unquantifiable capacities. The pungent odor of rape is active in its ability to "fill," "linger," and "state." This scent serves two functions—it not only describes the way a mother (Rosette) interacts with her daughter's (Angela) assault, it also acts as a trigger for Éliette to recall her own experience with rape. "Éliette avait refermé la porte se disant que sûrement sa manman Séraphine avait connu ses mêmes sentiments quand elle s'était jetée sur le démon avec l'envie d'assassiner" (271) ["Éliette closed the door, thinking to herself that her mama Séraphine had surely felt the same way when she'd thrown herself at the demon with a will to kill!" (194)]. In the act of closing the door, Éliette attempts to retreat to an insular place where she can lock out the scent and stain of trauma, but again, the memories persist.

I want to turn briefly to the role of the perpetrator in the representation of Angela's rape. Subjecting rape to "genealogical scrutiny" requires also observing the role of perpetrators of violation, as well as the discursive construction of the way they make sense of the sexual violence they perpetrate. Is there a way that examining Rosan's actions through his own eyes could provide us with a different conceptualization of this scene of sexual violence? I want to suggest here that it is particularly telling that, as perhaps indicative of its power, the cyclone metaphor is utilized not only by the narrator and the victim-survivors of assault. Everyone—the author, narrator, protagonist, perpetrators, and minor characters—participate in the same system of signification with a similar grammar for designating rape. When Rosan characterizes his violation of his daughter, he too draws a comparison between himself and a cyclone. The reader is thus instructed to view Rosan as a voracious consumer in his lust for his daughter's flesh. "Combien de fois s'était-il jeté pis qu'un cyclone sur le corps d'Angela. [. . .] Il ne pouvait pas se retenir. Il y avait une machine en dedans de lui, mécanique diabolique qui le poussait toujours dans la chambre d'Angela" (252) ["So many times . . . [he] had thrown himself more violently than a cyclone on Angela's body. He couldn't stop himself. There was a machine inside of him, diabolical mechanism that always pushed him into Angela's room" (180)]. Rosan's explanation of his compulsion adheres to a lasting myth about rapists—that they are carried away by uncontrollable urges. It would seem that the comparison of the cyclone to the rapist facilitates the perpetuation of such myths. Here there is an uneasy link between natural violence and sexual violence. Violence, as some early historians and philosophers have argued, is a natural part of "man."[54] By extension, it would seem to correlate that sexual violence is also natural. Doesn't imagining the relationship between sexual and natural violence also call upon us to view the former as natural? Read differently, the juxtaposition of the two might highlight the ways in which sexual violence is "unnatural" even though it takes place with the same regularity as natural violence. When we take this association in the context of the population she writes about, how do we interpret the racial politics of Pineau's work? I suggest here that yes, Rosan's character prompts us to imagine sexual violence as a natural insatiable urge, but Pineau's self-conscious raising of such questions challenges the accepted view of rape. It also challenges the culture of silence surrounding sexual violence because of which it is rarely interrogated. The cyclone operates as a signifier for sexual violence that is made use of by both the victim and perpetrator, a practice that attempts to blur the line between the two. As such, L'espérance-macadam proffers a distinctly black feminist iteration of sexual violence, refusing to obscure the realities of rape in deference to racial solidarity and demonstrates some of the ways that black women writers concern themselves with mapping the critical tensions of rape representation.

Pineau's careful rendering of this parallel, in which the violated female body is associated with the destroyed land, is largely animated by the idea of the cyclone as rapist. This strategy leads the reader to contemplate what metaphors of rape often elide: a close reading of the different actors involved. Untangling the sexual dynamics of the metaphor to look more closely at its implications fosters a greater understanding of the stakes of relegating sexual violence to a symbolic order. By this, I mean that despite Pineau's ostensible focus on the victim-survivor of rape, her explicit rendering of the perpetrator as beast also calls into question some of the dominant threads of feminist rape narratives. The perpetrator does not figure as voiceless or unrepresentable. Instead, he becomes hypervisible because his identity collapses into the cyclone, another topos-related figure with a crucial meaning in the Caribbean context. The Caribbean rapist as hurricane conjures different associations that can speak to the description of violence as simultaneously natural or unnatural.

I have cited the graphic passages of Angela's rape at length and in great detail throughout this section in an attempt to emphasize the lengths to which Pineau goes to show the depth and the breadth of sexual violence. As feminist philosopher Ann J. Cahill has observed, "Rape itself, as a phenomenon, is profoundly multiple, deeply differentiated by a host of diverse and at times conflicting discourses. Yet its possible meanings, while diverse, are always directly related to that complex interplay between the body and subjectivity."[55] The examples cited above exhibit the assorted reactions to sexual violence that one person can experience and the way these connect to a woman's bodily subjectivity. In the scenes of father–daughter incest, the tropical cyclone metaphor also operates as an illustration of the trauma's magnitude, demonstrating that reactions to assault are deeply psychological, in addition to being material and physical, and that they invariably influence the process of subject and identity formation.

The Reach of Rape: Vicarious Trauma in Pineau's Minor Characters

Throughout this chapter, I have argued that Pineau deploys different strategies for representing rape that strive to capture its far-reaching effects, as well as its inherently multiple meanings. I now turn to another way in which she does this through a discussion of the role vicarious trauma plays in the lives of two of the novel's characters, Anoncia and Séraphine. Anoncia, despite not having been directly abused, suffers from trauma as though she too was a victim. Her reactions broaden the scope of sexual trauma and further add to the "profoundly multiple" nature of rape. A victim of vicarious trauma, Anoncia's experience helps to index the various effects of sexual violence. The godmother and aunt of Éliette, Anoncia represents what happens when sexual violence is kept a secret, as is often the case given the stain of societal taboos—she is a literal manifestation of the choking hold of silence. "Plus d'une fois, elle avait voulu éclairer Eliette sur son père inconnu, sur la folie de sa maman. Las, les mots s'agglutinaient au tréfonds de sa gorge. La honte la possédait" (291) ["More than once she had tried to enlighten Éliette about her mysterious father, about her mother's madness. Alas, the words stuck at the back of her throat. She was consumed with shame" (208)]. As we saw in the harrowing example of Angela's rape, shame is a definitive emotion associated with sexual violence, but it is usually used to explain the way victims of rape experience the trauma.

Anoncia's intense shame is not just a result of being related to the rapist, who is her brother; I propose that it results from her being an extension of Éliette. This reality shows the reach of rape, as well as the collectivity of black women's experience. That "Marraine Anoncia savait tout de ce cyclone-là" [Godmother Anoncia knew all about that cyclone], indicates knowledge on a superficial level—she is aware of what happened and is the only one alive with the key to unlock Éliette's traumatic memories (272, 194). But the description goes on to suggest that the character is not only a witness, she also bears all of the marks of a woman also suffering from rape trauma syndrome. Trauma in her case is present through the language of contagion used to describe what she goes through. She has grown old and is constantly debilitated by the information to the point that the secret bears the mark of a disease that infects her daily: "Des poussées d'une peine sans nom la tenaient au lit, fiévreuse, désespérée" (288) ["Bouts of nameless sorrow kept her bedridden, feverish, on the verge of despair" (206)]. Her anguish is physical and psychological. She goes on to describe her feelings in relation to her brother: "parfois, le sachant du même sang qu'elle . . . [elle] se sentait souillée, putride et nauséeuse" (289) ["at times, knowing that he was of the same blood as she . . . [she] felt unclean, putrid, and repulsive" (207)]. Feelings of dirtiness introduce another affective response felt among victims of assault, who often feel stained by the penetrating act of rape. Rape comes to live in them psychologically as a mark or disease of trauma.

Anoncia's affective responses to sexual violence position her alongside Éliette and Angela making her a victim of secondary trauma. The extent to which she suffers as a guardian of the secret of the rape influences Anoncia's existence in the world, as well as in a metaphysical sense:

> Le Bon Dieu ne la laisserait jamais gagner le ciel tant qu'elle n'aurait pas délivré le secret qui la rendait complice des actes de La Bête . . . il y aurait toujours en dedans même de son corps un rongement dû à une peine infinie qui ne s'éteindrait qu'avec la décharge du secret. (272)

> The Good Lord would never let her go to heaven as long as she hadn't told the secret that made her party to the acts of the *Beast* . . . she would always feel something gnawing inside of her, due to an incalculable sorrow that could only be assuaged by unburdening herself of the secret. (194)

What is striking here is the way the secret literally consumes Anoncia, not only eating away at her (flesh) life on earth and but also preventing her passage from the world, so that she is held prisoner by her memories. These affective responses have consequences in Anoncia's daily life.

The struggle to keep the secret introduces difficulties into the women's relationship, and Anoncia's reluctance to share the full story with Éliette continues through the moment that she is confronted: "Anoncia serrait les dents sur son secret, prêtait l'oreille au vent, couvrait sa tête du drap, repoussait, repoussait le moment des aveux" (296) ["Anoncia clenched her teeth against the secret, listened to the winds, covered her head with the sheet, put it off, put off the moment of truth" (212)]. Anoncia shields Éliette from the truth that the novel's heroine desperately chases in the throes of the Hurricane. In her painful psychic retention of Éliette's rape, Anoncia becomes an archive for the memories of her niece's trauma. This is why Éliette seeks her out: not only to confirm her suspicions of the role rape played in her life, but also to obtain and claim ownership over the memories of her own trauma:

> Avant le Cyclone. Éliette voulait entendre, de la bouche de Marraine Anoncia, ce qu'elle savait déjà. Tout, elle voulait entendre de la bouche d'une vivante. Elle en avait le droit. Tout revivre, pour se relever enfin dessous cette poutre qui avait rompu son existence. (273)

> Before the cyclone. Éliette wanted to hear, from Godmother Anoncia's lips, what she already knew. Everything, she wanted to hear it all from the lips of a living being. She was entitled to that much. Relive it all, so she might finally get out from under that rafter that had crushed her life. (195)

The above quote is especially powerful for how it reminds us of trauma's lasting ability to haunt the individual, to not know what is nonetheless known. It also reinforces Éliette's need to be free from the memories as her mother told them and to have memories of her known. Through remembering, and the act of hearing from "a living being" she will finally be able to begin to move on from what has traumatized her over the years. Regardless of the united efforts of Séraphine, Anoncia, and Ethéna, Éliette sustains trauma from her horrifying experience. Living with incest in Savane precludes her escaping violence because other people's memories in this atmosphere of unmitigated violence enter her mind and stir up her own traumatic past. Thus Pineau indicates the difficulty of forgetting trauma and the ways that trauma functions as an *ineradicable mark*. Even the most precise exorcism, like the one Ethéna performed for Éliette, cannot prevent traumatic memories from eventually erupting.

Anoncia adds another layer onto this dialectic: she is traumatized because she remembers, whereas Éliette is traumatized because she forgets. Together these characters represent the tension between remembering and forgetting that sexual trauma gives rise to. Although Éliette suffers from the pains of trauma throughout the novel, she is able to live her life and grasp at attempts for peace and hope. Despite being sterile and afraid of men, she manages to marry twice. Despite being largely afraid of those around her, she is still a part of the community. What Éliette, who "n'avait connu que la noirceur de l'oubli, parole perdue d'hébétude en gage" [had only known the darkness of forgetting, for which falling mute and being left with a dulled mind were the dues she'd had to pay], must weather on a daily basis seems to be minimal compared with what Anoncia weathers (274, 196).

Like the narrator, the perpetrator, and the other characters in *L'espérance-macadam*, Anoncia reinforces the designation of a rapist as "The Beast." She uses this name to refer to Éliette's father, her "frère animal, crapaud des ténèbres, qui avait pourfendu Éliette" (288) ["brute for a brother, the slimy creature of the depths that had split Éliette in two" (201)]. All that we learn in terms of his actual name is that even as a child he was called Ti-Cyclone, prefiguring his subsequent appetite for sexual violence later on in life. Ti-Cyclone's actions as an adult wound his daughter for life, send his wife's mind into chaos, and inflict his sister with lasting psychic pain. When the people from the town mention him, Anoncia is overcome by an extremely visceral reaction.

> Et puis, d'un seul coup porté, ils assenaient le nom de La *Bête*. Lame de couteau, le nom étripait Anoncia d'une manière sauvage, tant et si bien qu'elle se croyait évidée, délivrée à jamais du rongement intérieur. Mais le nom prononcé n'était pas en vérité. Il laissait seulement Anoncia dans l'épouvante, debout droite au mitan de murs effondrés qu'elle rebâtissait chaque jour depuis l'enfer de 1928. (289)

> They dropped the name of the *Beast*. Like a savage dagger, the name tore Anoncia up, so much so that she believed that her entrails had been ripped out, delivering her at last from the inner gnawing. But the name pronounced did not really kill. It merely left Anoncia terror-stricken, standing stiffly amid the crumbling walls that she'd been rebuilding every day since the hell of 1928. (207)

Anoncia's bodily reaction to hearing her brother's name and carrying the secret adds her to the ranks of women—Séraphine, Angela and Éliette—who are traumatized by and because of rape. The language here mirrors descriptions of sexual violence, especially what we saw in the scene with Angela. Whether she is described as being disease stricken, voiceless, or shriveled in pain, the lasting effects of trauma are rendered in relation to her body.

Seeing Angela for the first time, Godmother Anoncia observes: "La petite qui t'accompagne te ressemble, tu sais, quand tu avais tes quinze ans, après que la parole t'a été rendue" (300) ["You know that girl you brought along looks just like you when you were fifteen, after you'd learned how to speak again" (215)]. Her comments are poignantly appropriate because Angela resembles Éliette in ways beyond the physical likeness—each is marked by the trauma of father–daughter incest. Their proximity complicates Angela's fulfillment of Éliette's lifelong dream to raise a daughter as her own, because the girl simultaneously embodies the trauma of the past and embodies hope for the future. Éliette's acceptance of their resemblance and her final decision to adopt Angela mark the end of the protagonist's tumultuous journey toward self-discovery. Angela thus becomes to answer to Éliette's lifelong quest for wholeness.

Deconstructing Rape Myths: Interpreting and Reacting to Sexual Violence

The story of Éliette's rape is muted; only in the last twenty pages of the novel do we learn that the source of the protagonist's pain is the residual trauma of rape and not the rafter having fallen on her during the 1928 Okeechobee hurricane. This is in contrast to Angela's assault, which is rendered with rigorous attention to detail and is untouched by ambiguity. On one level, the reasons for this disparity can be linked to the temporality of the two events: Éliette's rape occurred almost sixty years earlier, whereas Angela's has happened recently. But my view is that the differences between the two experiences also highlights the specificity of survivors of rape as another way of accounting for the protagonists' subjectivity, reminding the reader that individual female bodies experience sexual violence differently. My view is that this understanding is essential to a nuanced representation of rape because it challenges society's construction of a monolith in relation to sexual violence.

Whatever monolith exists is made up of a set of widely circulated myths about sexual violence, which can be considered as myths because, when measured against statistics and data collected from rape survivors, they are categorically proven to be untrue.[56] The myths are about where rape occurs, who the perpetrators are, what a rape victim looks or acts like, and how people respond to rape. Due to a lack of education about sexual violence, there is a widespread belief that so-called stranger rape is more prevalent; that black women are not victims of sexual violence; and that often when women are raped they have behaved in a way that warranted violent behavior based on their clothing, perceived promiscuity, etc. The existence of a monolith endangers victim-survivors' potential for subjectivity because it fails to account for individual experience. Instead it reduces their experiences with sexual violence to a single narrative and thus denies specificity. My view of the need for specificity is well articulated by Cahill, who writes, "rape needs to be thought of as . . . something that is taken up and experienced differently by different women but also holds some common aspects . . . as an experience that begins with the body but does not end there."[57] Relatedly, Tinsley calls for scholars to "remember the Caribbean not as a generality, but as a complicated specificity."[58] Taken together, these insights help to explain why Pineau's representation of rape in *L'espérance-macadam* critically negotiates the terms of how, when, and to whom sexual violence happens. How sexual violence occurs, how it is perceived, and how it is dealt with vary across individuals. A reading of Angela and Éliette's experiences in accordance with, and against, one another shows how Pineau further promotes such an intricate view of rape that places the embodied subject at its center but also moves beyond the body.

We can understand Angela's rape as the intermediary through which Éliette remembers her own experience with sexual violence. In this community, as Renée Larrier convincingly argues, "no one claims the torment of incest nor testifies about its trauma."[59] Up until Angela's arrival, Éliette's trauma had been steadfastly forgotten, buried deep within her. What we interpret as the lasting trauma of Éliette's life is not incest, but Cyclone 1928. As "the Beast" comes to serve as a metaphor for both the hurricanes and violators within the novel, Pineau deliberately confuses her reader with the overlapping narratives of rape. When Éliette is reminded of her experience as a child, she wonders: "Est-ce que Séraphine avait ouvert les mêmes yeux que Rosette quand elle avait compris ce qu'on avait fait à sa fille?" (269) ["Had Séraphine opened the same eyes as Rosette when she realized what had been done to her daughter?" (192)]. Later she asks again, "est-ce que Séraphine avait voulu se perdre aussi, entrer dans les grandes eaux, se noyer dans un flot de paroles pour repousser au loin la vision du grand mâle fourrageant dans la chair de l'enfant . . ." (271) ["had Séraphine wanted to disappear too, slip into the deep waters, down in a gush of words to stave off the vision of the tall man rooting around in the child's body?" (193)]. Through Rosette, Éliette considers her mother and, for the first time, does not focus on her madness or characterize her as a "poor woman" whose insanity is the result of The Passage of the Beast. Instead, she looks at her mother more complexly, wondering how the deceased woman reacted to the news of her daughter's rape. Although Rosette's behavior prompts Éliette to wonder about Séraphine, the two mothers are markedly different in the way they receive the news of their daughters' abuse.

On the one hand, Séraphine believes and is determined to defend her daughter. When Éliette recalls her mother's reaction at the end of the novel, she knows that "sûrement sa manman Séraphine avait connu ces mêmes sentiments quand elle s'était jetée sur le démon avec l'envie d'assassiner" (271) ["Séraphine had surely felt the same way when she'd thrown herself at the demon with a will to kill" (194)]. Éliette's conclusion reminds the reader that even if the two mothers had similar thoughts or feelings about the situation, their reactions we quite different. Rosette's response is more typical: initially she refuses to believe her daughter, accuses her of lying, and even physically abuses her. Her behavior displays attitudes commonly found in families in which incest occurs. The child, viewed as naïve or intellectually and emotionally inferior to the adult, is thought to be unaware of, mistaken about, or fabricating the situation. Several years before the appearance of *L'espérance-macadam*, an Antillean journal featured an article on childhood sexual abuse, describing the "lourd et dégueulasse" [heavy and disgusting] silence that usually accompanies sexual abuse. The author emphasizes the role of mothers in particular when faced with incest in the home.[60] Rosette, who does not believe her daughter, represents a common type outlined by the article.[61]

During the year in which the novel is primarily set, a group was formed in Guadeloupe to examine the rate of sexual violence on the island.[62] The results indicated that in 1988–1989, a total of eighty cases of childhood sexual abuse were reported: "Une enquête menée pendant 22 mois du 1e janvier 1988 au 30 octobre 1989 dans lequel ils ont recensé 80 cas d'abus sexuels des enfants mineurs" [A survey executed over the course of 22 months from January 1st 1988 to October 1999 in which 80 cases of sexual abuse against minors were recorded].[63] According to the study, "dans 6 cas sur 10 la protection de l'enfant n'est pas assurée par la mère" [in 6 out of 10 of these cases the child's protection is not secured by their mothers].[64] These numbers display a dominant pattern of behavior and reactions in response to incest. When Rosette unleashes her anger against her daughter; she revictimizes her, physically abusing her so badly that she knew she might kill her. "Quand elle avait commencé à frapper Angela, dans la noirceur de la chambre, c'était juste pour soulager sa peine qui lui pétait la tête, juste pour déloger le mensonge de la bouche de son enfant" (107) ["When she'd started beating Angela, in the dark room, it was only to ease the despair that was splitting her skull, only to knock the lie out of her child's mouth" (74)]. Here Rosette's violent treatment is motivated by her inability to believe Angela. The daughter is disbelieved, denied protection and then physically abused by her mother. Overall, many of the findings from the article, "L'inceste: Une réalité dans nos îles," are applicable to the context of Pineau's book. For example, "(1) Les victimes sont en majorité des filles [the victims are mostly girls] . . . (2) Elles sont âgées de 4 à 18 ans [they are between the ages of 4 and 18] (3) Particulièrement vers l'âge de 12 ans [especially around the age of 12] (5) Dans 70% cas ils n'osent pas dénoncer [in 70% of the cases they do not dare condemn (their assailants)] (6). Les pères dans 98% n'ont aucun handicap physique ou mental [in 98% of the cases the fathers have no physical or mental disabilities] (7). 70% pratiquent la pénétration vaginale complète [70% of the perpetrators engage in complete vaginal penetration]."[65] In 6 out of 10 cases the child is not guaranteed protection by the mother; as I noted previously, this was true for Angela but not Éliette. The same article notes that "la mère est souvent complaisante ou réduite au silence" [the mother is often complicit and reduced to silence], which is again the case for Rosette.[66] I draw these comparisons from my archival research here because it helps to draw attention to the ways that the representation of sexual violence necessarily intersects with the social reality of rape. Even the article's title "Inceste: Une réalité dans nos îles" attempts to do away with the notion that incest does not occur in the Antilles. Likewise, the article attempts to dismantle some of the misconceptions associated with the social response to sexual violence.

Although Pineau demonstrates these trends, she does not remain solely within documented statistics; she also offers a more supportive model through the response of Séraphine, who, when she learns of her daughter's violation, reacts as follows:

> Séraphine . . . s'était jetée sur le démon avec l'envie d'assassiner. Las, les forces lui avaient manqué. Ramollie dans un haut-le-cœur. Une seule oreille tranchée, un peu de sang serpentant le long du cou et puis bonsoir. Non, le démon n'avait même pas connu la geôle! (271–72)

> Séraphine had . . . thrown herself at the demon [Ti-Cyclone] with a will to kill. Alas she lacked the strength. Felt so nauseous her knees buckled beneath her. Only one ear slashed off, a little blood running down his neck, and that was it. No, the demon hadn't even seen the inside of a jail! (194)

Sickened and enraged, she also reacts violently, but in contrast to Rosette, Séraphine believes her daughter and then attempts to avenge the little girl. The role of the victims' mothers manifested in the novel thus diverges from the prescribed, recognizable one in which parents respond to sexual assault within the family. Through the examples of Séraphine and Rosette, Pineau demonstrates that incest elicits different responses from families.

The night before the 1928 Okeechobee hurricane, a disastrous cyclone that killed over five thousand people in Guadeloupe, Éliette is raped by her father. Sixty-one years later, Angela, having been molested for the past five years, is raped by *her* father the night before Hurricane Hugo in 1989. After finally disclosing the truth to her mother, and as a result of her mother not believing her, Angela is forced to leave home. But, as I have argued throughout this chapter, the two hurricanes do more than frame the occurrence and the aftermath of sexual violence; they also link our understanding of rape to the material body and to an embodied self. Furthermore, they reflect a rhetorical strategy that is animated by the grammar of natural violence. At times, as Éliette contemplates what happened, it is unclear whether "the Beast" she mentions is the cyclone (storm) or her father (the real perpetrator); it is also unclear whether she refers to herself or to Angela's experience. That she slips so easily from one to the other further aligns the two incidents:

> Cinq jours que Rosette se balançait, assise en tailleur sur le plancher. . . . Le même fer les avait brûlée toutes les deux. . . . Vies de mensonges. . . . Est-ce que Séraphine avait voulu se perdre aussi, entrer dans les grandes eaux, se noyer dans un flot de paroles pour repousser au loin la vision du grand mâle fourrageant dans la chair de l'enfant? (271)

> Five days Rosette had been rocking back and forth, sitting on the floor. . . . The same iron had branded them both. . . . Lives of lies. . . . Had Séraphine wanted to disappear too, slip into the deep waters, down in a gush of words to stave off the vision of the tall man rooting around in the child's body? (193)

"Both" seems to refer to Angela and Rosette, because Rosette is the one reflecting on the events and because their names are the last mentioned. But with the entry of Séraphine, another parallel is drawn, allowing us to read Éliette's experience into the preceding sentences. The use of the iron to characterize the "ineradicable mark" left by the fury of the husband/father's phallus is, as previously noted, a technique used throughout.[67]

One of the main differences between Éliette's and Angela's experiences of incest is the way they are written into the plot. In one case (Éliette's), the abuse is muted and unclear for most of the novel; and in the other (Angela's) case, several pages are devoted to full descriptions of incest. When Éliette eventually recognizes her own experience, the language of her story remains ambiguous:

> Ses pensées l'avaient menée loin, dans un temps avant Savane. Alors Éliette se revit hoquetant de rire dans les bras de son papa qui l'envoyait au ciel une fois, deux fois, cent fois. . . . C'est ainsi qu'apparut le visage de La Bête, bossuant d'abord la poutre de bois mol, et puis s'en détachant. Il chantait d'une voix rude, mal accordée aux éclats de rire qui sortaient dedans sa gorge. Tisons de désir, pépites de pacotille, ses yeux, tout lézardés aux remous de son âme, fouillaient déjà Éliette, la violentaient en songe. Tristes copeaux de la mémoire. (296)

> Her thoughts carried her far away, to a time before Savane. And Éliette saw herself, hiccupping with laughter in the arms of her papa, who tossed her up into the sky, once, twice, a hundred times. That is how the face of the Beast appeared, first bulging up unevenly from the soft wood of the rafter, then gradually detaching itself. He was singing in a coarse voice that didn't fit with the bursts of laughter coming from his throat. His eyes—embers of desire, shiny baubles, cracked through from the stirrings in his soul—were already rooting around in Éliette, assaulting her in thought. Sad crumbs of memory. (212)

For Éliette, there is no explicit description of what occurred, as opposed to what we saw in the blow-by-blow account of Angela's rape. What is interesting here is that narrative devices play an integral role, just as they did in the writing of Angela's experience, albeit in a different way. There is distance in how Éliette remembers the rape: she is "seeing herself," observing what happened rather than suffering through it. Ultimately, Angela and Éliette are united by their common experiences of sexual assault, but their relationship also transcends it.

Conclusion: The Feminist Politics of Rape Representation

Throughout this chapter I have argued that Pineau calls into question her own construction of the terms of the cyclone/rapist, land/female body parallel by offering subjectivity in the place of objectification. The conception of the rapist/Beast as a parallel for the hurricane/Beast thus escapes from becoming a simplified equivalence. A final example that highlights this effort is Angela's reaction to the hurricane. Unlike the older women in the novel, she is unafraid, and she finds opportunity for restoration in Hurricane Hugo. For Angela, the advent of further destruction will allow her to be completely renewed, shedding her body in favor of a new self that is not wounded by sexual abuse. This is a pivotal aspect of how she reconstitutes herself during and after the rape.

> Le cyclone ne terrifiait pas Angela. Elle l'espérait même, se figurant qu'il était un déchaînement envoyé par les cieux pour *la débarrasser de son papa Rosan*. Qu'il fonde sur la terre comme une grande guerre! Se disait-elle, qu'il répande des armes tourmenteuses, la foudre et des batteries de canons tonnants! Qu'il chavire le temps et me retourne dans le ventre de la manman! . . . Qu'il bombarde la geôle une bonne fois. Ruines, poussières, tout retournerait à l'état de poussière. Et même le souvenir, balayé par le grand vent. Soufflé, éparpillé, disséminé. (283; my emphasis)

> The cyclone didn't terrify Angela. She was even awaiting it, figuring that it was a fury unleashed by the heavens *to rid her of her papa Rosan*. She thought, 'May it swoop down upon the earth like a great war! May it turn around and send me back to my mama's belly!' . . . Ruins, dust, everything would turn back into dust. Even memories, swept away by the great winds. Blown away, scattered, dispersed. (203; my emphasis)

Angela imagines a force in Hurricane Hugo that can undo the wounds inflicted by her father. Her reaction makes an important remark about her belief in the possibility for healing from the trauma of sexual violence. Nature can be a harmful force, but it also contains healing possibilities. The healing elements that Angela discovers in the hurricane achieve a ritual significance as she crosses the bridge to Grande Terre. After her father's repeated rapes she would bathe in the basin of water beneath her bed; similarly, "derrière le pont de La Rivière Salée, Angela fit un vœu et demanda au cyclone de nettoyer son corps au plus profond, de la remettre tout entière comme avant, au temps de l'innocence" (284) ["on the other side of the Salée River bridge, Angela made a wish and prayed that the Cyclone would thoroughly cleanse her body, put it all back together again just like before, back in the days of innocence" (203)].

Throughout *L'espérance-macadam*, the recuperation of the rape-of-the-land analogy emerges as a specific strategy to undo the established dialectic of feminized Caribbean landscapes, a longstanding image that often negates female personhood. Pineau takes on the ways in which the "mythically rendered black body—and the female body in particular—was scripted to have no movement in a field of signification" and maps female personhood, the inherently multifaceted nature of rape, trauma and physical pain as a way to fill up the signifying field.[68] Angela's view of Hurricane Hugo as a healing element of nature challenges the author's construction of a parallel between violence of man and violence of nature. Whereas before the focus was on the body and then on family relations to indicate the specificity of the victim-survivor's experience of rape, now Pineau takes the notion further by pointing to the specificity of healing from rape. This gesture is a reminder that the trauma of sexual violence cannot be easily represented in simple metaphorical terms. It is an acknowledgment that, as the editors of *Rape and Representation* cogently put forth, although "rape resists representation," there are representational strategies and narrative techniques that can be deployed in an attempt to render it.[69] Reading *L'espérance-macadam*, as I have done here, negotiates one of the most vexing challenges of representing rape: locating a metaphor that is useful to describe its traumatic nature but that does not succumb to a desensitized version of violation by reducing it to a single image or experience. In many ways, Pineau recuperates the metaphor by rigorously revising and complicating it. The result is a nuanced depiction of gendered violence—one that accounts for the tensions embedded in the representation of rape. This disavowal is completed in the naming of *L'espérance-macadam*; it is a novel whose characters dare to hope. Angela, the wounded victim of sexual assault, emerges as the individual through whom our protagonist finds hope. Like a macadamized surface, the novel's heroines are weathered but not worn.

Though *L'espérance-macadam* is without question indebted to Simone Schwarz Bart's *Pluie et vent sur Télumée Miracle*, Pineau revises many of the novel's key concepts, particularly the biological matrilineal genealogy, which is so central to the elaboration of female subjectivity in Schwarz-Bart's novel.[70] In *L'espérance-macadam*, the genealogy is not triangulated through family ties but rather through fictive kin and the ties of trauma. Éliette is drawn to Angela because both women have experienced the pain of incest: Anoncia is a survivor of vicarious trauma, which shores up her connection to Éliette. In the face of the betrayal of incest, the book suggests an alternative to the familial ties that bind, and the book allows the women to construct an alternative community rooted in recognizing sexual trauma.

By way of conclusion, I return to Pineau's deployment of the cyclone-as-rapist analogy as a specifically black feminist rendering of rape. In her study of representations of sexual violence on screen, Tanya Horeck raises important questions about feminist representations of rape:

> Though what a feminist representation of rape might look like is certainly open to debate, the assumption here is that it is one that is inextricably connected to the 'real' of women's lives . . . is there . . . a such thing as a 'feminist representation' of rape, a specific image we can readily identify?[71]

The answer, I think, to this question, is a representation that succeeds in placing the female subject at its center, one that escapes reductive renditions of rape, one that accounts for the inexorable trauma of sexual violence, and one that pays careful attention to rape as a bodily experience—exactly what Gisèle Pineau achieves through her subversion of the woman-as-raped-land metaphor in *L'espérance-macadam*. By rewriting the master narrative of violated feminine Caribbean landscapes with exacting attention to subject formation and the vicissitudes of trauma, Pineau reimagines the lasting image of Caribbean woman as raped land. *L'espérance-macadam* releases the hold of one of the most enduring tropes of sexual violence in colonial and postcolonial literature, which collapses the violation of the land into the violation of the female body. In doing so, Pineau powerfully demonstrates that one can move from the conflict context to the body in conflict and remain attentive to the constitution of the subject and the elaboration of the scene of sexual violence.

4

Beneath the Layers of Violence
Images of Rape and the Rwandan Genocide

> La communauté internationale garde le silence sur le génocide du 1994 au Rwanda. Les Rwandais aussi. Pourtant, derrière les visages se cachent des profondes blessures.[1]
>
> The international community maintains silence on the Rwandan genocide of 1994. Rwandese do as well. Nonetheless, behind the faces are profound wounds.
>
> —Yolande Mukagasana

> This is the heart of the genocide narrative: it is ultraviolent, ultrapainful, ultrapowerful because the barriers to our sympathies, typically hedged by our identifications with ordinary characters, are here resolved as in the mirror stage into . . . a Manichean Aesthetic.[2]
>
> —Kenneth Harrow

ON APRIL 6, 1994, the presidents of Rwanda and Burundi were assassinated. Rwandan President Juvenal Habyarimana and Burundian President Cyprien Ntaryamira were flying together in Habyarimana's presidential aircraft. As the jet hovered directly over Kigali national airport, unidentified missiles attacked it and brought it down. Habyarimana was returning to his homeland from neighboring Tanzania, where he had been with Ntaryamira for the signing of the Arusha Peace Accords, a United Nations–sponsored peace agreement between the Hutus and the Tutsis intended to bring peace to Rwanda after decades of civil war. Habyarimana's assassination became a marker for the calamitous culmination of years of so-called "ethnic strife" between the groups. Following this event, unprecedented violence erupted as Hutu forces seized control of the government. What ensued for the next one hundred days was a ruthless barrage of violent crimes: murders, rapes, tortures, massacres, and mutilations of Rwandan Tutsis, Twa, and moderate Hutus. The systematic massacre of Tutsis by the machete-armed Hutu militants, or Interahamwe, drenched the entire nation in blood for seemingly endless days. The drama would end only when a group of Tutsi militants, the Front Patriotique Rwandais (FPR), captured Kigali and declared a ceasefire.[3] Approximately eight hundred people were killed each day, resulting in about one million deaths in total.[4] This international tragedy became known as the Rwandan Genocide—then Africa's largest genocide, and the third genocide of the twentieth century. This moment forever altered the image of Rwanda in the global imaginary, irrevocably situating the nation as (to borrow a phrase from Mahmood Mamdani) "a metaphor for postcolonial violence."[5] As a result of the genocide, Rwanda quickly became the African example of violence par excellence, one that would come to be a point of comparison for every subsequent conflict on the entire continent.

A few months into the steadily worsening disaster, prompted by Human Rights Watch, the U.S. White House called for Rwandan military leaders to "end the violence."[6] This characterization of the events appeared painfully flimsy relative to the reality—the word *violence* did not seem to wield enough power to accurately describe what was exploding in Rwanda. From a policy perspective, to use *violence* as a general term instead of *genocide* was to remain ambiguous about the details, seemingly negating the magnitude of the events gripping the small eastern African nation, where each day, hundreds were raped, wounded and killed. For Rwanda, the debate over the use of the term *genocide* was steeped in political implications; to articulate "genocide" was a choice differentiating those who were willing to act by sending peacekeeping forces or other types of military assistance from those who did nothing.[7] "Violence" was a nonpartisan quasi-acknowledgment of the events, whereas "genocide" was an admission of the colossal destruction and loss of life befalling Rwanda. Soon the painfully slow progression from "violence" or "civil strife" to "acts of genocide" and finally to "genocide" heard its echo throughout the international diplomatic community.

Almost two decades since these events unfolded, we know that by the time the events of 1994 in Rwanda finally came to be seen as genocide internationally, thousands of people had already died. Although it is important to note that *genocide* in this context is a political term with a set of policy-related consequences, the question of naming genocide is relevant to this study for how it carries into the cultural imaginary. As we consider what it means to represent violence, and the role that rape plays within a larger set of elaborated epistemologies of violence, these semantic shifts accentuate the failure of language to fully capture massive material or physical violence. This unavoidable problem of naming that occurred as the genocide unfolded prefigures the challenges of responding to and remembering the genocide through cultural production. Given our understanding of the enormity of this human rights catastrophe, how does one surpass a formulaic discourse of genocide? When representing genocide, how can cultural workers render its troubling realities and political connotations yet challenge its cultural construction? What does this layered, seemingly impenetrable historical and political context mean for the representation of sexual violence? Especially since rape was an essential component of the genocidal strategy, how do we account for the politics of its representation in this charged and conflicted context? In this chapter, I explore these questions by focusing on a range of cultural texts—the novel *Murambi: Le livre des ossements* (2000)/*Murambi: Book of Bones* (2006) by Boubacar Boris Diop, the travel narrative *L'ombre d'Imana: Voyages jusqu'au bout du Rwanda* (2001)/ *The Shadow of Imana: Travels in the Heart of Rwanda* (2002) by Véronique Tadjo, the film *Sometimes in April* (2004) by Raoul Peck, and the photographs in *Les blessures du silence: Témoignages du génocide au Rwanda* (2001)— each of which help to reframe the image of genocidal rape and, in so doing, challenge some of the dominant discourses surrounding the genocide.

Given the degree of essentialism and fixity associated with genocide representations, the topic raises a set of problems for knowledge production in the African context. On the one hand, it is clear that, as philosopher Sergio Cotta observes, "humanity did not wait until . . . [the twentieth century] to commit brutalities and heinous crimes such as torture and genocide; though the word is modern, the fact is ancient."[8] Yet narratives of African genocide slip easily into stereotypical pathologizing that reinforces the circulation of images portraying Africans as brutal savages. These images originated in the colonial project but seem to tenaciously endure through the twenty-first century. As a result, the representation of genocide becomes a creative task vexed with issues that are historical, political, rhetorical, and cultural and that link back to precolonial scripts contrasting the Western self with the African "other." Nicki Hitchcott refers to this as the "mystification of Rwanda": a polarizing narrative that positions Africans as abject and deviant.[9] There is a genocide-specific set of presuppositions that anchor analyses and representations of the events of 1994, prominently displaying a commitment to thinking about the genocide according to prescribed, formulaic, and reductive patterns that at times can even run counter to the facts.[10] Longing to subvert these scripts, scholars such as Ken Harrow thoughtfully wonder, "what would an alternative way of thinking the genocide look like?" I revise his question here by exploring how rape representation might be examined as an alternative way of "thinking" the genocide.[11] The primary goal of this chapter is to answer this question by examining *Murambi, L'ombre d'Imana, Sometimes in April,* and *Les blessures du silence* as models of cultural production that allow us to begin the work of rethinking genocidal rape. The methodologies I engage in this chapter are linked to the historic, political, and human rights analyses of the Rwandan genocide that do not treat the event for its singularity but rather view the catastrophe of genocide as multiply informed and interimbricated events. This perspective informs my readings of the books, photographs, and film; I continue searching for ways in which genocide can be understood in fuller dynamism rather than simply as a fixed moment in history. Indeed, the fact that the repercussions of the genocide continue to be experienced in the Democratic Republic of the Congo, and even inform the conflict unraveling there today, further establishes the need for such a multilayered approach.

New Geographies of Pain: Rescripting Genocidal Rape

Sketching a "geography of pain," Françoise Lionnet notes that, "women writers are often especially aware of their task as producers of images that both participate in the dominant representations of their culture and simultaneously undermine and subvert those images by offering a re-vision of familiar scripts."[12] I mention Lionnet's work here because she charts a theory—"a geography of pain," as she calls it—that locates subjectivity within the portrayal of violence and, often, through the use of violence. This is the case with the female characters she examines, each one being subject to and committing acts of violence. By looking at projects that are written with "meticulous attention to realistic detail, and the paradoxical desire to communicate, *in the most honest way possible,* the radically subjective, and generally incommunicable, experience of pain," Lionnet explores the critical intersection of the reality of violence and its representation.[13] Though Lionnet is not the first to identify the challenges that surface in the cultural production of violence, I mention her work as an important critical frame for the arguments in this chapter because of her concern with subjectivity in relation to the portrayal of violence.[14] My analysis strives to locate that inscription, the textual unfolding of violence, and explore its implications for rendering rape (in written form and visual culture) in the context of multiple forms of violence that explode simultaneously.

Lionnet's endeavor is especially provocative when we consider what I will refer to here as *layered instances of violence*, that is, different manifestations of violence that occur simultaneously. Gendered violence is often layered in this way, as attested by the frequent rapes of women during war. This chapter focuses on the how artistic representation excavates the layers of violence inherent to the Rwandan genocide, understanding that Rwanda is also an important example of layered violence because of the multivaried "locations" of Rwandese women—women from the global south, black African women—whose oppressions intersect.[15] For these women, the simultaneity of oppressions imbricates the experience of genocide, informing the way they are cast in the global imagination. These multiple, intersectional identities make transnational global feminisms an important framework for negotiating some of the challenges associated with the representation of genocidal rape. Given the ways that recent scholarship in transnational global feminisms has taken on the stakes of the human rights project in particular, many of my arguments in this chapter resonate with that field and build upon its insights.[16]

The use of rape in the context of war is an established and well-documented practice that dates back to the earliest centuries, including biblical times, and has become increasingly common in the twenty-first century. The illuminating study *Women and War: Gender Identity and Activism in Times of Conflict* describes the manifold uses of rape as a tool of war:

> Rape takes on important symbolic meanings tied to the gendered perspective of the state . . . rape in time of conflict afflicts symbolic damage to the nation/ethnic group by violating the group identity in the most primal form . . . [furthermore] the use of rape in wartime also reinforces the domination of men over women in general, and one group of men over another.[17]

Interestingly, this strategy demonstrates one of the social costs of the mentality elaborated in the previous chapter on the relationship between rape and the landscape, which relegates the role of women's symbolic significance. "First, violated women are represented as symbols of male power and conquest . . . [and] Second, violations against women contribute to the de-masculinization of conquered men, a symbolic process where some men are labeled as incompetent."[18] Here it becomes clear that the operation of women within a symbolic field positions her as a vulnerable victim and then further aggravates that vulnerability. In other words, because of what women symbolize, they become targets of rape warfare. The injury to women occurs at both a material and a symbolic level. In wartime, rape becomes important for (1) what it signifies as an attack on women, who are purveyors of the nation and vessels for childbearing, and (2) the injury it grafts onto masculinity.

Because of the deafening silence that eclipsed the original catastrophe of genocide in Rwanda, it may seem peculiar to speak of a dominant image. We can, however, discern several familiar representations, which traverse the mind through sight and sound, constantly surfacing in media and scholarship. These are: the grating hack of the machete, the bleached desiccated skulls arranged in a multitude of perfect rows, the truculent mobs proclaiming Hutu Power, the use of media to spread messages of hate, and the ubiquitous rape of women. I focus on this last figure or representation—the raped woman—to consider the way depictions of the Rwandan genocide can participate in and subvert its dominant representations. The central questions guiding this chapter are "How does one represent genocidal rape, and what are the different issues at stake?" This chapter relies on texts in different mediums to serve as the basis for this analysis: Tadjo's *L'ombre d'Imana*, Diop's *Murambi*, Peck's *Sometimes in April*, and Mukagasana's *Les blessures du silence*.

The first three examples count as creative interventions by artists who are not originally from Rwanda, but who position themselves as image-makers who bear responsibility for the way they represent traumatic events. These projects are explicitly global and transnational, calling attention to the genocide as an issue that extends far beyond the local. In my analysis of Diop's, Tadjo's, and Peck's projects, I argue that their representations of sexual violence complicate and enhance female subjectivity; that is, within these texts, raped bodies go from being a familiar image of genocide to possessing specific and unique functions in which lies a nascent subjectivity for the survivor/victim. For each of these scenes of rape, I am interested in considering not only how cultural workers render the excruciating image, but also in how these representations pay careful attention to the voices and to the experiences of gendered violence within the larger system of portraying genocide. I hope to show how non-Rwandese can participate in the effort to communicate images of genocide, in the "the most honest way possible," by eschewing reductive images that revictimize women. Finally, because I am especially interested in rape as a gendered form of violence whose ultimate goal is to deprive people of power, I argue that the reconstruction of rape narratives and representations can contextualize the Rwandan genocide without relativizing or denying the particularities of gendered violence. The examples analyzed here account for the atrocity of individual rapes, as well the traumatic use of rape as a genocidal strategy.

Boubacar Diop, Véronique Tadjo, and Raoul Peck each express a pre-existing urge to take on representations of the genocide. All were approached to participate in projects that would translate the trauma of the genocide into art. Similarly, all have identified their projects as moments of transformation in their creative trajectories. As such, their texts call forth the dialectics of transnational engagement, the problematics of representing genocide, and the tensions of grappling with traumatic remembrance. Their efforts also engage the responsibility and the role of the artist/intellectual in the face of sweeping violations of human rights. Moreover, their texts adopt a self-critical approach appropriate to their positionalities as image-makers of a genocide of which they were not victims. I begin with these three pieces in particular because they also constitute an effort on behalf of those outside of Rwanda to represent the genocide and thus allow us to enter into a discussion about subject positioning that is even more critically engaged in the following chapter on wartime rape in the Democratic Republic of the Congo. As such, they speak to the significance of testimony and witnessing present within the field of trauma studies, but also expose the limitations and challenges of this field. For example, Shoshana Felman argues, "testimony cannot simply be relayed, repeated, or reported by another without losing its function as a testimony."[19] However, I suggest that the Rwandan genocide, because of the original denial of its occurrence and the lack of international response, necessitates a different relationship to testimony wherein others who have not personally experienced the genocide are also called to account by listening to and relaying the trauma of others. When we also consider the Arusha International Criminal Tribunals and the Gacaca courts in Rwanda, the necessity for testimonies to be shared in multiple venues, media, sites, and formats comes into view as a crucial aspect of engaging traumatic memories.

The desire to explore and analyze testimony is the reason my analysis concludes with the final example—the photographic images used by Rwandese Yolande Mukagasana, one of the first genocide survivors to publish her written testimony. In the final section of this chapter, I move onto *Les blessures du silence: Témoignages du génocide au Rwanda* to complicate my readings of rape with another form of cultural representation of human rights violations. *Les blessures* raises a different set of questions because it combines testimonial narratives and photography. In the twentieth and twenty-first centuries, there has been renewed interest in the way visual representation and truth-telling discourses coalesce in the framing of atrocities and humanitarian responses to them. By investigating the way representations of genocidal rape figure into these conversations, I open up a space for scrutinizing the way the intimate violations of black African women fit into global discourses of gender, power, and human rights. Mukagasana can be counted as one of the many Rwandese who have not only taken up the task of writing their own testimonies but also of helping others to tell their own stories by compiling the testimonies of survivors, victims, and perpetrators in *Les blessures du silence*. Mukagasana took on this project only after publishing her testimonial narratives, *La mort ne veut pas de moi* (1997) and *N'aie pas peur de savoir—Rwanda: Une rescapée tutsi raconte* (1999).[20] Reproducing narratives of those who witnessed and survived the genocide privileges the subjectivity of people who actually experienced the events and appears to be one of the main objectives of Mukagasana's project. Here the witnessing and the testimony are doubled by the realization that these are *stories to pass on* and by the active participation in the effort to pass them on.

Rape as a Genocidal Strategy and Strategies of Genocidal Rape Representation

Rape was an influential genocidal strategy used to violate both women and men in Rwanda. As one feminist scholar describes wartime rape, it is often "ethnic rape as an official policy of war. . . . It is rape as an instrument of forced exile. . . . It is rape under orders. . . . It is rape as seen and heard by others, rape as spectacle . . . it is rape as genocide."[21] MacKinnon's extended example speaks to the different operations and effects of rape warfare as a specific form of state-sanctioned violence. To write about representing rape within the genocide, we can begin with information documenting the widespread use of sexual violence. Rape was an essential component of the Hutu strategy.[22] By raping women, they could accomplish several goals simultaneously: (1) inflict pain on women considered as the enemy, (2) force women into shame, (3) symbolically emasculate Tutsi men by forcing them to watch the "taking of their women," and (4) further ensure the future obliteration of the Tutsi ethnicity by impregnating women with Hutu genes. *Shattered Lives: Sexual Violence during the Rwandan Genocide*, a report by Human Rights Watch, details the atrocities against women. I cite this report at length here in an attempt to uncover some of the ways that the genocide was explicitly gendered.

> During the 1994 genocide, Rwandan women were subjected to sexual violence on a massive scale, perpetrated by members of the infamous Hutu militia groups known as the *Interahamwe*, by other civilians, and by soldiers of the Rwandan Armed Forces . . . including the Presidential Guard. . . . Although the exact number of women raped will never be known, testimonies from survivors confirm that rape was extremely widespread and that thousands of women were individually raped, gang-raped, raped with objects such as sharpened sticks or gun barrels, held in sexual slavery . . . or sexually mutilated. These crimes were frequently part of a pattern in which Tutsi women were raped after they had witnessed the torture and killings of their relatives and the destruction and looting of their homes. According to witnesses, many women were killed immediately after being raped. . . . Rapes were sometimes followed by sexual mutilation, including mutilation of the vagina and pelvic area with machetes, knives, sticks, boiling water, and in one case, acid.[23]

The accounts in the report are excerpted directly from the personal testimonies of survivors who have increasingly come forward with their traumatic narratives in the past two decades. Through these acts of telling, the women bear witness to the violence that invaded and branded them physically and emotionally. Given the prevalence of rape—it is estimated that 250,000 to 500,000 rapes were committed—it is not alarming that rape as an act of war has emerged as a dominant representation of the Rwandan genocide. To analyze sexual violence in the context of state conflict—in particular, unpacking the issues that surround the use of rape as a tool of war or genocidal rape—is a fraught and often frustrating exercise. As I have illustrated throughout this book, far too often focusing on sexual violence in the context of conflict obscures its occurrence in other contexts, as well as its material and psychological toll. As the late feminist legal theorist Rhonda Copelon insightfully observes,

> The recognition of rape as a war crime is . . . a critical step toward understanding rape as violence. The next step is to recognize that rape that acquires the imprimatur of the state is not necessarily more brutal, relentless, or dehumanizing than the private rapes of everyday life, nor is violation by a state official or enemy soldier necessarily more devastating than violation by an intimate.[24]

Yet following the representations of sexual violence against women in the Global South, whether it is Mexican women in Tijuana, Haitian women in displacement camps after the earthquake, Somalian women fleeing famine on the Kenyan border, or Congolese women in the Democratic Republic of the Congo, the affective sentimentality exploited in their representation seems to suggest otherwise. That is to say, too often the ostensible focus on rapes that take place in the context of conflict not only fail to account for the high incidence of rape in peacetime, they also objectify the subject of this violence by positioning wartime rape as a particularly gendered spectacle. Rendering the pain of rape for its brutality and dehumanization without falling prey to the prescription that Copelon critiques is a creative and theoretical challenge for representation. Thus, one of the persistent issues at the core of rape representation becomes the way to anchor its portrayal in a broader context without minimizing its various dimensions in a specific setting. The concern at the heart of this chapter is the way different forms of cultural production can construct representations of genocidal rape that critically and thoughtfully intervene in the extant discourses at the intersection of genocide and sexual violence. Given all of the different issues at play and the stakes of genocide representation, how does one begin to think productively about rape representation?

The African Stakes of Genocidal Representation

One of the main problems of representing the Rwandan genocide lies in the way it aligns with central axioms about the prevalence of violence on the entire African continent. On the one hand, the problem is discursive because the very occurrence of genocide affirms the conception that there is a supposedly "'intrinsic' culture of violence that defined the 'Dark Continent.'"[25] Discourses surrounding the genocide often employ vocabulary of savagery with references to carnage, horror, and ethnic or tribal clashes that come together in a system of knowledge that is specifically African. As such, "for many in the West, the particular nature of the violence in Rwanda seemed both to validate deeply ingrained and historically rooted images of an inherently aggressive African identity, and to confirm the genocide as proof of an anthropological aberration."[26] When linked to the question of writing to remember genocide, these additional layers add further complexity. As Aedín Ní Loinsigh provocatively asks in his study of fictitious renderings of the genocide, "Is it even acceptable to focus attention on the act of writing if this risks distancing the subject itself?"[27] In other words, does not cultural production of the genocide adumbrate configurations of Rwandese subjects whose lives were lost or inexorably altered by its violence? Because of the different types of silences at work in genocide discourses, both as it unfolded and as it is being remembered, lacing the threads of the divergent narratives requires careful attention whether in representation or in analysis.

In response to the question of how to theorize the events leading up to the Rwandan Genocide and its effects in the Great Lakes region, Harrow offers this point: "All this vocabulary around genocide stresses its exceptional nature. It is that exceptionality that I want to rethink now. And I want to rethink the historicist approach that asks us to understand it as the product of an historical process that dates back in time to the beginning of the Tutsi-Hutu conflict, back to the mists of time when the 'truth' of the conflict had its origins."[28] Harrow's analysis hinges on the postmodern question of what constitutes truth and the way truth is constructed in relation to political events. Asking that we fundamentally rethink scholarship on the genocide and the propensity to focus on false points of origin, Harrow reveals the instability of truth in the production of genocide images, whether written or oral. "Its narrativization of the 100 days starting in April, the flights to Goma, the aftermath in the Congo—all this reads like Greek tragedy, and is entitled tragedy, unfortunately, time and time again. And it leads, always, inevitably, inexorably, to that moment of anagnorisis, of genocide, that culminating, defining moment, ontologically separate from, albeit explained by, that which went before it."[29] Like Harrow, I take issue with the logic that undergirds many studies and the representations of the history of the genocide, but I am particularly interested in the way we can extend this retheorization to the specific portrayal of genocidal rape. My aim is to understand the way envisioning truth as slippery and unstable impacts the reception of testimony, calling into question the narratives of rape survivors in ways that are both problematic and productive. To this end, I argue that rape distills a greater range of possibilities for unraveling the complex layers of genocide.

Sites of Genocide and Seeing Rape in Boubacar Boris Diop's *Murambi: Le livre des ossements*

Boubacar Diop and Véronique Tadjo began traveling to Rwanda as participants in the project *Rwanda: Écrire par devoir de mémoire*, whose genesis was in Fest'Africa, an annual gathering that takes place in Lille, France and is organized by l'Association Arts et Métiers d'Afrique [African Arts and Media Association]. Initiated by Ivorian Maïmouna Coulibaly and Tchadien Nocky Djedanoum, the festival celebrates African literature through workshops, discussions, and roundtables that emphasize the importance of collectivity and community. Several African writers who met during the Fest'Africa meeting of 1997 established *Écrire par devoir de mémoire* in an attempt to use their art to bear witness to the enduring trauma of the Rwandan genocide.[30] The project was born out of frustration with the way the international community responded to the genocide and was motivated by discontent over the dearth of commentary on and analysis of the genocide, especially by non-Rwandese African writers. Jean-Marie Rurangwa, who fled Rwanda for exile in Burundi, vividly expressed this sentiment: "I was very indignant about the silence and the indifference of the international community in the face of the Rwandan tragedy. After the genocide I thought: I have no power to stop the genocide, but I have at least the possibility to perpetuate its memory by writing. So I wrote poems."[31] To address this problem in a proactive way they decided to travel to Rwanda, visit sites of genocide, and write about their experience. The collective, made up of ten writers, set out to spend a two-month period in Rwanda in an effort to use their creative expression as a tool for commentary and analysis.[32]

The title of the effort emphasizes "devoir de mémoire," the concept of writing born out of a duty to remember. This designation implicitly acknowledges that in the context of genocide, memory develops into duty and obligation to constitute a form of commitment. In its proximity to the title of Yambo Oulouguem's *Le devoir de violence*, the title of the *devoir de mémoire* project also posits remembering, commemoration, and collectivity as alternatives to violence. Rather than focus on the violence, the project emphasizes the wounds of memory. *Écrire par devoir de mémoire* draws attention to problems of genocide representation, such as "the duty to remember," the role of witnessing, and the use of writing to represent violent histories. Indeed, it was a "global act of commemoration both in terms of the ways it negotiates Rwanda's relationship with Western imperialism, in particular with France and 'la francophonie' as a more enabling network of transnational relationships through which the genocide is remembered."[33] This initiative should be considered as a creative act of intervention into the global postcolonial imaginary that calls into question the discourses that have continued to characterize Africa in relation to the West.

Describing the *Écrire par devoir de mémoire* goals, Fest'Africa director Nocky Djedanoum explains:

> Artists, especially writers, wanted to fill a gap in their hearts; we wanted to take a position [in the] mourning for Rwanda, Africa and the world had to take an immortal dimension. And therefore we came to Rwanda, listened to the Rwandese and thus produced works, thereby opening an important page in the history of Rwanda. *It was a case of Africa being committed to Africa.*[34]

The important page to which Djedanoum refers is one on which African writers from outside of Rwanda work to participate in the telling of a traumatic moment in history. Here the goal was not for the Fest'Africa group to speak *for* the writers but rather *with* them. In the spirit of collectivity, their goal was to take part in remembering and in responsibility. This incentive calls attention to the way that these writers envision their work as having a role related to social justice. Pan-African and transnational, the project marks out a new direction for the function of the arts in the postgenocide global imagination. Furthermore, as Hitchcott has convincingly argued, the Fest'Africa project is without parallel because as "an organised, collective, artistic commemoration of the genocide, [it] is unique. The emphasis on fiction is also unusual since, although a great deal of academic scholarship on Rwanda has been published in the last fourteen years, very few fictional works have appeared."[35] Djedanoum's declaration that "it was a case of Africa being committed to Africa" also suggests a need for subject recognition based on a mutual understanding of European misrecognition. In other words, in the face of misconceptions and misrepresentations of the genocide, Africans are uniquely positioned to undercut these frames with alternate representations. This plurality is especially significant given the ways in which postgenocide Rwanda has emerged as a fixed site of "Otherness."

In 1998, Fest'Africa collective traveled to the Rwandan capital Kigali to begin their project of translating trauma into text; each writer agreed to produce a piece of work after the journey. There were no aesthetic conventions in terms of genre or what they were meant to write; rather each one was free to use the form that best suited them.[36] By embarking on this project, they actively sought to resolve the conflict that questions of naming, remembering, and reconciling the Rwandan genocide posed to creativity. For the participants of *Écrire par devoir de mémoire*, the act of witnessing is linked to their postcolonial condition and has a global significance. Overall, the project, "for all its shortcomings, attempted to drag Rwanda out of the 'heart of darkness' and into the global imagination" through the use of creative expression.[37]

Together, the writers intended to create texts that would remember the far-flung atrocities of the genocide, an exceedingly difficult task, given the enormity of the events and the outsider perspective occupied by most of them. What need could there be for an artistic rendition of the mass carnage and international mayhem whose description was already chilling? Why delve into the artistic when reality did not require graphic detail because eye-witness accounts alone could achieve a ruthlessly appalling demonstration of humanity at its worst? In the description below, taken from the *Association Internationale pour la mémoire du génocide au Rwanda*, which was born as a result of *Écrire par devoir de mémoire*, there is no need for embellishment:

> [Le génocide] a été rendu possible par la participation active d'une très large partie de la population rwandaise, toutes couches sociales, tous sexes et toutes catégories d'âges confondus: des hommes, des femmes, des vieillards et même des enfants qui ont tué leurs voisins, leurs semblables . . . déchiquetés par les grenades, abattus au fusil, brûlés à l'essence ou au feu de bois, écrabouillés par des massues cloutées, balancés dans les latrines ou dans les eaux des lacs et des rivières, mais le plus souvent découpés à la machette. Des bébés fracassés contre les murs des maisons ou les roches. Des dizaines de milliers de personnes exterminées dans des églises et autres lieux de culte. Des femmes enceintes éventrées pour en sortir et martyriser le fœtus, d'autres violées et empalées, d'autres encore, dont de vieilles dames, promenées nues sous les yeux de leurs tortionnaires.[38]

> [The genocide] was made possible by the active participation of a very large part of the Rwandan population, all levels of society, all the sexes, and all the categories of age were involved: men, women, the elderly and

even children killed their neighbors, those who looked like them . . . shredded by grenades, vanquished by guns, burned by oil or by firewood, crushed by studded masses, thrown into latrines or in the waters of lakes and rivers, but the majority were hacked by machetes. Babies were thrown against walls of houses or rocks. Tens of thousands of people were exterminated in churches and other places of worship. Pregnant women were disemboweled to make martyrs of their fetuses. Others raped and impaled, and still others, old ladies among them, paraded naked underneath the eyes of their torturers.

This type of characterization asks that we turn again to the relationship between the reality of violence and its representation, because here the "reality" is dense and is graphically portrayed. Recognizing that their project to record the history of the Rwandan genocide from an outsider perspective could have several problematic implications, the Fest'Africa group used different strategies to engage the dialectic of fact and fiction in their works. Given their mission to write a version of history for Rwanda, there are a number of challenges this project introduces, such as the problem of perspective and responsibility, or the question of who can speak for the personal experience of trauma. Another major problem was related to funding because *Écrire par devoir de mémoire* was funded by *Fondation de France*. This financial backing could be seen as a tactical approach on behalf of the French administration to rectify the complicity of the French government in the genocide.[39] To combat some of the complications that might arise in their work, they employed various techniques to record their findings, each time privileging the account of Rwandese survivors and witnesses.[40]

Given the predominance of violence as an "African theme," it is important to question the way these narratives of violence are constructed and circulate in a postcolonial global context. As many scholars have noted, this is of particular importance in the case of the Rwandan genocide. Hitchcott writes, "Of course the relationship between fact and fiction is all the more complex in this case since there exist so many different versions of the Rwandan genocide, which has been variously described in terms of ethnic rivalry, tribal killings, anarchy and even a kind of natural disaster."[41] This problem is one of the main issues faced by genocide representation—the diversity of accounts, histories, and factors involved. Conscious of the need to uproot the hegemony of discourses reducing the genocide to its African context alone, the writers of *Écrire par devoir de mémoire* were particularly invested in offering a view complex enough to accommodate this multiplicity of factors involved. Again as Hitchott notes,

> This decision to present the genocide from a wide range of points of view implicitly challenges the self-interested, monolithic narratives of Belgian colonialism, 'la francophonie,' Hutu Power, RTLM (Radio Television Libre des Mille Collines) and the Western media, all of which help to essentialise Rwanda in the global imagination, and directly or indirectly contributed to the success of the genocide.[42]

This commitment to wresting the hold of genocide representations from a single, over-determined narrative is evident in the forms of the texts that emerge from *Écrire par devoir de mémoire,* many of which take on polyphonic structure, manipulate generic conventions, or make use of temporal shifts to destabilize fixed ideas about what happened in Rwanda before and during the genocide.

Despite the collective's best efforts to remain vigilantly aware of the flaws in their perspective, the project has also been the object of virulent criticism.[43] As Diop explains years later, many Rwandese were cautiously wary of the initiative at first. Explaining some of the problematics at the core of the project he writes,

> Il faut dire que la présence d'une majorité d'écrivains francophones dans un projet soutenu par la Fondation de France n'était guère de nature à les rassurer. Ces réserves étaient bien compréhensibles, car c'était en partie pour la défense de la langue française que Mittérand et les réseaux de la Françafrique s'étaient rangés sans états d'âme sur la côté des organisateurs du génocide.[44]

> One must say that the presence of a majority of francophone writers in a project supported by the Fondation de France was hardly likely to reassure them. These reservations were understandable because it was partially due to the defense of the French language that Mitterand and the Françafrique networks had no qualms about situating themselves on the side of known organizers of the genocide.

Here the problem of the use of the French language as a barrier to transnational engagement is prominently on display. The source of funding is problematic because of its alignment with the French government, which was complicit in the genocide and the lack of response to it. The project was also criticized for having too few Rwandan writers, given the inclusion of only two Rwandese, Vénuste Kayimahe and Rurangwa. Other criticisms have been leveled against the general objectives; the notion of non-Rwandan artists feeling obligated to remember the genocide and write a version of its history. In particular, their texts have been critiqued for a lack of authenticity and insufficient alignment with the people of Rwanda. Another problem with the project was that it failed to address other atrocities taking place in other parts of the African continent, where thousands of people had died previously and were still dying in wars related to the genocide, as was the case in the Democratic Republic of the Congo or Burundi. Nonetheless their commitment to Rwanda persisted beyond the realization of *Écrire par devoir de mémoire*, and they continue to be driven by *"le devoir de mémoire."* Six years after the original journey, in 2004, they held the annual Fest'Africa conference in Rwanda to mark the tenth anniversary of the genocide. Some, like Boubacar Boris Diop have been consistently vocal about the aftermath of the genocide. Through articles in newspapers and public forums, and most notably in his collection of essays, *L'Afrique au-delà du miroir* (2007), Diop has deployed his renown to critically engage genocide scripts from a historic, cultural, and political perspective.

In *Murambi: Le livre des ossements*, Diop overlaps the occurrence of the genocide (in the past) with the present through the story of Cornelius Uvimana, a history teacher who returns to Rwanda after having lived abroad for twenty-five years. Uvimana's profession as a history teacher and writer is not lost on the reader, who understands that his task to come to terms with the history of the genocide is at once personal, political, and professional. In her introduction to the English translation, Eileen Julien explains that, "those ninety days are the focus of the novel, but in every sense the full story exceeds that frame, taking in us readers, too."[45] The title comes from the massacre of 50,000 people at the Murambi Technical School during the genocide. Written after Diop's visit to the site, *Murambi* is a "commemorative work of fiction" that pays homage to the events and also calls into question acts of material memorialization.[46] *Murambi* is a multivoiced narrative primarily narrated in the third person, with interspersed accounts of survivors told in the first person. The inclusion of these different voices creates a polyphonic rendering from both inside and outside perspectives. The use of a multivoiced narrative is significant, and demonstrates the author's desire to render more than one perspective on the history of the genocide. Yet, as the protagonist discovers his father's complicity in the genocide, his role as an outsider is compromised, uncomfortably implicating him.

The novel grapples with the problem of memorialization, the insufficiency of language, and the contested nature of truth. In fact, the entire text seems to be a struggle to document stories of the victims and the perpetrators from the outside perspective of a man who was not present in

1994. Thus, the story becomes a way of piecing together what happened and what the role of his family was through the voices of those who lived it. This dynamic of course mirrors Diop's positionality as an outsider looking in. The creation of an archive also reflects the creative process of the Fest'Africa group as they visited different sites of genocide. Yet in its constructed nature and difficult rendering of testimonies, the novel also problematizes the idea of a genocide archive. Sustained attention to sexual violence occurs at two different moments in the text. First in the testimony of Jessica Kamanzi, who hears the testimony of another woman held as a sex slave and recounts the experience in the first person. The second example is from Gérard Nayinzira, a general for the Hutu army who witnesses soldiers raping women. These two perspectives on genocidal rape are consistent with the novel's larger project of mapping insider and outsider perspectives of the genocide alongside and almost onto one another.

In the chapter narrated by Jessica Kamanzi, she encounters a young woman who lives in fear of being raped. Jessica understands that because the woman is beautiful, "Ils [les soldats] allaient la violer mille fois avant de la tuer. Elle le savait, et elle était en train de perdre la raison" (119). ["They (the soldiers) were going to rape her a thousand times before they killed her. She knew it, and she was going out of her mind" (92)]. The woman's psychological state is prominently on display in these pages. As with many representations of genocidal rape, "son histoire [était] si banale" ["her story (was) so commonplace"] (119/92). After she finds refuge in an abandoned church, the Interahamwe come every night and "emmènent des douzaines de gens pour les tuer" (119) ["take away dozens of people to kill them" (92)]. The priest in charge of the church uses this situation to his advantage: "Le prêtre fait du chantage aux gens qui sont là-bas, dit-elle. Il envoie à la mort celles qui refusent de coucher avec lui" (119). ["'The priest blackmails the people who are there,' she says. 'He sends the women who refuse to sleep with him to their death'" (92)]. Genocidal rape operates differently here, with the women being blackmailed in exchange for sex. The priest's blackmail is elaborately intertwined with the practice of genocidal rape. In their conversation, the women discuss the details of what this violence entails. When the woman asks Jessica if she knows how they rape women, Jessica thinks to herself,

> Oui, j'avais vu cela. Vingt ou trente types sur un banc. Certains d'un âge respectable. Une femme, parfois juste une frêle gamine, est étendue contre un mur, jambes écartées, totalement inconsciente. Il n'y a aucune violence

chez ces braves pères de famille. Cela m'avait glacé le sang de les voir ainsi parler de choses et d'autres à l'instant où toute une vie se défaisait à jamais sous leurs yeux. Et parmi les violeurs il y a presque toujours, exprès, des malades du sida. (120)

Yes, I had seen it. Twenty or thirty guys on a bench. Some of them old enough to know better. A woman, sometimes just a frail child, is stretched out against a wall, legs spread, totally unconscious. These good family men aren't into violence. It has chilled my blood to see them chitchatting right at the moment when a whole life was coming apart under their very eyes. And among the rapists there are almost always, by design, some who have AIDS. (93)

This description occurs only in the narrator's internal monologue. She would rather not hear the details from the women she speaks to. "'Je sais comment ils font,' fis-je. 'Quand ils ont fini, ils te versent de l'acide dans le vagin ou t'enforcent dedans des tessons de bouteille le ou des morceaux de fer.' 'Oui.' J'avais parlé très vite. Cela me faisait honte d'entendre des choses pareilles" (121). ["'I know how they do it,' I said. 'When they've finished, they pour acid in your vagina or stick in pieces of broken bottle or pieces of metal.' 'Yes.' I had spoken too quickly. I was ashamed to hear such things" (93)]. Her shame as a listener implicitly evokes the shame experienced by rape survivors. These displaced feelings of shame structure the two women's interaction.

A desire for recognition also shapes this passage, though not from the speaker but from Jessica, who longs to let the woman know that she hears, sees, and understands her. "'Je te jure que je comprends,' dis-je à l'inconnue. J'avais envie de l'appeler par son nom. Elle me fit une description obscène de ses relations avec le prêtre. Il lui avait rasé le pubis en prenant tout son temps, le regard fou de désir. Il restait hypocrite jusque dans l'abjection. Il voulait lui faire dire qu'elle était consentante" (121). ["'I swear to you that I understand,' I said to the unknown woman. I wanted to call her by name. She painted me an obscene description of her relations with the priest. He had shaved her pubic hair, taking his sweet time, his gaze mad with desire. He remained hypocritical even in his depravity. He wanted to make her say that she consented" (94).] As the narrator attempts to get more details from the speaker, she asks. "J'arrêtai ma visiteuse d'un geste de la main. 'Comment t'appelles-tu?' 'Je n'ai pas de nom. Je suis celle qui va mourir.' 'Mais tu me racontes des choses intimes, ce n'est pas la peine d'entrer dans les détails.' 'Oh! Si!' fit-elle avec véhémence. Oh! Si! Je ne veux pas mourir avec cela'" (122). ["I stopped my visitor with a gesture of my hand. 'What's your name?' 'I have no name. I'm the one who's going to die.' 'But you're telling me the intimate details, it's not worth going into every detail.' 'Oh yes it is!' she said vehemently. 'Oh yes it is! I don't want to die with that secret'" (94).] The desire to know the woman's name becomes a way for Jessica to recognize her more profoundly, to achieve a greater intimacy and somehow dim the shadow of guilt that plagues her.

Two important factors frame the way we understand the women's exchange. First, the fact that Jessica is in danger of being caught positions her as a potential victim as well as a survivor. Fear for her own life informs the way she understands and interacts with the woman. But by refusing to tell her name, the speaker defies the logic of testimony. She denies Jessica the recognition that the other woman wishes to confer upon her. Her refusal provides her with some autonomy over her story. By reading the scene in this way we can discern the transactional nature of testimonies—the exchange of the rape story for empathy here is foreclosed, despite the hearer/viewer's longing to interact according to these terms. What the anonymous woman gains, however, is the ability to have her story passed on because *she* wants to, not because Jessica wants to hear the details but because the woman needs to release them. Here the inclusion of details plays a crucial role for the person who tells the story.

In the final chapter, Gérard Nayinzira tells the protagonist what he witnesses and the way he escapes Murambi. He too describes the scenes of rape that he witnesses in the second person. The correlation between the book's title and this concluding chapter reinforce its culminating nature; it is the chapter in which the main character finally receives the information for which he has been searching during the entire novel. General Nayinzira explains what happens to him during the genocide and includes a story about witnessing sexual violence.

> J'ai vu un Interahamwe violer une jeune femme sous un arbre. Son chef est passé et lui a crié: 'Hé toi, Simba, partout où on va, c'est toujours la même chose, les femmes d'abord, les femmes, les femmes! Dépêche-toi de finir tes pompes, on a promis à Papa de bien faire le travail!' Le chef a fait quelques pas, puis se ravisant, est revenu écraser la tête de la jeune femme avec une grosse pierre, et il y a eu d'un seul coup juste cette bouille rouge et blanche à la place du crâne. Cela n'a pas interrompu le Interahamwe qui a continué à besogner le corps agité de légers soubresauts. . . . J'ai vu cela de mes propres yeux. (221–22)

> I saw an Interahamwe rape a young woman under a tree. His boss came by and shouted at him: "Hey Simba, everywhere we go it's always the same story, first the women, the women, the women! Hurry up and finish your push-ups, we promised Papa we'd do a good job!" The boss took a couple of steps, then, changing his mind, came back to crush the young woman's head with a big stone, and in a single blow there was just this red and white pulp in place of the skull. That didn't stop the Interahamwe who kept working away at the twitching body . . . I saw that with my own eyes. (175–76)

Again I am interested in *how* rape is represented rather than *what* it represents, so I analyze this scene from that perspective. It is worth lingering here to understand what such a perspective offers. This is not a scene of rape rendered by a perpetrator or victim, but by an observer, a bystander who happens to witness the violation. From his vantage point, the reader also witnesses the scene. The victim is virtually absent—present only as a raped body. We learn nothing of her identity, her story, or her embodied person. We do know that she is killed, a fact that does not end her rape. The only description of her body is of the way it twitches after her skull is crushed. We also know that she is like one of many—"it's always the same story, first the women, the women, the women!" We imagine the boss, both exasperated and amused by the rapaciousness of his troops for whom sexual violence is the first priority. As it figures here, sexual violence is at once a product of and a distraction from genocide. The disregard for the victim is completed when the boss kills her. The perpetrator's proclivity for sexual violence is rendered even more gruesome and grotesque as he continues to rape the woman. The crushing of her skull is described with greater detail than the rape, because the latter horrifies the general even more. Here sexual terror is completed through murder. The violence of rape is amplified by the brutal killing of the woman in the middle of the act. The general's perspective does not equate these forms of violence but rather implies a subtle hierarchy in which murder is a way to punish the enemy, whereas rape (push-ups) is merely a form of recreation for soldiers.

In *Murambi*, the protagonist's internal complexity lies in an ethical dilemma about not being present during the genocide (for which he feels both guilty and grateful) and an inability to know what actually happened in 1994. At first, it seems that the final chapter could offer some kind of resolution to the problem of knowing, or at least answer a number of questions that percolate in Cornelius' mind throughout the novel. But Diop refuses to offer such closure. The novel also comments on the utility of testimonial narratives in the aftermath of genocide. To this end, the General cautions:

> Si tu préfères penser que j'ai imaginé ces horreurs, tu te sentiras l'esprit en repos et ce ne sera pas bien. Ces souffrances se perdront dans des paroles opaques et tout sera oublié jusqu'aux prochaines massacres. Ils ont réellement fait toutes ces choses incroyables. Cela s'est passé au Rwanda il y a juste quatre ans, quand le monde entier jouer au foot en Amérique. (222)

> If you prefer to think that I imagined these horrors your mind will be at peace and that's not good. The pain will get lost in opaque words and everything will be forgotten until the next massacre. They really did incredible things. It happened in Rwanda only four years ago, when the entire world was playing soccer in America. (175–76)

By asking Cornelius (and, by extension, the reader) if "[we] believe" him, the General invokes the dialectics of witnessing and testimony after the genocide when survivors share their experiences in a field fraught with the past that ignored them. Again the general's words seem to directly address the reader and the original response to the genocide by the international community. The reader of *Murambi* should not leave the book with a "mind at peace." Observing these scenes and hearing the testimonies of the survivors in the book, viewing the bones to which the title refers, understanding the layers of violence endemic to genocide makes achieving any kind of peace unimaginable. The construction of rape in *Murambi* functions as a way to reveal some of the inner workings of how survivors, perpetrators and those in between interpret the role of sexual violence during the genocide. In the two drastically opposed examples examined above, the representation of rape is first explicit and then skimmed over. But in both cases it offers reflections on the way the problem of retelling rape adds layers to genocide testimonies.

An Aesthetic of Multiplicity: *L'ombre d'Imana: Voyages jusqu'au bout du Rwanda*

L'ombre d'Imana: Voyages jusqu'au bout du Rwanda by Véronique Tadjo resists the fashioning of a monolithic discourse of genocide by adopting what I refer to as an "aesthetic of multiplicity" that proceeds in several directions. An aesthetic of multiplicity is the term I am using to describe the form and the content of Tadjo's text, which embraces plurality at the levels of perspective, voice, style, history, and genre. This aesthetic of multiplicity acts as a new form of inscription that attempts not only to translate violence and trauma but also to negotiate some of its attendant difficulties. As an example of violence that has received international attention, the Rwandan genocide brings into focus the yield of shifting from the context of conflict to the body in conflict as I am proposing. Throughout this book we have seen that different strategies of rape representation attempt to offer modalities for writing violence in which plurality can thrive—as an example of such an impulse, *L'ombre d'Imana* is significant for its refusal to adhere to the generic conventions of travel writing.

Within Tadjo's aesthetic of multiplicity, we find journalistic account, fictional prose, personal testimony, and poetry coalescing in a manifestation of the author's *engagement*. Whereas Loinsigh has identified "the resulting play with the generic identity [of *The Shadow of Imana* as a way to] highlight her personal artistic dilemma," I read this innovative use of form not as indecision on the author's part but as an intentional technique that attempts to negotiate the challenges of writing the genocide.[47] Reading *L'ombre d'Imana*, we become aware of the way Tadjo realizes the scope of her ideology to confront violence on an international scale. The text poses no central question; instead, the author lays out multiple goals. Addressing the aftermath of the genocide, she broaches its themes of loss, trauma, healing, and reconciliation. She struggles with the question of how to represent violence in the written word, as well as how to account for, analyze, and remember it. Interestingly, this has been identified as a characteristic of Tadjo's writing even prior to the publication of *L'ombre d'Imana*. Cécile Lebon has duly noted the variegated style of the author describing how Tadjo has dipped in and out of genres throughout her writing career. For Lebon, Tadjo is "une voyageuse qui, au plus profond d'elle même, se sent concernée par les maux qui rongent sa terre africaine" [a traveler, who, in the most profound part of herself, feels concerned with the ills that plague her African land].[48] My reading extends Lebon's point to propose that there are elements unique to the experience or occurrence of genocide that necessitate an aesthetic of multiplicity, and it is as such that we should read the diversity of genre in *L'ombre d'Imana*. Thus Tadjo's generic and stylistic choices, and her deliberate confusing of generic conventions that constitute the form of her text, must be linked to its content and context. This reading attempts to account for the mutually dependent relationship between form and content in a way that questions some of the suppositions laid out in previous chapters of the present study.

Like Diop, Tadjo travels to Rwanda as a member of the *Écrire par devoir de mémoire* initiative, though her text takes a different shape. As the full title, *L'ombre d'Imana: Voyages jusqu'au bout du Rwanda*, suggests, Tadjo attempts to acknowledge this journey by a non-Rwandese writing version of the history as a potentially problematic act. Her nod to Louis-Ferdinand Céline's *Voyage au bout de la nuit* is an invocation of one of the most celebrated, yet negatively charged, novels in French literature.[49] The interpellation of Céline is an extratextual move that signals recognition of her own positioning with regard to the Rwandan genocide. She is conscious of merely becoming, like Céline, a writer-turned-Conradian-hero delving into the "heart of darkness" to discover the truth about the self. The ubiquitous search for "the Self" in relation to "the Other" is not this Ivorian writer's mission. Her title alerts readers that she is positioning herself as critically aware and open to dialogue. Along with the Céline reference, the fact that she pluralizes her use of "voyage" is another autocritical gesture. Unlike Gide, Léry, or many of the other French canonical writers who set out on a voyage in the singular, she does so in the plural.[50] Though this is evidently because Tadjo made more than one journey to Rwanda, it also serves as a way to dehegemonize the French tradition of the *récit de voyage*, or travel narrative, that is, to upset whatever the reader may already think she or he knows about travel writing. She writes to move this tradition away from its canonical structure in which white European males embark on a quest for "the Other" in order to validate "the Self." One journey is never enough, Tadjo's title avers; a voyage in the singular can never be the only source of analysis because it will never be enough to begin to comprehend the different layers of the country. One must travel more than once to foster deeper understanding.

In *L'ombre d'Imana* Tadjo adopts what I am calling an *aesthetic of multiplicity* not just as a literary technique, but also as a mode of writing specifically used to grapple with the representation of genocide. With the phrase "an aesthetic of multiplicity," I mean to indicate a new form of inscription that attempts to translate violence and trauma through multifaceted techniques, among which we find journalistic account, fictional prose, personal testimony, and poetry coalescing into a single formation. This technique, I argue, is a strategy that mirrors the occurrence of rape; because it occurred so frequently, it invariably took on different forms. My goal here is to show the way Tadjo's aesthetic of multiplicity foregrounds the fact that there is no monolithic story of genocidal rape, but that different narratives exist.

When Tadjo embarks on the first thorough description of someone killed by the genocide, it is of a female subject, *la femme ligotée*—the bound up woman. As first expository act of representing genocide in the entire text, *la femme ligotée* uncovers layers of violence. The woman she describes was raped and had her throat slit by the murderers:

> Eglise de Nyamata/Site de génocide/La femme ligotée Mukandori. Vingt-cinq ans. Exhumée en 1997. Lieu d'habitation: Nyamata centre. Mariée. Enfant? On lui a ligoté les poignets, on les a attachés à ses chevilles. Elle a les jambes largement écartées. Son corps est penché sur le côté. *Elle a été violée.* Un pic fut enfoncé dans son vagin. *Elle est morte d'un coup de machette à la nuque.* On peut voir l'entaille que l'impact a laissée. Elle porte encore une couverture sur les épaules, mais le tissu est maintenant incrusté dans la peau. Elle est là pour l'exemple, exhumée de la fosse où elle était tombée avec les autres corps. Exposée pour que personne n'oublie. Une momie de génocide. Des bouts de cheveux sont encore collés sur son crâne.[51] (my emphasis)

> Nyamata Church. Site of genocide . . . A woman bound hand and foot. Mukandori. Aged twenty-five. Exhumed in 1997. Home: the town of Nyamata. Married. Any children? Her wrists are bound, and tied to her ankles. Her legs are spread wide apart. Her body is lying on its side. She looks like an enormous fossilized fetus. She has been laid on a dirty blanket, in front of *carefully lined skulls* and bones scattered on a mat. *She has been raped.* A pickaxe has been forced into her vagina. She died from *a machete blow to the nape of her neck.* You can see the groove left by the impact. She still has a blanket over her shoulders but the material is now encrusted into the skin. She is there as an example, exhumed from the ditch where she has fallen with other bodies. On show so that no one can forget. . . . A mummified victim of genocide. Remnants of hair are attached to her skull.[52]

In this graphic description, we can note the initial clinical reportage of the scene—the naming of the location, followed by the subject to be described, assigns to it an archival nature. Beginning with basic methods for categorization, home, marital status, etc., it reads like a scene displaying the collection of evidence, an endeavor to deliver the victim's condition in an objective and almost sterile nature. But the rawness of the details makes it impossible to be indifferent. In the original French, the use of the *passé composé* reminds us of the completion of the action, accentuating death, although the details make it seem more current, along with the fact that the body remains exposed, in another act of violation. This results in a discursive tension in the representation. As we draw additional conclusions beyond the material context, we can note the effects of the textual clinicization—the attempt to create distance is undercut by the reality. No technique can distance the terror of genocide, so the use of a more distant tone becomes a reminder for the consistent power that subsumes the reality of genocide. Tadjo utilizes three of the familiar representations named in the introduction of this chapter—"carefully lined skulls," "a machete blow," and "she has been raped." But the deployment of these images does not undermine the focus of this passage that pivots around the identity of the victim and the gendered aspect of the incident.

A close reading of this example reveals that there are additional corporeal elements of memory, that is to say, the literal embodiment of memory, wherein the female body becomes a *site of embodied memory*. This in turn raises the question of encountering rape through embodiment rather than through the knowing perspective of the victim. We are reminded of the ways in which the body can reflect trauma even when the victim resists or suppresses awareness. In cases such as these, the body offers a different vantage point from which to understand rape. Here we can return to Cahill's work encouraging an understanding of rape that reinforces bodily experience, but that does not deny a space in which individual specificities can flourish. As she explains, "rape needs to be thought of as . . . something that is taken up and experienced differently by different women but also holds some common aspects . . . as an experience that begins with the body but does not end there."[53] Marked by the unrelenting trauma of rape now, in addition to the unequivocally traumatic experience of genocide, these women can never escape the memories. As a site onto which the memory of genocide is inscribed, *la femme ligotée*'s body becomes a site of traumatic memory. This realm of memory is different than Pierre Nora's concept of *lieu de mémoire*, but Nora's formulation is fitting in this case because the body of *la femme ligotée* is a literal point where history and memory converge, a place "où se cristallise et se réfugie la mémoire" [where memory crystallizes and secretes itself].[54] We can further conceive of the raped body as a *lieu de mémoire* because of the way it bears upon collective memory—according to the passage, it is this potency of the memory that even allows it to be transferred onto other bodies. Immediately after seeing the body, Tadjo notes:

> L'horreur de la terre souillée et du temps qui passe déposant des couches de poussière. Les os des squelettes-carcasses se désintègrent sous nos yeux. La puanteur affecte les narines et s'installe dans les poumons, contamine les chairs, infiltre le cerveau. Même plus tard, plus loin, cette odeur restera dans le corps et dans l'esprit. (23)

[T]he horror of the sullied earth and of time laying down layers of dust in its passage. The bones of the skeletal corpses are disintegrating before our very eyes. The stench infects our nostrils and settles inside our lungs, contaminates our flesh, infiltrates our brains. Even later on, this smell will linger in our bodies and our minds. (12)

This transference (from the victims' bones, to the earth, to those who are present viewing the sites) reinforces the power of the remembered rape as a site of memory. The language of contagion brings to life the pungent odor being conveyed, but also travels beyond scent and the visceral into the intellectual, emotional, and spiritual effects of genocide. Inclusion of the mind and the spirit designates the manifold spheres of influence that genocide traverses. Everything is contaminated by the smell; the odor becomes a metaphor for the pollution pervading the minds, bodies, and spirits not only in Rwanda and Africa but throughout the world. It is an unrelenting infection that remains in the hearts and bodies of those who inhale it even years afterward. The resulting disease is a perverse sickness where genocide is forgotten, the victims' voices are silenced, and the world can turn its eyes away, never denouncing violence in a refusal of recognition. The mechanisms of contagion and contamination highlight the duration of the genocide, further establishing it as a type of trauma. In the expository act of writing rape as infectious memory, Tadjo points to the way the violation of a dead woman can have effects that outlast the genocide. As she becomes a site of memory that impacts those around her, *la femme ligotée* is endowed with an identity and a self that establishes her subjectivity.

Tadjo locates the retelling of genocide within individual voices, and within their interstices—that is, the gaps in which the stories are not shared explicitly but instead their effects are enumerated. Narratives, in their subjectivity, are useful vessels of countermemory and are crucial because without the voices of those that experienced the genocide, their memories would be destroyed. Though the narratives of survivors are an integral part of Tadjo's project, in another scene where rape is made explicit, she goes beyond voice by focusing closely on the emotional aftermath of sexual violence. Thus she shows the forms of trauma that accompany layers of violence—beneath post-traumatic stress disorder there is rape trauma syndrome. The story that follows features Anastasie, whose flesh imprisons her as the memory of her rape steadily asserts and re-asserts itself. From the minute she wakes up, the rape assaults her mind, "Anastasie se réveillait brusquement à l'heure où l'aube pointait et se sentait envahie par la mémoire de son viol" [Anastasie would wake suddenly as dawn was breaking and be invaded by the memory of her rape (75/63)]. The portrait of Anastasie suffering from rape trauma syndrome continues:

> Elle restait emmurée dans la prison de sa chair. Sa langue était pâteuse et l'empêchait de prononcer le moindre mot. Ses envies étaient érodées comme des rochers frappés par une mer en furie. Elle ne connaissait plus l'intérieur de son corps [et] se sentait étrangère à cette masse lourde qui écrasait son esprit. Elle se sentait épuisée avant même d'entrevoir le début de la journée. (73)

> She was trapped in the prison of her flesh. Her tongue felt furry, and prevented her from uttering the slightest word. Her desires had been worn away like rocks lashed by a stormy sea. She no longer recognised the inside of her body, felt a stranger to this heavy mass, which was crushing her spirit. She felt exhausted even before glimpsing the beginning of the day. (63)

As with rape survivors in various contexts, for Anastasie the rape constitutes an "ineradicable memory," which is the way Catherine Clinton describes the mark of sexual assault.[55] The memories of her rape prevent Anastasie from wanting to do anything or to go anywhere. She is unable to recognize her own body, feeling like a stranger, even alien to it. This lassitude is the result of the unremitting trauma of her rape, of which we learn as soon as the chapter opens. Tadjo's refusal to re-create the rape is a rhetorical strategy that refuses the spectacle of suffering. Rather than describe the rape first, Tadjo again takes the site upon which the rape occurs (the woman's body) and describes the effects. By doing so, she emphasizes disembodiment, disempowerment, and distance, showing us the way the body has been severed and fragmented. The distancing of the body is further performed through its description as a prison and a heavy mass, and by its comparison to a group of rocks. Tadjo uses visual imagery to articulate tumultuous emotions. Now the distance between the body, marked as a traumatic memory of genocide, and the survivor's self governs her existence. Anastasie longs to "disparaître dans l'oubli, naviguer doucement, se laisser emporter par les flots souterrains" (73) [disappear into oblivion, sail along gently, let herself be carried away by the underground stream (63)]. Here the refusal to recreate the rape is also a rhetorical decision that denies the spectacle of suffering as it simultaneously demonstrates the survivor's ambiguity about what happened to her.

The use of water provides another multilayered metaphor. In the first half of the paragraph, water is an image used to conjure violence. It is a reminder of the violent rushing and overflowing nature of the rape, and as Anastasie describes her eroding desires "étaient érodées comme des rochers frappés par une mer en furie [worn away like rocks lashed by a stormy sea], we witness the violent motion of the water slapping the rocks. A few sentences later, water becomes her refuge, as she longs to navigate *les flots souterrains*—"the underground stream." The two images do not contradict one another; instead, they signal the intricately woven nature of sexual violence and the torrents of emotions that ensue in its wake. These images depicting the troubling realities of rape disclose the persistent memory of rape as they expose the woman's body after violation, and describe the way one survivor feels emotionally and physically.

What is particularly remarkable about this example is the ambiguity surrounding *when* Anastasie was actually raped; it could have been during the genocide or during another time of violence. Overall, this haze over temporality serves as a reminder that rape is not only a crime of war. This gesture is a significant acknowledgment of the war waged on women's bodies outside of the context of genocide, and one that accedes to their multiple locations. Ultimately Anastasie's affective response to the memory of her rape underscores the fact that "men do in war what they do in peace, only more so . . . when it comes to women the complacency that surrounds peace time extends to war time . . . ."[56] Adding yet another layer of intricacy to Anastasie's situation is the fact that her rapist is also her brother, aptly named Anastase. An understanding of this incestuous relationship gives the reader pause. Could it be that a part of Tadjo's point in writing this story is to indicate and prefigure the ways in which Rwanda eventually becomes a nation (family) turned against itself? Is the act of incest meant to foreground the ways in which the violence of genocide operates as a deviant perversion from the model of stable statehood? In other words, might we read the story of Anastase and Anastasie as a metaphor for the Rwandan genocide, and were we to do so, would Tadjo then be characterized as an author who uses the sexual violence to symbolize or metaphorize national problems? I propose that reading the story of Anastase and Anastasie— whose names mirror one another almost in the same way that the Hutu and Tutsi reflect one another as one people, though divided—as a metaphor for the genocide, can serve to complicate the utility of rape metaphors in the context of violence. Even if Tadjo makes use of metaphor, she does so in a noticeably self-conscious way. The fact that this is not the only example of rape in the book further emphasizes multiplicity as a way to understand

and engage genocidal rape. The use of the metaphor here disturbs any facile conclusions about its efficacy as a way to talk about violence, thereby allowing us to destabilize some of the basic assumptions of this study.

These carefully rendered figurations of rape in *L'ombre d'Imana*, as I have sketched out here, focus our attention on the distinctions inherently present in the experience of rape. Realization of the victim/survivor's subjectivity pivots around discursive modes (as in the union of body and memory), narrative modes (as in the choice of reportage), and textual modes (as in the use of the water image) that underscore the specificity of rape for those who are subject to it in the context of the Rwandan genocide. Ultimately, Tadjo's aesthetic of multiplicity in *L'ombre d'Imana* manages to reveal an embodied female subject beneath layers of violence.

Resistance, Agency, and Genocidal Rape in Raoul Peck's *Sometimes in April*

As in the work by Véronique Tadjo, the representation of genocidal rape in *Sometimes in April* marshals existing narratives of sexual violence and renders them according to embodied female subjectivities that also position women as agents. In his portrayal of the Rwandan genocide, Haitian filmmaker Raoul Peck worked assiduously to incorporate the experience of survivors by seeking out their voices and participation for *Sometimes in April*. Peck's efforts remind us that the "outsider" as creator is potentially problematic. He reveals during an interview for *Making of* Sometimes in April, the documentary short that aired prior to the HBO premiere, that "it was always important that step by step I had the trust of the people over there and they felt I was telling their story."[57] The story that Peck tells is an attempt to "explain the . . . political background around genocide," and as he divulges further, he was not "interested in doing a sort of Black Schindler's List."[58] The director's professed desire to distance his representation of the genocide from references to the Holocaust seizes upon the need to situate the genocide only in relation to itself. This is significant in the production of genocide discourses, which often refer back to the Holocaust as the original urtext for unspeakable violence. Peck's commitment to reframing the genocide is made manifest throughout the film as well as in its marketing—the world premiere was in a Kigali stadium for a Rwandese audience. If the affirmative response by this population is any indication, the film will contribute to providing a nuanced understanding of the complexities surrounding the genocide.

Sometimes in April is a film about the Rwandan genocide as it unfolded and the events that followed it. It relates the story of two Hutu brothers, one struggling to rebuild his life after losing everything during the genocide, and the other held for trial at the Arusha Tribunal. The significance of the two sons is not lost on the viewer; not only does *Sometimes in April* stage a Cain-and-Abel-like story of two Hutu brothers torn apart by violence, but the protagonist Augustin is himself the father of two sons, and the boys he encounters in Arusha later on are also brothers whose relationship refracts his relationship to his brother as well as to the boys he lost. In the first words of the film, we hear the voice of the older brother, Augustin:

> Yes, it's April again. Every year April the rainy season starts. And every year, every day a haunting emptiness descends over our hearts . . . every year in April I remember how quickly life ends . . . and every year I remember how lucky I should feel to be alive. Every year in April I remember.[59]

This lugubrious chorus of reflections begins the fictional story of protagonist Augustin Muganza, a former-Hutu-soldier-turned-schoolteacher, whose entire family was killed during the genocide. Because he refused to join the ranks of the slaughtering Hutus, Augustin and his family had to hide and flee from the genocide. He entrusts care of his Tutsi wife and their children to his brother, Honoré, a radio journalist well loved by the Interahamwe for supporting their politics of hate. *Sometimes in April* begins ten years after the genocide and shows the way these two brothers still struggle with the traumatic wounds of memory, visible through flashbacks and overlapping time frames. The film proffers a grim look at the genocide that does not evade the details of the way the massacres occurred. Unlike the Oscar-nominated film on the same subject, *Hotel Rwanda* (2004), *Sometimes in April* goes to great lengths to demonstrate the complexity of genocide without crowning a heroic figure, and without diminishing the horrific details of the slaughter that lasted one hundred days but whose origins are embedded deep within history. Some images are common to both films—the white-painted/black–letter-branded U.N. trucks, the intermarriage of a Hutu protagonist and a Tutsi woman, the actual Hotel Mille Collines, and the radios blaring their hate propaganda. However, the films are totally different in their approach to remembering the genocide and in how they engage rape representation.

Peck captures three distinct moments in an attempt to illuminate our understanding of the genocide. First, through a lengthy introduction, he offers a written history of the events leading up to the genocide, beginning with Belgian colonialism. Then throughout the film, he alternates between the present (ten years after the genocide and during the International Criminal Tribunal) and ten years previous (during the days of the mass killings). Like Véronique Tadjo and her Fest'Africa colleagues, the participants in the making of *Sometimes in April* felt an overwhelming need to participate in the project as a way to speak out against the lacking and limiting views of media and international responses to the genocide. Idris Elba, the actor who plays Augustin, explains this desire in an interview:

> In [his native] England the news was Africans killing Africans . . . again. Little did I know a million people had been slaughtered in three months. I had to do this film for the sake of those people so their story could be told in full reality, not through some CNN or BBC reporter's edit.[60]

Again, I focus on scenes that portray the rape of women—Valentine's testimony at the Tribunal and the fate of Jeanne, Augustin's wife. I aim to show that these scenes point to the integral role of women in the unfolding history of the genocide. The first is the testimony of Valentine, a secret witness for the Tribunal in Arusha. When she first appears, Valentine speaks to Augustin through the walls of his hotel room. The scene of the conversation shows them on opposite sides of the wall, with their backs against the hard surface separating them. As a mark of separation, the wall signifies one of the many divisions of the film—a separation through which there can be communication only with the determined effort of both parties. Rather than serving as a barrier to communication, the wall protects and opens the possibility of dialogue; the actors' visible emotional openness with one another penetrates the wall and reminds the viewer of the possibility that perceived boundaries can be overcome.

Although she has never met him, Valentine asks Augustin to come hear her testify the following day. Her vulnerable request is a cry for humanization. By inviting someone she chooses to be present at her testimony, Valentine selects her own witness and empowers herself. Hers is a strategic call for recognition and control in the face of a process that offers neither, and instead renders her anonymous. Valentine's request allows her to subvert the dialectics of the international human rights legal process by controlling who recognizes her as a subject. The following is her testimony:

> The first one, he took my baby off my back and put it on the floor. He penetrated me. He came to me and he had me a second time. Later, I don't

remember exactly where, the interahamwes held us in another room and they raped all the girls. A young man threw himself on me. . . . After that he did humiliating things to me, he did not even remember that I was a mother. . . . When the second man was finished, the third one came and he forced me to lie down again. He raped me. . . . At that moment I just wanted to die. . . . Then the fourth one came and he took me . . . At that moment I thought, God in heaven who are these men? . . . The next day the interahamwes came and they made us go back to that house but they had to drag me there like a dead person. . . . I was dead.[61]

The scene of Valentine's testimony of her rape at the cultural community center is based on a true story of the trial of former mayor Jean-Paul Akayesu, whose conviction marked the second time someone was charged and convicted of rape as an "act of genocide" in a Rwandan International Tribunal.[62] The inclusion of the Akayesu trial told only from the perspective of a raped survivor redresses the impact of these monumental political strides on an individual. As such, we are given an intimate look into what the international human rights success meant at the personal and individual level. In Valentine's monotonous tone, the listener discerns pain, courage, and perseverance. The lingering effects of trauma cause her to seek out Augustin for support. She asks him to attend the testimony so that her words can be heard by someone other than the officials and the judges at the trial, someone inevitably close to her but removed from her experience as a survivor. By framing the rape from a female perspective, Peck continues where Tadjo leaves off with the description of Anastasie's feelings. The portrayal of Valentine is historically accurate; some of her words come directly from the testimonies of survivors in the previously cited United Nations report. It assigns voice and authority to the rape survivor, for her testimony at the Tribunal is crucial to the (pivotal) sentencing of Akayesu. By allowing Valentine to tell her story, a story that is based on a specific reality, Peck demonstrates the way rape victim-survivors make up an indispensable component of the reconciliation process. At the same time, Valentine's example reveals a woman "making sense of [her] experience and channeling their pain into a struggle for justice, which involves . . . recognizing themselves as subjects before the international community."[63]

Augustin's presence as a listener to the testimony is as important as the contents of the testimony itself. The invitation by the witness to select her listener, and the assumption that he is in solidarity with her, can be interpreted as a way to challenge the construction of international human rights practices as exemplified by the Arusha Tribunals. A survey of the different faces listening to her testimony, actors whose faces remain more or less expressionless as Valentine speaks, reinforces the implicit critique of a system that obviates those it intends to empower. This trial scene reproduces one of the vaunted procedures of human rights legal intervention, demonstrating the role of rape victim-survivors therein. The scene also critiques the efficacy of human rights testimonies as a mode of recognition. Listening to Valentine, the viewer is made uncomfortably complicit in the spectacle of human rights testimonies. Watching the reactions of those to whom her testimony is supposed to be directed, we become sensitized to the limitations of the process. In this way, the film addresses the limitations of the Arusha Tribunal as a forum for recognition and reconciliation.[64]

The mother of two sons, Valentine is also the double of Augustin's dead wife, Jeanne, who we learn (in two subsequent scenes) suffered a similar fate. The scene opens with the voice of Honoré recounting to his brother what he learned about Jeanne's death. The camera lens pans to the setting of a church where a number of women are being held inside. Peck never shows us the actual rape on screen. Instead we see the women immediately after what is only called "a horrific night." There are obvious signs of what took place in the room: the women's ripped clothes, crippled demeanor, and position cowering in the corner. The sight of the men zipping up their pants, buckling their belts, and all but congratulating one another with slaps on their backs leaves us with no doubt that multiple rapes have just taken place. After her rape, Jeanne pulls a grenade that leads to the demise of her perpetrators, as well as her own death. When she asks them, "Do you think I am afraid to die?" she voices the cry of women such as Valentine, who, after multiple rapes, "just wanted to die."[65] Her suicide–murder is an act of bravery and agency because by sending the women away before killing their assailants, she protects them to the greatest extent possible within the circumstances. Jeanne's selfless act of vengeance also bears symbolic significance through which we imagine all of the women who were crippled into inaction after being raped. Her character, whose name symbolically resonates with the ubiquitous fifteenth-century French martyr, issues an alternative to the role of the eternally vulnerable and victimized raped woman. The focus on Jeanne's act promotes a combination of empowerment, resistance, and agency that is not frequently associated with stories about women in the Rwandan genocide.

The examples from *L'ombre d'Imana* and *Sometimes in April* highlight four methods for representing "positive" subjectivity for rape survivors of the Rwandan genocide: reflection on a dead woman who was a victim of sexual assault, memories of a woman uncertain about when she was raped, testimony of a survivor of gang rape, and a woman retaliating against her perpetrators. I propose that there is an underlying progression in the view of subjectivity for the four narratives of rape I have drawn out in the first half of this chapter. First, in *la femme ligotée*/the bound woman, we see the raped body exposed, which functions as metonymy for genocide. The triple violation of the body—that the woman was first raped, then had the pickaxe thrust into her vagina, and then had her body left outside the grave to be exposed as an example—is a haunting warning of the way genocide can always repeat itself.[66] This is also similar to what Diop coined *le double génocide*—the original genocide and the subsequent silence surrounding it.[67] The example of Anastasie is an elaborate exploration of the effects of rape on the psyche, an expository act that renders rape trauma syndrome, focuses on the body and situates it as a site of subjectivity. In the case of Valentine, we have a woman voicing her own story (despite its harrowing nature) for a political end whose larger goal is accountability and reconciliation. Finally, in Jeanne we see a raped woman who goes from being a hapless victim of sexual assault to an empowered agent of her final destiny and that of her perpetrators.

This progression of narratives can be seen as a chain of subjectivities that with each step goes further in pursuit of creating women who are subjects, and not just the "spoils of war"—women whose experiences of sexual violence are not forgotten, discarded, or lost in representations of the Rwandan genocide. Ultimately, the progression that we see in these different works in different forms attests to the growing possibility that genocide can be rendered in complex terms that excavate its multiple layers of violence.

Adding another medium to these forms, in the following section, I examine *Les blessures du silence* in which the author explains that a reductive image of genocide is just as detrimental as a forgetting of the past:

> Ne retenir du génocide rwandais que les images des corps déchiquetés par des machettes pour aussitôt s'apitoyer sur des camps de réfugiés atteints de cholera, comme si celui-ci avait aussi choisi ses victimes, c'est transformer d'un coup de baguette magique des personnes concernées par ce génocide—bourreaux, complices, survivants, innocents—en simple victime d'un drame humanitaire. C'est surtout refuser d'analyser le mécanisme et le fonctionnement de ce génocide, c'est accepter qu'il puisse se reproduire au Rwanda ou ailleurs.[68]

> To only retain from the Rwandan genocide the images of bodies torn to pieces and machetes in order to immediately have pity on the refugee

camps suffering from cholera, as though the former had also chosen its victims, is to transform, with the wave of a magic wand, the people affected by the genocide—the killers, accomplices, survivors, innocent— into mere victims of a humanitarian drama. In particular, to do this is to refuse to analyze the mechanism and the function of this genocide; it is to accept that it can reproduce itself in Rwanda or elsewhere.[69]

Mukagasana warns that formulaic images engender revictimization because they forgo analysis and freeze the accounts of the genocide into the snares of a monolith that rehearses colonial scripts. This critique of the genocide monolith echoes Harrow's and Hitchcott's observations about the way genocidal discourses re-issue colonial scripts by fixing the African continent as a locus of violence and abject atrocity.[70]

As I have argued throughout this book, numerous challenges surface as one renders rape. When we then consider a layered experience of violence as we did here, with representations of rape within genocide, the challenges persist and intensify. By delivering portrayals of rape that are neither reductive nor limiting in their renditions, Diop, Tadjo, and Peck deftly negotiate the challenges Mukagasana expresses. They achieve this in a number of ways: by turning their attention to the elaboration of subjectivity, by displaying episodes of rape with different outcomes for the victim/survivor, by applying different narrative modes to tell the stories of rape, and by indicating the significance of sexual violence within a larger system of violence. By showing what lies beneath layers of violence, their compelling representations indicate an unflagging commitment to privileging the voices of genocidal rape survivors.

Les blessures du silence: The Visual Production of Genocidal Rape

Throughout this study, I have been attentive to the ways in which rape representation, instead of symbolizing national and international concerns, offers a productive way to engage and unpack some of the different problems posed by representing violence. Given representation's limited ability to communicate pain, cultural workers often deploy a diverse range of forms and strategies to conduct the task of translating trauma into art. Photography offers a dense field of translation for the irrevocable incommunicability of pain by embarking on visual representation. As a representational practice, photography has been one of the dominant modes used for circulating human rights abuses, catastrophic events, and atrocity in the context of war, genocide, and torture. Rather than document atrocity per se, *Les blessures du silence* seeks to put a face on the victims and perpetrators of the Rwandan genocide and to place them alongside one another as a way to address some of the traumatic wounds still visible and painful a decade after the genocide. In addition to being a collection of photographs assembled in a book, *Les blessures du silence* later traveled as a worldwide exhibit marking the fifteen-year anniversary of the genocide.[71]

As one of the first survivors of the genocide to publish her written testimony, Mukagasana has remained passionately invested in encouraging people to educate themselves about the events that transpired during 1994, as well as what led up to it and what has followed it. Mukagasana initiated the project as a way to bring together reflection, reconstruction and reconciliation through oral testimonies and visual images. She sought photojournalist Alain Kazinierakis to assist her by photographing the people she interviewed. Much scholarship has been devoted to the ways that photography enters into the visual and affective politics of spectatorship, staging an encounter between the viewer and the viewed that comes with a set of troubling politics in the spectacle of suffering. Though primarily a visual field, photography (and particularly photography of catastrophe) not only documents historical events, it also allows the viewing subject to interact with the historical event as a belated witness. Photographs can help to influence emotion, and thus they are operative mechanisms for the production of affect. At the same time, the intersection between photographs and emotion is neither unproblematic nor unmediated. As Carrie Rentschler has noted, "Witnesses can also act complicitously in others' suffering by watching it without seeking to alleviate it, and they can empathize, or 'feel with,' others who suffer—an imagined form of affective participation."[72] The dynamics that Rentschler describes here can be applied to photographs of the Rwandan genocide—the viewing of these images and their popular circulation can objectify and diminish. In this regard, *Les blessures du silence* stands apart as images that focus on portraits—faces of victims and survivors—as well as an effort to place those victims and perpetrators in front of and in conversation with one another. The emphasis is not on the portrait subjects' suffering, but rather on the unwieldy project of reconciliation.

This collection offers a point of departure to explore the legibility of rape in visual representations of the genocide. At first, using photography as a form of rape representation might appear contradictory, but in its documentation of survivors and of the enduring effects of the genocide, *Les blessures du silence* allows the reader/viewer to encounter rape survivors, rapists, and children born of rape, thus serving as a rich archive for the diverse experiences and outcomes of genocidal rape. Documenting the faces of the survivors as well as the perpetrators also functions in another way for the collective memory in Rwanda, because photography can "provide special access to experiences that have remained unremembered and yet cannot be forgotten," essentially acting as a trigger.[73] Thus, as a commemorative act, the photographs contribute to the history of the genocide, not only by documenting the narratives of survivors, but by offering recognition for those who were not in the book but may benefit from their stories. The dialogic structure places individual Rwandese in conversation with one another. The politics of recognition here takes on a completely different tone that privileges the standpoint of genocide survivors and that does not require a Western subject to legitimate their testimonies.

Together the photographs, the interviews and the paratext open a space for thinking about the genocide as a multilayered event with effects that are also myriad. *Les blessures du silence* stands out as a complicated exploration of genocide that refuses to capitulate to facile renderings of the event and the history that preceded it. This unsettling of genocidal scripts is particularly discernible in the commitment to dissolving the boundaries between victim and perpetrator to stage the encounter between the two on the page. The image on the back of the collection captures this dynamic (see fig. 3). Mukagasana sits facing the camera with a man in front of her. His back is to the camera, and his hand appears to be in motion, as though he is in midsentence. Mukagasana sits with pursed lips and a furrowed brow as though struggling with what she hears. The caption underneath explains, "Dans une prison au Rwanda, Yolande, survivante du génocide, est devant Patrice qui avoue avoir tué cent personnes" [In a prison in Rwanda, Yolande, a genocide survivor, is in front of Patrice, who admits to having killed one hundred people]. Yolande's position mirrors the situation of those living in Rwanda, forced to encounter one another on a daily basis, literally living with the wounds of silence. Mukagasana approaches genocide representation by relying on form to negotiate complex dynamics at play before, during, and after the genocide, refusing to fix the event into a singular narrative logic. In the remaining section of this chapter, I examine the way *Les blessures du silence* reconceptualizes genocidal discourses by exploring its dialogical structure, its shifting relationship to testimony, and its inclusion of diverse rape narratives.

Figure 3. "Dans une prison au Rwanda, Yolande Mukagasana, survivante du génocide, est devant Patrice qui avoue avoir tué cent personnes." Photo credit: Alain Kazinierakis, *Les blessures du silence*

A Dialogic Encounter with Genocide

The dialogic aspect of *Les blessures du silence* lies at the center of its ability to disrupt many of the genocide's core ideologies; it comes forth first through the featuring of victims and perpetrators as mentioned above, the interview process of Mukagasana posing questions to be answered by other survivors, and the interplay between text and image. The metatextual relationship between the testimonies and the photographs functions dialogically as a more dynamic way to engage the genocide. This practice also mirrors the juxtaposition of victims/killers who are interviewed, as well as the insider/

outsider positioning of the writer and photographer. These relations stage a binary that they proceed to call into question. Together, the visual and written registers help highlight genocide as "the oscillation between a crisis of death and the correlative crisis of living; between the story of the unbearable nature of an event and the story of the unbearable nature of its survival."[74] Like the *flots souterrains* that splash around Anastasie, the pattern of this oscillation laps and flows around the survivor, who can never be certain of which way its flow will take them. There is an inherent uncertainty to living after the genocide and in testifying about the genocide. The use of the "silence" works largely to indicate this uncertainty, just as the book attempts to make these silences productive through the use of the camera lens.

Alongside the back and forth between Mukagasana and those featured in the book, there is another dialogic relationship at work between the text and the images in *Les blessures du silence*. This dialogic relationship functions in several ways, especially as it appears that the photographs themselves reference and interpellate one another. The text is introduced by four prefaces, including one written jointly by Mukagasana and Kazinierakis, and one by an official of Médecins sans frontières. Following this is the first section, consisting of photographs, each offering a full-page image of the survivors and perpetrators. Underneath each of these images is an identifying marker with the person's name, age, role in the genocide, and status afterwards. For example, "Valérie B.: 44 ans, journaliste, actuellement en prison" [Valérie B. 44 years old, journalist, currently in prison] (18). Each photograph stands on its own, suggesting an isolated image telling the events for themselves as they lived them. However, the narratives in the following section tell a different story, as we learn that the photographic subjects tell their stories in response to questions from Mukagasana, revealing their highly mediated form. By choosing one line from their narratives to place as a caption underneath the large photographs, Mukagasana and Kazinierakis assign meaning to their subjects. More than even Tadjo and Peck, Mukagasana enters into the complexity undergirding the genocide because of her own experience of having been saved by a Hutu woman. As a result, "Elle refuse les schémas ethniques qui veulent que celui qui est hutu est génocidaire et que celui qui est tutsi est victime" [She refuses the ethnic schemas according to which the one who is Hutu commits genocide and the one who is Tutsi is a victim] (7).

Les blessures du silence was financially supported and published by Médecins sans frontières, a humanitarian institution which, unlike Fondation de France, had a history of investment in Rwanda. According to the authors, it was "une des rares ONG qui soit restée au Rwanda pendant le génocide" [one of the rare NGOs that stayed in Rwanda during the genocide] (82). While Mukagasana acts as author and editor for the project, the eye behind the lens is the photojournalist Alain Kazinierkakis; their collaboration is key to animating the project of commemoration, testimony, and witnessing. In the first introduction to the book, Alex Parisel explains the importance of the photographs as a way to mediate what genocide renders incommunicable.

> C'est dans les visages captés par le photographe . . . que l'on aborde l'indicible. Ces photos condensent avec sobriété la complexité et la difficulté d'être simplement vivant quelques années sans lumière après le génocide. Et à y regarder de plus près, je me demande si ces visages sont encore des visages des êtres vivants . . . ces visages des témoins . . . sont bien plus insoutenables que l'imagerie habituelle de l'horreur faite de machettes et de crânes fracassés. (8)

> It is in these faces captured by the photographs that we begin to approach the unspeakable. These photographs condense with sobriety and complexity the difficulty of simply being alive a few years without light after the genocide. And to look more closely, I ask myself if these faces are still faces of living people. These faces of the witnesses are even more unbearable than the habitual imagery of the horror done by the machetes and the shattered skulls.

These observations reveal that one of the difficulties of thinking about cultural productions of human rights violations is how the problem of spectatorship is structured around the politics of recognition. The author searches for humanity in the faces he observes on the pages of the book—a conceptualization of recognition that informs and mobilizes human rights discourses in ways that de-emphasize Third World subjects as human. The politics behind this rhetorical practice must be investigated for the way they foreclose the elaboration and mobility of the viewed subject. Furthermore, the comparison of the faces of the witnesses with the recognized signs of genocide objectifies the photographs of the subjects in a way that is troubling. By stating the obvious, the author of the Médecins sans frontières introduction uncritically rehearses the subject/object dichotomy that has plagued visual representations of Africans since long before colonialism, again displaying the currency of these dynamics in genocide discourse.

Kazinierakis, on the other hand, directly addresses this prevailing discourse by citing the limited view inherent to media representations of Rwanda, critiquing the ways that "les journalistes et les photographes n'ont pu donner qu'une image partiale, voire caricaturale, de ce qui se passait au Rwanda. La presse s'est intéressée à ces images parce que c'était une représentation spectaculaire du Malheur" [journalists and photographers were able to give only a partial image, in other words a caricature, of what was going on in Rwanda. The press was interested in those images because they were a spectacular representation of Evil] (11). The question of positioning and the relationship between the eye behind the camera and the body in front of the camera comes sharply into focus as Kazinierakis foregrounds Mukagasana's role as a mediator and translator between the camera lens and the Rwandese subjects it captured. He attributes any success of the images to her presence:

> C'est grâce à elle, à sa présence de survivante, que j'ai pu me mettre en face des survivants du génocide, car elle m'a invité à voir et à sentir les blessures profondes de la destruction, la souffrance de chaque instant, le chagrin d'avoir perdu tout ce que l'on aimait, la culpabilité de rester vivant—autant de sentiments qui, sans elle, seraient demeurés secrets, et à moi, inaccessibles. (11)

> It is thanks to her, to her presence as a survivor, that I was able to place myself in front of survivors of the genocide, because she invited me to see and to feel the deep wounds of destruction, the suffering of each instant, the pain of having lost everything that we loved, the guilt of remaining alive—so many feelings that, without her, would have remained secret and inaccessible to me.

By referencing both his position as a photographer and her position as a writer, he actively underscores the stakes of witnessing and of photographing the Rwandan genocide from the perspective of an outsider as well as an insider. On the one hand, Mukagasana appears to be a vehicle that renders the experience of the other survivors translatable to her photographer. On the other hand, her presence legitimates and authenticates the gaze of his lens, allowing him to become a mere spectator in the exchange between Mukagasna and the various subjects of *Les blessures du silence*. Here again we can observe the politics of recognition at work. His comments seem to reinforce the dynamics consistent with "the history of human rights . . . as a story of selective and differentiated visibility, which has positioned certain bodies, populations and nations as objects of recognition and granted others the power and means to look and to confer recognition."[75] Mukagasana describes their working relationship in similar glowing terms, "Ainsi nous avons décidé ensemble de rompre le silence autour de ce génocide; il est vrai que l'union fait la force!" [In this way we decided together to break the silence around the genocide; it is true that there is strength in unity!] (81). However, it is important to be mindful of the potentially problematic dynamics that come into play in this collaboration.[76]

Nowhere is the question of positioning more clear than in Mukagasana's written reflection, "Une nuit sans sommeil" [A Night Without Sleep], which precedes the testimonials and interviews. The author passionately expresses her desire to learn more of these stories and to share them with others. The imperative we learn here is deeply personal, as she attempts to reconstruct both herself and the fabric of Rwanda, linking the quest directly to her own personhood as well as a larger nationhood. "Tenter de me reconstruire et de reconstruire le tissu social rwandais" [Attempt to reconstruct myself and to reconstruct the Rwandan social tissue] (82). Mukagasana's essay describes the ways in which she, as an escapee, was haunted by the genocide.

She also expresses discomfort with the extant narratives of the Rwandan genocide, describing them as both limited and limiting. Openly challenging the rhetoric of human rights, she states, "on m'a toujours parlé des droits de l'homme. . . . Est-ce que le survivant du génocide au Rwanda ne serait pas un homme? Non, nous n'avons jamais connu ces droits" [I have always heard about human rights . . . is the genocide survivor not human? No. We have never known those rights . . .] (81). In the place of human rights discourses that obviate and obscure survivors, Mukagasana offers careful, critical, and patient attention. She writes, "C'est par un patient et parfois laborieux travail d'écoute que j'ai pu pénétrer le cœur de mes interlocuteurs" [it is only by a patient and at times laborious labor of listening that I was able to penetrate the heart of my interlocutors] (82). She tells us that listening is the most fundamental aspect of her interviews. Yet, this active listening is challenging for Mukagasana. Only by listening can she hear the wounds of silence to which the title refers. Here silence is particularly operative as an element of listening. By listening, one undercuts the systematic silencing of survivors' stories. Furthermore, in the act of listening one renders oneself silent, choosing not to offer one's own perspectives, observations, or judgments of the genocide.

Although she privileges active listening, Mukagasana also names the unstable quality of truth telling in the form of testimony. "J'ai témoigné comme survivante du génocide. Je dois aider d'autres survivants à le faire. Mais la vérité que nous connaissons n'est qu'une partie de la vérité [I testified as a witness to the génocide. I have to help other survivors to do so as well. But the truth that we know is only one part] (81). Whereas the use of the verb *connaître* rather than *savoir* serves as a way to contest the nature of knowing in relation to genocide, the subsequent use of *savoir* in the following sentence suggests that there is truth to be known and that this truth is in fact knowable. The statement is doubly coded because it also refers to the need for perpetrators to testify and to speak their own experiences.

The collection of witness accounts *Les blessures du silence* includes the stories of both perpetrators and victims of the genocide. This can be read as a concerted effort to destabilize the binary oppositions between the two by giving equal weight to all Rwandese in the aftermath of the genocide, even those who helped perpetuate it. It stages the challenging pursuit of truth and reconciliation. Mukagasana acknowledges that this formula has become almost platitudinous in its inefficacy in addressing most of the genocide's core issues. The politics of this practice attempt to unravel the ideology of pernicious division that lies at the core of thinking about genocide outlined by scholars such as Mamdani and Harrow.

Mukagasana lists the material costs of the genocide as specifically gendered. "Les survivants, eux sont toujours seuls, livrés à la misère morale et matérielle. Les femmes, les filles et même les petites filles violées pendant le génocide meurent tous les jours par manque de soin ou par le sida [The survivors, they are always alone, left to their moral and material misery. The women, the girls, and even the little girls raped during the genocide are all dying from a lack of care or from AIDS] (81). Though the photographs do not document rape directly, they help plot the use of photography as a way to document atrocities and as such offer an example how rape surfaces in instances of layered violence. Acting as a visual mode, photographs serve more than one purpose throughout the project. They attempt to communicate what is otherwise incommunicable in a way that exceeds the use of words because the image moves beyond it. The photographs also act as a site of memory, serving as a visual archive that documents the faces of those involved in and hurt by the genocide. In their focus on faces, the photographs also shift attention away from pained and maimed bodies (as in the severed limbs and heads infamously used to symbolize the genocide) to focus on the humanity offered through the look, the gaze, and the face of individual Rwandese. By privileging the photographs of living faces rather than of those of corpses, Mukagasana reckons with the dominant visual images of the genocide that err on the side of bodily ruin and objectification.

Les blessures du silence carefully articulates the double victimization of genocide survivors in a way that focuses on their experiences and remains attentive to the ways in which survival carries a burden of its own. "Les rescapés sont doublement victimes d'être encore en vie: nous avons trop honte de n'avoir pu sauver les nôtres" [The escapees are doubly victims for still being alive: we have too much shame from not having been able to save our own] (7). Such a view of survival serves to complicate the significance of the survivors in telling their stories—stories that are wracked with pain and hackneyed with memories hampered by guilt. Further reinforcing this point, we read, "les victimes s'éprouveront doublement victimes: victimes d'avoir été la cible du génocide, ils sont aujourd'hui victimes d'avoir été victimes, quand les grandes puissances voudraient qu'ils se contentent d'une réconciliation amnésique" [the victims prove to be double victims, victims of having been the brunt of the genocide, they are today victims for having been victims, while the powers that be would like them to be content with an amnesiac reconciliation] (10). Kazinierakis begins his own introduction, tellingly entitled, "Des visages qui parlent" [Faces That Speak], with a reflection on what role photography can play in light of catastrophic events. He writes, "Les images fixes nous marquent durablement. Elles hantent nos consciences et structurent notre imaginaire. . . . Victimes sans images, donc sans visages. . . . Il est temps de rendre leur humanité au Rwandais" [Fixed images mark us forever. They haunt our consciences and structure our imaginary. . . . Victims without images, so without faces. . . . It is time to give their humanity back to Rwandese] (11). These words echo Susan Sontag's observation that "photographs . . . haunt us."[77] Again here the photographer enters into the familiar logics of human rights frameworks, which interface with the politics of visibility and recognition as concepts integral to personhood. The title of Kazinierkis' introduction stages an equivalence between visuality and voice, allowing the faces of survivors to speak for themselves, positing that for Rwandese, their own looking is more significant than the way others look at them.

The photographic image on the cover of the book stands as one example of these ocular logics (see fig. 4). The cover shows a black–and–white photo of a woman with eyes downcast and mouth slightly ajar. The contrast between her white shirt and the dark background of the frame serve push her into prominence in the spectator's visual field. The woman, whose name we learn is Eugénie, has a forehead with a deeply indented scar that creates a cleavage in her forehead. The scar is the unquestionable sign of a machete, a wound that is all but silent and that cries out to the viewer as well as to the context of the project. Yet the wound is not the focal point of the image. It is Eugénie's open mouth, drawing attention to

Figure 4. Eugénie N from *Les blessures du silence*. Photo credit: Alain Kazinierakis, *Les blessures du silence*

her position as a speaking subject is just as present in the frame. "Je ne raconte mon histoire à personne, parce que je suis dégoûtée de la nature humaine. L'homme a détruit tout en moi" [I do not tell my story to anyone, because I am disgusted with human nature. Man has destroyed everything in me] (14). By linking this desire for anonymity (not wanting to share her story) with recognition of society's inhumanity, Eugénie refutes one of the most significant claims of rights discourses—that sharing one's story is a necessary feature for the advocacy process. Eugénie's statement implies either that sharing her story will lead to nothing, or that what it will lead to (empathy? recognition? breaking silence?) is insignificant compared with the gaping wounds of memory. Located on the collection's cover, Eugénie becomes an example through which we first observe the way the wounds of silence operate. Yet with her downcast eyes and barely opened lips, she does not invite the spectator's gaze but rather seems to refuse it or to be ashamed of it. She is the reluctant witness who shares her story only at Mukagasana's request because her interlocutor is also a survivor. "Je n'ai accepté de témoigner que parce que toi aussi tu es une veuve qui a perdu ses enfants. Nous avons une histoire semblable. C'est pourquoi je te fais confiance" [I only accepted to testify because you are also a widow and you lost your children. We have a similar story. That is what I confided in you] (85). The politics of recognition and visibility function here in a way that Wendy Hesford never explores when we understand that Eugénie shares her story because she recognizes herself in Yolande and therefore desires to speak to her. A mutual understanding is born out of the women's ability to look at and to be seen by one another. This pair effectively inverts the relationship between spectatorship and recognition that is key to human rights logic, because rather than conferring unto the survivor the humanity that allows her to speak and to be seen, the survivor makes a choice to speak because she sees herself in the interviewer. This interaction, which simultaneously acknowledges and then dismantles the dialectic of silence at work in commemorations of the genocide, can take place only because both women are survivors of the genocide.

Central to the narrative constructed in *Les blessures du silence* are the testimonies, which, along with the act of bearing witness, serve as an important index for the literatures of trauma. Whereas some critics have argued that recording traumatic testimony can serve as a form of subaltern agency, here I focus on the unstable relationship between the construction of genocidal memory, the act of witnessing, and the way framing witnessing in this way poses new challenges for rape representation. Understanding that testimonials are socially constructed and constituted, problematically informed by the context in which they emerge, I am interested in considering the function of the testimony in relation to the other forms of cultural production explored in this chapter. Furthermore, I argue that both Mukagasana's and Kazinierakis' awareness of these issues mediates and even structures the form of *Les blessures du silence*. In many ways, this final analysis departs from the examples used earlier in this book, which are centrally focused on rape representation. However, in light of my argument about the Rwandan genocide as an incident of layered violence, I first explore genocide representation as constructed through visual images. My goal here is to critically engage the use of testimony and photography as modes of rape representation, questioning some of their key ideologies in the construction of narratives of sexual violence. Through the combination of testimony and photography, *Les blessures du silence* also stands as an example of the way remembering the genocide can generate productive possibilities that attend to destabilizing many of its core ideologies.

Human Rights Testimonies and the Spectacle of Suffering

Two conceptualizations of witnessing are useful to help think through the ways that *Les blessures du silence* negotiates the politics of bearing witness and the role of testimony in representations of suffering. *Testimony* authors Dori Laub and Shoshana Felman argue that "a textual testimony . . . can penetrate like an actual life," making the case for the usefulness of testimony as a genre.[78] In their exploration of the relationship between witnessing and secondary trauma, Laub and Felman argue that, "translation, as opposed to confession . . . becomes a metaphor for the historical necessity of bearing witness."[79] *Les blessures du silence* helps to illustrate the way this process takes shape, especially because the translation of the languages spoken in Rwanda—Kinyarwanda and Swahili—present an initial layer of challenges. In their awareness of their positionality and determination to situate themselves in relation to their interviewed subjects, Mukagasana and Kazinierakis exemplify the ways that "human rights scholars and advocates [can] situate ourselves among a series of traumatic representations . . . calling for an understanding of witnessing as a historically contingent rhetorical act, which is implicated in and mediated by sociopolitical relations, discourses, and technologies."[80] As narratives of atrocity that bring together witnessing, testimony, and memory, the stories in *Les blessures du silence* can be understood as a form of human rights narrative that is attendant to some of the limitations of the genre.

Human rights testimonies have been problematized for their representational practices, which often rely on the politics of recognition and visibility to lay claim to human subjectivity and agency. In *Spectacular Rhetorics: Human Rights Visions, Recognitions and Feminisms,* Wendy Hesford rightfully argues that, "Human rights testimonies, like human rights images, risk voyeurism and commodification."[81] Despite their predominant use in the field of international human rights advocacy, these testimonies pose methodological and ethical challenges. First, in their highly structured format, these testimonies are viewed as acceptable purveyors of "the real," a construction that leaves little room for critique and does not account for the unstable characteristics of truth. Second, testimonies often adhere to a logic of humanity rooted in spectatorship, vocality, and spectacle. Third, these testimonies are often viewed as static and as locked into a temporality that denies the subject's continued experience of trauma. In her call for "representations that do not simply turn passive or silent voices into compelling speech, to reproduce the traumatic real, but that reconfigure witnessing in rhetorical and ethical terms," Hesford proposes a different way of constructing, analyzing, and accounting for the manifold operations of human rights testimonies.[82] I agree with Hesford that often "oral and written human rights testimonies may shift attention away from the visualization of suffering [and that] individual testimonies are shaped by culturally available scripts and an international moral economy attached to an identity based politics of recognition."[83] However, I propose that, as a survivor of genocide herself, Mukagasana mitigates the extent of these dynamics through the dialogic structure of the project.[84] Because the testimonies are framed by questions that Mukagasana asks, the extent to which the speakers shape their testimonies according to cultural scripts is less straightforward, or even pronounced. Thus we see that one way of rethinking the testimony genre is to stage the encounter between the speaker and the listener differently.

The photographs serve as a rich repository that further informs the narrative and influence readings of the text as straightforward testimonies. Because the photographs are essentially portraits, they can function powerfully as a visual representation that refuses to objectify the survivors. This refusal means not participating in the display of the abject that usually accompanies images of genocide. Nowhere do we see the dominant images referred to at the beginning of this chapter—the grating hack of the machete, the bleached desiccated skulls arranged in a multitude of perfect rows, the truculent mobs proclaiming Hutu Power. The rape of women, rather than becoming a sign of the sexually deviant nature of genocide, reflects a common practice experienced by too many. As examples of simple portraits of people's faces that do not focus on their mangled, broken bodies, these photographs offer another way to commemorate atrocity that refuses both the objectifying/othering gaze and the spectacle of suffering. Kazinierakis and Mukagasana manage to do this mainly in two ways. First, the presence of text in the book draws attention away from the spectacle of violence apparent through photography and instead focuses the reader on the relationship between text and image, and the words of both survivors and perpetrators. Second, through the inclusion of perpetrators alongside victims, the editors openly address and undo some of the binaries that seem to animate most discussions of the genocide. This practice also helps to dismantle the facile relationship between victim and victimizer—and by extension the relationship between victim and agent—that saturate representations of human rights abuses.

By effectively denying the spectacle of suffering and its related voyeurism through a refusal to focus on severed limbs or visible wounds, *Les blessures du silence* performs a dialogic wink of the eye. Whereas the title foregrounds the wound, the actual content of the book is more focused on the ubiquitous "wound that cries out," the traumatic memory of the genocide rather than its physical and material legacy. As suggested by the title, the wound is an organizing symbol of the entire collection. Again, in the introduction Kazinierakis and Mukagasana write, "La communauté internationale garde le silence sur le génocide du 1994 au Rwanda. Les Rwandais aussi. Pourtant, derrière les visages se cachent des profondes blessures" [The international community maintains silence about the Rwandan genocide of 1994. Rwandese do also. However, behind the faces deep wounds are hiding] (9). The wounds referred to here are psychological and emotional; the fact that they are hidden means that they cannot possibly refer to the physical toll, the material damage done to thousands of bodies. Likewise, they point out, "On peut visiter le Rwanda aujourd'hui sans entendre parler de génocide, les blessures sont si profondes qu'elles ne sont visibles que grâce à un travail sensible, patient, humain et dépourvu de tout jugement. C'est ce travail-là que nous avons voulu prendre" [We can visit Rwanda today without hearing any mention of the genocide, the wounds are so profound that they are visible only through a sensitive, patient, and human project without any judgment. This is the type of work that we wanted to do] (10). In their invisibility, hidden wounds are far less spectacular than are physical wounds, which are a material sign of the extreme nature of genocidal violence.

Throughout *Les blessures du silence,* Mukagasana situates herself as an insider and describes the ways in which this type of status informs her desire for sensitized portraits of the genocide. For example, the author's commitment to dismantling key ideologies of genocide and postgenocide discourses is manifestly invested in the undoing of the carefully crafted oppositional framework of a genocide consisting of Hutus versus Tutsis as the main players. "Au Rwanda il n'y a pas deux camps" [In Rwanda there are not two camps] (9). This determination to remove the masks of genocidal discourses straddles historic and geopolitical imperatives, which she clearly lays out: "... maquiller un crime contre l'humanité en guerre civile, tribale, en massacres interethniques, c'est oublier que le génocide n'est pas tombé du ciel, mais a été soigneusement, politiquement préparé pendant plus d'un demi-siècle" [to disguise a crime against humanity as a civil war, as tribal, interethnic massacres, is to forget that the génocide did not fall out of the sky, but that it was carefully, politically prepared for more than half a century] (9).

The questions posed by the author guide most of the testimonies included in the collection. Constantly aware of the relationship between herself as the gatherer of these stories and the position of the interrogated subject, she asks questions that chip away at the layers of meaning beneath how individual survivors interact with memories of the genocide. For example, in one revelatory conversation with a little girl, she asks, "Mais dis-moi, pourquoi tu ne me regardes pas dans les yeux? Tu peux, pourtant. Mais tu baisses les yeux. (*Silence.*) Et pourquoi tu ne me réponds pas? (*Silence.*) On t'a dit de ne pas me répondre? (*Silence.*) Pourtant, tu sais parler" [But tell me, why do you not look me in the eye? You can, you know. But you lower your eyes. (Silence) . . . And why do you not answer me? (Silence) Were you told not to answer me? (Silence). Yet you know how to speak] (108). Questions such as these demonstrate Mukagasana's awareness of her own location in the same way that we saw at work with Tadjo. Far too many representations of the Rwandan genocide rely on the narratives about battles of ethnic strife of two groups constantly in opposition to one another. In contrast, by including the perpetrators, Mukagasana attempts to render a post-genocide Rwanda in which victims and killers live side by side one another, and she presents the possibility that dialogue could happen between the parties involved.

Y a-t-il eu des viols là où tu étais?
[Were there rapes where you were?]

In a conversation with one of the imprisoned perpetrators, Jean N., Yolande asks directly, "Y a-t-il eu des viols là où tu étais?" [Were there rapes where you were?] (132). The man, Jean, answers, "C'est quoi un viol? C'est prendre de force une femme?" [What is a rape? To take a woman by force?]. Jean's question reveals a lack of understanding of what can be called one of the most commonly used tools of the Rwandan genocide and what subsequently became one of its most referenced atrocities. The man goes on to tell Yolande that he actually saved women from being raped and that at one point his brother wanted to rape a woman who consented to sexual relations. The inclusion of this testimony recasts one of the most common genocidal rape narratives, stories in which women are held captive for days and are repeatedly gang raped. Yet the inclusion of his testimony does not contradict these other stories, which are so prevalent throughout the book. Instead, it reveals a difference, an instability of the terms under which rape takes place in the genocide. In another interview, Mukagasana asks Valérie, a journalist being held in prison, "Qu'est-ce que vous pensez du viol pendant le génocide? [What do you think about the rape during the genocide?] (96). The woman responds: "Les gens qui ont été torturé peuvent témoigner. En tant que femme, c'est très choquant. Là on voit pas le respect du sexe féminin" [The people who were tortured can testify to that. As a woman, it is very shocking. In that we see no respect for the female sex]. The inclusion of numerous female perpetrators is significant here, especially because the role of women as complicit in and as perpetrators of war crimes has been given less attention. As another study of the topic points out:

> The case of the Rwandan genocide underscores the need for practitioners of women's studies not to overlook ethnic politics when examining violence against women. . . . Women were not just victims they were also perpetrators. Hutu women from all walks of Rwandan life participated in the killing. In Kibuye, the militia mobilized the local prostitutes to kill children. Rwandan nuns refused to harbor refugees, turned them over to the militia, provided lists of those yet to be killed, and even participated in the killings themselves. Some Hutu female medical personnel became killers, too. Schoolgirls killed their classmates.[85]

To effectively consider these gender dynamics is to include, as Mukagasana does in *Les blessures du silence*, female perpetrators in the dialogue. This moment with Valérie is telling for the way the speaker places the burden of testimony on those who were tortured. Rape, she seems to suggest, must be told by those who were victimized by it; the story is theirs to tell. There is a way that this determination to have the story told only by rape survivors deflects the accountability of the perpetrators. At the same time, Valérie's comment suggests a different rubric for remembering rape in the context of genocide. With these questions to the perpetrators, the interviews open a broader perspective on the occurrence of genocidal rape. The uncomfortable nature of this perspective moves far beyond facile visions of the genocide.

The testimony of Agnès offers examples of women who developed different strategies in the hopes of not being raped. She describes, " . . . ma tante, qui s'était habillée de pagnes et d'un short très serrant pour décourager les violeurs, a été abattue d'un coup de machette" [My aunt, who dressed herself with a traditional skirt and a pair of tight shorts underneath in order to discourage the rapists, was defeated by one strike of the machete] (101). The aunt's experience tells a delicate story that, although it points to the possibility of resistance, finally suggests the futility of agency despite innovative efforts to secure it. But upon second reading, the longer term effects of this rape could also suggest options for future resistance when we think about the way Agnès is haunted by the events. Along with the implicit evocation of the wound, the notion of haunting appears to be more than an abstraction in these narratives: "Ma tante a été battue d'un coup de machette. Son bébé qu'elle portait sur le dos est tombé avec elle dans la fosse. J'entends encore les cris de cet enfant" ["My aunt was killed by one strike of the machete. The baby that she was carrying on her back fell with her into the ditch. I can still hear the cries of this child today"] (24). Even more telling is that for Agnès, "son plus grand souhait est de faire des études de psychologie pour aider toutes les femmes violées" ["her greatest hope is to study psychology in order to help all raped women"] (101). This desire demonstrates an individual desire to reconstitute life in the aftermath of rape, as well as a collective vision for rehabilitating victim-survivors of sexual violence.

Featured along with Agnès, Clémence's experience speaks to one of the postgenocide issues that is prevalent in Rwanda: children born of rape. Clémence's testimony describes her rape and captivity in great detail (see fig. 5).

> Finalement, l'un d'eux m'ont emmenée et enfermée toujours nue, dans une pièce sombre. Le jour il allait travailler, c'est-à-dire tuer, piller, violer, humilier. . . . Le soir il me battait et me violait. . . . Lorsque je me suis retrouvée enceinte, j'ai d'abord eu honte. Mais aujourd'hui, je dois reconnaître que cette enfant est la seule richesse qui me reste. Je l'ai appelé Umumararungu, c'est à dire "celle qui me sort de la solitude." (103)
>
> Finally, one of them took me and locked me up, still naked, in a dark room. The day he would go out and work—by this I mean kill, pillage, rape and humiliate. . . . At night he would beat me and rape me. . . . When I found out I was pregnant, I was at first ashamed. But today, I have to recognize that this child is the only richness that is left to me. I named him Umumararungu, which means the one who comes to me out of solitude. (103)

As an example of the postgenocidal social problem of children born from rape, Clémence manifests one of the many fraught legacies for Rwandan society to confront. Like many of the women raped during the genocide, Clémence bears a child who will have the face of one of her perpetrators. She sits with her head tilted to the side, her mouth open as though mid-sentence, and her hands clasping either side of her daughter's face. The shadows of rape appear in these photographs through the faces of children who are the products of rape such as Clémence's daughter Umumararungu (27).

Figure 5. Clémence K., 22 ans, survivante du génocide and Agnès from *Les blessures du silence*. Photo credit: Alain Kazinierakis, *Les blessures du silence*

Two photographs are placed on a single page, one on top of the other and aligned with the binding of the book (see fig. 6). Both subjects are photographed with a dense forest of woods behind them. The trees and the bushes are not in focus; the women's faces are in the foreground against the blurred background of the woods. In the bottom photograph, the woman's eyes closed and her hands are raised, she appears to be in the process of remembering. The words beside her photograph read: "Il disait qu'il fallait que les enfants qui naîtraient à l'avenir soient obligés de demander à leurs parents à quoi ressemblaient les Tutsi et que toute femme tutsi devait être déshabillée afin que l'on sache comment étaient le sexe et la cuisse d'une Tutsi quand il n'y en aurait plus sur la terre" [He said that the children who would be born in the future must be able to ask their parents what Tutsis looked like and that every Tutsi woman had to be

Figure 6. Victoire M. from *Les blessures du silence*. 37 ans, survivante du génocide au Rwanda. Bernadette N. 59 ans. Photo credit: Alain Kazinierakis, *Les blessures du silence*

undressed so we could know what the sex and the thigh of a Tutsi woman was like for when there would no longer be any of them on earth] (68). It is only when we read her testimony later on in the book that we learn that she is quoting the words of Paul Akayezu, one of the ringleaders of the genocide who instructed men to rape and kill. The caption confirms the use of rape as a gender-specific way to affect the subsequent generations. Because the photographs do not always disclose the rape immediately, the documentation of the sexual atrocities primarily takes shape through the testimonies. As *Les blessures du silence* progresses, these stories occupy an increasingly important role and point to the diversity of experience within the genocide.

As an example of an older woman affected by the genocide, Bernadette gives further meaning to the range victims whose lives were irrevocably altered in 1994. She is a Hutu woman married to a Tutsi man who immediately names the longer history of the genocide, not fixing it in 1994. "Je n'ai vécu que les massacres des Tutsi, car je n'ai eu que des Tutsi comme époux. Mon premier mari a été tué en 1959" [I have lived nothing but the massacres of Tutsis, because I have only had Tutsis as husbands. My first husband was killed in 1959] (146). More than any of the other speakers, Bernadette references and points to her body, foregrounding the physical effects of the genocide and disclosing the details of her experience with torture. She emphasizes her corporeality in a way that draws the speaker to the wound. In the image her hand is up, palm facing her as though she herself contemplates the wounds on her flesh (fig. 6 top). "Regarde mes poignets, j'ai été ligotée avec une chambre à air. Regarde mon thorax, j'ai eu les clavicules et des côtes brisées. Regarde ce trou dans ma nuque. Regarde mon dos, mes genoux. Je suis handicappé à vie. On disait que j'étais une Hutu qui se battait pour les Tutsi. C'est pour cela qu'on m'a torturée" [Look at my wrists, I was tied up with a tube. Look at my chest, I had my collarbone and ribs broken. Look at this hole in my neck. Look at my back, my knees. I am handicapped for life. They said I was a Hutu who fought for the Tutsi. This is why they tortured me] (147). In her mention of the explicit injuries Bernadette calls attention to the corporeal elements of genocide. By doing so she actively refuses to have her experience with torture denied.

The final example that I would like to take under consideration is Victoire, a survivor interviewed who, like Valentine from *Sometimes in April*, describes the cultural center where Akayezu instructed the Interahamwe to rape Tutsi women in large numbers (see fig. 6). Victoire recounts the comments Akayezu made as he encouraged the men to rape Tutsi women. "Akayezu disait au Interahamwe: 'Vous devez sentir vous-mêmes le plaisir que l'on éprouve à violer une femme Tutsi.' Et les Interahamwe commençaient alors le viol. Les filles hurler de douleur" [Akayezu was telling the Interahamwe: "You should feel for yourselves the pleasure that one gets from raping a Tutsi woman." And the Interahamwe then began the rapes. Girls were screaming in pain"] (147). Here Victoire's words help to illustrate how, "the hate propaganda before and during the genocide fuelled the sexual violence by demonizing Tutsi women's sexuality."[86] As Victoire goes into the details of her testimony, we learn that she is raped repeatedly by at least ten different men and that her baby is also killed. Her interaction with Mukagasana demonstrates the "struggle shared between the speaker and the listener" in concrete ways.[87] Here, the listener has trouble receiving the story in a way that reflects (though it cannot not begin to mirror exactly) the difficulty the speaker has sharing it. Victoire's eyes are particularly striking—seeming half way closed they focus intently in front of her. Both her hands are held up and curved towards her body as though she is gesturing to herself. Victoire leans forward and is positioned as tilted in the frame as though to enhance our visual interpretation as a subject moving forward. The image of Victoire is striking for its active component that stands in contrast to the experience she describes. Taking her testimony from the interview and the image of her together suggests different ways of seeing Rwandese rape survivors. This view proves invaluable in wresting genocidal rape narratives from familiar scripts of violence.

Les blessures du silence also displays an interface between word and image that challenges preconceived and widely circulated notions about the genocide. Taken together, these images help mediate the ways in which spectators interact with viewed subjects who are often rendered both as abject and as object through their visual representation. The presence of interviews and the types of questions she asks allow Mukagasana to undo some of the traditional relations in which the "spectator is configured as the holder of rights and as their distributor to those who are unable to claim them independently."[88] Mukagasana's professed misunderstanding of human rights as a concept shows that she is aware of how human rights discourses fail to include the complex subjectivities like those of genocide survivors. We can read this as her pointed critique of the failures of human rights in the face of genocide. Even more, she offsets the traditional formula according to which a voiced listener takes the testimony of a voiceless speaker in order to confer rights upon the latter. By positioning herself as neither the one with the ability to confer human rights nor the advocate who brings the survivors to speech, Mukagasana does not succumb to the failures of traditional human rights testimonial narratives.

As such, her work invokes and challenges the visual field of human rights advocacy. Purposefully combining visual and narrative fields, *Les blessures du silence* takes on the difficulty of relating the testimonies of genocide survivors with some measure of fidelity to the complexity that their narratives engender. This complexity can be seen as a guiding principle for the entire genocide itself despite the desire to fix it into time and space and assign a singular meaning to it. Previous discourses of genocide demonstrate the ways that it is rhetorically similar to sexual violence—understood for what it symbolizes, but left uninterrogated for its multiple meanings and tangled operations.

Parsing out some of the dynamics at work in the visual representation of human rights discourses, in *Spectacular Rhetorics* Hesford questions the affective and political operations at work in the production of signs and images designed to do human rights work. As an example that engages the politics of recognition from multiple perspectives, *Les blessures du silence* is an especially provocative site of analysis in this regard. Given the ways in which "the visual field of human rights internationalism often functions as a site of power for and normative expression of American [and Western] nationalisms, cosmopolitanisms, and neoliberal global politics," it is important to think critically about the way visual images of the Rwandan Genocide operate in the larger context of human rights advocacy.[89] The examples in the collection demonstrate that "human rights defenders fight for international recognition and visibility in a global marketplace that tends to recast structural inequalities, social injustices, and state violence as scenes of individual trauma and victimization," a practice that is especially applicable to rape representation both within and outside of the context of war.[90]

Conclusion: The Politics of Rape in Postgenocide Rwanda

Almost two decades after the Rwandan genocide, the twenty-first century has brought forth multiple cinematic and literary representations of its occurrence.[91] Especially because of the media recognition of *Hotel Rwanda*, these representations have garnered attention from larger audiences for whom the actual genocide went on practically imperceptibly. In many ways, the popularity of these texts signifies international guilt and anxiety about the way the genocide was ignored when it first occurred. Like former President Bill Clinton's creation of the Clinton Global Initiative which he explains as a way to rectify the wrongs of his authorization of U.S. inaction in Rwanda, these initiatives often tell us more about who articulates them rather than about what they actually express.[92] A larger project can be perceived in much post-genocide cultural production: educating people about what happened so that, as Mukagasana implored, it will not be acceptable for genocide to be "reproduced elsewhere." Yet, currently another genocide rages on in Sudan, and the effects of Rwanda are still causing deadly conflict in the Democratic Republic of the Congo. To discuss the implications of *Murambi, L'ombre d'Imana, Sometimes of April* and *Les blessures du silence*—texts that offer textured understanding to the layers of violence endemic to genocide—is to hope that the necessity of these types of projects for remembering genocide will not continue in perpetuity. In the context of rape, the international trials that followed the genocide marked an important moment: one of the first times that perpetrators of rape were tried for crimes against humanity.[93] The recognition of rape as a crime against humanity is one of the groundbreaking, though overdue, achievements of the Arusha Tribunals, underscoring that this success should be met with cautious, measured enthusiasm.

When we consider rape representation and genocide in the context of literary and cultural criticism, we are still left with the problem of representation. The problematics of trauma and memory ensure that representation will remain at issue when literature, photography, or film seeks to portray the genocide. Likewise, the global existence of a "rape culture," denying the experience and the significance of rape narratives, ensures that representations of rape will map contested spaces.[94] Perhaps the most important accomplishment of the examples under consideration from *Murambi, L'ombre d'Imana, Sometimes in April,* and *Les blessures du silence* is that they suggest that alternative representations are possible. These possibilities are embodied by representations that do not revictimize the victim-survivors of genocidal rape, do not trivialize the experience of those who suffered during the genocide, do not erroneously suggest that rape occurs only in times of war, and do not dilute the traumatic experience of thousands and their dead.

Examining genocidal rape is one way to understand the layers of violence grafted onto Rwandan history. Instead of standing as a sign for something of fixed and stable meaning, rape becomes a figure of dynamic divergent multiple meanings, indicative of the different registers, origins, and implications that result from it. This is not to say that rape becomes a sign of everything else rather than being the sign only of violation. Indeed, rape figures as a symbolically dense iteration of violence that illuminates its complexity rather than freezing its significance. Whereas the previous chapters of this study challenge, question, and unsettle the use of rape metaphors, here I have focused on the deployment of rape representation as a more useful and fruitful way to portray genocidal violence. By mapping a cartography of genocide that closely considers rape, I have attempted to abandon some prevailing genocide mythologies, showing that focusing on the multiple meanings of sexual violence in this context is a way to think about genocide *differently* and that cultural production is a useful way to imagine these possibilities.

5

Regarding the Pain of Congolese Women

Narrative Closure, Audience Affect, and Rape as a Tool of War

> Everyone speaks on behalf of Congolese women, but when do we really hear their voices?[1]
>
> —Shana Mongwanga

> Where there [are] mines [in eastern Congo], there are communities. But it's not easy for them to exploit it with the presence of the communities. That's why they use their weapons and sexual violence to intimidate the population to move from places where there are mines. Because they know that the woman is the heart of the community, so they fight on her body, by using rape.[2]
>
> —Chouchou Namegabe

IN HIS REFLECTIONS on the use of drama as a vehicle for social change, Robert Skloot writes, "plays do things to people. What the theatre can provide uniquely is a connection between human beings and among groups *through the creation of empathy*. It is a connection that, however brief, creates visible, remarkable humane possibilities.'"[3] Still, the pursuit and achievement of empathy have limitations when viewed in relation to representations of sexual violence. What is the line between the need for the empathic connection and the articulation of personhood for those in whose name these connections are made? What ramifications come into play when achieving connection through empathy obscures the subjects of drama or documentary? Specifically, I question the cultural and rhetorical significance of empathy and sympathy, which often run the risk of resulting in misrecognition and affective denial of the so-called "subaltern subject" of wartime rape in the Democratic Republic of the Congo (DRC).

This chapter explores these questions by looking at the way rape as a tool of war in the DRC has been documented, dramatized, fictionalized, and visualized on screen, on stage, and in print. As the longest and deadliest ongoing war on the entire continent, the conflict in the DRC has resulted in the highest loss of life—up to 5 million dead today—since the Second World War and has earned the title of "Africa's World War." Turning to the subject positions of Congolese women victimized through wartime rape, I examine the construction of personhood in relation to the use of narrative closure both as an attempt to resolve the conflict and as a way to generate intimate affective responses from the audience. I argue that the appeal to the audience's affect infringes on rape victim-survivors' subjectivities, and I expose the problems with these techniques. The chapter analyzes a series of texts about the use of rape as tool of war in the DRC to explore what the subject positions of the women involved in these conflicts reveal about the limitations of the human rights project, a framework that these texts often invoke.

The approach of this chapter is interdisciplinary across genres, mirroring the technique used in the previous chapter and specifically by Véronique Tadjo in *L'ombre d'Imana*. First, I argue that the form, the aesthetic of multiplicity, offered in *L'ombre d'Imana* is an explicit and intentional attempt to grapple with the inexpressibility of the genocide. Then, I consider the effectiveness and limitations of specific genres as well as visual, narrative, and dramatic techniques to represent the lives of wartime rape survivors in the DRC. I am interested in how formal choices inform projects centered on representations of wartime rape, and the ways that grappling with the use of form can be more broadly situated in terms of the confines dictated by scripts of violence. In my discussions of Lisa Jackson's documentary *The Greatest Silence: Rape in the Congo*, Sherrlyn Borkgren's photodocumentary *Forever Changed: Berrlyze's Story*, the plays *Ruined* by Lynn Nottage and *Les recluses* by Koffi Kwahulé, and finally the documentary *The Road to Bukavu* by Shana Mongwanga, I critique the investment in narrative closure as a way to manage these stories of suffering, asserting that the deployment of devices to garner empathy, sympathy, and compassion can severely compromise the visibility and viability of Congolese women as subjects. In an effort to articulate the problems with cultural production that tries to render the idea of wartime rape manageable for the audience through an appeal to emotion, this chapter unpacks how these stories cohere and asks why techniques to represent the conflict in the DRC so often return to emotion as a way to lay hold of the conflict.

I interpret these techniques as attempts to achieve narrative closure that seek to resolve the conflict not as a way to suggest possibilities for the subject but rather as a way to provide a manageable, more enjoyable experience for the viewing audience. In its critique of human rights logics and its attention to the way women and girls are configured in these representations, this chapter is in theoretical conversation with Hesford's *Spectacular Rhetorics: Human Rights, Visions, Recognitions, and Feminisms*, Rebecca Wanzo's *The Suffering Will Not be Televised: African American Women and Sentimental Political Story Telling*, and Susan Sontag's *Regarding the Pain of Others*. Hesford is particularly instrumental in helping me illuminate the way the rhetorical framework and underlying logics of human rights law are inflected by the politics of recognition and visibility in ways that limit its advocacy for the human. Wanzo's *The Suffering will not be Televised* helps foreground the legibility and audibility of black women's suffering in relation to the use of sentimentality and emotion, whereas Susan Sontag's study articulates problematics and politics at play in the visualization of global atrocity. Together, these studies lay the groundwork for the my intervention that critically interrogates the role that other people's emotions and human rights discursive frames play in the way we "regard the pain" of Congolese women. The methodologies I deploy offer frames for thinking more deeply about black women's visibility in ways that are affective, bodily, psychological and material. To this end, the texts are each informed by different visions, presented in the visual mediums of documentary, drama, and photodocumentary. By beginning with Jackson and ending with Mongwanga, I chart a path of possibilities for the relationship between viewing and visibility.

Can the Subaltern Survivor Speak? Lisa Jackson's *The Greatest Silence*

Lisa Jackson's documentary film *The Greatest Silence: Rape in the Congo* (2008) introduces provocative questions about the usefulness of the documentary genre in rape representation. Along with the stories of the women who have been raped, the film also uses interviews with experts in the Congo, including government officials, women activists, and anti-rape advocates. Among the anti-rape advocates there is a clinician, Dr. Denis Mukwege, the gynecologist founder of Panzi Hospital, renowned for treating women with injuries caused by sexual violence.[4] Jackson uses her personal narrative of sexual violence as a point of departure for documenting the stories of women who were raped during the war. The documentary links a general culture of impunity and the war zone atmosphere to the incidence of rape. The first words of the film establish that "rape has always been used as a weapon of war," so the viewer has a context for the type of sexual violence to be portrayed.[5] Citing the long historical use of rape a tool of war signals that the DRC is not, and should not be considered, unique. Jackson is careful to delineate that the use of rape as a weapon of torture and as a military strategy is far from exclusive to the DRC.

The film's title, *The Greatest Silence: Rape in the Congo*, invites questions about the use of silence as a discursive practice for anti-rape advocacy in the region. Throughout this book, I have argued that the use of silence as a textual and extratextual trope of rape representation requires steadfast interrogation. The language of silence surrounding sexual violence suggests that only through literal speech acts can survivors begin to dismantle these discursive hierarchies. Phrases like "stop the silence," "break the silence," and "shatter the silence" instruct survivors to vocalize their experiences of violation. The omnipresence of silence should be understood in at least three ways. First, it signals the societal lack of response to rapes that occur. Second, it is the silence surrounding the subject of sexual violence in general. Third, it denotes the power of rape to force survivors into silence about their experiences, stripping them of voice and of the power of enunciation. Indictments of silence assume that the act of enunciation allows the subject to articulate posttraumatic pain and to become an agent of change in transforming a rape culture of silence.[6]

In a world that perpetually disbelieves narratives of rape and in a society in which stigma cleaves to sexual violence, breaking the silence is an important constitutive step on the journey into selfhood, personhood, and healing. Yet focusing on silence inevitably re-inscribes binaristic terms that entrench the opposition of rape victims and survivors. Demanding silence restricts the victim/survivor's right to subjectivity, whereas emphasizing silence can deny the experiences of those who actively resist it. The unequivocally negative interpretations of silence also fail to enable recuperative readings in the way silence functions for rape survivors. It is especially important to consider more fully the way silence could be interpreted as an essential part of the survivor's chosen response to trauma. As Tom Maguire explains, "in work on trauma narratives, attention is drawn to the importance of silence within the testimonies of survivors. Such moments of silence are regarded as sites of witnessing which are bounded by, but not articulated within, language."[7] But the notion of witnessing has its own problems. The affective politics of witnessing displace, replace, and often objectify the suffering subject. From this point of view, silence should be analyzed in terms of its structural presence and narrative significance rather than merely as part of a larger discursive framework for describing inaction and ignorance toward rape.

To which silence does the writer-director refer in her title *The Greatest Silence*? The use of the superlative positions this silence in relation to other silences, but which silences? For whom does this silence exist? On the one hand, she seems to reference the international community's lack of awareness about rape in the Congo. Scholars, journalists, and activists working on the subject also use this lack of knowledge to frame their work. Referring to the "silence and inaction of the international community in the case of the Democratic Republic of the Congo," Ngwarsungu Chiwengo points out that "the atrocities—the massacres, rapes, displacements of population, assassinations and Hutu genocide remained veiled in silence because of the Rwandan genocide."[8] Chiwengo's point is that the Rwandan genocide has eclipsed surrounding conflicts in the Great Lakes Region that have emerged in its wake. Despite the fact that the war in the DRC is a direct result of the Rwandan genocide, discussions of the latter too often exclude the former. Likewise Jan Goodwin writes, "many are . . . unaware that the [DRC] is 11 years into a brutal conflict in which up to 4.7 million people have died—the highest number of fatalities since World War II."[9] References to silence as a way to portray the crisis in the DRC tacitly invoke the dynamics of recognition according to which silence is undone when the problems in the region are audible and visible to a Western audience.[10] In view of this, the "greatest silence" Jackson highlights through her title could relate to the specific geopolitical space of the Congo and the scope of the ongoing war. In public lectures, Jackson has indicated her desire to incite feminists and anti-rape advocates based in the United States into action regarding sexual violence in the Congo, suggesting that the silence belongs to her American peers.[11] However, in analyzing this reference to the international community, we are presented again with the problem of positioning. We are left wondering if the "subaltern survivor" can speak and when she does speak, to whom is she speaking? Can she be heard? Taken this way, the film suggests a need for the subaltern subject to speak directly to the West, duplicating the problems global feminists have had with mainstream Western feminist analyses of issues in the Global South. This troubling dynamic has long been a concern for transnational global feminists. In "Under Western Eyes," Chandra Talpade Mohanty explains, "universal images of 'the third world woman' (the veiled woman, chaste virgin, etc.), images constructed from adding the 'third world difference' to 'sexual difference,' are predicated upon (and hence obviously bring into sharper focus) assumptions about Western women as secular, liberated, and having control over their own lives."[12] That is to say that too often so called Third World women are constructed only in opposition to white western women—these power dynamics are especially apparent when the self-presentation and re-presentation are juxtaposed. *The Greatest Silence* offers one example for how this works because of the presence of women from the United States and the DRC. When we consider what Hesford has referred to as the "ocular epistemology that underlies both documentary [filmmaking] and human rights advocacy," Jackson's film title can be read as further reifying the need for recognition by the West as a way to confer human rights.[13] These ocular logics are significant in the context of human rights advocacy, which relies on making visible people who suffer human rights atrocities. Seeing is an important part of advocacy, and victims are often called to testify to their experiences before others in order to attract interest in their causes. The power dynamics at work in the way the subject is configured to be seen or made visible become especially troubling when these visions are orchestrated through vehicles ranging from documentary film and still photography to journalism. Visual representation plays a role in human rights discourses that situate the spectator as the one who can see and the victim of atrocity as one to be seen, creating a dynamic that can easily undermine the personhood of the latter.

The film's title unintentionally rehearses neocolonial scripts about Third World women that position First World women as fundamental to their liberation. Jackson is unknowingly complicit in some of the damaging dynamics that imbue the discourse of sexual assault with stereotype. On the one hand, she is at times self-critical about her practices. For example, she questions her original impulse to bring the women gifts of nail polish and perfume. Commenting on what she brings to the women, she says, "now the gifts feel meager and a little pathetic. These women need their lives back and I bring them J. Lo's new fragrance." This type of awareness shows that Jackson is able to think critically about her position and her project.

Jackson also poses questions that reveal less awareness of her positionality. She asks "questions that [she] always wanted to ask her own rapists," as though the Congolese men can stand in for the Washington, D.C. men who attack her.[14] The implicit racial dynamics here are disturbing despite the statistics that most rapes in the United States happen intraracially rather than interracially. We are left to wonder why Jackson must travel to the African continent to find men who can stand in for her attackers. Because the Congolese women are left out of the opening scene in which the director questions the perpetrators, here we are pointedly reminded of the way the suggestive myth of the black male rapist who violates white women obscures the stories of black women.[15]

As the film opens, the women (the "subaltern" survivors) do not speak. Ironically, despite the expressed desire to overcome "the greatest silence," the documentary begins with interviews of men, dressed in military fatigues or rebel uniforms, who have identified themselves as rapists. The perpetrators are given voice and the capacity to mount their defense. Later on, these perpetrators tell their tales of war: "If she says no I have to take her by force."[16] The first stories that the film relays belong not to Congolese women victim-survivors but to armed militiamen responsible for rapes. Another potential problem with filming victims of rape in the DRC is how overdetermined that particular representation has become, making it almost an urtext for the spectacle of sexual violence. One need only think of the constant reference to the DRC as "rape capital of the world" to recall how spectacular representations of rape in the Congo have become. How cultural workers can productively negotiate that spectacularity is one of my concerns here. Jackson's conversations with these perpetrators do little to disengage or complicate the spectacular nature of rape in the Congo. The perpetrators qualify their actions, explaining that "this is all happening because of the war."[17] According to them, rapes occur through no fault of their own but rather because of the current state of conflict. Participation in the war explains acts of sexual violence. Their flawed logic explaining why they rape suggests that to them, rape is acceptable and that rape is an expected and inevitable consequence of war. Displacing accountability portrays them as victims; their actions are dictated by the war. Through them, we learn that in the DRC, rape and other forms of gender-based violence are pervasive war tactics and that the female body is but one more combat zone.

The film is unabashedly self-reflective. Jackson repeatedly associates her personal narrative as a rape survivor with the stories of the women she documents. In the first twenty minutes, she uses different techniques to connect her own survivor story to those of the women she interviews. She explains, "I understand a little bit of what they are going through. I [go] to the Congo hoping that if I tell them a little bit of my story [they] would break the silence surrounding theirs."[18] Positioning herself as an exemplar for standing against rape, Jackson's empathy and experience are the documentary's point of departure. She describes her own experience: when she was walking home from work one day in Washington, D.C., she was gang raped by three men. The case made headlines; although the men were never found, there were articles by and about her in well-known national media outlets such as *The Washington Post* and *Newsweek*. By asserting her hope that telling this story will allow the women to "break the silence" surrounding theirs, Jackson positions herself as an agent of transformation enabling these women to disclose their own rape stories.

Here the positioning of African women as suffering object recalls Wanzo's carefully elucidated argument that "the reliance on the subject/object split through sympathetic identification [adheres to] the sentimental tradition."[19] Empathy and sympathy are central to *The Greatest Silence* because Jackson's empathy establishes her as the one to tell this story, and the Congolese women are situated as the object of spectator sympathy. On the one hand, the distinction between empathy and sympathy is significant in that they each denote different emotional registers, but on the other hand the emphasis on either destabilizes the affective authority of their objects. Whereas one of the important roles of testimony is that it "is given the value of accumulated knowledge when it positions the listener as enabling the victim to work through trauma," Jackson's film appears to foreclose this option for the victim by circling back to her own story and back to the way the testimony enables her as a victim and a listener to work through her trauma.[20] Missing from this dynamic is the way the telling influences the women who share their testimonies with the director. I am critical of the way empathy (which designates the ability to *feel* the experience of others because you have experienced it yourself or can imagine it) and sympathy (which centers on feelings of care for the suffering of others and a desire to comfort them) function in these examples because they obviate the women who are on the receiving end of those emotions. The Congolese women's stories are curiously absent, with the exception of a few shadowy presences in the film. The problem with the way empathy and sympathy function in this documentary lies in how they become the dominant focus that obfuscates other parts of the story. In her sustained analysis of how empathy and sympathy figure into the stories of black women's suffering, Wanzo argues cogently that "a major ethical problem with using sympathy and compassion as the primary mechanism for political change is that sentimental politics depends on the cultural feelings of those in power, and the disempowered must depend on patronage."[21] Similarly, here the overreliance on empathy diminishes the standpoint of the black women survivors who are intended to be the subjects of the documentary. This dynamic reproduces conventional power relations.

Jackson's stance seems to assume that the women in the DRC require a (Western) vehicle in order to be able to tell their story; before arriving, she anticipates occupying this role. The documentary's stated objective is to make audible the voices of Congolese women. Moreover, it demonstrates Spivak's corollary to the question of whether the subaltern can speak—the question is not whether subaltern women can speak but rather whether they can be heard. To this I would add that even beyond this dialectic of speaking, silence, and voice is the issue of hearing and listening. As the introduction of the book demonstrates, there is no longer any doubt as to whether or not the subaltern *can speak*, the more compelling questions are now about listening. As the so-called subaltern speaks is she listened to and by whom? How does listening take place? At issue for me is how Jackson's overidentification with the women she seeks out leads to a disidentification of the Congolese women, or hyperawareness of the difference between the women. This in turn results in the othering of the Congolese survivors. The insistent insertion of Jackson's narrative suggests the need of a Western subject to mobilize awareness and understanding of the rape of Congolese women.

Despite these troubling beginnings, as the film advances, Jackson's story becomes less prominent. The women's testimonies of their rapes are scattered throughout the documentary. Marie-Jeanne is the first to relate her experience with rape: "They found me in my house. I was ill and five months pregnant. They held me. My husband ran away. Then the soldiers took me. There were five soldiers. They all raped me. . . . I know that wherever I go people will say 'that woman was raped.' I hated myself and blamed myself for what had happened."[22] Here she explains what happened before and during the rape, as well as the emotions she experienced afterward. By naming self-hatred, self-blame, and shame over this experience, she reproduces the psychological effects of rape, feelings that Jackson identifies with. The filmmaker tells her that "she [Marie-Jeanne] was wrong to blame herself for being raped but that I [Lisa] had done the same thing," to let Marie-Jeanne know that she understands and empathizes with her situation. As the first of the stories told by one of the Congolese women in the film, Marie-Jeanne's approach emblematizes the way the rape narratives of these survivors are present in *The Greatest Silence*.

The stories are told in multiple settings to different people. We see a center that helps women who have been victimized by rape. We meet women being treated in Panzi Hospital. There are also the women who belong to the church group that was created for survivors. Some of the women running the program in the church also travel to small villages to assist other women who have been raped. This diversity is also reflected in the way the stories are told and to whom they are told. Marie-Jeanne tells her story directly to the filmmaker, whereas Chantal tells her story to Honorine, a police officer who is "Bukau's one woman special victims unit." Honorine listens to and documents Chantal's testimony in order to prosecute the perpetrator. That Chantal chooses to testify against her perpetrator sets her apart from many of the women in the film. Jackson is quick to point this out, as well as to point out that Chantal's age is what makes an eventual conviction possible. Still, Chantal's story agitates the conception of Congolese as silenced victims unable to respond or react to their rapes.

In another setting at someone's home, a woman talks about being impregnated after her rape. "I was 15 years old when they raped me. . . . It was the Interahamwe, and they raped me. And I became pregnant. I have a daughter. Her name is Lumière. Light." Hearing this, the interviewer asks, "Is she a light for you?" to which the woman responds, "No I was obliged to take her. . . . There is nothing I can do about the past. But sometimes I spend the day crying." This interaction is telling because the woman cannot be fixed into a simple story of healing and redemption after rape. This story of children conceived out of rape diverges significantly from what we saw with Clémence's story in *Les blessures du silence*, for whom the child offers consolation. In this case Chantal gives her child the name Light not because she has been healed or moved to see the light in her experience; she has just chosen that name. Through her, the viewer observes the different ways to respond to sexual violence, reminded of how difficult it is to achieve coherent stories of healing and to move beyond rape.

During one of the film's final scenes, a group of women gathers to share stories of sexual violence with one another in the church. At least five or six different women are filmed sharing their experiences with rape. They comment on the patriarchal culture: "And more than once we went to the village chiefs to explain the problem, and they did nothing. They talk about parity between men and women, but this is a dream for us, impossible! We are considered half human beings." The women acknowledge the ways that telling their stories to one another offers an outlet for what they experience. Their understanding is important because they are gathered not for the purposes of the film, but as part of a regular gathering of women there to tell their stories to one another. Hidden from view, Jackson drops from the position of privileged spectator. Instead, we get the sense that the women tell the stories for each other as a way to recognize and to be recognized.

This desire for self-recognition is also reflected in the moment when Jackson turns the screen around on the camera and allows the women to see themselves. Aware that their stories will be disseminated for a foreign audience, they long to also see for themselves. This moment is especially profound when considered in light of the politics of recognition that inform human rights advocacy projects. In this practice, the viewer must recognize the victim of human rights atrocity; less important is the way the victims see themselves or whether they even see themselves at all. Though fleeting, this glimpse into the camera presents the opportunity for resignification because it literally shifts the gaze from object to subject.

Like all films, *The Greatest Silence* calls forth questions about the gaze and the locus of power used to document sexual violence. From her place behind the camera, Jackson is positioned as the film's principal gaze. She looks at the women, hears their stories, renders their bodies visible and their voices audible for the audience. The audience sees what Jackson sees; we occupy her vantage point in witnessing what the women have endured. This dynamic also reinforces the idea that "the other, even when not an enemy, is regarded only as someone to be seen, not someone (like us) who also sees."[23] Several techniques reinforce the outsider positioning of the audience in relation to the film. For example, Jackson's documentary is also about the Congolese landscape from a historic, political and geographic perspective. The film first premiered on HBO, and the historical sketch at the beginning of the film reveals that it is intended for Western spectators without basic knowledge of Congolese history. These descriptions take the viewer from King Leopold's exploitation of the country's riches to the end of colonialism, and from the brief career of Patrice Lumumba to the thirty-year plunder under dictator Mobutu Sese Seko. The narration of these events occurs in Jackson's voice as the camera surveys the land. In long shots of nature, the narrator extols the beauty of the land and its fecundity, citing natural resources as the camera displays lush fields and mountains.

The beauty of the land contrasts starkly with the brutalities that unfold there. As the camera lens glides over the idyllic countryside, the narrator's voice confirms, "looking at the beauty you would never know the country is at war."[24] This narrative implicitly alters the legacy of colonialism by connecting the land (and by extension its indigenous inhabitants) with violence. The majesty that Jackson introduces alludes to a premodern African topos, unbrutalized by war. The landscape tells another story, which proves crucial to understanding the Congo crisis as a story about the land. The land and especially its resources—whether gold, diamonds, or coltan—can stand in opposition to or in union with the female bodies that are similarly plundered. Filling the lens with this look at the land calls forth the significance of the Congolese context, a history that is precolonial, colonial, and postcolonial. When we consider that so many of the Congo's crises have been bound to the country's topography, the easy deployment of symbolic language that establishes a parallel between the plundering of the land and the ravaging of women's bodies we saw at work in Chapter 3 of this study come into view once again.

From a cinematic standpoint, these panoramic views introduce us to the majesty of the Congolese countryside in the course of several minutes.[25] Focus on the land foregrounds the physical context of the war in a way that attempts to tell another story. By juxtaposing the beauty of the land and the "horrors of war," Jackson invites questions from the audience. The viewer is prompted to wonder, "How can such horrific things be happening in such a beautiful place?" In this way, she unwittingly participates in stereotypes about sexual violence that are inherent to a rape culture telling us that rape happens in certain places, to certain kinds of people.[26] Rape happens in the context of a man jumping out from behind the bushes, to a woman wearing a short skirt, during wartime. Even as she attempts to undo the notion that rape does not happen only to specific types of people in certain circumstances, Jackson's lens enables the discourses that she attempts to subvert. These narratives relate the exterior context of sexual violence to its interior occurrence, establishing a false dichotomy between the existence of rape and outward appearances. Jackson's stance and the film's intended audience combine to further distance us from the survivors who are enshrined in the greatest silence—othering them as a subaltern group and short-circuiting their ability to speak.

One of Jackson's first visits in the film is to a local non-profit established to support the needs of rape survivors. She endeavors to connect with the women in a number of ways: showing them pictures of her home, her family, and her partner, and offering them gifts of perfume and nail polish, all as a prelude to sharing her rape story with them. The women's responses relay one of the film's most profound points, obscured in the determination to focus on subaltern narratives of rape. After Jackson discloses her personal experience with rape, one of the women asks how long the war in her country, the United States, has been going on. Like many, the woman who poses the question does not realize that both "developed" and "developing" countries are included in the global statistic that 1 in 3 women will be sexually or physically assaulted in her lifetime; Jackson does not dwell on this point either. This missed occasion represents one of the film's most significant limitations, not meeting its potential as a transnational project that addresses and engages the problem of sexual violence from a perspective that moves dialogically between the local and the global. In other words, by not pausing to consider the incidence of rape as a problem in terms of its specificity and then connecting it more broadly, *The Greatest Silence* constructs a binary that reinforces the distance between Third World rape victim-survivors and their Western counterparts.

Lisa Jackson is transparent about her subjective stance. In fact, Jackson's use of herself not only foregrounds the role of empathy, but also appeals to audience sympathy. This dynamic adheres to sentimentality, especially because, as Wanzo argues, "sentimentality is, above all, focused on the affect of the consumer . . . [and] . . . the sentimental narrative is often an important first step in attracting an audience for political issues; it simply cannot mark the end of political analysis."[27] *The Greatest Silence* is prototypical of a wave of twenty-first-century documentary films that shift away from objectivity to become increasingly individual and personal. As such, the film follows trends of the documentary genre, which depart from offering a set of representations that are unaffective and that are unaffected by personal inclinations. Yet in Jackson's documentary, this personal point of view comes with another set of problems when analyzed from the perspective of subaltern subject positioning. In its rhetorical structure, the documentary reinforces the notion that audience empathy and self-identification are necessary for entry into discussions about wartime rape, especially when the subjects are distant and different (in this case, Congolese). *The Greatest Silence* ultimately reveals that the desire to speak for the subaltern undermines the fact that survivors can speak and know their own conditions without mediation of a Western subject to facilitate discussions about their plight.[28]

When viewed in the context of Mohanty's landmark essay, "Under Western Eyes," which highlights the construction and "production of third world woman as a singular monolithic subject," it becomes especially clear that Jackson presents a script in need of interrogation and the critical lens of transnational global feminist praxis.[29] The reliance on this Western liberal framework for discussing Congolese women is common in the context of some strands of global or international feminisms that exploit the gendering of sympathy, according to which African women are eternally oppressed, subjugated, and victim to a patriarchal culture of violence. *The Greatest Silence* provides an example of the use of documentary film to unveil human rights atrocities, and how these films can be structured around the "framework of a modernized First World that should go in and rescue those facing yet another crisis in the Third World, always imagined as a region of aberrant violence."[30] The use of empathy provides a vehicle for the rescue to occur, and sympathy offers a gateway for negotiating the aberrant violence of rape as a tool of war. Together, these affects connect with the power relations that undergird the retelling of survivor stories through the nonobjective and object-rendering lens of documentary film.

"Staging a Woman's Complicated Relationship to the War": Lynn Nottage's *Ruined*

Lynn Nottage's play *Ruined* seems to stand in stark contrast to *The Greatest Silence*, although the artists' methods are similar. Both women travel to the DRC and, in Nottage's case, to the surrounding area to conduct interviews with women who have been sexually violated during the war and fled to refugee camps in neighboring countries. Nottage fictionalizes the accounts of the women she has spoken with, sliding their stories into the creation of characters. Like Jackson's documentary, Nottage's play demonstrates the need to achieve narrative closure that mobilizes affective responses from the audience. In *Ruined*, Nottage represents the use of rape in the DRC conflict by (1) subtly weaving the historic and political context of the war throughout the play, (2) creating a physical and literary vocabulary to "speak the unspeakable," and (3) dramatizing "a woman's complex relationship to the war" by focusing on female characters. Although these devices appear to be initially promising, the final move in which Nottage concludes the play with an appeal to audience affect undercuts the production of subjectivities that were previously at its core.

Ruined is based on interviews from women who were raped in the DRC, Uganda and Rwanda, although these narratives are never presented in a linear or straightforward manner. The title "Ruined" describes the condition of women who have suffered multiple rapes and mutilation to the point that they are physically disabled—permanently damaged and destroyed. Many of these women also suffer from a condition known as fistula, a hole or tear in the uterus leading to incontinence and excruciating discomfort. To tell this story, Nottage translates her interviews into a loose contemporary adaptation of Bertold Brecht's play *Mother Courage*. As a narrative strategy, the use of adaptation moves the drama away from the testimonial/interview genre from which it originates while it positions the African continental-based conflict according to a recognizable Western framework. Anchoring the play in this established dramatic tradition also calls attention to the theater as a medium for relating stories of war. But Nottage's play is markedly different than Brecht's in its establishment of women's bodies as a militarized zone in which conflict occurs. Director Kate Whoriskey traveled with Nottage to conduct the interviews of the women whose stories appear in the play and whose faces occupy the halls of the theaters where *Ruined* is performed. The photographs are also included in the written play's coda published by Theatre Communications Group in 2009. In the prefatory note, Whoriskey invokes a relationship between human rights and theatrical production that echoes Robert Skloot's point from the introduction of this chapter: "[Theater] has an incredible capacity for illuminating the unseen, reshaping history, bringing out empathy, and providing social commentary."[31] Likewise, in interviews, Nottage is especially adamant about offering a "theatrical experience not a journalistic message."[32] Her comments suggest that the lack of media attention, the scope of these human rights abuses, and the overwhelming numbers of women raped during the war motivate the form of and the need for *Ruined*. She also reveals that while creating the play, she searched for ways to negotiate and mediate these elements. Scholars on the intersection of gender and human rights like Elizabeth Goldberg have forcefully argued that "the place of women and children [is] in the global background to both event and representation in the context of human rights," yet the bodies of women and children are profoundly impacted by these conflicts.[33] For example, rape is often listed as one of the major atrocities of war. However, these references to rape as a tool of war serve as markers for the brutalization of women, without actually naming the specificity of their material, bodily and psychic injuries.

Taking on the effects of wartime rape, *Ruined* is heavily invested in global human rights issues, which it engages through the use of images and references, often leveling critique and social commentary about the way the war is being handled and perceived by the international community. But this positioning, the effort to shed light on the conflict for a Western audience, must be called into question as we consider the fraught topic of war and representation in Africa. As Goldberg indicates, "strategies for narrative representation of grave human rights violations share a common problem with the struggle against such violations."[34] The language of human rights has consistently fallen short as a framework with which to engage atrocities occurring on the African continent. Often "subaltern" women are merely situated as victims of so-called "backward" regimes of the Global South, in a discursive frame that positions them as victims and receives little interrogation.

Noting some of the problematics that emerge in images of war on the African continent, Susan Sontag explains:

> The more exotic the place, the more likely we are to have full frontal views of the dead and dying. Thus postcolonial Africa exists in the consciousness of the general public in the rich world . . . mainly as a succession of unforgettable photographs of large-eyed victims, starting with figures in the famine lands of Biafra in the late 1960s to the survivors of the [Rwandan] genocide. . . . These sights carry a double message. They show suffering that is outrageous, unjust, and should be repaired. *They confirm that this is the sort of thing which happens in that place.* The ubiquity . . . of those horrors . . . cannot help but nourish the belief in the inevitability of tragedy in . . . poor . . . parts of the world.[35]

Sontag's logic relies on the establishment of a local subject "we" (this place) and a distant "they" (that place), similar to what Lisa Jackson leaves implied in *The Greatest Silence*. By naming broken limbs and large eyes, Sontag highlights the use of the body in these narratives. Transforming from subjects into sights, they are emptied of their subjectivity, and they operate metonymically as the sign of suffering all over the African continent and in the Global South in general. Absent from these narratives is the way structural and institutional marks of the colonial legacy or contemporary cultures of globalization contribute to and in many ways provide a context for this suffering.[36] Some failures of human rights narratives involve the use of shorthand to frame conflict, the appeal to emotion to cause people to "care more," and the focus on resolutions that offer only short-term, unsustainable closure.

Although the project attempted to call attention to the crisis in the Congo, throughout the play Nottage places the war in the background or "at the door."[37] One way she achieves this is through design and technical elements, which create a space where war circulates but does not penetrate the main stage. By displacing the story from the conflict to how different women have been affected by the war and the way they respond to it, Nottage focuses on what becomes of the women during war rather than on the war itself. Through characters and settings, she places the war in the background and the women—the violence to which they are subjected and the ramifications of the violence—at the center of the narrative. Nottage accounts for the economic, social, and historic factors contributing to the war only through the use of sound and fleeting references in the dialogue. Interspersed social commentary by the characters also provides some context for the complexity of the conflict. The first mention of the war occurs in the second scene of the first act, as Mama describes how her life has changed as a result. "I open my doors, and tomorrow I am a refugee camp overrun with suffering. Everyone has their hands open since this damned war began. . . . I keep food in the mouths of eight women when half the country is starving" (14). Mama Nadi's comment reveals one of the paradoxes of her character as one who simultaneously provides for and exploits the women working for her. As the brothel owner, she orchestrates one of the patterns of war; because of the war, women's bodies are enlisted as prostitutes to provide pleasure for military and civilian men. In a way, these women in *Ruined* engage in in a form of survival sex—receiving shelter in exchange for the use of and profit from their bodies. For them being prostitutes benefits Mama Nadi more than it benefits them individually. Despite her professed protection of and care for the girls, Mama Nadi is complicit in their sexual exploitation.

Technical devices, such as the scene backdrop, props, and shrubbery surrounding the stage, call attention to the brothel environment. In the background, we hear shots, grenades, and bombs; at times, we see smoke. Soldiers burst into Mama Nadi's where they are instructed to leave the weapons (and the war) at the door. For a moment, and for most of the play's scenes, Mama Nadi's provides the illusion that the war can be kept at bay. As the doors to the space closes, the chaos of the conflict retreats. And yet it is omnipresent as a subtext that undergirds the script. A casual conversation about coltan seems to indict the global community's complicity in the war. The presence of a diamond that Mama obtains from a miner occasions a plot twist as well as a reminder that the conflict also revolves around natural resources. A quick reference to Mobutu vaguely reflects a fraught history of the DRC. These moments of dialogue offer a larger context for the conflict, though ultimately this conflict—its origins and details—is not as important as what happens to women as a result.

Perhaps one of the richest elements of the play is the use of music, which is used to distract from the war (see fig. 7). Music is a driving force in the play's plotline. Sophie's angelic voice combines with mellifluous soukous cadences, punctuated by rhythms to which characters like Josephine incessantly gyrate. In these boisterous scenes of club dancing, with Sophie's dulcet lyrics captivating the ears, the war dissipates further into the background. The music acts as another way to generate emotional responses from the audience by serving as a shield from the harshness of war and the insidiousness of prostitution. Sophie's songs inform this process of forgetting with the words, "You come here to forget/And drive away regret/

Figure 7. *Ruined*, Josephine (Zainab Jah) dancing for soldiers. Photo credit: Kevin Berne/*Ruined*, La Jolla Playhouse

And dance like it's the ending of the war" (20). The words of the song could apply to any of the characters in the play, not only to the soldiers and miners to which the bar caters. The girls have in many ways arrived at Mama Nadi's "to forget," just as Mama Nadi has managed "to forget" by creating her business. The song's irony lies in the impossibility of forgetting.

The illusion of forgetting continues through the use of the term *ruined* to describe the injuries sustained from repeated rapes and penetration with various objects. As the title of the entire play and the only word in the title, the word *ruined* is accorded immediate significance, and invites a series of questions. What does it mean to be ruined? What or whom precisely is ruined? Is this a term created by the playwright, or is it indigenous to the Democratic Republic of the Congo? According to Congolese radio journalist and feminist activist Chouchou Namegabe, *there is no word for rape* in Kikongo or Lingala, so the word used—*ubakaji*—was borrowed from neighboring Tanzania.[38] On the one hand, it could have been a technical or logistic choice because the language lacked a better word. But I want to suggest that *ruined* is used to establish the play's vocabulary of war to convey the act as having physical, social, and psychological ramifications. *Ruined* is used to name the unspeakable; it is a shorthanded way to recount an extreme amount of violence that in a way cannot even be quantified. The use of the past tense highlights the finite nature of what the women have experienced. Not only are they ruined, they have been ruined—it is a verb that describes what was done to their bodies and lives.

Although this suffering is evoked through the title and the use of the term, in the actual play, the word *ruined* is used sparingly. As few as the instances are in which "ruined" is spoken, there is more that is unspoken surrounding it. In the first scene of the first act, we learn via her uncle Christian that "Sophie. Sophie is . . . is . . . ruined" (12). The written text uses an ellipsis to sever the verb in two, indicating how difficult it is for Christian to speak the words. This happens again shortly thereafter as he attempts to urge Mama Nadi to take on Sophie; telling her, "the village isn't a place for a girl who has been . . . ruined. It brings shame, dishonor to the family" (15). As Jennifer DeVere Brody has argued, ellipses often act as "supplements to the printed matter in/of the text."[39] Here the supplemented knowledge evokes the difficulty of using the word ruined, leaving the devastating nature of what it means implied. In these early references, at no point do we learn exactly what is meant by this terminology. Leaving the audience without a definition or an explanation of what it means to be "ruined" establishes the literally unspeakable nature of what Sophie endures.

Instead of being spoken or written, her pain is performed through the visual—confirmed only through her physical presence, as she shuffles around the stage—and through her uncle's inability to discuss what had happened to her. Sophie's limp acts as a physical sign of being ruined; throughout the play, every time she moves on the stage, it is clear not only that she has trouble walking but also that she can barely move her lower body. Here the production of *Ruined* offers insight that the written script does not.[40] Attempting to convey to Mama Nadi the full extent of the damage, Christian explains, "Look, militia did ungodly things to the child, took her with . . . a bayonet and then left her for dead. And she was." Before he can finish the sentence, Mama cuts him off brusquely, the stage directions telling us that she "snaps"; "I don't need to hear it. Are you done?" (13). Here Christian's attempts to explain the way Sophie became "ruined" are halted and quickly cut off by Mama, who "does not need to hear it." In the final scene, we learn that Mama was also "ruined," changing the way we understand her refusal to hear these details. Reading the play, every time someone utters "ruined"—which itself becomes a euphemism for the brutality, extremities, and extent of sexual violence—the word is accompanied by a pause, a hesitation, or an ellipsis confirming the difficulty in naming the act and foregrounding the unspeakability of the violence, emphasizing the inexpressibility of the pain. In this way, silence becomes productive, telling us that when something is not voiced it is because there is more to be said, there are no words to describe it. Silence serves as an index of pain performing the unspeakability that Christian previously named.

Nottage has stated her interest in "staging a woman's complicated relationship to war," an intervention that is especially significant given the way that women's bodies, faces, and experiences during wartime have been obscured.[41] As Cynthia Enloe puts it, "rape evokes the nightmarishness of war, but it becomes just an indistinguishable part of a poisonous wartime stew called 'lootpillageandrape'"[42] To stage this relationship, Nottage uses the protagonist character, Mama Nadi, the owner of the bar/brothel who is equal parts shrewd businesswoman and doting mother hen. Interestingly, closely reading how Mama Nadi and each of the female characters operate in relation to the war suggests feminist politics implicitly at work in the play. Rather than present the expository act of writing sexual violence and showing the way the women were violated, Nottage goes a step further in making them subject by showing what the women do afterward and the way they attempt to go on in the face of lives that are supposed to be ruined. For some (Salima), the choice is death at their own hands. For some

(Josephine), the choice is to live sensually in sheer abandon, creating fantasies of escape with one's clients. Others (Sophie) plot to escape in other ways, whereas some (Mama Nadi) profit off the misfortune of women rendered homeless in the war.

Ruined relies on the grandeur of Mama Nadi to balance the narrative of women's pain, victimization and vulnerability (see fig. 8). Her story and person dominates both the text of the play and the material space on the stage. The character's narrative significance is underscored by the fact that she is the owner of the bar in which all of the action takes place, and she is performed as a loud, regal, and imposing woman who overtakes any scene she is in. As the stage instructions describe, she is "an attractive woman with an arrogant stride and majestic air" (5). Unafraid of standing up to rebel leaders or government commanders, Mama Nadi is a complex and often contradictory subject. These contradictions are especially apparent in her relationships with the younger women she claims to protect.

By the play's conclusion, this message of Mama Nadi's strength is compromised when Mama is forced to engage in sexual relations with one of the soldiers in order to protect Sophie. The final resolution also undermines this model of empowerment and independence because eventually Mama Nadi joins together with Christian, creating a love story that ends happily ever after. Mama's initial resistance to his advances were based on her desire for independence, recognition for how much she had sacrificed to intentionally construct a world where men were disposable. Although men were omnipresent and certainly were the reason for Mama's success (their business fuels her income), Mama's world appeared to be a matriarchal enclave in which she alone reigned. The fact that she simultaneously protects, harms, and threatens the girls also speaks to the ironic complexity of the character.

Establishing Mama Nadi as an independent, pioneering figure, *Ruined* presents another way of imagining Congolese women victimized by the war. Though victimized herself, she perpetuates patriarchy by running an establishment that caters to men. At the same time, however, by placing the girls in sexual relationships that operate transactionally, she diminishes the likelihood of them being assaulted as a tool of war. Mama Nadi's savvy business sense and shrewd nature inform the play's dialogues. She explains to Salima and Sophie that "If things are good, everyone gets a little. If things are bad, then Mama eats first" (17). The physical space of the play, which takes place entirely inside the walls of the brothel/bar, is dominated by Mama's presence. Her ownership and authority over the physical space stands in contrast to the control exerted over women's bodies in the

Figure 8. *Ruined*, Mama Nadi and Sophie (Tonye Patano and Carla Duren). Photo credit: Kevin Berne/*Ruined*, La Jolla Playhouse

war being waged outside her doors. Everyone who enters the place knows that, as Mama says to Commander Osembenga, "once you step through my door, then you're in my house. I make the rules here" (42). Mama Nadi's word of caution to the menacing commander places her in a position of power from which she is able to articulate the destiny of those in her surroundings. This power is compromised by the play's climax, when the soldiers storm the brothel in search of rebels, destroying the bar and brutalizing the women.

Up until the moment when she must cede power to Commander Osembenga, Mama Nadi holds her ability to maintain the brothel at a high premium, a sign of her ability to be independent despite being "ruined." At several intervals, she explains how she built her business with her own hands. "Since I was young people have found reasons to push me out of my home, men have laid claim to my possessions, but I am not running now. This is *my place.* Mama Nadi's" (91). The repetition of her name, after citing that this is her place, evokes a deliberate pride of ownership and belonging that Mama Nadi refuses to relinquish. This ownership defines who she is and who she becomes in the war. Explaining why she takes on the girls in order to give them a better life and to protect them from the war, Mama Nadi engages in a twisted postfeminist logic of patrimony. "My girls . . . ask them, they'd rather be here, than back out there in their villages where they are taken without regard. They're safer with me than in their own homes" (86). According to her logic, because they have been raped and shamed away from their villages, the girls are supposedly safer with her where they are not raped, even if they are still sexually disempowered. Girls like Josephine, whose "father was a village chief," now become prositutes to make life livable. The notion of ended and suspended lives informs our understanding of the play's unfolding and structures the narratives of each main character. Entry into the brothel is on the one hand a form of protection, and on the other hand the sign of an end of the lives the girls once knew. The only exception is Sophie, who is determined to find a way out of Mama Nadi's in order to escape the violence behind the forest trees and to find physical healing through reconstructive surgery by a doctor in Kivu. The irony here is that Sophie, the girl who is "ruined," refuses to resign herself to this fate and instead seeks to create alternatives for herself. She mirrors Mama Nadi's trajectory, the ways in which Mama, though "ruined," opened a bar and brothel, recreating herself as a businesswoman who offers temporary (if fleeting) refuge from the harshness of the war.

At no point in the play is rape explicitly staged, although the sexual aggression of the soldiers culminates in what appears as if it will be the rape of Josephine, until Mama Nadi offers to tell them where Salima is hiding. In "Signifying Rape: The Problems of Representing Sexual Violence on Stage," Lisa Fitzpatrick notes that "the difficulties of representing rape . . . are the problems of shaping physical, lived experience into a narrative that is heavily influenced by social and cultural discourses in both its construction for the theatre, and its reception in performance."[43] Reception might be one of the main reasons rape and sex are absent from the stage in *Ruined*. The story is difficult enough for the audience without the staged presence of the physical act of rape because it is materially present through Sophie's body. Every time Sophie winces, shuffles, limps, and stretches, she communicates her pain to the audience. For this reason, seeing *Ruined* performed influences how we perceive the pain in the play. The performance of sexual violence is relegated to and expressed through Sophie's pained body. Her lived experience of pain courses through her fractured body as she moves across the stage. The staging of this pain focuses our attention on the body's movements in different scenes.

One of the most harrowing scenes of *Ruined* calls attention to the body in a different way. This scene features a woman being "ruined" not through a scene of rape but rather through Salima's self-inflicted violence (see fig. 9). Although Salima is not physically "ruined" like Sophie, her life has been permanently damaged because of the war, and she chooses to die rather than continue to live in the ruins of the war, because of which she lost her family, her husband, her baby, and her ability to live in her village. Salima is held for five months in a pit where she is repeatedly gang raped by soldiers. When she finally escapes and returns home, her family and the entire village shun her. Her husband accuses her, saying that she brought the rape upon herself; as she says in her own words, "he called me a filthy dog and said that I had tempted them" (67). She arrives at Mama Nadi's brothel heartbroken and, as she soon learns, pregnant. The pregnancy drives one of the major plotlines in the play as she attempts to hide it from Mama, and Sophie devises a plan for both girls to leave the brothel. The story of Salima's relationship with her husband, a soldier who initially rejected her but then returns fully repentant and in search of his wife, is another major narrative arc that leads to the play's climax. In a scene where he enters Mama Nadi's to find Salima, she refuses to come out, then finally stumbles onto the stage covered in blood. Before her fatal collapse, she proclaims, "you will not fight your battles on my body anymore!" (94). Salima prefers to take matters into her hands and to cause her own death rather

Figure 9. *Ruined*, Salima's death. Photo credit: Kevin Berne/*Ruined*, La Jolla Playhouse

than be subject again to the varying degrees of violence she has endured in her lifetime. The cry, "you will not fight your battles on my body anymore," is an indictment of a culture in which women's bodies become spoils of war. War is gendered as masculine—the men are fighting, they are seen in fatigues dressed as soldiers and toting guns. But the women are often war's hapless victims for whom war translates into sexual violence. This dynamic militarizes women's bodies, subjecting them to constant violence. Sophie, Salima, and Mama Nadi's examples demonstrate that rape in the Congo happens because men wage war. It is unclear whether Salima was attempting only to remove the child from her womb or if she was committing suicide. But whether it is a botched abortion or suicide, Salima's act is an attempt to reclaim her body. By turning violence unto herself, she simultaneously participates in and terminates the cycle of violence in her life. When she declares, "you will not wage your battles on my body anymore," Salima acknowledges thousands of victims like her whose bodies have been enmeshed in the conflict in the Congo. Whether they are women who are held captive and are retained for men's sexual pleasure or women who (like Sophie) have been violently entered so many times that they are mutilated and "ruined," their bodies have become battlegrounds that men tread and trample over. But the statement and the act also express the hope for a future. She demands that women's bodies no longer be spaces of war; they will no longer be battlegrounds not because the war is ending, but because women will take matters into their own hands.

These feminist alternatives are fleetingly possible but ultimately untenable. The most glaring suggestion secured by the end of the play is that a character like Mama ultimately cannot exist. For women, independence is not possible in an atmosphere where their bodies are battlegrounds on which men wage war. A union with Christian is necessary for her survival. Though she initially resists this claim, protectively guarding her independence and self-made sources of power, eventually Mama succumbs to the advances of her suitor. In this way, the text segues into a romantic success narrative of overcoming that makes intimacy possible for the protagonist. By using romance to conclude *Ruined*, Nottage succumbs to the simplicity of narrative closure. Though the drama initially offers a female-dominated and female-inspired universe as an alternative to the war, or perhaps in spite of the war, it ultimately reproduces the notion that such a world is unsustainable and that women need men for protection, partnership, and romance. This romantic ending destabilizes the previously articulated messages of female survival devoid of male protection. The use of the romance as a method of narrative closure for the play appeals to the viewer's sensibilities and emotional need for a felicitous ending to a bleak story.

The desire for audience's empathy and sympathy can result in the objectification of the intended subject. As the subject becomes object, the empathic or sympathetic spectator's position is privileged. Sara Ahmed describes this in *The Cultural Politics of Emotion* when she points out that the "pain of others is continually evoked in public discourse, as that which demands a collective as well as individual response."[44] More emphasis is placed on the response, which can continue action and is therefore dynamic, whereas the original pain at issue remains static and frozen. This focus also displaces the significance of the character in question, replacing it with the viewer. The romantic turn at the end of the play can be interpreted as Nottage's attempt to transform *Ruined* from a narrative that moves beyond Congolese pain, suffering, and violence into a love story. By making the play into a love story, Nottage maneuvers away from creating a text in which audience empathy takes on the most central role, but this end result has its problems.

What Nottage offers as an alternative to grappling with the harshness of war is heterosexual coupling as a way to conclude the narrative neatly and harmoniously, leaving the audience to depart with positive feelings. The romance between Mama Nadi and Christian provides the narrative closure that the audience may desire and displays the tendency of "fictions about rape to depict rape survivors' successfully finding intimacy" as a way to create positive stories of restoration and healing.[45] The resolution displaces the story of Mama Nadi as a subject because immediately preceding her acceptance of Christian as her husband she reveals that she is "ruined." The short time between her disclosure and her collapse into his arms makes the resolution appear even less plausible. The problem with such a conclusion is that it flattens out the complexity of Mama Nadi as a character who has been "ruined" by suggesting that a solution to her condition is to be found in union with Christian. The elaboration of what happened to Mama Nadi is foreclosed in favor of appealing to the audience's emotional need for a happy ending. Concluding in this way, *Ruined* ends as a sentimental script that elides the multiple meanings of rape and upsets the formation of subjectivity, which seemed to be at its core.

Les recluses: Disrupting Narrative Closure

Koffi Kwahulé's play *Les recluses* complements and complicates this discussion of the role that narrative closure and audience affect play in stories of Congolese women's suffering. *Les recluses* is a poignantly feminist dramatic work that counters the depiction of Congolese women as suffering objects through technical, visual, and written strategies. Whereas the human rights framework emphasizes the need for resolution, Kwahulé's multidimensional understanding of conflict compels the audience to reflect on the difficulty of survival. Likewise, as an avant-garde theatrical piece, *Les recluses* diverges significantly from the realist model of Nottage's *Ruined*. Here I consider *Les recluses* for the way it underscores the intricacies of war by refusing a manageable, resolved narrative that would elicit a sympathetic response from the audience. This is achieved through techniques such as (1) the use of masks and gender-blind casting, (2) the use of technology through projected images of testimonials between each scene, and (3) the role of staging and dialogue to undermine the play's conclusion.

Like many of the cultural workers whose texts I examine, Koffi Kwahulé's exploration of sexual violence in *Les recluses* is consistent in his oeuvre. Violence figures prominently in Kwahulé's works in the form of incest, rape, war, torture, and serial killings. As John Conteh-Morgan and Dominic Thomas put it, "Kwahulé's theatrical sensibility is more immediately shaped by a contemporary world of social and domestic violence, a genocidal world of moral ambiguity."[46] For the playwright, the representation of violence is an essential aspect of his theatrical vision, which is ostensibly informed by his politics. *Les recluses* continues in and extends this practice of writing violence by focusing on the conflicts in the Great Lakes region.

Les recluses is an all-female production about a group of women who were raped during the war and who offer their stories as a testimonial to what they endure. The director's note specifies that this should be an all-female production: "Il est souhaitable que tous les personnages, y compris les personnages masculins, soient tenus par des femmes" [It is the author's wish that all the characters, including the male characters, be played by women]. This choice marks the beginning of Kwahulé's effort to use gender and performance as a way to challenge conventional understandings of the use of rape as a tool of war. Whereas *Ruined* was dominated by women because their stories were the focus of the plot, and their narratives more intimately explored, *Les recluses* goes further to achieve this focus through casting. The all-female universe can be interpreted as a way of re-imagining the dynamics of war, as it suggests that the absence of men offers a form of liberation that is otherwise impossible. The women in the play often move in union with one another, operating in the style of a Greek chorus tinged with the formations of a dance ensemble (see fig. 10). When viewed in the context of male absence, the play's insistent handling of women's stories of war highlights the multiplicity of these experiences and foregrounds the gendered dynamics of war and postwar reconciliation.[47]

Figure 10. Les recluses in Greek chorus. Photo credit: Danièle Pierre, *Les recluses*, Théâtre Varia

The role of the mask marks another technical decision that playfully undermines the straightforward and linear approach to representing the war (see fig. 11). The masks underscore the invisibility of the women, casting them as literally faceless. They also suggest that there is something else about the DRC conflict in general, and the use of rape as a tool of war specifically, that we cannot see and that is not readily visible, available, or penetrable. In many ways, the form of *Les recluses* is typical of Kwahulé's body of work. As Conteh-Morgan and Thomas explain, in the context of francophone theater, Kwahulé is part of a generation of "assertive practitioners who were critical and sometimes polemical exponents of new dramatic forms."[48] Indeed, the use of the avant-garde genre is particularly instrumental in creating a complex version of the war for the audience. The masks distance the audience from the characters emotionally and deny them access to fully engaging the subject matter at hand. This performance of distance and accessibility creates a power differential between the spectator and the actors because of which those on the stage are in the position of privilege. Ultimately the use of the masks inverts the power relations of postcolonial domination, neo-imperial intervention, spectator positioning, and African subject erasure through the denial of access. The denial of access creates a disturbing, unsettling experience for the audience that refuses to appeal to affective responses as a way to manage representations of war. Put differently, the masks help maintain a distance between the audience and the actor that effectively undermines the spectator/spectacle dynamic so essential to the logics of cultural recognition. By masking themselves, the actors refuse to be seen, indicating that recognition and visibility are not central concerns in the drama.

Les recluses revolves principally around the character of Kaniosha, a woman who was raped by soldiers and who is soon to be married to Nzeyimana, to whom she has not disclosed the violence in any detail.[49] Although they marry at the end, the marriage is not presented as a solution to Kaniosha's violent past or as a subversion of her independence, as we saw in *Ruined*. Kaniosha's is the main story, but it is only one of many that emerge. Overall, Kwahulé does not avail himself of the strategies for narrative closure at work in the previously examined works by Jackson and Nottage. Nonetheless, Kwahulé employs many of the rhetorical and thematic tropes of rape representation, such as the breaking of silences, the need for healing, the onset of shame and blame in the aftermath of rape, and the chaos of war. Those referred to as *"les recluses"* form a collective of women who have suffered wartime rape. This type of nomenclature signals a choice on the women's part to come together and to separate themselves from people

Figure 11. Les recluses masked. Photo credit: Danièle Pierre, Les recluses, Théâtre Varia

who have not been violated. The term is ironic because by definition a recluse leads a solitary life, yet the women by living together as a solitary collective contradict a pure definition of the term. The choice to separate is particularly significant in a larger context because of the social exclusion of women who are raped. As we saw with Salima in *Ruined*, women who are raped are often banished from their villages, forced to live outside of the community.

Even as it gathers these women together under the title of *Les recluses*, the play conserves their heterogeneity by staging a dialogic encounter with the multiple voices, registers, and perspectives. Overall, the play stages a jarringly disjointed and fragmented rendering of war and its effects. In contrast to the solutions offered by Jackson (self-referential and empathic entry to enable subaltern survivor story telling) and Nottage (sentimentally romantic conclusion), Kwahulé offers no resolute narrative closure for how to imagine, understand, survive, heal, and continue on after the war. The fractured dialogue underscores the dissolution of the subject in conflict; that is the way that conflict poses challenges to personhood. Emphasizing the voices of survivors, the play fluctuates between fictitious account and autobiographical narratives intersecting with human rights intervention, which privilege use of autobiographical testimony. The idea of testimonial as truth telling is central to human rights discourses, but many feminist scholars have forthrightly cautioned "feminists to resist seeking 'experience' or 'truth' outside of discourse . . . the challenge is to listen and learn from testimonials, visual evidence, and other markers of human rights abuses without presuming this evidence is transparent."[50] Adding the testimonies to the play as a part of, yet separate from, the main scenes, Kwahulé conjures the instability of the testimonial genre. Placing the projections on the stage as a part of the drama invites the audience to question their performance as well as their veracity. Including the projections in the play implicitly invokes their own constructed meaning.

Enunciation, through telling and speaking about rape, is central to *Les recluses*. The dialectics between remembering and forgetting, between telling and not telling, and between remaining silent and speaking are prolonged throughout the play in the dialogue and action. The play opens with Kaniosha's friends urging her to share the details of the rape with her fiancé. "Il comprend, tu sais. Il dit, l'essentiel c'est que vous en parliez. À moi ou à quelqu'un d'autre, peu importe, parlez-en [He understands, you know. He says it is essential for you to speak. To me or to someone else, it doesn't matter, talk about it]" (10). This directive to speak is similar to what we encounter with discourses in the rape crisis advocacy field where speaking is held at a high, undifferentiated premium. The possibility of disclosure is performed as a realizable possibility in the context of the play because so many of the survivors speak throughout. The decision to speak, and to whom to speak about her rape, is an important aspect of subject formation that Kaniosha grapples with throughout *Les recluses*. Even if she does not tell her story, her awareness that the story is hers to tell prolongs the idea that she has an ability to render what happened to her according to her own terms.

Still, the stigma of rape, a clear reason for silence in the first place, also informs the dialogue. Kaniosha explains that her wedding dress must be "la plus blanche possible" [as white as possible] . . . Pour couvrir. Effacer [To cover. To erase]." (11). Her reasoning is separated into different sentences (*Pour couvrir. Effacer.*) Isolated from one another in this way, the words question their possibility. The rhetorical question becomes, "Can rape be effectively covered or erased?"

Even in the presence of such far-reaching stigma, Kwahulé indicates different responses to sexual violence. Though he recognizes the overwhelming shame and guilt, the play also documents another response that is more attentive to the needs of the victim-survivor. Kamegué plays the role of a therapist, helping the survivor to negotiate the aftermath of rape: "Tu n'a rien fait, on t'a fait quelque chose, tu ne demandais rien, tu ne cherchais rien, mais c'est à toi d'expliquer au monde pourquoi cette chose-là t'est tombée dessus" [You did not do anything. They did something to you, you did not ask for anything, you were not looking for anything, but you are the one who has to explain to the world why this thing has fallen upon you] (11). The play's struggle with genre is stated in the first scene, which questions the role of theater addressing atrocity: "De toute façon, personne ne voit comment le théâtre pourrait soigner ça" [Either way, no one could see the way this theater could heal these things], as though to inquire into the role of theater in exploring narratives of wartime rape.[51] By openly asking how theater/performance could heal the aftermath of war, Kwahulé interrogates both the form being used and his position as playwright. Rather than suggest that theater makes healing and understanding possible, as Whoriskey and Skloot express, Kwahulé leaves the question about the role of the theater unanswered. As it continues, the form of the play contributes to leaving the question unanswered.

Perhaps the most consistent element holding *Les recluses* together is the repeated telling of women's stories. I will consider these stories in detail because unpacking their representation and the frequency of their occurrence reveals women's multiple subject positions and shifting relationships to the war. At the same time, analysis of the role of testimonials and the use of rape stories must be carefully executed. To this point, Ann Grossman has a helpful admonition: "Women's rape stories were framed in incredibly complicated ways, shaped by their audience and the motives behind their telling. Their experiences were ordered and given meaning within a complex grid of multiple images and discourses."[52] Analyzing the way these testimonies operate in the play means questioning the ways war rape stories are given meaning, especially when they adhere to the acceptable tropes of war. As we saw in the previous chapter, rape warfare often involves captivity, gang rapes, banishment, and children produced from violation. Unfortunately, quite often the reproduction of these scenes participates in atrocity spectacles that cast the tellers of the story as victims and those who hear the story as voyeuristic witnesses. Though these risks are undeniably in play, aesthetic innovation and creative strategies can help to recontextualize their effects. In other words, stylistic choices can create room for reframing the way rape testimonies operate in a larger system of representing violence.

WHEN KANIOSHA first tells the story of her rape, she recounts: "ils m'ont arraché mes vêtements, et ils m'ont jeté à terre, et ils m'ont menacé. . . . Ils étaient neuf, peut-être dix, peut-être plus. J'avais mal comme je n'avais jamais eu mal. Et surtout je me sentais comme de la boue, une boue dans laquelle se roulaient des porcs. . . . Mais c'est mon histoire! [They ripped off my clothes, and they threw me on the ground, and they menaced me. . . . There were nine of them maybe ten, maybe more. I was in pain as I had never been in pain. And more than anything I felt like mud, mud that pigs were rolling in . . . But this is my story!]" (14). Kaniosha relates how she feels both physically ("I was in pain") and psychically ("I felt like mud"). By characterizing herself as mud, she invokes the feelings of dirtiness and worthlessness that invade victims of rape.

In contrast to Kaniosha, Hélène M., who offers the second screen-projected testimony, goes into great detail about whom she spoke to after being raped. Hélène presents an example of someone who learns not to be silent:

Pendant la nuit, des hommes ont surgi dans la maison de ma grande sœur où je dormais. *Ce n'étaient pas des militaires, mais des bandits.* . . . J'ai souffert de ne pouvoir en parler à personne jusqu'à ce que quelqu'un me parle de la Maison des Femmes; elle m'a dit que l'on y accueillait les femmes comme moi, et qu'on les aidait à *guérir de leurs blessures*. Je me suis mise alors à fréquenter les groupes de la parole de la MDF et j'ai pu apprendre comment en parler à mon mari qui ne m'a pas répudiée. (25)

During the night, some men burst into my older sister's house where I was sleeping. *They were not military men, just robbers*. . . . I suffered from not being able to talk to anyone until someone spoke to me from the House of Women, she told me that they welcomed women like me, and that they helped them to *heal from their wounds*. I then began to frequent the speaking groups of the House of Women and I was able to learn how to speak to my husband who did not repudiate me. (my emphasis)

Hélène's testimony takes on three recurring ideas, or myths, about rape in the context of war. First, because she is raped by a group of bandits and not by soldiers, these remarks explicitly acknowledge that rape is used not only as a tool of war by men engaged in conflict. This distinction proves crucial to understanding rape as a global epidemic that occurs regularly both in and out of the context of war. By highlighting that the men were not in the military, Hélène reminds us that women's bodies have become militarized zones routinely subject to violence. Second, she points to the work being done on the ground in the region to help women heal, tell their stories, and gain support. Third, that her husband did not repudiate her also upsets the dominant perception of the way men in general react to rape. Projected onto the screen and offered as a live testimony, Hélène's story registers visually, thematically and discursively as a counternarrative to the stories that are shared on the physical stage.

Nahima also tells her story, which bears a resemblance to what happens to Kaniosha. "Voici l'histoire à laquelle j'ai toujours préféré celle de Kaniosha. Voici mon histoire. L'histoire de ce qui m'est arrivé" [Here is the story that I always preferred to Kaniosha's story. Here is my story. It is the story of what happened to me] (29). Introducing her testimonial narrative in this way foregrounds the ownership over the story as well as the inherent differences in the experiences of rape. Nahima's language articulates that even though there are many women subject to rape in the context of war, there are places where these stories converge and diverge. Her narrative also underscores the possible banalization that could occur through the frequent occurrence of rape when she states that *toutes les femmes que je connaissais l'avaient déjà subi* [all the women she knows had already experienced it (rape)], so to some degree she was expecting it. But even the frequent occurrence of rape cannot mitigate or reduce the pain she experiences when she is raped, a detail that effectively pushes against banalization. Throughout the description of what she suffers, Nahima also highlights both the similarities and the differences between her experience and that of other women.

> Toutes les femmes que je connaissais l'avaient déjà subi. Alors chaque fois je me disais, prépare-toi ma grande, bientôt ce sera ton tour; il n'y a pas de raison que tu n'y passes pas. Donc quand je les ai vu entrer, je me suis dit au moins après, ce ne sera plus que derrière toi. Ils étaient trois. Pour la forme, je leur ai parlé de mes bijoux contre. . . . Enfin disons ma vie. Ils m'ont dit, c'est la guerre, et la guerre est faite pour tuer. Mais ce qu'on va te faire, c'est plus que te tuer. Ils ont pris les bijoux et ils m'ont plus que tuée. La guerre vous réduit à n'être que de la viande. (29)

> All the women that I knew had already experienced it. So every time I told myself, get ready my dear, soon it will be your turn, there is no reason for you not to also experience this. So when I saw them enter [into my home] I told myself at least after this it will only be behind you. There were three of them. As for what happened, I talked to them about my jewelry instead of . . . well let's call it my life. They said to me this is war, and war is made to kill. But what we will do to you is more than kill you. They took the jewelry and they more than killed me. War reduces you to being no more than a piece of meat.

The speaker's understanding that she would eventually be subject to rape speaks to how frequently it occurs as well as how deeply women are socialized to understand it as a normal part of war. The widespread incidence of sexual violence causes women to expect that they will eventually fall prey to the use of rape as a tool of war. At the same time, it is still shocking when it happens to them. Defining what they did to her as "more than kill her," Nahima articulates one of the metaphors for rape sustained throughout *Les recluses*, in which the word *viol* (rape) is not once used, similar to what we saw in *Ruined*. The attackers are enumerated: "Ils étaient sept [There were seven]" (17). Their actions are referenced: "ce qu'ils venaient de nous faire . . . [what they just did to us]" (25) and "Quand le chef de poste a eu fini [When the chief of the post was finished]" (32). The time is stated: "Quand c'est arrivé" [when it happened] (39). The women alternately describe what happened to them as "what the men did" or "what the men took" and "when they finish" without ever explicitly naming it *rape*. These ambiguous descriptions do not merely reflect cultural norms for dealing with sexual violence. Rather than appearing to be an inability to name rape, this omission acts as a forceful commentary on the universality of rape. This omission at once undercuts and sustains the unspeakability of rape. On the one hand, the word *rape* is never used, making it unspeakable, but on the other hand the women access so many ways to articulate rape that is proves to be hyperspeakable. If the unspeakability of rape adheres only to the word itself rather than to its physical and material aspects, along with the trauma that follows, it remains significant at the level of semantics rather than the level of politics. Renaming rape becomes an important signifying practice in the face of trauma because it allows victim-survivors to speak of rape the way they want to speak of it rather than through a predetermined codified vocabulary used in advocacy and human rights discourses.

The individuated narrative testimonials interspersed throughout the text accentuate the multiple subject positions inhabited by Congolese women rape survivors. These testimonials remind us that in addition to being multivocal, *Les recluses* is also a multimedia performance. Through the use of projected images, Kwahulé presents the testimonies of survivors of war in between each scene of the play. The women whose stories we hear have been raped, and in the projected scenes they narrate the story of what happened to them. Set against the backdrop of the primary story unfolding in the play, Kaniosha's imminent marriage to Kamegué, these visual images tell a different story. In the text of the actual play, they are separated onto their own pages, numbered and contained in the space of one paragraph with the title "Témoignage d'une recluse" [Testimony of a recluse]. The testimonies are structured in identical ways. First, the "recluse" gives her first name and first initial of her last name, her occupation, and where she lives, followed by her age and an explanation of what happened to her. This form is quite similar to what we saw at work in Mukagasana's use of testimony in *Les blessures du silence*. In *Les recluses*, Rose N. states:

> La première fois, c'étaient des militaires. Ils ont surgi dans la maison avec des voisins. J'étais enceinte. Ils étaient sept. Ils ont exigé que mon mari soit présent pour tout voir. . . . La seconde fois, cela s'est passé sur le bord de la route. J'allais chercher des marchandises. Ils étaient deux. Ils n'étaient pas militaires. Sur le bord de la route. Des gens allaient et venaient. (17)

> The first time, it was military men. They burst into the house with some neighbors. I was pregnant. There were seven of them. They demanded my husband to be present to see everything. . . . The second time, it happened

on the side of the road. I was going to buy some provisions. There were two of them. They were not military men. On the side of the road. People were coming and going.

The structure of Rose's testimony brings together several elements useful for interpretation. Like many of the women, she was raped more than once. As is common in the use of rape as a tool of war, the soldiers require her husband to be present to visually witness the rape to exact patriarchal punishment on him as well. The second time it is especially important to note that she is raped by men who are not soldiers, the implication being that rape as a weapon of war does not limit the perpetrators to soldiers. Women's bodies are constantly under siege, both in their homes and outside, vulnerable to different types of perpetrators. That "people were coming and going" as she is being raped on the side of the road suggests lack of attention and a culture of impunity surrounding sexual violence. Taken together, these testimonies create a comprehensible narrative that contradicts the narrative chaos of the play's main story. In their similarity and coherence, these stories put forward a unified vision of what rape as a tool of war means in the lives of survivors, yet this vision is nonetheless differentiated. The testimonials mediate and inform the rest of the performance because they are inserted between each scene, reminding the audience of actual women who have suffered similar forms of violence. The testimonials also operate diagetically by seeming to directly address the audience rather than being restricted to the stage. The use of projection to achieve this effect succeeds in adding another dimension to the drama unfolding (see fig. 12).

Although these testimonies are structurally identical, their content suggests a wider range for the ways that women experience rape as a tool of war in the DRC. Only once do we see the victim-blaming trope present in *The Greatest Silence* and *Ruined*. Francine B. describes:

> Quand c'est arrivé j'étais en 4e année primaire. Des rebelles. Ils ont surgi dans la maison. Ma mère était absente. . . . Après cette chose, certaines personnes de mon entourage m'ont montrée du doigt. Ces gens disaient que c'est moi qui ai profité de l'absence de ma mère pour exciter les rebelles. On disait beaucoup d'autres choses encore. Des choses vraiment sales contre moi. . . . Actuellement je vis seule. (39)

> When it happened I was in my fourth year of primary school. Some rebels. They burst into the house. My mother was absent. After this thing, certain people from my area pointed the finger at me. Those people said

Figure 12. *Les recluses*, projected images. Photo credit: Danièle Pierre, *Les recluses*, Théâtre Varia

that I was the one who benefited from my mother's absence to excite the rebels. They said much more as well. Really dirty things against me. . . . Now I live alone. (39)

Francine's experience makes a literal recluse of her. She withdraws from the community because of what is said about her. In this descriptive passage, Francine never mentions the way *she* feels about what happens to her; she describes with journalistic detail and relates only the way others felt about what happened to her. Here the presence of emotion is important because of whose emotion is foregrounded; the absence of a description of Francine's feelings about her rape reflects the social dynamic. The outcome of her situation is determined by what people say and think about her, not by the way she responds or what she thinks or feels. Replicating the reception and nonrecognition of her rape reinforces an understanding of the way rape functions within structures of sociality. Francine repeats this experience in sparse detail as though to negotiate an existence in which what happens to her is significant only for the way others interpret it. Yet, her rehearsal of this script tacitly offsets its pervasive force by exposing the encoded message of erasure.

The confusion throughout the play's dialogue reaches its culmination in the final wedding scene. Again the use of the wedding suggests formulaic closure in the same heteronormative frame that we saw in the play *Ruined*. But in this case the formal and technical elements of the avant-garde style undercut the romantic ending, throwing it into confusion. We do not know who is speaking, who is present, or who participates in the ceremony. Each of the recluses wears a mask, cutting off access once again and adding to the confusion for those viewing the performance. The dissonance of the scene disrupts the highly rehearsed structure typically associated with marriage ceremonies. The stage directions further instruct: "On assiste à un rituel syncrétique fait de citations de différentes cérémonies de marriage" [We are attending a syncretic rite made up of quotations from different marriage ceremonies] (40). They further indicate that the people on stage do not seem to be paying attention, and that the public cannot hear what the "priest" is saying to the bride and groom. What follows are a series of lines spoken by different people with no indication of who is speaking. The resolution of the wedding finally occurring is thus undermined both by the staging and the actors' dialogue. The dialogue is completely nonsensical in the context of a wedding ceremony scene: "Oui bien sûr" [Yes, of course], the first lines of this scene tell us, but who is agreeing, and to what do they agree? (40) "Qu'est-ce qu'il ne faut pas entendre?"

[What are we not supposed to hear?] To whom is this question directed? "Ma casserole, quand est-ce que tu me la rends, ma casserole?" [When are you going to give me back my pan?] (40). This last line is the most bizarre of all, because it introduces a dispute over a pot that was lent. As opposed to the coherent narrative closure offered by the romantic union between Christian and Mama Nadi in *Ruined*, *Les recluses* destabilizes the use of marriage as a concluding trope through narrative and dramatic mechanisms. The scene reaches its culmination through music, and finally Kaniosha speaks. The stage directions instruct: "Silence. Kaniosha prend la parole" [Silence. Kaniosha begins to speak] (43).

> Moi. / J'ai quelque chose à te dire, Nzaeyimana. . . . / Pendant la guerre, mon frère a tué un chef du camp en face. / Ses hommes sont venus chez nous. / C'est un des nôtres, un voisin, qui les a conduits jusqu'à la maison. . . . Et ils ont fait, les uns après les autres, ce qu'ils étaient venus faire en réalité. / J'ai eu très mal, dans mon âme plus que dans ma chair. . . . Aujourd'hui je fais partie du groupe de ces femmes recluses en elles-mêmes que celui qui est parti et qui n'est jamais arrivé essaie de guérir par la parole. (44)

> Me. / I have something to tell you, Nzaeyimana. . . . / During the war, my brother killed a chief from the camp across the street. / His men came to our house. / It was one of our own, a neighbor that drove them all the way to our house. . . . And they did to me, one after the other, what they really came there to do. / I hurt very badly, in my soul more than in my flesh. . . . Today I belong to the group of women recluses off to themselves that this one here is a part of and who have never stopped trying to heal through the spoken word. (44)

This passage marks the first time that Kaniosha describes the entirety of what happens to her in explicit detail. The rhetorical structure of Kaniosha's monologue calls attention to her experience and her position. Separating the "moi" literally on its own line in the written text and choosing the reflexive *me* form rather than the "je" refers back to herself in a way that makes her both subject and object. The juxtaposition of "moi" and "j'ai" further emphasizes Kaniosha as the speaker. She clearly identifies whom her words are directed to, yet the story is as much for the designated character as for the audience. This monologue also offers the only explanation of where the term *recluses* originates despite the fact that the word is used to identify the women from the first scene of the play. After Kaniosha's monologue, she reveals the evidence against the judge who blackmailed her; then a dramatic sequence follows, in which the identities of the *recluses* are revealed. According to the stage directions, "Les autres recluses viennent se mettre sur la même ligne que les 'mariés.' Les unes après l'autre, elles ôtent leur masque et déclinent leur identité, la date ou les dates de leur traumatisme" [The other recluses come to put themselves in the same line as the bride and groom. One after the other, they remove their masks and they reveal their identities, as well as the date or the dates of their traumas]. (46). The psychic harm that the women have suffered is evident in the way they cling to one another. They are recluses not because society has cast them out, but because they need one another for survival.

Les recluses stages the intricacies of representing conflict in the Democratic Republic of the Congo by continuously unsettling the principal narrative playing out in the main plot. Through this avant-garde style coupled with theatrical and thematic innovations, Kwahulé shows the way identity remains multiply configured even in the context of war. Together, these techniques emphasize subject formation and articulation in relation to stories of sexual violence, even (especially?) in the context of war. Kwahulé's portrayal of *les recluses* underscores the mutable and shifting nature of war, a context in which anything can be altered from one day to the next. By offering multiple meanings of what violation entails, the way trauma is endured, and what life looks like in the aftermath of wartime rape, Kwahulé calls attention to the individuated experience and the situated knowledge of Congolese women in a way that challenges their personification as suffering, abject Other.

Forever Changed: Berrlyze's Story by Sherrlyn Borkgren

More than any other of the texts considered in this chapter, the photo-documentary *Berrlyze's Story*, is particularly attentive to the role and position of the subject after the conflict, without exoticizing suffering. The generic conventions of photography initiate visual conversations about the subject's position in relation to war that is imaged through lighting, positioning, angles, and lens. Focusing on images of suffering in the context of war, in *Regarding the Pain of Others* Sontag probes crucial questions that come into view for the spectator, artists, and subjects of photography. To document suffering, first comes the question of "what can be shown, what should be shown—few issues arouse more public clamor."[53] When we consider Sontag's point that, "the more remote or exotic the place, the more likely we are to have full frontal views of the dead and dying," Borkgren's strategy to show neither of these becomes striking in the context of war photography.[54] Borkgren also indicates the multiple and shifting meanings of what being a subject of war can look like by focusing on the way Berrlyze negotiates different contexts.

In the visual iconography of suffering, "the appetite for showing bodies in pain is as keen, almost, as the desire to show bodies that are naked," the question of the way photographic images engage with rape as a tool of war offers different angles.[55] To represent the use of rape as a tool of war in the DRC, photographer Sherrlyn Borkgren focuses on the story of one girl survivor rather than on multiple narratives. *Forever Changed* is told through the bright eyes of Berrlyze, a nine-year-old girl who was gang raped by a group of men. That these eyes are bright and not haunting or hollow is the beginning of the way the story differentiates from so many stories about the DRC and the rape victim-survivors there. Despite the fact that this is the story of a single protagonist, *Forever Changed: Berrlyze's Story* gathers different threads of the issues to offer a narrative of what rape as a tool of war means for a young girl and the way her life continues in the aftermath.[56] Borkgren followed Berrlyze and took photographs of her in various moments of daily life to piece together a story of wartime rape. The images are not the usual collage of sunken eyes, armed gunmen, and destitution one expects to see in a photo gallery of images of war on the African continent. Instead these pictures impart a different type of narrative that shifts the focus from victimization. Borkgren expands the aesthetic possibilities for documenting war by focusing more on Berrlyze than on the violent conflict that surrounds her.

From the beginning, the title offers us a single story, that of Berrlyze and not an "unnamed [subaltern] subject" without her own specificity.[57] Rather than offering a dislocation of reality, the images in *Berrlyze's Story* anchor her locally in the context of her village where war is ongoing, as daily life continues. The photographs compose a space where subjectivity separate from war remains possible. We begin with the sound of Congolese voices singing a capella and a quote from Berrlyze in white font across the black backdrop. "They put a bag over my head and pulled me into the bushes and the soldiers got me."[58] Berrlyze tells her story in stark white letters against a black screen. She does not indicate what she means by "got me," but then the words of her father leave no room for equivocation. "Berrlyze's father says that Berrlyze has changed since the soldiers raped her." The photographs piece together a life that appears to go on, one that has no choice but to continue: Berrlyze reading at school, sitting in an almost

Figure 13. Berrlyze attending school. Photo credit: Sherrlyn Borkgren, *Berrlyze's Story*

empty classroom where the teacher stands in front of a few children (fig. 13). Berrlyze making her way down the road with one other girl on a dirt road, each one balancing packages on her head (fig. 14). Berrlyze sitting in front to a pile of vegetables at the market; whether she is buying or selling remains unclear. Berrlyze's praying head bowed in front of an enormous image of the Virgin Mary. Berrlyze running hand in hand with another girl, the unmistakable look of glee punctuating her strides. Berrlyze walking with her father, whose stern face and steeled eyes communicate a look of protection (fig. 15). In this final image we see the unforgotten pain of a father wounded by his inability to protect his daughter—protection is one of the dominant tropes that accompanies stories about war, as well as one of the main vehicles through which victim's experience collapses into the way others view their rape. The shift in focus from Berrlyze to her father happens fleetingly, sparingly and without compromising Berrlyze's story, which the title reminds us of in the focus of the camera's eye.

The next words Berrlyze shares are about a culture of impunity in which no one is punished for rape, even when the victims are nine-year-old girls who can name their rapists: "I know who they were, I told their names, but no one did anything." Accountability and inaction here are cast locally, not globally toward the lackadaisical international community but

Figure 14. Girls fetching water. Photo credit: Sherrlyn Borkgren, *Berrlyze's Story*

Figure 15. A young rape survivor and her father weave through the local market in the DRC. Photo credit: Sherrlyn Borkgren, *Berrlyze's Story*

rather to the supposed authorities on the ground. This quote expresses the power of the young girl who unabashedly tells her story and names her perpetrators without hesitation. Recentering the narrative of war on the story of a girl provides critical insight into the way discourses of rape as a tool of war function in relation to audience perception. By avoiding some of the typical tropes of wartime rape representation and wartime photography, Borkgren advances an individuated subject whose experience with conflict varies from others.

This is not a spectacular story about what has been called "Africa's World War," a ceaseless conflict that has resulted in almost five million deaths. Nor is it the story of the exploitation of natural resources: diamonds, oil, and coltan, each of which has been fuel in the fires of corruption and conflict that create the atmosphere of war. This is not the story of a beautiful landscape whose fecundity springs forth conflict minerals and stones. This is the story of one girl, like whom there are countless others. Berrlyze is one girl who is living life each day in the aftermath of rape. She is one girl for whom the trauma of sexual violence persists. The indelible images of pain that we are used to viewing to tell the stories of war in Africa are nonetheless present in this photodocumentary. However, the story of one girl accompanies them. The photodocumentary is a single narrative of one nine-year-old victim-survivor. Borkgren's photographs invoke and agitate predetermined strategies for war photography, particularly the use of the spectacular to relay suffering, and the "exploitation of sentiment (pity, compassion, indignation) that occurs in different registers."[59]

On the one hand, it is well known that images of children are often strategically deployed in human rights advocacy as a way to generate outrage, sympathy, and action. In fact, as Wendy Hesford argues, "within the last few decades children have replaced women as the public emblems of goodness and purity . . . [to] become the moral referent and motives for action."[60] Children are particularly effective in mobilizing sympathy and exemplifying moral decay because of the universal appeal of youth and "the ideology of innocence that surrounds childhood."[61] There are moral and ethical challenges posed by situating children as the spectacular objects of human rights discourse because the children have even less power to determine their own narratives. Children's rhetorical agency; that is, their ability to represent themselves is usually compromised in their representation. In contrast, my analysis of Berrlyze's story explores the ways it attempts to frame her narrative from the perspective of her ability to speak on her own behalf. Rather than "reinforce [her] disenfranchisement," the photodocumentary anchors Berrlyze in a geopolitical and material context in which she is an actor as opposed to a passive recipient.

The focus of the pictures is on neither the war nor the trauma of rape but rather the fact that life continues despite the violence. The fact that life continues is different from the ability of the individual to continue, because the latter lapses easily into narratives of overcoming and resilience that can quickly deny individual humanity. By chronicling Berrlyze going through daily life, Borkgren successfully unfreezes her subject's experience with sexual violence. She is a moving subject and not merely a girl broken from the pain of sexual violence; she moves through space as more than a victim of rape warfare. In the volatile setting of war, Berrlyze continues about the mundane aspects of life: fetching water from a well, carrying a load on her head, running with a friend in a wide open field, and poring over books with a schoolmate. Berrlyze does nothing spectacular; the marked refusal of the camera's eye to spectacularize her suggests a more refined relationship between the viewing lens and the object of that lens, which affirms her subjectivity. As we saw in *Les recluses*, this refusal to cave to the logics of spectatorship, recognition, and the spectacle of suffering subverts some of the dynamics of human rights advocacy narratives.

Despite the use of the child as the subject of the photodocumentary, Borkgren's lens situates Berrlyze as a subject both visually and rhetorically. The pictures demonstrate that narratives of childhood victimization can move beyond reproducing children as static noncitizen subjects caught in conflict that forecloses any possibility of personhood. In this way, *Berrlyze's Story* becomes a powerful example that "recognizes children as complex moral and political subjects who must negotiate the economic and social inequities of globalization at the local level."[62] Berrlyze interacts with and analyzes her story in a way that signals her narrative autonomy. The title, *Forever Changed: Berrlyze's Story*, announces the end of anonymity by situating the subject and her story in the center of the narrative. The premise that Berrlyze is "forever changed" suggests finality without resolution. Ultimately *Berrlyze's Story* upsets the "spectacle of suffering," and refuses to imagine pain and violence through a narrative of sublime overcoming.[63] Instead, the photodocumentary presents a repository of images that neither shock nor excuse, calling for neither sympathy nor pity. Berrlyze's story can be framed through the black feminist optic of both/and, which illuminates her position as a victim-survivor, rather than only one or the other.

This interpretation of Berrlyze's story contradicts many of Sontag's arguments when she posits, "photographs objectify: they turn an event or a person into something that can be possessed."[64] The documentary refuses this objectifying gaze. Ironically, given the set of arguments designating the shortcomings of war photography in *Regarding the Pain of Others*, *Berrlyze's Story* goes further than any of the other texts in this chapter in its disavowal of objectification. Together, the photographs surpass the narratives in their ability to document the unknown. Sontag argues, "narratives can make us understand. Photographs do something else. They haunt us."[65] However, in *Forever Changed* it is precisely the haunting that makes us understand. Here, the concept of haunting calls for closer reading. The assumption for Sontag is that the haunting images would engage the spectacle of suffering by displaying human rights violations. *Forever Changed* is not a simple triumphant narrative of victory over the war. In fact, the story makes plain that although Berrlyze sought justice, she was categorically denied. These details simultaneously highlight Berrlyze as a survivor willing to pursue her perpetrators and as a victim who cannot be read according to the overcoming trope that denies invulnerability and inviolability.

As *Regarding the Pain of Others* attests, war photography as a genre intersects with questions about spectatorship, subject positioning, and human rights advocacy narratives. Sontag notes, "compassion is an unstoppable emotion. It needs to be translated into action, or it withers"; she thereby invokes the logic of human rights advocacy, which often uses visual representation to move people to compassion and then to charity or other action.[66] The unstoppability that Sontag refers to here suggests that there are emotions that inevitably must be translated into action. This idea also lies at the core of how human rights discourses appeal to emotions to mobilize international concern and advocacy. Sontag's conclusion draws upon the line between politics and affect, one that few contemporary studies of affect have addressed as cogently as Ahmed in *The Cultural Politics of Emotion*, in which the author explores the relationship between everyday lived emotions as a part of the discursive structures of the nation-state. Ahmed argues that when pain enters the political register, it risks sliding quickly into fetishized and commodified signs of suffering in which the subject of suffering is flattened into object: "And yet the pain of others is continually evoked in public discourse, as that which demands a collective as well as individual response."[67] When pain functions this way, the concealed presence of Congolese women is one of the tacit outcomes of the way rape as a tool of war is represented. Even the phrase "rape as a tool of war" shrouds the violated subject in ambiguity, placing emphasis on the tools of war and the act of rape rather than on the material bodies and psyches affected by it, let alone their individuated personhood. Cultural production like *Les recluses* and *Berrlyze's Story*, on the other hand, help to illustrate the different locations and subject positions beneath the use of rape as a tool of war.

I conclude here with Berrlyze's story to suggest other modes for rape representation in the context of war and to posit that perhaps the answer to the problems of representation lies in shifting the focus from the conflict to the body, though not necessarily the pained body. Seeing Berrlyze in each of these different scenes anchors her in the myriad social, cultural, and political contexts that inform her life. Rather than isolating her from strands of her identity, *Forever Changed* illuminates a different way to foreground subjugated knowledge that does not use emotion to draw in the viewer. Borkgren foregrounds Berrlyze's subjectivity and makes her identifiable as a victim-survivor of sexual violence and much more. This insistence on personhood provides more balanced alternatives for narrating and viewing the pain of Congolese women and girls.

Conclusion: Representing Wartime Rape beyond Empathy and Sympathy

One of the main questions that feminist theorists have grappled with in analyses of violence against women as a human rights issue concerns the spectacularization of women's bodies. The problem of "how to avoid reproducing the spectacle of victimization while also not erasing the materiality of violence and trauma, and recognizing the interdependence of material and discursive realms" shapes rape representation in particular.[68] None of the texts considered in this chapter actually reproduces scenes of sexual violence. Instead, the final two examples rely on representational configurations that seek to imagine the affective responses of their subjects, allowing them to feel rather than place the liberty of emotion on the audience, the spectator, or the viewer. The latter contributes to the misrecognition of the "subaltern survivor's" ability to feel. Instead of constructing Congolese women as eternal victims, unable to speak, to be seen, to feel, or to act, *Ruined, Les recluses,* and *Forever Changed* negotiate the representation of wartime rape by providing different frames for establishing the subject's complex positioning in a field of human rights shortcomings that include the politics of recognition, the optics of visibility, and the spectacle of suffering. Foregrounding the individual subjectivities of the women in these various works provides alternative models that move beyond the question of whether or not the subaltern can speak, but rather taking speaking (or deliberate silence) as a fact and then elaborating the forms and functions of speech acts, performative gestures, and affective responses to violation.

The use of empathy, whether present through sentimentalism or romance, reveals larger representational strategies or trends in human rights narratives, which tend to activate affective responses in order to gather attention for various causes. Though much of the work critiquing these practices has centered on narratives of Arab and Islamic women, throughout this book I have focused on the black bodies of African and African diasporic women to incorporate a larger number of identifications that traverse race, class, nation, and gender.[69] Ngwarsungu Chiwengo has rightly pointed out, "bearing witness to African events in literature, the media, or human rights discourse is challenging because of the power relations that undergird its representation and visualization."[70] As is evident in *The Greatest Silence*, these power dynamics can infringe upon subjectivity through the use of camera angles and narrative structures. The quest for affective and structural resolutions to the use of rape as a tool of war leads cultural workers to employ aesthetic techniques that have vexed political implications. The forms of cultural production brought together in this chapter indicate varying levels of visibility for regarding Congolese women's pain. The focus on wartime rape in these representations positions victim-survivors in several ways: for Lisa Jackson, it involves empathy as a point of departure, understanding that "this could happen to you too," as it did to her. In *The Greatest Silence*, the combination of an empathic protagonist and attempts to attract sympathy from the audience displace the position of the Congolese women. For Nottage, it entails offering the viewer another alternative to war, using romance to suggest a way of overcoming human rights atrocities. In *Ruined*, a combination of narrative, visual, and dramatic strategies foregrounds the women's variegated subject positions in relation to the war, but these efforts are eventually undermined by the romantic conclusion, a turn that invests more in the audience than in the characters whose lives unfold on stage. For Koffi Kwahulé, wartime rape representation means presenting polyphonic stories that are performed in multiple registers. In *Les recluses*, Congolese women are profoundly visible and are made present through their stories in various media. Through techniques that disrupt the ease of narrative closure, the play throws into question the possibility of resolution, ultimately uncovering different types of stories about rape as a tool of war and multiplying the possibilities of responses to these stories. In contrast to these previous examples, *Forever Changed: Berrlyze's Story* focuses on one protagonist whose subjugated knowledge of her experience is transmitted through sight and sound, with an emphasis on the halting aftermath of rape.

As a conflict that has been branded impossible to resolve, the crisis in the Democratic Republic of the Congo has generated divergent responses. Most of the texts examined in this chapter are remarkably consistent with the discourses of human rights intervention in the region. Empathy and sympathy from the audience are in many ways essential to the project of human rights advocacy, which relies on support from foreign spectators to generate responses and action. In order to get people to care more, these narratives invariably attempt to inspire sympathy, empathy, and compassion. Cultural texts of atrocity provide a different index for considering human rights issues, introducing stylistic, thematic, generic, aesthetic, and ethical questions about representation and consumption. Representations of rape as a tool of war, whether in the form of documentary or drama, have the ability to sustain or undermine the personhood of individuals subject to sexual violence. That the need to manage audience emotion so often overtakes the expression of personhood for Congolese women displays the competing narratives about the role of subject formation in discourses of sexual violence. By examining the discursive process through which Congolese women are peripherally located in stories that are supposed to be about their suffering, I have tried to broach why empathy, despite its ability to "do things to people," poses problems that shroud the "subaltern survivor" in silence. By turning to Kwahulé's drama and Borkgren's photodocumentary, I include re-visions of these familiar scripts regarding the pain of Congolese women. Throughout this chapter, I have critiqued the way narratives of sexual violence are structured around scenes of recognition that require an affective response from the audience or spectator. In the affective economy in which these cultural workers traffic, empathy is especially significant for what it means about the relationship between the viewer and the viewed. By projecting identification onto the audience, these narratives displace the subjects of the stories they seek to amplify. Although scholars such as Dominick LaCapra have articulated some forms empathy as a meaningful mode of recognition despite its ostensible limits, I am skeptical of the deployment of techniques and formal choices that rely upon empathy to structure the text of wartime rape. The problem with empathy, in my view, is not that it exists, but rather where its focus lies. Empathy often obscures and compromises the personhood of the subjects are supposed to be featured; instead it flattens out their experience as one that matters more because of whom it matters to.

In closing, I offer alternatives to the marginalization of Congolese women in the construction of their stories of suffering by turning to the example of two Congolese women who use activism to respond to the crisis in the DRC through a different lens: journalist and activist Chouchou Namegabe and filmmaker Shana Mongwanga. The Congolese radio journalist and founder of *Association des Femmes des Médias du Sud Kivu* (AFEM)/The South Kivu's Women's Media, Chouchou Namegabe uses community broadcasting to air women's stories of sexual violence in the region. Literally taking back the radio airwaves and proclaiming them a space for women's stories to be heard, Namegabe features testimonies of women who have been raped. Describing the women who came forward to share their stories, Namegabe describes the way "they were desperate to share their secrets and suffering," a point that undermines the overwhelming silence used to characterize stories of rape.[71] Through AFEM, Namegabe encourages and trains more Congolese journalists to use the media as a way to advocate for the needs of women who have been raped. This practice exemplifies a black feminist intention to address women's human rights from the vantage point of the women themselves, recognizing that their subjugated knowledge is essential to advocacy. Namegabe's work highlights the way Congolese women participate in the struggle to bring attention to and to end rape in their region. The notion that the women she encounters are "desperate to share their secrets and suffering" provides a distinct index for the way we understand the role of women in the representation of wartime rape.[72] The desperation to disclose their stories and to refuse silence unravels the image of women unable to articulate their stories of pain. Namegabe's activism also contradicts the notion that these women are held captive by silence, unable to embark upon any forms of resistance to the rampant rapes that have been taking place since the war began. As she explains the urgent need for this work, Namegabe shares in an interview,

> The issue is important for me because it's touching the right of men, the right of women. And I feel concerned because I'm a woman too. And also I'm a journalist. I saw that I couldn't do anything. I don't have guns to fight against it, but I've got my microphone, to use it, to fight against the rape and sexual violence. That's why we give the microphone to victims, to tell their stories. Because somewhere it's the first way to heal their internal wound, to talk about it, to make it known, to call for actions, because we want it to end.[73]

The points she makes here are crucial to our understanding of how cultural production and technology come together for others to regard the pain of Congolese women in a way that foregrounds their individual situated knowledge. First, she names sexual violence as a community and human issue, one that affects both men and women. Second, Namegabe expresses her own desire to find and make use of the tools she has at her disoposal in order to combat the rape of women. Finally the equipping of other women with these tools is not only for a larger audience to hear so that the war can end, but also as an element of their own personal healing. In this way, Namegabe's activism is a fitting counternarrative for representations of Congolese suffering that rely on a Western advocate for change, that emphasize the need for empathy, or that call for the pain of wartime rape to be mediated and managed from the outside.

This book began with a protest scene of women marching in Bukavu to oppose the mass rape of women in the Democratic Republic of the Congo. I now return to that scene through the lens of the film *The Road to Bukavu*, a documentary directed by Congolese filmmaker Shana Mongwanga. Mongwanga's work foregrounds the activism and agency of Congolese women involved in the conflict. This transnational project should be understood as an act of feminist praxis that unsettles the boundary between local and global activism. The film highlights a transnational global feminist movement of women organizing in the DRC and abroad to draw attention to the use of rape as a tool of war there and to cover a counterpoint to the inaction surrounding the conflict. One of the guiding principles of the film and of Mongwanga's work in general is foregrounding Congolese women's voices. Whereas human rights advocacy has been structured around others speaking for Congolese women in order to create empathy for the cause, Mongwanga begins with Congolese women speaking for themselves about the cause in order to emphasize their activism and concrete actions.

Her documentary on the march of Congolese women that introduces this book presents a new politics of recognition that is manifestly dialogic, similar to what Mukagasana offers in *Les blessures du silence*. Explaining her goals, Mongwanga writes:

> I chose to structure the film as a diary of their journey as it happened from the moment they arrived in Kinshasa, their travel to Bukavu and Goma by boat, on their way to the demonstrations and the visit to Mwenga—a very important place where *forty Congolese women were buried alive in 1999 because they resisted the occupation of their land*. Mwenga is almost never in

the media. The work and resistance of Congolese women are scarcely mentioned in the media.

The film shows the memorial that was inaugurated to honour their bravery and is dedicated to these women who inspired me. I would really like the media to focus more on the courage, resistance, resilience and extraordinary work of the women in the region rather than parading celebrities in sunglasses carrying presumed African orphans to promote their own image.[74]

By associating the structure of the film with a longer history of women's activism in the DRC, Mongwanga stages an encounter between history and current events. This technique posits a genealogy of women's activist engagement. Mongwanga's reproduction of the march intervenes in several important ways. Framing the film as an intimate diary, she exploits one of the most well-known forms of travel narratives used as a tool of African subject erasure. Like Véronique Tadjo, she reclaims the intimate diary and travel narrative and reconfigures it according to terms that are both African and feminist. Mongwanga further issues a historic challenge to the erasure of Congolese women's agency by citing the example of the women buried alive in 1999. Second, she critiques the silence that encloses the activism of Congolese women as coming from the dominant (read Western) media. Third, she expresses a desire for a new repository of images that includes Congolese women's activism and does the work of beginning to create such an archive herself.

Perhaps what these examples of documentary film, drama, and photodocumentary foreground most of all are limitations of different forms of representation, especially when they attempt to render wartime rape in the context of a conflict as spectacular as the war in the Democratic Republic of the Congo. Through generic innovation, narrative strategies, and formal techniques, the modes of representation that I have examined in this chapter attempt to connect the materiality of violence and trauma to the discursive realm of performance and visual art. Ultimately, they help highlight not only the problem of representation, and the way victimhood and personhood operate in critical tension with one another, but also the way rape representation can do more than reproduce scripts of violence that gain meaning only through their reception. By this I mean, texts that rely too heavily on how and by whom they are received in order to make the conflict matter will inevitably overlook the important ways in which those caught in these conflicts not only figure as subjects but also how they process and analyze their experiences with violence. The examples of creative expression by Kwahulé, Namegabe, and Mongwanga posit an alternative to the reliance on audience affect because what matters is not the way others receive these stories, but rather the way these representations and productions reconceptualize human rights discourses centered on the spectacular. Namegabe and Mongwanga are invested in actively regarding Congolese women as subjects and agents. Their interventions are especially critical in a climate that has tended to turn subjects into objects of advocacy, and what the cultural work is supposed to do to the person who consumes/views/hears becomes more important than those featured in the actual work. This alternative reformulates tropes of visibility, vocality, and agency that dominate studies of the "subaltern." More importantly, it moves beyond affective responses and suggests other possibilities for what cultural work can achieve in the context of wartime rape in general, and in the DRC in particular. By imagining more dynamic possibilities for the critical and creative labor that rape representation can perform, these examples wrest figurations of wartime rape from the realm of affect-laced human rights preoccupations, offering a way to refuse the objectification and spectacularization of Congolese rape victim-survivors.

EPILOGUE

Not Just (Any) Body Can Be a Global Citizen

Rape and Human Rights Advocacy in the Twenty-First Century

> . . . unequal distribution then and now in a country stratified as *moun anwo, moun anba/. . . moun lavil, moun andeyo/. . . moun ki moun, moun ki pa moun/*. . . unequal distribution by *gran manjè, ti manjè* big thieves, small thieves/local exploiters, foreign moguls as our girls are raped and preyed upon/How many cups of revolution will it take to reconstruct and rebuild Haiti?/How many cups of revolution will it take for little Faila to throw away her whistle and dream of a new Haiti?
> —Claudine Michel, *Unequal Distribution*

> It bothers me when someone says raped women . . . Abused women, women victims of war, find some other appropriate term. But raped women—that hurts a person, to be marked as a raped woman, as if you had no other characteristic, as if that were your sole identity.[1]
> —Nusreta Sivac, *Calling the Ghosts*

EARLY IN SEPTEMBER 2011, a story about an 18-year-old Haitian man who was raped in the small coastal town of Port-Salut, was revealed on the internet. Johnny Jean's perpetrators were members of the Uruguayan forces of the United Nations Stabilization Mission in Haiti (MINUSTAH), who had been occupying the southwestern town for years. The incident took place on July 20, though it was made public three months later. The video, taken by a cell phone camera, shows two officers holding him down while two others rape him. Shot upside down, the video was apparently taken by one of the soldiers, then accidentally sent to a resident from the town and subsequently leaked.[2] In the footage, the victim is pressed down against a mattress, his hands pinned down behind him and turned upwards so that he cannot escape the grip of his perpetrators. With their military fatigues and light blue hats (*les casques bleus*), the soldiers are donned in the familiar attire of the UN troops known throughout the island. One of the most troubling aspects of the profoundly disturbing footage is the chorus of raucous laughter echoing in the background. These peals of laughter are heard throughout the entire video, an eerie marker of the tone of that reaffirms the soldiers' pleasure and play. Since the video surfaced, the UN chief of MINUSTAH has confirmed its authenticity, and Jean has filed the crime with a local police unit. He has also received a medical exam, which confirmed his injuries as being consistent with those of someone who had been sexually violated. Following it all, a wave of protests surged throughout the island and in the diaspora demanding once again that MINUSTAH must go. The Uruguayan troops were later expatriated to their country of origin. In May of 2012, Jean also went to Uruguay to offer his testimony after the men were charged with "private violence."[3]

The footage of Jean's rape quickly became an index for the flagrant abuse of MINUSTAH, whose human rights violations against Haitian civilians, though not as widely publicized outside of Haiti, are well known to those on the island. In the coverage, the victim is always identified as a boy, a move that underscores the predatory nature of the crime and its attendant power dynamics, but also one that falls unwittingly prey to narratives of emasculation, which often arise in stories of rape where the victim is male. The use of the cell phone camera highlights the ways technologies of visual representation now influence the landscape of human rights advocacy, having become fundamental in documenting twenty-first-century human rights abuses. As Wendy Hesford has noted, "visual and audiovisual media are important features of contemporary human rights advocacy . . . [and] over the last decade, for example, amateur video has played an important role in the trial for major leaders in the International Criminal Tribunal."[4] As the video circulated and became appropriated for advocacy purposes, the power and the utility of scenes of suffering also rose to prominence as a broader public became aware of MINUSTAH's crimes against humanity. At the same time, "visual exposure to violence [can] fail to produce sustained attention or action," so although the visual evidence offered by the video initially sent shockwaves over the Internet, the question of what real impact the video could have in postearthquake Haiti certainly remained at issue.[5] Even more problematically, questions surrounding the protection of the perpetrator—his identity and his rights as a victim-survivor, or what is commonly referred to as revictimization of those who go forward and report sexual violence, gained traction as the video circulated. Especially beyond the specter of Abu Ghraib, it has become clear that though new technologies figure in how visual evidence of human rights abuses circulate and gain prominence, their effects on policy can remain at issue. The power of this particular spectacle was compounded by the actors involved, members of the MINUSTAH, whose presence in Haiti began with the 2004 controversy when former president Jean-Bertrand Aristide was forced out of office amidst political turmoil.

What occurred in the aftermath of this incident brings into greater relief the way the discursive framing of rape, citizenship, victimhood, and human rights are intertwined. Johnny Jean is made visible first as a victim of sexual violence who becomes an icon of suffering at the hands of the MINUSTAH, and second as a citizen with legitimate claims to belonging to a sovereign nation. When viewed in the context of Haiti's "postearthquake rape crisis," discussed at length in Chapter 2, the incident works against the standard image of rape victims as women residing in the insecurity of tent cities all over Port-au-Prince.[6]

The incident puts the anxieties, confusions and complexities of rape rhetoric and discourses prominently on display, revealing the ways these situations dovetail with the problems of invasion, occupation, and neo-imperial and globalized power, which have been difficultly mapped onto Haiti. The level of outcry surrounding the Port-Salut incident, which was named "viol collectif" (collective rape) by Haitian President Michel Martelly also introduces an uncomfortable characteristic of rape representation. The narrative that unfolded to envelop Jean was that of the abuses of the MINUSTAH, which many had been protesting at least since 2006. Johnny Jean symbolized the recklessness of MINUSTAH, a peacekeeping force, whose protection of the Haitian people just as frequently involved their mistreatment. As a result, this spectacle of rape did not become one of gendered victimization, but rather a sign of neo-imperial domination and exploitation to be situated in the same context of military intervention. The young man at the center of the incident became named and interpellated as a citizen whose claim to rights was abused by MINUSTAH. He came to occupy the role of at once symbolizing the violation of the nation, and existing as someone with a claim to the rights that make him a citizen.

Johnny Jean therefore serves as poignant a reminder of Jacqui Alexander's argument in her remarkable essay "Not Just (Any) Body Can Be a Citizen," when she asserts, "Citizenship . . . continues to be premised within heterosexuality and principally within heteromasculinity."[7] Here the occupation of the symbolic did not circumscribe or restrict his national identity of belonging. A victim-survivor of rape, he is also a citizen-subject able to "invoke the national to (re)establish identity within shifting geopolitical contexts."[8] Interestingly, the protests against the rape were also led by women who deployed the language of human rights claims in their outcry. Their activism echoes the scenes of protest that introduced this book and that serve as a reminder of how anti-rape activism is not restricted to one gender. The Port-Salut rape thus suggests that obscuring the details of sexual violence and eclipsing those subject to it happens regardless of gender.

Concluding with this scene adds another layer to the knotted web of rape discourses that situate gender as a primary field through which sexual violence is represented, processed, and reacted to. While the representations of sexual violence I examine throughout *Conflict Bodies* primarily feature the heterosexual rape of women and girls, it is important to note that sexual violence, while predominately meted out against women, extends to men and boys as well.[9] If standpoint theory helps to differentiate between the gendered experience of the world through subjugated knowledge, then the act of rape and its aftermath diminish the distance within that gap.[10] Even more if "in its extremity, rape makes manifest the specifics of a given culture's understanding of the female subject in society," what does this mean for the male subject of rape?[11] The example also delineates the way public responses to rape are undergirded by the politics of sex and power. Contrary to the ways in which the rape of women and girls is often depoliticized in this context, the conversations surrounding Jean affirm the machinations of global politics because of which bodies are rendered submissive to and penetrable by foreign sources. As the incident was discursively co-opted by national forces, Johnny Jean was framed as a symbolic marker. He came to operate as a fully embodied citizen-subject whose violation surpassed its symbolic meaning. This incident offers another example of the way rape intersects with political context and implies political machinations, inevitably becoming a story about something *other than* the subject of the violation. This practice, as the Port-Salut case indicates, generates discussions of history and geopolitical relationships and effectively transcends gender even while it supports prevailing gender hierarchies.

For the newly elected Haitian president, the Port-Salut rape served another function. The day after the video leaked, he vigorously condemned the act, stating that, "The President shares the feelings of all Haitians and guarantees that those who are guilty of, or complicit in, this act will not go unpunished."[12] Calling it "an act that revolts the national conscience," Martelly's rhetoric uses the language of nationalism to unite the affective response of the Haitian people as an important indicator of what must take place as a result of the rape.[13] By referring to the rape as "collective," Martelly implicitly evokes the ubiquitous rape of the nation trope as a marker of violation with national consequences. In his official comments, the president also touched on the departure of MINUSTAH, linking the incident to his campaign promises, "Il est important de commencer à travailler sur le retrait de la Minustah, comme je l'ai prôné lors de la campagne" [It is important to begin to work on the retreat of MINUSTAH, just as I promised during the campaign].[14] Invoking human rights violations and the abusive behavior of UN peacekeepers also allowed Martelly to frame the incident as one about protection of Haitian sovereignty and the destructive advance of neo-imperialism. The official statement from the president's administration read as follows:

> La Présidence condamne vigoureusement cet acte qui révolte la conscience nationale et attend un rapport détaillé rétablissant l'exactitude et les circonstances des faits.
>
> Tout acte de viol, sans égards au genre de la victime, ni du bourreau, constitue un délit grave qui ne saurait être toléré. Il est ainsi demandé aux instances concernées de se réunir en urgence avec les responsables de la Minustah pour que des mesures soient immédiatement prises pour éviter la reproduction de tels actes.
>
> En attendant que toute la lumière soit faite sur ce délit, et que justice soit rendue, la Présidence partage l'émotion de tout le peuple haïtien et donne la garantie que les coupables et complices d'un tel acte ne resteront pas impunis.[15]

> The Presidency vigorously condemns this act that revolts the national conscience and awaits a detailed report establishing the exactitude of the circumstances of the facts.
>
> Any act of rape, without regard to the gender of the victim or of the perpetrator, constitutes a serious offense, which cannot be tolerated. It is thus applied to the relevant bodies to meet urgently with leaders of MINUSTAH so that immediate steps be taken to prevent the recurrence of such acts.

> Until that light is shed on this crime and that justice is done, the President shares the emotion of all the people of Haiti and provides assurance that the perpetrators and accomplices of such an act will not go unpunished.

Despite the claim that "tout acte de viol, sans égards au genre de la victime, ni du bourreau, constitue un délit grave qui ne saurait être toléré" [every act of rape, without regard for the gender of the victim or the perpetrator, is serious offense that cannot be tolerated], the fact that the Port-Salut case generated such public outcry from the government suggests otherwise. In a different context, Hesford has commented on the circulation of the Abu Ghraib torture photographs as a "a critical occasion to examine the rhetorical politics of staging empire."[16] Her point is relevant here because the Jean incident's circulation can open critical discussions about how rape, spectatorship, the spectacular relate to the performance of national discourses.

For Martelly, the video occasioned an opportunity to critique the modalities of intervention and empire that have structured Haitian politics for years and especially in the contemporary moment. This political refiguration of Jean's rape turned it into a national cause, an opportunity to denounce MINUSTAH in particular and neo-imperial occupying forces in general. Visualizing torture plays an important political role that has implications for the entire nation; here the visual reproduction of rape was a mobilizing call to action. Martelly's gesture denounces the existence of sexual violence in Haiti but in so doing also suggests that certain types of rape by certain actors matter more than others. Because the circulation of the video can also be linked to the reduction of the number of MINUSTAH troops by fifteen percent, which took place less than a month after the incident was made public, we are reminded that the event itself had tangible and expediently executed policy effects, despite the fact that MINUSTAH remained in Haiti.

Serving as visual documentation of MINUSTAH human rights violations, the video told a story with a longer history. Far in the background of this rape lies the fact that this is not the first time members of MINUSTAH have been accused of raping or proven to have raped Haitian citizens. In 2005 and 2006, United Nations' peacekeepers were accused of raping young women in the cities of Gonaives and Leogâne. In 2007, more than one hundred Sri Lankan troops were sent home after being accused of sexual abuses, including prostitution with young girls.[17] MINUSTAH have perpetrated numerous infractions, and their continued presence has been met with disdain, discord, and protest. Overall, the organized response to the Port-Salut rape more closely resembles the reactions to a 2005 raid in Cité Soleil that resulted in the death of a dozens of people. Likewise, we also know that, according to the well-known Haitian anti-rape organization Commission of Women Victims for Victims (KOFAVIV), "the presence of MINUSTAH (UN peacekeeping mission) in poor neighborhoods has done little to prevent rapes from occurring on a daily basis. The number of cases we have received from Village de Dieu and Cité Soleil alone shows us that MINUSTAH has failed to provide real security for women in these areas."[18] In the responses to the video, the violation of this universal human right was more at issue than was the particularity of Jean's experience with sexual violence.

Transnational global feminists have consistently argued that epistemologies of the human and the universal can fail to include women and survivors' subjectivities, identities, and social relations. In the human rights field, conflict zones occupy a central role as locations for which activists garner support, marshal humanitarian aid, and work at peacekeeping. The example of the Jean incident illustrates, just as I have maintained throughout this book, that the relationship between human rights discourses and the black suffering body is an uneasy one, wherein the bodies are given meaning more because of what they represent and to whom rather than what they represent for the individual being represented. As a point of departure to explore the modalities of speech and voice evident in representations of the rape, the scene of Congolese women demonstrating against rape warfare at the beginning of this book foregrounds the way sexual violence can be premised as a human rights issue. Adding to it this closing scene of the Port-Salut rape, we come to understand that speaking is as much about being seen and that in the twenty-first century new technologies have once again altered the field of vision. It also reveals that the vocabulary of human rights frameworks falls short in its failure to complicate perspectives on sexual violence. Public engagement with human rights in the twenty-first century has been manifestly informed by conflicts in which sexual violence is deployed as a weapon of war or sex trafficking is used to destroy women's mobility. My analysis of the way expressive cultures negotiate the visibility, legibility, and audibility of rape presents ways to theorize violence that extricates it from overdetermined narratives. Despite my focus on the incidents of sexual violence and the trauma that ensues in their wake, I am aware that "trauma is part of what makes subjectivity othered, but it is not what makes subjectivity subjectivity."[19] This idea challenges the presuppositions of this study on the one hand, yet also calls us to look for more textured elaborations of subjectivity.

The present wave of global human rights activism swelling in countries in Africa, Latin America, and the Caribbean do little to account for the ways in which representation problematically informs these politics. These narratives of violence construct only part of a material whole that the realm of the imagination helps to nuance. By reframing the discourses of rape representation through a comparative, interdisciplinary, and feminist consideration of the symbolic, my goal here has been to trace and to call for new ways of relating rape to violence. This impulse follows Françoise Lionnet's directive making the case for a "truly comparative feminist criticism, one performed on the border [of] disciplinary categories. Such an approach aims not at conflict resolution but rather at reframing issues in such a way that dialogue can remain open and productive, allowing critics to map out new articulations of cultural expressions."[20] The example of Port-Salut demonstrates the pervasive hold that scripts of violence have over interpretations and representations of sexual violence. In contrast, many of the texts in this study highlight the possibilities for the representation of violence to move from portrayal to portrait—following a continuum that accedes to a new level of understanding. As a re-creation of someone's likeness that can occur in many forms (painting, sculpture, written), a portrait is a richer and more dynamic form that suits representations of rape in which the viewer or reader must pause to see what more is at work in its rendering. A portrait offers a way to see multiple faces and hidden lines rather than simply a static or straightforward re-imagining. In fact, the viewer may never be able to see every aspect of a portrait from the subject or the creator's perspective.

These works and my analyses of them challenge scripts of violence according to new perspectives that are portrait-like in their rendition. In today's global climate, "rape is not a side effect but is actually a new frontline. Widespread and systematic sexual violence is both a crime against the victim and a crime against humanity. And sexual violence is the only crime against humanity that is routinely dismissed as being random or inevitable."[21] My understanding of this global climate is manifestly informed by many different locations, and certainly not restricted to the geographic areas mentioned in this book. I am convinced of the importance of imaginative work in helping us to not only think critically about sexual violence, but to begin to transform the pervasiveness of a global rape culture.

Because poetry, with its oral/aural resonance, offers a different way to listen, I give the final words of this book to Claudine Michel's poem *Unequal Distribution*. The poem is emblematic of the way cultural production, creative expression, and activism by Haitian feminists extend the legacy of fallen feminists Myriam Merlet, Anne-Marie Coriolan, and Magali Marcelin, three important figures who perished in the earthquake of 2010. The loss of these women was mourned as a serious blow to the movement because each of them was considered a *poto-mitan* in the history of Haitian women's activism. Since the 1950s, feminists in Haiti have been working toward women's rights. Whether in the institution of a new criminal code for the classification of rape, or in the organization of the first International Tribunal for Violence against Women in Haiti, during which women were able to speak about the atrocities unleashed upon their bodies after the coup of 1994, their activism has steadfastly taken on the issue of sexual violence. Today feminist journalists like Samia Saloman are joined together with grassroots organizations in order to tell the stories of rape survivors and to protect women and girls from vulnerability in today's postearthquake tent cities. The activist and cultural work of Haitian feminists since the earthquake serves as a reminder that this movement did not die with the activists in January 2010. If anything, the loss of these *poto mitan* has reinvigorated feminist attention to Haitian women's rights.

Claudine Michel's poem "Unequal Distribution" follows in the same trajectory. It appears in a special segment of the feminist journal *Meridians* entitled "Pawol fanm sou douz janvye" [Women's Words on January 12th] in which writers, scholars and activists weigh in on the catastrophe through their chosen form of creative expression. Edited by Haitian feminist scholar/performer/anthropologist/activist Gina Ulysse, *Pawol Fanm* is a polyphonic multigenre collection that enriches the archive of Haitian women's cultural production while adding a resolutely feminist innovative point of view. "Unequal Distribution" has a particular relevance for the arguments presented in this book, which attempt to account for the widespread incidence of sexual violence while not reducing rape-victim survivors' to their experiences with sexual violence. Dedicated to "our young Haitian girls who carried whistles and Faila herself," Michel's poem invests layered meaning in the personhood of these rape survivors:

> Unequal distribution that forces five-year-old Faila to wear around her neck that whistle so she is not raped at night going to the makeshift bathroom in tent city Pétion-Ville

> Unequal distribution and a whistle and a flashlight that do not stop her ten-year-old sister from the pouncing hands of her assailants flashlight and all

> unequal distribution of food water energy shelter
> different lives different destinies

two nations in one *before* the quake / and *after* the earth cracked open / two nations in one / Unequal distribution caused by unequal exchanges with imperialist powers that fleece Haiti for four hundred years unequal distribution by neo-liberal policies and organizations that took more than they gave two nations in one

Unequal distribution from succeeding irresponsible governments that never represented the people

Unequal distribution by corrupt civil servants who dominated and betrayed those they were in charge of educating and protecting two nations in one

unequal distribution then and now in a country stratified as *moun anwo, moun anba*
... *moun lavil, moun andeyo*
... *moun ki moun, moun ki pa moun*

... unequal distribution by *gran manjè, ti manjè* big thieves, small thieves/ local exploiters, foreign moguls as our girls are raped and preyed upon

How many cups of revolution will it take to reconstruct and rebuild Haiti?

How many cups of revolution will it take for little Faila to throw away her whistle and dream of a new Haiti?[22]

The poem deploys many of the strategies of rape representation elucidated in this book. First, in its dedication to Faila, it is a reminder of how sexual violence is one issue within the panoply of problems faced by poor girls and women in Haiti *before* and *after* the earthquake. Security in the tents, lack of access to resources, and corruption of nongovernment and government agencies interimbricate Faila's life informing her multiple oppressions. Taken alone, the term *unequal distribution* emphasizes multivalent forces at work that create uneven, unequal, and unjust circuits of power. Refusing to reduce Haiti's "rape problem" to a single factor or moment, Michel makes it clear that the maldistribution she references is as much a product of history and internal forces on the island as it is a problem of globalization and systematic impoverishment. The repetition of "unequal distribution" is both a reminder and a rallying call. Lastly, the final line, "how many cups of revolution will it take for little Faila to throw her whistle away and dream of a new Haiti," links Faila to a larger historical context also complicit in maintenance of her status as a poor girl living in an IDP camp. The dream to which Michel gestures at the poem's conclusion is left unresolved and unrealized and left in suspension—it is the broken promise of revolution that restricts and reduces women and girls' bodies to objects. Through these distinct and sonorous verses, Michel identifies classism, sexism, neo-imperialism, structural inequality, and social injustice as problems that date much further back than January 12, 2010. Evincing a heartbreaking present and a fraught past, she nonetheless gestures toward an imagined future where a new Haiti can be dreamt of.

The need for a dream expressed here reminds us that, "transforming a rape culture involves imaginative leaps from our present state of institutionalized violence to a future that is safer and more just. We must summon our imaginations for this task, because history and society have so few precedents for us . . . transforming a rape culture is about changing fundamental attitudes and values."[23] Creative expression is an important terrain in which these imaginative leaps must take place. Transformation becomes possible because in addition to being a social reality, rape culture functions discursively and rhetorically through different forms of representation. When thinking about sexual violence, the imagination becomes a space of freedom. It is a space where we can imagine a more safe and just future, a world free of sexual violence, a world in which victim-survivors are not reduced to their status as victims, and a world in which bodies are not battlegrounds. By looking at the symbolic and material realms together, we are better able to re-imagine the ideologies that seek to contain us. Focusing on cultural production as a way to shift our understanding of rape narratives means reading and re-reading to unearth keys that unlock codes about sexual violence that persist in our imaginaries. The task of creative expression is often to transmit these codes, but it can also lay bare the problems within, challenge them, re-imagine them, and ultimately suggest new possibilities and directions for those areas where reality and representation collide. This practice renders rape legible for the way it functions in epistemologies of violence and effectively begins the work of transformation.

NOTES

Introduction

1. Mama, "Sheroes and Villains: Conceptualizing Colonial and Contemporary Violence Against Women in Africa," 264.
2. Higgins and Silver, *Rape and Representation*, 2.
3. 5.4 million people have been killed and hundreds of thousands of women have been raped since the conflict began in 1996. One figure estimates that in 2009 alone 15,000 women were raped in the region.
4. Despite the signing of peace treaties in 2002 and the "official end" of the war, various armed conflicts continues with no signs of abating in the eastern Congo.
5. BBC, "DR Congo women march against sexual violence" 17 October 2010 http://www.bbc.co.uk/news/world-africa-11562059. Accessed 20 October 2010.
6. First lady Olive Lembe Kabila was also present on the march; yet given the Kabila government's ineffectiveness in dealing with the mass rapes in the DRC, it is only appropriate to question her role in this movement.
7. BBC, "DR Congo women march against sexual violence" http://www.bbc.co.uk/news/world-africa-11562059.
8. In using this phrase I am purposefully, though cautiously invoking Gayatri Spivak's legendary essay. Subaltern identity (who is subaltern and relation to whom?) and the concept of silence (which does not unequivocally oppose agency) are fraught. As Ania Loomba states, "too inflexible a theory of subaltern silence, even if offered in a cautionary spirit, can be detrimental to research on colonial cultures by closing off options even before they have been explored." Loomba, *Colonialism/Postcolonialism*, 196. My use of Spivak here is to signal the ways in which black women in general and Congolese women in particular have been marked as Other due to the rape crisis unfolding in the DRC.

9. This term is also a reminder of Angela Davis' description of the violation black women were subject to under slavery. Davis, "Rape, Racism, and the Myth of the Black Male Rapist," *Women, Race and Class* (Vintage Books: New York, 1987) 172–201.

10. Hunt and Rygiel, *(En)Gendering the War on Terror,* 3.

11. Nkrumah, *I Speak of Freedom,* 91.

12. For discussions of the use of victim and survivor in the rape crisis advocacy field see *Abused Women and Survivor Therapy* by Lenore Walker (Washington DC: American Psychological Association, 1994) and *Surviving Sexual Assault,* edited by Rachel Grossman and Joan Sutherland (New York: St. Martin's Press, 1983).

13. Mama, "Sheroes and Villains," 264.

14. While some such as Nigerian scholar Onyèrónké Oyewùmí have made critical interventions challenging the feminist focus on the body as a useful category of analysis, in the context of sexual violence, I find it crucial to consider and to highlight the corporeal aspects of rape, especially given the ways that women of African descent have been configured as inviolable. Oyewùmí, *The Invention of Women: Making African Sense of Western Gender Discourses* (Minneapolis: University of Minnesota Press, 1997).

15. Michel le Bris et al ,"Pour une littérature-monde en français," *Le monde* 15 mars 2007. See also LeBris et al., *Pour une literature monde en français* (Paris: Gallimard, 2007).

16. Glover, "The Ambivalent Transnationalism," 99.

17. Forsdick, *Francophone Postcolonial Studies,* 3.

18. Ibid., 7.

19. Jenson, "Francophone World Literature," 16.

20. Kaplan and Grewal, "Transnational Feminist Cultural Studies," 358.

21. Hesford and Kozol, *Just Advocacy?*, 13.

22. Collins, "The Social Construction of Black Feminist Thought," 747.

23. Hekman, "Truth and Method: Feminist Standpoint Theory Revisited," 342.

24. White, "Talking Feminist, Talking Black," 79.

25. Most of the texts of rape cultural criticism that are focused on the Global South are in the context of African American women. Recently the study *State of Peril: Race and Rape in South African Fiction* (New York: Oxford University Press, 2012), by Lucy Graham, expands the Anglophone African work in this area.

26. Horeck, *Public Rape,* vii.

27. Robertson and Rose, *Representing Rape,* 3.

28. This is not to say that no effort has been made to analyze gender violence in the field. Most recently, Marie Chantal Kalisa, takes on such a project in *Violence in Francophone African and Caribbean Women's Literature* (Lincoln: University of Nebraska Press, 2009) which focuses on the ways that African and Caribbean women writers give prominence to violence in their work. Focusing largely on the notion of "herstory," Kalisa's main objective is to insert the female perspective into narratives of violence by looking at novels written by women. In its attention to the exclusion of women's voices from discussions of violence, Kalisa's study is a significant precursor to this study. Likewise, James Day, ed., *Violence in French and Francophone Literature* (Amsterdam and New York: Rodopi, 2008) does important work in excavating the subject of violence and its literary manifestations. Here the focus on francophone and French regions together marks a departure from comparative analyses that separate the hexagon from its former colonies. Prior to each of these, Lorna Milne served as editor for *Postcolonial Violence, Culture and Identity in Francophone Africa and the Antilles* (New York: Peter Lang, 2007) in which the authors are particularly concerned with the examining representation of physical and material violence rather than exploring epistemic violence and other conceptual models in the production of discourses about violence.

29. Hartman, *Scenes of Subjection*.

30. See Frantz Fanon's *Les damnés de la terre* and Aimé Césaire, *Le discours sur le colonialisme* (Paris: Présence africaine, 1989).

31. Throughout this book I use black feminist theoretical approaches based on intersectionality to call in to question the critique of experience offered by postmodern feminists, see for example Joan Scott *Gender and the Politics of History* (New York: Columbia University Press, 1989). My use of standpoint theory as an alternative to this formulation offers one way to rethink these critiques.

32. Mardorossian, "Towards a New Feminist Theory of Rape," 743.

33. See Saidiya Hartman, *Scenes of Subjection: Terror, Slavery, and Self-Making in Nineteenth Century America* (New York: Oxford University Press, 1997) and Christina Sharpe, *Monstrous Intimacies: Making Post-Slavery Subjects* (Durham, NC: Duke University Press, 2010).

34. In *Rape Warfare: The Hidden Genocide in Bosnia-Herzegovina and Croatia* Beverly Allen defines genocidal rape as "a military policy of rape for the purpose of genocide. . . ." She goes onto to note that rape is "often part of torture preceding death" and that it "furthers the genocidal plan of ethnic cleansing." Beverly Allen, *Rape Warfare*, vii.

35. Scarry, *The Body in Pain*, 4.

36. Ibid., 6.

37. See Nicholas Kristof and Sheryl WuDunn, *Half the Sky*, 61–62.

38. As feminist cultural critic Beverly Guy Sheftall has recently noted, black feminism has been especially instrumental in making violence against Black women legible to the point that "any examination of violence against black women is Black Feminism 101, and a testament to its viability."

39. I use feminist politics to mean: those actions and schools of thought that oppose and challenge inequality of women through acts varying from writing to political action. Despite whether or not the artists studied here are self-proclaimed feminists I argue that their texts can be marked by feminist politics and be read according to this framework. My vision of feminist politics takes its cue from such as Chandra Talpade Mohanty, Carole Boyce Davies, and Patricia Hill Collins, who also focus on the simultaneity of oppressions such as race, gender, class, nationality, sexuality, culture, and other "locations" (what such designations have been termed by Mohanty) in *Third World Women and the Politics of Feminism*. The view of Third World feminism as outlined by Mohanty entails four interrelated concepts: "(1) the idea of the simultaneity of oppressions as fundamental to the experiences of social and political marginality and the grounding of feminist politics in the histories of racism and imperialism; (2) the crucial role of a hegemonic state in circumscribing their/our daily lives and survival struggles; (3) the significance of memory and writing in the creation of oppositional agency; and (4) the differences, conflicts, and contradictions internal to third world women's organizations and communities." Chandra Talpade Mohanty, "Cartographies of Struggle," 10.

40. de Lauretis, "The Violence of Rhetoric: Considerations on Representation and Gender," 240.

Chapter 1

1. Boni, "Violences familières dans les littératures francophones du sud," 110.

2. Clinton, "'With a Whip in His Hand': Rape, Memory, and African-American Women," 205.

3. The newly translated version appears with two other texts in Yambo Ouo-

loguem, *The Yambo Ouologuem Reader: The Duty of Violence, A Black Ghostwriter's Letter to France, and the Thousand and One Bibles of Sex*, trans. and ed. Christopher Wise (Trenton, NJ: Africa World Press, 2008).

4. Wise, *Yambo Ouologuem: Postcolonial Writer, Islamic Militant*, 4.

5. Fanon, *Les damnés de la terre* (Paris: S.A.R.L, 1961). Frantz Fanon, *The Wretched of the Earth*, trans. Constance Farrington (New York: Grove Press, 1963).

6. Tracy Sharpley-Whiting presents a feminist re-reading of Fanon's work as "not only advocating gender equity and liberation, but representative of a *pro*feminist consciousness" in *Frantz Fanon: Conflicts and Feminisms*, 3.

7. Sielke, *Reading Rape: The Rhetoric of Sexual Violence in American Literature and Culture*, 10.

8. Fanon, *Damnés*, 65/Fanon, *Wretched*, 35. Fanon mentions countless forms of violence, in the first chapter he speaks of "pure violence" (69), "violence absoule" (66), "le caractère totalitaire de l'exploitation coloniale" (71). Subsequent citations will be by page number in the text hereinafter.

9. Waller, *Contradictory Violence*, 12.

10. Avelar, *The Letter of Violence*, 7.

11. Fanon, *L'an V de la Révolution algérienne*, 25. Fanon, *A Dying Colonialism*, 46. Subsequent citations will be by page number in the text hereinafter.

12. Donadey, "Francophone Women Writers and Postcolonial Theory," 205.

13. Mbembe is a justifiable endpoint to the group I have presented because, in his inclusion of women, he signals a possible departure from the earlier view, at least recognizing the interplay of political power and female oppression. "The unconditional subordination of women to the principle of male pleasure remains one pillar upholding the reproduction of the phallocratic system." But he does not insist on the role of gender. Achille Mbembe, *On the Postcolony*, 110.

14. Ibid., 113.

15. Ibid., 25.

16. Ibid., 102.

17. Ibid., 57.

18. *Ville cruelle* (Paris: Éditions africaines, 1954), *Le pauvre Christ de Bomba* (Paris: R. Laffont 1956), and *Remember Ruben* (Paris: Union générale d'éditions, 1974) are some examples of this tendency.

19. Beti, *Main basse sur le Cameroun*, ii.

20. Britton, "In Memory of Edouard Glissant," 668.

21. Kemedjio, "Rape of Bodies, Rape of Souls," 69.

22. Ibid., 71.

23. Garraway, *The Libertine Colony*, 22.

24. In relation to Africa this is perhaps especially true in the case of the Maghreb, the northern region, particularly for Algeria, which waged a war for independence from 1957–60, but in my work I focus on only Sub-Saharan Africa.

25. See Dayan, *Haiti, History and the Gods*.

26. Brutus, *L'homme d'airain*, vol. 1:264 (quoted in Dayan 1998).

27. Saint Arnaud Numa first fictionalized a story of the Taino queen in his play *Anacaona, reine martyre: Tragédie en trois actes* (Port-au-Prince, Haiti: Fardin, 1981). Later on Haitian-American writer Edwidge Danticat creates a fictionalized account of the Taino queen in her young adult novel *Anacaona: Golden Flower, Haiti, 1490* (New York: Scholastic, 2005).

28. For a history of the Caco Rebellions, a series of uprisings against the U.S. Occupation in the northern and southern parts of Haiti, see Abbott, *Haiti: The Duvaliers and Their Legacy*.

29. Peck, *L'homme sur les quais*, 1993.
30. Bell, *Walking on Fire*, 9.
31. See Beverly Bell's *Walking on Fire* which goes into great detail about this period after the coup.
32. The exact details of what took place during February 2004 are as of today are still contested, some have labeled the incident as a coup, others as the resignation of Aristide, and still others as his kidnapping.
33. Dash, Review, "*Ecrire en pays assiégé: Haiti, Writing Under Siege*," 163.
34. The recent article by journalist Mac McClelland that appeared in *Mother Jones* in the spring of 2011 helps to make this point. Mac McClelland, "Aftershocks," *Mother Jones* 36 Jan–Feb 2011): 30–42.
35. McClintock, *Imperial Leather*, 377.
36. Ormerod, "The Representation of Women in Caribbean Fiction," 101.
37. Sembene's later books also include minor references to rape in writing and on screen. For example, in *Black Docker* (1975) rape is present subtextually. This book has already been intertextually linked to Richard Wright's *Native Son*. Like Wright, Sembene makes subversive use of the "black male as rapist" trope that can be found in various texts of the African diaspora. What we see here is that rape is used as a theme to draw attention to the oppression of Black men by French people. Narratives of the black male rapist deny the subjective experience of Black women as T. Denean Sharpley-Whiting has pointed out in "When A Black Woman Cries Rape: Discourses of Unrapeability, Intraracial Sexual Violence, and the State of Indiana vs. Michael Gerard Tyson," in *Spoils of War: Women of Color, Cultures and Revolutions* (Lanham, MD: Rowman and Littlefield Publishers, 1997).
38. See Ousmane Sembene, *Ô pays mon beau peuple!* (Paris: Presse Pocket, 1957).
39. Faye states that "Les plus pernicieux sont les colons; ils disent: 'Il n'y a rien à tirer de ses nègres qui sont tous des fainéants, des voleurs. Pour les faire travailler, il n'y a rien de tel que la chicotte. Ils prétendent que leur vie ici est un enfer. Ils se prennent pour des héros.' . . ."/"The most pernicious are the colonizers, they say 'there is nothing we can pull from these [Blacks] who are all lazy, they are stealers. To make them work there is nothing like the lash. . . . They pretend that their lives here are hell. They take themselves for heroes,'" Sembene, *Ô pays mon beau peuple!*, 99.
40. When Sembene later adopts the medium of film he revisits the theme, addressing the largely ignored massacre of hundreds of *Tirailleurs* in *Le Camp de Thiaroye*.
41. For a study of violence in the context of francophone African literature that treats this novel along with several others, see Odile Cazenave, "Writing the Child, Youth, and Violence into the Francophone Novel from Sub-Saharan Africa: The Impact of Age and Gender," *Research in African Literatures* (Bloomington: Summer 2005, Vol. 36, Iss. 2): 59–72.
42. Sembene, *Ô pays mon beau peuple!*, 117.
43. Ibid.
44. In Sembene's oeuvre we find one of the few exceptions to representations of gender violence as a part of the nationalist project: the character of Penda in *Les bouts de bois de Dieu: Banty Mam Yall* (Paris: Livre contemporain, 1960). Penda is a prostitute who is determined to join in the railway strike struggle.
45. Ouologuem, *Le devoir de violence*, 26.
46. Ouologuem, *Bound to Violence*, 4.
47. When it was first published, *Le devoir* was lauded for the impact of its historic project: "*Le devoir de la violence* marque un nouveau tournant dans les lettres africaines qui deviennent dès lors, une littérature incontestablement courageuse dans cette époque qui suit les indépendances" [*Le devoir* marks a new turn in African letters

that have become since then, an undeniably courageous literature in this new era that follows the independence era] (Introduction, *Le devoir de violence* by Yambo Ouloguem 7).

48. Ahmadou Kourouma's second novel, *Monnè, outrages et défis* also treats the theme of violence and power, for an analysis of this work, see Amadou Koné, "Violence du pouvoir et pouvoir de la violence dans *Monnè, outrages et défis.*"

49. For a complete study of Kourouma's use of language in his work, see Makhily Gassama's *La langue d'Ahmadou Kourouma ou le français sous le soleil d'Afrique* (Paris: Karthala, 1995).

50. In his own words on this subject Kourouma refers to the "rape of language" by saying, "Je crois que les français ont leur langue. Ils ont violé beaucoup de peuples, mais ils voudraient que leur langue reste pure [I believe the French have their own language. They violated a lot of people, but they want their language remains pure]." *Chat* sur RFI 5/9/2001. http://aviquesnel.free.fr/Direlire/kourouma-le-soleil-des-independances.htm. Here Kourouma's logic follows a distinctly Fanonian impulse, a response to "le viol des langues africaines" with his own "viol de la langue française."

51. Kourouma, *Les soleils des indépendances*, 33. Kourouma, *The Suns of Independence*, 20.

52. *Les soleils des indépendances*, 41. *The Suns of Independence*, 25.

53. Dominic Thomas conducts such a reading in *Nation-Building, Propaganda, and Literature in Francophone Africa*.

54. Ibid., 66.

55. *La vie et demie*, 62.

56. Ibid., 69.

57. Tansi's novel *Les septs solitudes de Lorsa Lopez* (Paris: Seuil, 1984) pivots around the death of a woman whose murder results in women-centered change for the entire community. Although, a few years later Tansi uses the theme of gender violence as an organizing principle within the novel, I use *La vie et demie* as an example because of the intricate and explicit use of violence throughout the entire text.

58. For example, as Thomas observes, "[i]n *L'état hontueux*, the penis is described as a 'rape utensil.'" Thomas, *Nation-Building, Propaganda and Literature in Francophone Africa*, 68.

59. Although this study does not focus exclusively on women writers, it is indebted to previous works by scholars who do so, especially during the 1980s and 1990s. These are: Renée Larrier, *Francophone Women Writers of African and the Caribbean* (Gainesville: University Press of Florida, 1990); Irène Assiba d'Almeida, *Francophone African Women Writers: Destroying the Emptiness of Silence* (Gainesville: University Press of Florida, 1994); Odile Cazenave, *Femmes rebelles: Naissance d'un nouveau roman africain au féminin* (Paris: Harmattan, 1996); *Postcolonial Subjects: Francophone Women Writers*, ed. Mary Jean Green et al. (Minneapolis: University of Minnesota Press, 1996); Nikki Hitchcott, *Women Writers in Francophone Africa* (Oxford: Berg, 2000); and Kenneth Harrow, *Less Than One and Double: A Feminist Reading of African Women's Writing* (Portsmouth, NH: Heinemann, 2002). Likewise, later studies which take on different methodological approaches to analyzing francophone African and Caribbean women's writing together have also broke important ground. See for example Julie Nack Ngue, *Critical Conditions: Illness and Disability in Francophone African and Caribbean Women's Writing* (Lanham: Lexington Books, 2012) and Bernard Ekome, *Le corps des africaines décrites par des romancières africaines* (Paris: Harmattan, 2012) both of which expand extant vies on how female bodies and corporeality are rendered through literature.

60. Mehta, *Notions of Identity*, 5.
61. Cazenave in Smith 95.
62. Schwarz-Bart, *Pluie et vent*, 159. My translation.
63. See Abena Busia, "This Gift of Metaphor: Symbolic Strategies and the Triumph of Survival in Simone Schwarz-Bart's *The Bridge of Beyond*," in *Out of Kumbla: Caribbean Women and Literature*, ed. Carole Boyce Davies and Elaine Savory Fido (Trenton: Africa World Press, 1990), 289–301; Ronnie Scharfman "Mirroring and Mothering in Simone Schwarz-Bart's *Pluie et vent sur Télumée Miracle* and Jean Rhys' *Wide Sargasso Sea*," *Yale French Studies* 62 (1981): 88–106; and Clarisse Zimra, "What's in a Name: Elective Genealogy in Schwarz-Bart's Early Novels," *Studies in 20th Century Literature* 17.1 (1993): 97–118.
64. Schwarz-Bart, *Pluie et vent sur Télumée Miracle*, 112–13. *Bridge of Beyond*, 72.
65. Ibid., 113. Ibid., 72.
66. Ibid., 115. Ibid., 73.
67. Scharfman "Mirroring and Mothering in Simone Schwarz-Bart's *Pluie et vent sur Télumée Miracle* and Jean Rhys' *Wide Sargasso Sea*," 95.
68. Dash, "Vital Signs in the Body Politic," 312.
69. Condé, *Moi, Tituba, Sorcière noire de Salem*, 15./*I, Tituba, Black Witch of Salem*, 3.
70. Andrade, "The Nigger of the Narcissist," 216.
71. Beyala, *Tu t'appelleras Tanga*, 46. *Your Name Shall be Tanga*, 30.
72. Volet, "A Literary Feast in a Violent World," 187.
73. Ibid., 191.
74. Trouillot, *Rosalie l'Infâme*, 40.
75. Of course this is not to say that women have not also deployed the vocabulary of sexual violence to describe the postcolonial dynamic of epistemic violence that continues today. Aminata Traoré's *Le viol de l'imaginaire* (Paris: Fayard, 2002) is a significant example in this regard.
76. My use of the term "rhetoric of rape" borrows from Sabine Sielke's analysis in *Reading Rape* in which she defines the rhetoric of rape as "what we talk about when we talk about rape;" see Sielke, *Reading Rape*, 2.
77. Ibid.
78. Scott, *Gender and the Politics of History*, 44.
79. Hannah Arendt begins *On Violence* by noting that "No one engaged in thought about history and politics can remain unaware of the enormous role violence has always played in human affairs, and it is at first glance rather surprising that violence has been singled out so seldom for special consideration." Hannah Arendt, *On Violence*, 8.
80. Aiming her critique at the New Left, militant African Americans, Frantz Fanon and all who espoused the use of violence as a means for liberation, Arendt described the ways in which more violence leads to less power, writing that "Violence can always destroy power; out of the barrel of a gun grows the most effective command, resulting in the most instant and perfect obedience. What never can grow out of it is power." Arendt, *On Violence*, 53.
81. Ibid.
82. See Hartman, *Scenes of Subjection*.
83. MacCannell and MacCannell, "Violence, Power and Pleasure," 227.
84. Like many feminist scholars, I am skeptical of Foucault's usefulness for a study of gender violence. There are many instances in which it is necessary to depart from Foucauldian constructions; for example, his assessment of power as neutral has problematic implications for gender: "[A]s illuminating as his [Foucault's] work is to our

understanding of the mechanics of power in social relations, its critical value is limited by his unconcern for what, after him, we might call 'the technology of gender'—the techniques and discursive strategies by which gender is constructed" in de Lauretis, "the Violence of Rhetoric," 245; see also Michel Foucault, *Discipline and Punish*, 93.

85. Foucault defines "technology of power" as "one of the four types of technologies, a matrix of practical reason that determines the conduct of individuals and submit them to certain ends or domination, and objectivizing the subject" although Foucault neglects this angle, this is often what happens to women in the representation of violence. Michel Foucault, *Technologies of the Self*, 18.

86. Ferly, *A Poetics of Relation*, 60.

87. Stockton, *The Economics of Fantasy*, 3.

88. Elizabeth Willey conducts an analysis of Ouologuem's "subversive" politics in the context of gender, arguing that "An extension of the feminist critique to [all of Ouologuem's corpus] seriously weakens any representation of Ouologuem's work as subversive." She goes on to also cite the work of Eileen Julien who "points out that though Ouologuem's text is radically critical of the hierarchy inherent in European colonialism, it does not challenge hierarchical gender relations; in fact, on a textual level in reinscribes female passivity;" see Willey, "Pornography or the Politics of Misbehaving?," 160.

89. Julien, "Rape, Repression and Narrative Form in *Le devoir de violence* and *La vie et demie*," 161.

90. Sielke, *Reading Rape*, 62.

91. In the final chapter of *Les damnés de la terre* entitled "Guerre coloniale et troubles mentaux," Fanon presents a number of analyses on the experience of Algerians who suffer from varying degrees of posttraumatic stress disorder (PTSD) as a result of the Algerian war for independence. One of the cases is that of an Algerian soldier whose wife was raped during the war. In this instance, only the man's reactions to his wife's rape are presented as relevant. I will return to this particular example in chapter 2. See Frantz Fanon, *Les damnés*, 196–97.

92. Fanon's example of Algerian women carrying the bomb beneath the veil is one of the best examples of how women can play a role in anti-colonial insurgency.

93. See Christiane Makward's *Mayotte Capécia ou l'aliénation selon Fanon* for an indepth study of Fanon's troubling characterization of Capécia and her novel *Je suis martiniquaise*. I do agree with Sharpley-Whiting, who has problematized analyses of Fanon's evaluation of *Je suis martiniquaise*; however what interests me here is how sexual violence fits into these discourses. Interestingly, from a black feminist perspective, Fanon's preoccupation with the cultural mythology of the Black male rapist in *Black Skin, White Masks* also poses a challenge to the black female subjectivity since the contestation of this myth has also contributed to the silencing of Black women's narratives of rape. I am not contesting that Fanon "views rape as a form of colonial oppression directed explicitly toward colonized women"; rather, I am critiquing how this link between rape and colonial oppression is analyzed as well as how it tends to focus the effects of sexual violence on colonized men (Sharpley-Whiting, *Frantz Fanon: Conflicts and Feminisms* 15).

94. Lionnet, "A Politics of the 'We'?: Autobiography, Race, and Nation," 380.

95. Anne McClintock offers an important analysis of how nationalism, gender, and race often operate in concert with one another in the oppression of women in *Imperial Leather*, 353: "Nationalism [is] radically constitutive of people's identities through social contests that are frequently violent and always gendered."

96. Alexandre, "From the Same Tree," 917.

97. Willey, "Pornography or the Politics of Misbehaving?," 149.
98. Mardorossian, "Towards a New Feminist Theory of Rape," 743.
99. Siebers, "Language, Violence and the Sacred," 215.
100. Higgins and Silver, *Rape and Representation*, 3–4.
101. Buchwald, Fletcher, et al., *Transforming a Rape Culture*, Preface.
102. Higgins and Silver, *Rape and Representation*, 248.
103. Sharpe, *Allegories of Empire: The Figure of Woman in the Colonial Text*, 8.
104. Mouralis, "Les disparus et les survivants," 14.
105. "Parmi les femmes, c'est assurément Calixthe Beyala qui va le plus loin dans l'audace langagière. [Among the women, it is assuredly Calixthe Beyala who goes the furthest in linguistic audacity."] Mwatha Musanji Ngalasso, "Langage et violence dans la littérature africaine écrite en français," 75.
106. Bonnet, "Villes africaines et écritures de la violence," 24.
107. Boni, "Violences familières dans les littératures francophones du sud," 110.
108. Boni actually mentions Ilboudo's novel *Le mal de peau* in her footnote: "Chez Monique Ilboudo, le viol a pour conséquence la couleur de la peau. . . . " [In the work of Monique Ilboudo, skin color is a consequence of rape. . . .]).
109. Dominique Mondoloni, "Comprendre," 3.
110. In an article for *Le monde diplomatique*, Boubacar Boris Diop takes another approach to understanding the presence of violence: "Selon une idée répandue mais jamais clairement formulée, la culture de la violence a des racines profondes en Afrique. Cet a priori mène tout droit à une lecture raciale des luttes pour le pouvoir sur le continent comme expression de haines ethniques séculaires." [There is a widespread belief, never clearly formulated, that the culture of violence is deeply rooted in Africa. The underlying assumption is racist: that power struggles in the continent are the expression of secular ethnic hatreds.] Diop, "Avertissement ivoirien à la Françafrique," 9.
111. Chemain-Degrange, "Violence destructrice, violence régénératrice: originalité de la littérature africaine subsaharienne," 15.
112. Fratta, "Violence destructrice, violence régénératrice: originalité de la littérature africaine subsaharienne," 7.
113. This reading of *viol* as neuter is important because although rape is an act of violation that can be issued against men and against women, it is often not specified that men too can be victims of sexual violence.

Chapter 2

1. Chancy, "There are No Giraffes in Haiti," 306–7.
2. Francis, "Silences Too Horrific to Disturb," 75.
3. Dayan, *Haiti, History and the Gods*, 48.
4. See for example Ronnie Scharfman, "Theorizing Terror: The Discourse of Violence in Marie Chauvet's *Amour, colère, folie*," 230.
5. *Amour, colère, folie* has been describes as a trilogy, a novel in three movements, a triptych, and three separate novellas.
6. The list of Haitian dictator novels includes, Marie Chauvet, *Amour, colère, folie* (1968); Franketienne, *Ultravocal* (1972); Anthony Phelps, *Moins l'infini* (1973); Gérard Etienne, *Le nègre crucifié* (1974); Jean-Claude Charles, *Sainte dérive des cochons* (1977); René Depestre, *Le mât de cocagne* (1979); Roger Dorsinville, *Mourir pour Haïti ou Les croisés d'Esther* (1980); Emile Ollivier, *Mère-Solitude* (1983); J. J. Dominique, *Mé-

moire d'une amnésique (1984); Lilas Desquiron, *Les chemins de loco-miroir* (1990); Lyonel Trouillot, *Rue des pas perdus* (1996); Dany Laferrière, *Le cri des oiseaux fous* (2000); Edwidge Danticat, *The Dew Breaker* (2004); Ludovic Comeau, Jr. *Les bâtisseurs du lendemain* (2007); Marie-Célie Agnant, *Un alligator nommé Rosa* (2007); Kettly Mars, *Saisons sauvages* (2010); Evelyne Trouillot, *La mémoire aux abois* (2010).

7. The term *la terreur*, translated the terror, is commonly used to refer to the regime.

8. Mehta, *Notions of Identity, Diaspora, and Gender in Caribbean Women's Writing*, 11.

9. See Beverly Bell's *Walking on Fire: Haitian Women's Stories of Survival and Resistance*.

10. Zarifis, "Haitian Women Speak Out Against Violence," *Inter-American Commission on Human Rights*, (2008) online http://www.oas.org/es/cidh/.

11. Sheller, *Citizenship from Below: Erotic Agency and Caribbean Freedom*, 161.

12. Myriam Chancy notes in *Framing Silence: Revolutionary Novels by Haitian Women* that "A report made in 1927 by the United Nations' Women's International League for Peace and Freedom revealed that U.S. troops had been responsible for numerous 'war crimes' against women." Chancy, *Framing Silence*, 39.

13. Francis, *Fictions of Feminine Citizenship*, 80.

14. Trouillot, *Haiti, State Against Nation*, 167.

15. See Elizabeth Abbott's *Haiti: The Duvaliers and Their Legacy*, 78–80 for a detailed account of Hakim-Rimpel's story.

16. Dietrich and Burt, *Papa Dac et les Tontons macoutes*, 105.

17. Myriam Chancy argues a similar point in both *Framing Silence: Revolutionary Novels by Haitian Women* and "No Giraffes in Haiti."

18. Charles, "Gender and Politics in Contemporary Haiti: the Duvalierist State, Transnationalism, and the Emergence of a New Feminism (1980–1990)," 140.

19. Francis, *Fictions of Feminine Citizenship*, 81–82.

20. Beverly Bell's *Walking on Fire: Haitian Women's Stories of Survival and Resistance*, an important intervention featuring the testimonies of Haitian women goes into great detail about gender violence, and in particular rape that took place during the *deshoukaj* and *machin enfènal* periods.

21. Charles, "Gender and Politics in Contemporary Haiti," 135.

22. United Nations Population Fund (UNFPA) 25 November 2005. http://www.haiti info.com/article.php3?id_article=4073.

23. The most publicized incident occurred in February of 2005 when a Haitian woman reported being raped by three members of the U.N. Stabilization Mission. According to the Commission of Women Victims for Victims "The presence of MINUSTAH (UN peacekeeping mission) in poor neighborhoods has done little to prevent rapes from occurring on a daily basis. The number of cases we have received from Village de Dieu and Cité Soleil alone shows us that MINUSTAH has failed to provide real security for women in these areas." http://www.haitisupport.gn.apc.org/Rape2005.htm.

24. See the report by Ann-christie d'Adesky and the Poto Fanm + Fi Collective, *Beyond Shock: Charting the Landscape of Sexual Violence in Post-Earthquake Haiti, 2010-2012* for important insights into understanding sexual violence in the aftermath of the earthquake.

25. Francis, "Silences Too Horrific to Disturb," 78.

26. Tracy Wilkinson, "Rape flourishes . . . " *Los Angeles Times*, 4 February 2011 and Olesya Dmitracova, "Post-quake chaos fuels . . . " Reuters, 6 January 2011.

27. Amnesty International, "Aftershocks: Women Speak Out Against Sexual Violence in Haiti's Camps," http://www.amnesty.org/en/library/asset/AMR36/001/2011/en/57237fad-f97b-45ce-8fdb-68cb457a304c/amr360012011en.pdf. Accessed 6 January 2011.

28. International Institute for Justice and Democracy in Haiti, KOFAVIV, MADRE, *Our Bodies Are Still Trembling: Haitian Women's Fight Against Rape*, http://www.madre.org/images/uploads/misc/1283377138_2010.07.26%20-%20HAITI%20GBV%20REPORT%20FINAL.pdf. 4. Accessed 9 September 2011.

29. Ibid., 4.

30. d'Adesky et al., *Beyond Shock*, 13.

31. Ibid., 15.

32. This is in contrast to human right reports during the 1990s which covered the increase of sexual violence during the coup. As Lucia Suarez points out during this time, "rape without political motivation . . . receives little if no attention in recent human rights/political studies." Suarez, "What Happens When Memory Hurts?: The Haunting of Rape," 63.

33. The French definition of these words from *Le Robert dictionnaire de la langue française* makes this distinction clear "Politique: nom masculin, 1. Relatif à l'organisation et à l'exercice du pouvoir dans une société organisée. *Pouvoir politique, pouvoir de gouverner*." [masculine noun 1. On the organization and exercise of power in an organized society. Political power, power to govern] and "Politique: nom, feminine. 1. Manière de gouverner un État (politique intérieure) ou de mener les relations avec les autres Etats. *Politique conservatrice, liberale, de droite etc.*" [feminine noun. 1. How to govern a state (domestic policy) or conduct relations with other states. Conservative politics, liberal, right etc.] *Le Robert dictionnaire de la langue française*, 3ème édition, (Paris: Dictionnaires Le Robert, 1998) 1017.

34. While *Amour, colère, folie* is the novel by Chauvet that has received the most attention, violence is present throughout her corpus. Of particular note is the novel *Fille d'Haïti* (1954) in which the protagonist Lotus is raped as a result of her political activities. A recent article by Kaiama Glover conducts a thoughtful and thorough analysis of the novel "'Black' Radicalism in Haiti and the Disorderly Feminine: The Case of Marie Chauvet, *Small Axe* 17.1 (2013): 7–21.

35. Walcott-Hackshaw, "My Love is Like a Rose," 40.

36. "The use of rape . . . as an instrument of state-instituted violence has increased massively over the last ten years [between 1987 and 1997], which is not to say that the same form of violence was not used under Duvalier (Marie Chauvet's novels disabused us of such naïveté)." Chancy, *Framing Silence*, 44.

37. Ibid., 307.

38. Rose Normil is not the only woman who is sexually violated in *Amour, colère, folie*. There is also the case of Dora Soubiran in *Amour*, who is punished for her privileged status with sexual mutilation. In the final section, *Folie*, policemen who represent the Tontons Macoutes also sexually violate several women while they are held in custody.

39. Vieux-Chauvet, *Amour, colère et folie*, 200. Vieux-Chauvet, *Love, Anger, Madness* trans. Réjouis and Vinkour, 192. Subsequent citations will be by page number in the text hereinafter.

40. Kempadoo, *Sexing the Caribbean*, 3.

41. This view was most recently reinforced in the translation of the novel. For example, in the introduction Edwidge Danticat describes Rose as "a self-sacrificing

counterpart to *Love's* Claire Clamont ... " (Danticat, "Introduction" *Love, Anger, Madness*, trans. Réjouis and Vinkour, x). Yet the translators in their preface express that "there is torture-rape in each of the novellas in Marie Vieux-Chauvet's 1968 trilogy." Réjouis and Vinkour, "Sharp Minds, Raw Hearts: A Translator's Preface," in *Love, Anger, Madness*, vii.

42. Back matter, Marie Vieux-Chauvet, *Amour, colère et folie* (Paris: Soley, 2006).
43. Rajan, *Real and Imagined Women*, 73.
44. Scarry, *The Body in Pain*, 5.
45. Rajan, *Real and Imagined Women*, 72.
46. N'Zengou-Tayo, "'Fanm Se Poto-Mitan': Haitian Woman, the Pillar of Society," 130.
47. Ibid., 129.
48. At only one point does Paul make note of the psychological effects of what Rose goes through: Paul notices that his sister is suffering internally "Elle a l'air de détester le monde entier. Elle a un drôle de regard fixe, comme si intérieurement elle suivait un affreux spectacle ... " (Vieux-Chauvet, *Amour, colère, folie*, 247).
49. Tal, *Worlds of Hurt*, 155.
50. N'Zengou-Tayo, 135.
51. Such a legacy is especially noticeable when we look at contemporary Haitian writers. Ranging from a mother's excruciating "testing" of her daughter in Danticat's *Breath, Eyes, Memory* (1992) and Marie-Célie Agnant's use of the theme in *La dot de Sara* (1995) to *Le diable dans un thé à la citronnelle* (2005), Gary Victor's representation of the precarious journey to heal from rape after many years. Such examples clearly demonstrate that different forms of sexual violence are being drawn explicitly.
52. For a recent article that helps to make this point, see Clare Counihan, "Desiring Diaspora 'Testing' the Boundaries of National Identity in Edwidge Danticat's *Breath, Eyes, Memory*," *Small Axe* 37 (March 2012): 36–52.
53. Danticat, *The Dew Breaker*, 21. Subsequent citations will be by page number in the text hereinafter.
54. See Kamala Kempadoo's *Sexing the Caribbean* for an in-depth analysis of "transactional sexual relations" including prostitution and sex working.
55. Danticat, "We Are Ugly But We Are Here."
56. Placide, *Fresh Girl*, 98. Subsequent citations will be by page number in the text hereinafter.
57. For a series of essays on childhood representations of sexual assault in literature see Deirdre Lashgari, ed., *Violence, Silence, and Anger: Women's Writing As Transgression*.
58. Mars, *Saisons Sauvages*, 136. All translations of *Saisons Sauvages* are mine. Subsequent citations will be by page number in the text hereinafter.
59 Cazenave, "Francophone Caribbean Women Writers," 94.
60. Kempadoo, *Sexing the Caribbean*, 3.
61. Tinsley, *Thiefing Sugar*, 104.
62. Mardorossian, "Towards a New Feminist Theory of Rape," 745.
63. Danticat, *Breath Eyes Memory*, 61.

Chapter 3

1. Aimar, "Rencontre avec Gisèle Pineau," 17–19. Unless otherwise noted, all translations in this essay are my own.

2. See novel of the same name, Raphaël Confiant, *Bassin des ouragans*, 1994.

3. I use the term "natural violence" here to denote catastrophes of nature that have causes beyond human influence, such as hurricanes, floods, earthquakes, and volcanoes. Indeed, these forces exist in many different environments, but tropical islands are particularly vulnerable to them.

4. Aimar, "Rencontre avec Gisèle Pineau," 19.

5. Some helpful examples include Aliyyah Abdur-Rahman *Against the Closet: Black Political Longing and Sexual Figurations* (Durham: Duke University Press, 2012).

6. Ferly, *A Poetics of Relation*, 34.

7. Barnes, *Incest and the Literary Imagination*, 2.

8. Valerie Orlando's idea of subjecthood is helpful here: "Female subjecthood as defined by current African and Caribbean francophone women authors is formed not only from new ideals of the mind but also from the conceptualization of an original body politics; a corporeal reality that promotes a sexually differentiated structure of the speaking subject. Such a new speaking subject is no longer understood as an ahistorical object, but rather is viewed as a body linked to, and interwoven with a plurality of systems: political, cultural, economic and historical. The new feminine subject is a site of contestation where sociocultural and political struggles play themselves out, are heard by all, refashioned and retransmitted to a woman's own terms." Valerie Orlando, *Of Suffocating Hearts and Tortured Souls*, 2.

9. Cahill. *Rethinking Rape*, 8–9.

10. Ibid., 10.

11. Ibid.

12. Feminist theorists of the body such as Judith Butler, *Bodies that Matter: On the Discursive Limits of Sex* (New York: Routledge, 1993), Elizabeth Grosz, *Volatile Bodies: Towards a Corporeal Feminism* (Bloomington: Indiana University Press, 1994), and Rosi Braidotti, *Nomadic Subjects: Embodiment and Sexual Difference in Contemporary Feminist Theory* (Columbia University Press, 1994), among others have generated an impressive body of work that addresses issues of the body, difference, and subjectivity.

13. Tinsley, *Thiefing Sugar*, 15.

14. Ippolito, *Caribbean Women Writers: Identity and Gender*, 9.

15. Mehta, *Notions of Identity, Diaspora and Gender in Caribbean Women's Writing*, 4.

16. Kalisa, *Violence in Francophone African and Caribbean Women's Literature*, 119.

17. Walcott-Hackshaw, "My Love is Like a Rose," 46.

18. Roumain, *Gouverneurs de la rosée*, 39.

19. Benítez-Rojo, *The Repeating Island*, 5.

20. Ibid., 300.

21. Ibid., 302.

22. Ibid., 201.

23. Ibid., 215 (my emphasis).

24. Ibid.

25. Ibid.

26. Ibid., 5 (my emphasis).

27. Tinsley, *Thiefing Sugar*, 42.

28. Ibid.

29. Tinsley, "Black Atlantic, Queer Atlantic Queer Imaginings of the Middle Passage," 215.

30. Rosello, *Littérature et identité créole aux Antilles*, 7.

31. Walcott-Hackshaw 46.

32. Tinsley, *Thiefing Sugar*, 23.

33. Ibid.
34. Jackson, "Subjection and Resistance . . . " 92.
35. Ibid., 92.
36. Naudillon, "Le continent noir du corps: représentation du corps féminin chez Marie-Célie Agnant et Gisèle Pineau," 81.
37. Duvivier, "My Body is a Piece of Land," 1108.
38. Ibid., 1109.
39. Njeri Githrie, for example, writes that Pineau is "often referred to as one of the voices of Créolité" in "Horizons Adrift: Women in Exile, at Home, and Abroad in Gisèle Pineau's Works," 74.
40. Condé, "The Stealers of Fire: The French-Speaking Writers of the Caribbean and their Strategies of Liberation," 163.
41. Cazenave, "Francophone Caribbean Women Writers," 98.
42. Like many feminist writers and intellectuals, I am suspicious of Créolité dogmatism as a way to approach rape representation, as Brinda Mehta observes "Créolité's linguistic absolutism has unwittingly become an inverted image of francité, or Frenchness, in absolute bonds of departmental affinity." Mehta, *Notions of Identity, Diaspora and Gender in Caribbean Women's Writing*, 7.
43. Belugue, "Entretien avec Gisèle Pineau," 89 (my emphasis).
44. Tinsley, *Thiefing Sugar*, 35.
45. Pineau and Abraham, *Femmes des Antilles: Traces et voix, cent cinquante ans après l'abolition de l'esclavage*, 4.
46. Naudillon, "Le continent noir du corps," 81.
47. Pineau, *Chair Piment*, 23.
48. Another issue that informs narratives of rape for people of African descent is the "myth of the black male rapist" first coined and described by Angela Davis. "Rape, Racism, and the Myth of the Black Male Rapist," *Women, Race and Class*, 172–201 (New York: Vintage Books, 1981).
49. In order to distinguish between the textual references to the storm ("the Beast") and my own contextual use of the term, I place references from the novel in quotations.
50. Caruth, *Unclaimed Experience*, 6 (my emphasis).
51. Cahill, *Rethinking Rape*, 13.
52. Haigh, *Mapping a Tradition*, 41.
53. See for example, A. W. Burgess and L. L. Holmstrom, "Rape Trauma Syndrome," *American Journal of Psychiatry* 131 (1974): 981–86; Judith Lewis Herman, *Trauma and Recovery* (New York: Basic Books, 1992); Jenny Petrak and Barbara Hedge, *The Trauma of Sexual Assault: Treatment, Prevention, and Practice* (New York: Wiley, 2002); and Susan J. Brison, *Aftermath: Violence and the Remaking of a Self* (Princeton: Princeton University Press, 2002).
54. See *On Violence: A Reader* (Durham, NC: Duke University Press, 2007) for a useful collection of classic perspectives on violence from Walter Benjamin to Slavoj Žižek.
55. Cahill, *Rethinking Rape*, 118.
56. I am referring here to studies conducted in Guadeloupe, in the United and in France, each of which point to a discrepancy between the public perception of rape and the statistics regarding the circumstances and frequency of its occurrence. Myths about rape are commonly addressed in anti-sexual assault advocacy; in fact, the "Myths and Facts" doctrine is a staple of many rape awareness and prevention education programs.
57. Cahill, *Rethinking Rape*, 5.

58. Tinsley, *Thiefing Sugar*, 67.
59. Larrier, *Autofiction and Advocacy*, 101.
60. Canneval, "Viol à Domicile: les enfants en danger!" 43.
61. The issue of mothers' reactions to incest is not specific to Guadeloupe. Gisela Norat explores this theme in literature by addressing the problems that incest often presents in mother–daughter relationships. She writes, "another characteristic of an incestuous family is a poor mother-daughter relationship, which undermines the daughter's ability to confide in another adult. . . ." See Gisela Norat, "The Silent Child Within the Angry Woman: Exorcising Incest in Sylvia Molloy's *Certificate of Absence*," in *Violence, Silence, and Anger*, ed. Deirdre Lashgari (Charlottesville: University of Virginia Press, 1995), 219.
62. I am thankful to Harvard University Graduate School of Arts and Sciences and the Mellon-Mays Program through which I was able to obtain funding to conduct research on anti-violence movements in Guadeloupe and the work of Gisèle Pineau.
63. Fabrice, "L'inceste: Une réalité dans nos îles," *Sept Magazine* 592 (25 octobre 1990): 15.
64. Fabrice, "L'inceste: Une réalité dans nos îles," 13–17.
65. Ibid.
66. Ibid.
67. Catherine Clinton argues that "[i]n every case of rape, whether the mark is invisible or permanent, life or death, a mark remains: the memory of a violation—force without consent. . . . The mark may only be *an ineradicable memory*." Clinton, "With a Whip in His Hand': Rape, Memory, and African-American Women," 205 (my emphasis).
68. Brooks, *Bodies in Dissent*, 5.
69. See Lynn A. Higgins and Brenda R. Silver, eds., *Rape and Representation* (New York: Columbia University Press, 1991) 4.
70. Ferly, *A Poetics of Relation*, 26.
71. Horeck, *Public Rape*, 120.

Chapter 4

1. Mukagasana, *Les blessures du Silence*, 9.
2. Harrow, "*Un train peut en cacher un autre*": Narrating the Rwandan Genocide and *Hotel Rwanda*," 223.
3. The Front Patriotique Rwandais-inkotanyi, also known for its English name Rwandan Patriotic Front (RPF), is a predominantly Tutsi group of militants who had been in exile in Uganda. For an analysis and history of RPF see Gérard Prunier, "Éléments pour une histoire du Front Patriotique rwandais," *Politique africaine* 51 (octobre 1993): 121–38.
4. 800,000 is the most widely accepted number of official deaths, but others have also been recorded in these sources, with the highest being placed at 10,000 a day. As Mahmood Mamdani states, "no one can say with certainty how many Tutsi were killed between March and July of 1994 in Rwanda." Mamdani, *When Victims Become Killers: Colonialism, Nativism, and the Genocide in Rwanda* (Princeton: Princeton University Press, 2001), 5.
5. Mamdani, *When Victims Become Killers*, 14.
6. "Rwandan Genocide," BBC *Special Reports*, 28 May 1994 http://news.bbc.co.uk/2/hi/in_depth/africa/2004/rwanda/default.stm. Accessed 21 May 2011.

7. For example, although Human Rights Watch would begin using the term genocide on April 19, it would take almost two months for the United States to agree with the genocide terminology. Samantha Power, *A Problem from Hell: America in the Age of Genocide* (New York: Perennial, 2002) 357. For a detailed explanation on the debate surrounding the use of the term in relation to genocide, see Samantha Power's chapter "Rwanda: Mostly in Listening Mode" 329–89 in Power, *A Problem from Hell*.

8. Cotta, *Why Violence?* 2.

9. Hitchcott, "A Global African Commemoration: Rwanda, Écrire par devoir de mémoire," 153.

10. Mahmood Mamdani's work stands as a clear point in this regard. In *When Victims Become Killers*, he delineates some of the central mythologies of the genocide and frames them in terms of three silences concerning the history, agency, and geography of the genocide. See Mamdani, *When Victims Become Killers*, 5–6.

11. Harrow, "'Un train peut en cacher un autre,'" 224.

12. Lionnet, "Geographies of Pain: Captive Bodies and Violent Acts in the Fictions of Myriam Warner-Vieyra, Gayl Jones, and Bessie Head," 137.

13. Ibid., 137 (emphasis mine).

14. Elaine Scarry pursues the topic in her study *The Body in Pain: The Making and Unmaking of the World*, an exegesis on the incommunicability of pain. Although, as Rajeswari Sunder Rajan has argued, "Scarry created out of pain the very condition of the female subject . . . 'the radical subjectivity of pain' as Scarry calls it, referring to its essential privacy and incommunicability can also serve as the basis of subjectivity in the sense of . . . the constitution of the identity of the self/subject." Rajeswari Sunder Rajan, *Real and Imagined Women*, 20.

15. I borrow this term from Chandra Talpade Mohanty, who, like many global feminist theorists, has focused on the simultaneity of oppressions such as race, gender, class, nationality, sexuality, culture, and other "locations" that inform my vision of feminist politics. In the case of Rwanda we must consider race, gender, nationality, culture, and ethnicity.

16. See for example transnational feminist scholars such as Inderpal Grewal, *Transnational America: Feminisms, Diasporas, Neoliberalisms* (Durham: Duke University Press, 2005), Wendy Hesford and Wendy Kozol, *Just Advocacy?: Women's Human Rights, Transnational Feminisms, and The Politics of Representation* (New Brunswick, NJ: Rutgers University Press, 2005), Chandra Talpade Mohanty, *Feminism Without Borders: Decolonizing Theory, Practicing Solidarity* (Durham: Duke University Press, 2003).

17. Kaufman and Williams, *Women and War: Gender Identity and Activism in Times of Conflict*, 39.

18. Ibid.

19. Felman, "Education and Crisis, or the Vicissitudes of Teaching," 15.

20. Yolande Mukagasana, *Les blessures du silence: Témoignages du Génocide au Rwanda* (Arles: Actes sud, 2001); Yolande Mukagasana, *La mort ne veut pas de moi* (Paris: Fixot, 1997); and Yolande Mukagasana, *N'aie pas peur de savoir* (Paris: Laffont, 1999).

21. Catherine MacKinnon, quoted in Hesford *Spectacular Rhetorics*, 93.

22. It should be noted that Tutsi women were not the only women raped during the genocide. Part of the Interahamwe strategy was to also eliminate, torture, kill, and rape moderate Hutu men and women.

23. Nowrojee, "Shattered Lives: Sexual Violence during the Rwandan Genocide and Its Aftermath," 1.

24. Copelon, quoted in Goldberg, *Beyond Terror*, 212.

25. Loinsigh, "Lying to Tell the Truth," 83.

26. Ibid.
27. Ibid., 85.
28. Harrow, "*Un train peut en cacher un autre:* Narrating the Genocide and Hotel Rwanda," 223.
29. Ibid., 222.
30. Participating writer Boubacar Boris Diop explains that the idea was initiated by Fest'Africa director, Nocky Djedanoum, "Le directeur du festival, Nocky Djedanoum, a pensé que ce serait bien d'envoyer au Rwanda des auteurs africains puisque, quand il y a eu le génocide, tout le monde en a un peu parlé mais pas les auteurs africains. C'est Nocky qui a donc eu cette très belle idée. . . . Le Rwanda m'a appris à appeler les monstres par leur nom" [The festival director, Nocky Djedanoum, thought it would be good to send African authors to Rwanda, since at the time there has been genocide, and everyone talked about it a bit about but not African authors. Nocky is the one who had this wonderful idea. . . . Rwanda has taught me to call the monsters by name]. See "Entretien avec Boubacar Boris Diop," 15.
31. Rurangwa, "Why I Write, What I Write, How I Write It," 20.
32. The following is a list of the ten writers, their countries of origin and the titles of their works from the project: Boubacar Boris Diop, Sénégal. *Murambi, le livre des ossements* (Stock, 2000); Monique Ilboudo, Burkina Faso. *Mukratete* (Le Figuier et Fest'Africa editions, 2000); Koulsy Lamko, Tchad. *La phalène des collines* (Kuljaama, Kigali, 2000); Tierno Monenembo, Guinée. *L'ainé des orphelins* (Seuil, 2000); Meja Mwangi, Kenya. *Great Sadness* (forthcoming); Vénuste Kayimahé, Rwanda. *France-Rwanda, les coulisses du génocide;* Véronique Tadjo, Côte d'Ivoire. *L'ombre d'Imana: Voyages jusqu'au bout du Rwanda* (Actes sud, 2000); Jean-Marie Vianney Rurangwa, Rwanda. *Le génocide des Tutsi expliqué à un étranger* (Le Figuier Fest'Africa Editions, 2000); Abdourahman Ali waberi, Djibouti. *Terminus: Textes pour le Rwanda* (Le Serpent à Plumes, 2000); Nocky Djedanoum, Tchad. *Nyamirambo!* (Le Figuier Fest'Africa Editions, 2000).
33. Hitchcott, "A Global African Commemoration,"154.
34. Interview of Nocky Djedanoum by Chaacha Mwita, "Writing to Remember Genocide," *Sunday Nation,* 13 (my emphasis).
35. Hitchcott, "A Global African Commemoration,"152.
36. Yet according to Loinsigh even this assignment imposes a set of limitations because "the specific aesthetic demands imposed on the authors were accompanied by an unspoken moral and ethical responsibility to ensure that their writing," Loinsigh, "*Un dimanche à la piscine à Kigali:* Writing the Rwandan Genocide," 86.
37. Hitchcott, "A Global African Commemoration," 159.
38. *Maison de mémoire.* "Manifeste," http://www.africultures.com/partenaires/evenements/rwanda94/aimgr.htm. Accessed 16 April 2011.
39. For more on the French government's involvement in the Rwandan genocide, specifically in the form of militia training of the Hutu forces, see Linda Melvern's *Conspiracy to Murder.*
40. The Rwandese that the Fest'Africa writers encountered made specific requests of the collective. Boubacar Boris Diop explains that they were repeatedly asked, "N'écrivez surtout pas de romans avec nos souffrances." *Cahier d'études africaines* n°150–52, Boubcar Boris Diop, Entretien 16.
41. Hitchcott, "A Global African Commemoration," 156.
42. Ibid., 156–57.
43. Malgasy writer Jean-Luc Raharimanana was one of the most outspoken critics of the project.
44. Diop, *L'Afrique, au-delà du miroir,* 21.

45. Julien, Foreword to *Murambi: Le livre des ossements*, xi.
46. Hitchcott, "Writing on Bones," 56.
47. Loinsigh, 87.
48. Lebon, "Véronique Tadjo: Voyages en tous genres littéraires," 50–52.
49. In a 1932 article from *Le Figaro*, the critic André Rousseaux captures the debate surrounding Céline's work: "Quoique le *Voyage au bout de la nuit* de M. Louis-Ferdinand Céline n'ait pas eu le prix Goncourt—que tout le monde lui attribuait à l'avance—il passionne l'opinion littéraire plus qu'aucun livre n'avait fait depuis longtemps. On prend violemment parti pour ou contre lui. Pour les uns, ce livre est une ordure; pour les autres, une œuvre de génie." André Rousseaux, "Le cas Céline," *Le Figaro*, 10 décembre 1932.
50. Jean de Léry has written *Histoire d'un voyage fait en la terre du Brésil* (1557), and André Gide, *Voyage au Congo* (1927). Both of these texts have received critical acclaim and membership in the French literary canon, they have also been hailed as travel narratives that continue the tradition of an ethnographic study of the other.
51. Tadjo, *L'ombre d'Imana*, 19–20 (my emphasis). Subsequent citations will be by page number in the text hereinafter.
52. Tadjo, *The Shadow of Imana*, 11 (my emphasis). Subsequent citations will be by page number in the text hereinafter.
53. Cahill, *Rethinking Rape*, 5.
54. Nora, *Les lieux de mémoire I*, 7/Nora, "Between Memory and History," 284.
55. Catherine Clinton, "With a Whip in His Hand, 205.
56. MacKinnon, "Rape, Genocide, and Women's Human Rights," 53.
57. *Making of Sometimes in April*. HBO Films Documentary Short (2005).
58. Ibid.
59. Dir., Peck, Raoul. *Sometimes in April*. United States, HBO Films (2005).
60. Elba, "Interview with Idris Elba."
61. Peck, *Sometimes in April*.
62. The first time that rape was recognized as a crime of genocide was in 1993 during the International Criminal Tribunals for the Former Yugoslavia (ICTY). See Beverly Allen, *Rape Warfare: The Hidden Genocide in Bosnia-Herzegovina and Croatia* (Minneapolis: University of Minnesota Press, 1996) for more information about rape during this ethnic cleansing.
63. Wendy Hesford, *Spectacular Rhetorics: Human Right Violations, Recognitions, Feminisms* (Duke University Press, 2011), 113.
64. The limits of the Arusha Tribunal with regard to reconciliation is especially evident in the encounter between Augustin and Honoré, the two brothers for whom there is no reconciliation. The report *Your Justice Is Too Slow: Will the ICTR Fail Rwanda's Rape Victims?* by Binaifer Nowrojee highlights the many problems with the results of the ICTR ten years after the genocide.
65. Peck, *Sometimes in April*.
66. Nowhere is this repetition more evident than in the current situation in Darfur, Sudan.
67. Boubacar Boris Diop made these comments at the annual African Literatures Association meeting in 2005. To Diop's observation we could add a third element that took place in between—the initial international refusal and failure to name the events in Rwanda as genocide.
68. Mukagasana, *Les blessures du silence*, 11. Subsequent citations will be by page number in the text hereinafter.
69. Translation mine.

70. There is a disturbing link between *Les blessures du silence* and the work of Boubacar Boris Diop. Diop was asked to write an introduction to the collection, but in it he included a scathing critique of then-French President François Mittérand, who infamously stated in 1994 that "Dans ces pays-là, un génocide n'est pas trop important." Cited in Hitchcott, "Writing on Bones: Commemorating Genocide in Boubacar Boris Diop's *Murambi*," 55.

71. Although Boubacar Boris Diop wrote the original introduction to the collection, his contribution was refused by the publisher because of his implication of François Mittérand's complicity in the genocide. The Diop introduction was later published as an essay in Diop's *Afrique au-delà du miroir*.

72. Rentschler, "Witnessing: U.S. Citizenship and the Vicarious Experience of Suffering," 298.

73. Hesford, *Spectacular Rhetorics*, 7.

74. Caruth, *Trauma*, 7.

75. Hesford, *Spectacular Rhetorics*, 30.

76. In the essay we learn that this union extends beyond *Les blessures du silence*. Together Mukagasana and Kazinierakis create an organization whose main goal is to remember the genocide in the form of Nyamirambo Point d'Appui.

77. Sontag, *Regarding the Pain of Others*, 89.

78. Felman and Laub, *Trauma*, 2.

79. Felman and Laub, *Trauma*, 54.

80. Hesford, *Spectacular Rhetorics*, 56.

81. Hesford, *Spectacular Rhetorics*, 122.

82. Ibid.

83. Hesford, *Spectacular Rhetorics*, 116.

84. Ibid.

85. Jones, "Gender and Genocide in Rwanda," 93.

86. Nowrojee, "Your Justice is Too Slow," 2.

87. Felman and Laub, *Trauma*, 16.

88. Hesford, *Spectacular Rhetorics*, 4.

89. Hesford, *Spectacular Rhetorics*, 3.

90. Hesford, *Spectacular Rhetorics*, 29.

91. The following is a list of fiction/dramatic films and documentaries on the genocide: *100 Days* (2002); *Sometimes in April* (2004, drama); *Hotel Rwanda* (2004); *Shooting Dogs* (2005); *A Sunday at the Pool in Kigali* (2005, drama); *Shake Hands with the Devil* (2007, dir. Roger Spottiswoode); *Munyurangabo* (2007, dir. Lee Isaac Chung); *Le jour où Dieu est parti voyage* (2009, dir., Philippe Van Leeuw); *Kinyrwanda* (2011, dir. Alrick Brown). A great number of the documentaries, listed as follows, are directed by journalists who covered the genocide and its aftermath. *A Culture of Murder* (1994, dir. Steve Bradshaw); *Journey into Darkness* (1994, dir. Fergal Keene); *The Bloody Tricolo* (1995); *Valentina's Story* (1997, dir. Fergal Keene); *When Good Men Do Nothing* (1997, dir. Steve Bradshaw); *Triumph of Evil* (1998, dir. Steve Bradshaw); *Gacaca: Living Together in Rwanda?* (2002, dir. Anne Aghion); *Umurage* (2002, dir. Gorka Gamarra Laguntzailek); *Keepers of Memory* (2004, dir. Eric Kabera); *Shake Hands with the Devil: The Journey of Roméo Dallaire* (2004, dir. Peter Raymont); *Beyond the Gates* (2005, dir. Michael Caton-Jones); *Ghosts of Rwanda* (2005, dir. Greg Barker); *Rwanda: How History Can Lead to Genocide* (2006, dir. David Munoz); *Intended Consequences* (2008, dir. Jonathan Torgovnik); *Flower in the Gun Barrel* (2009, dir. Gabriel Cowan); *Gacaca Film Series* (2002–2009); *Rwanda: Les collines parlent* (2006, dir., Bernard Bellefroid); and *A Generation after Genocide* (2010, dir. Torey Koraha and Jonathan Weiman).

Indeed, many of the titles of these films reflect the telos that Mamdani and Harrow outline, explained at this beginning of this chapter.

92. Former President Clinton has repeatedly apologized for US non-intervention in Rwanda in different venues. As one news article puts it ". . . on Mr. Clinton's fourth visit to Rwanda, it was clear the efforts by his foundation had personal meaning. He said he was sorry his administration failed to intervene during the 1994 genocide. "The United States just blew it in Rwanda," he said flatly . . . Paul Kagame, Rwanda's president, said he had accepted Mr. Clinton's repeated apologies." Celia W. Dugger, "Clinton Makes up for Lost Time in Battling AIDS," *The New York Times*, 29 August 2006. Accessed 11 August 2013.

93. Because the International Criminal Tribunals for the Former Yugoslavia punished rape as a form of ethnic cleansing, the Rwandan genocide represented the first time individual acts of rape were prosecuted as acts of genocide.

94. It is worth noting again here that "rape culture" as I use in throughout this book is defined well in *Transforming a Rape Culture*, "A [rape culture] is a complex of beliefs that encourages male aggression and supports violence against women," Preface.

Chapter 5

1. http://africanwomenincinema.blogspot.com/2011/08/shana-mongwanga-for-common-cause.html. Accessed 17 June 2011.

2. Lisa Mullins, "Exposing the Brutality of Sexual Violence in the Congo". *PRI, The World*, 23 September 2011. Accessed 6 August 2013. http://www.theworld.org/2011/09/namegabe-rape-sexual-violence-congo/.

3. Skloot, "Old Concerns and New Plays in the Theater of Genocide," *Genocide Studies and Prevention* 5, 1 (April 2010): 114–120, 114.

4. Panzi hospital was founded in 1999 by Dr. Denis Mukwege who has served more than 20,000 women since. In November of 2012, Dr.Mukwege was forced to flee his home and the hospital in Bukavu after armed men attacked him and his family.

5. Jackson, *The Greatest Silence: Rape in the Congo* (Jackson Films Inc., 2007).

6. Here I am purposefully invoking same definition provided in earlier chapters, "a rape culture is a complex of beliefs that encourages male aggression and supports violence against women." *Transforming a Rape Culture*, eds. Emilie Buchwald, Pamela R. Fletcher, and Martha Roth (Minneapolis, MN: Milkweed Editions, 1993), Preface.

7. Cubilié, *Women Witnessing Terror*, 10.

8. Chiwengo, "When Wounds and Corpses Fail to Speak: Narratives of Violence and Rape in the Congo (DRC)," 79.

9. Goodwin, "Silence = Rape," *The Nation* (8 March 2004).

10. Similarly, *The New York Times* journalist Nicholas Kristof, has consistently mentioned international ignorance and inaction in his articles on the incidence of rape in eastern DRC. Recent examples from *The New York Times* include "Orphaned, Raped and Ignored" 31 January 2010, and "The Grotesque Vocabulary in Congo," 10 February 2010.

11. I am thankful to Rosanne Adderley who gave me this information in her helpful comments after a conference paper presentation at ASWAD (Association for the Study of the Worldwide African Diaspora) in Accra, Ghana during July 2009.

12. Mohanty, "Under Western Eyes," 74.

13. Hesford, *Spectacular Rhetorics*, 185.

14. Jackson, *The Greatest Silence*.
15. In *NO! The Rape documentary* Farah Jasmine Griffin uses examples from African-American literature to note the ways in which "the myth of the Black male rapist" occludes black women's stories of rape.
16. Jackson, *The Greatest Silence*.
17. Jackson, *The Greatest Silence*.
18. Jackson, *The Greatest Silence*.
19. Wanzo, *The Suffering Will Not Be Televised*, 85.
20. Felman and Laub 58.
21. Wanzo, *The Suffering*, 229.
22. Jackson, *The Greatest Silence*.
23. Sontag, *Regarding the Pain of Others*, 72.
24. Jackson, *The Greatest Silence*.
25. Others have made note of the paradoxical beauty of the Congo and other countries in the Great Lakes region to frame their discussions of violence that began with the Rwandan genocide and continues today.
26. In the field of sexual assault victim advocacy there are widely circulated "Myths and Facts about Rape" which explain the different social factors that influence how rape is perceived.
27. Wanzo, *The Suffering Will Not be Televised*, 115.
28. Spivak, "Can the Subaltern Speak?" 295.
29. Mohanty, "Under Western Eyes: Feminist Scholarship and Colonial Discourses," *Third World Women and the Politics of Feminism*, eds. Chandra Mohanty, Ann Russo, and Lourdes Torres (Bloomington: Indiana University Press, 1991), 51–80, 51.
30. Wendy Hesford and Wendy Kozol, *Just Advocacy?: Women's Human Rights, Transnational Feminisms, and the Politics of Representation* (New Brunswick: Rutgers University Press, 2005), 17.
31. Nottage, *Ruined*, ix. Subsequent citations will be by page number in the text hereinafter.
32. Nottage interview with Charlie Rose.
33. Goldberg, *Beyond Terror*, 18.
34. Goldberg, *Beyond Terror*, 20.
35. Sontag, *Regarding the Pain of Others*, 71.
36. As Chimamanda Ngozi Adichie writes, "beginning the story from the broken limb of the Sierra Leonian as opposed to the capitalistic insatiability for diamonds that fuels the conflict, yields a completely different story that accounts for the shifting historic and geopolitical dynamics at play." Adichie, "African Authenticity and the Biafran Experience," 53.
37. Mama Nadi tells the soldiers to "leave their weapons at the door."
38. Minoui, "Congo's Anti Rape Crusader," *The Daily Beast* 28 June 2010 http://www.thedailybeast.com/blogs-and-stories/2010-06-28/chouchou-namegabe-and-the-rape-crisis-in-congo/?cid=tag:a112#. Accessed 6 September 2011.
39. Brody, *Punctuation*, 62.
40. I am referring to The Huntington Theater Boston premier of *Ruined* in January 2011.
41. Nottage, *Ruined*, ix.
42. Enloe, *Maneuvers: The International Politics of Militarizing Women's Lives*, 110.
43. Fitzpatrick, *Feminism, Literature, and Rape Narratives*, 196.
44. Ahmed, *The Cultural Politics of Emotion*, 20.
45. Wanzo, *The Suffering Will Not be Televised*, 118.

46. Conteh-Morgan and Thomas, *New Francophone African and Caribbean Theatres*, 171.

47. In this way the play recalls Monique Wittig's feminist drama *Les guerillères* in which the author imagines a collective female personhood and inter-subjectivity for liberation and through exclusive use of the French pronoun "elles," the feminine plural to describe the protagonists.

48. Conteh-Morgan and Thomas, *New Francophone African and Caribbean Theatres*, 154.

49. The photographs in this manuscript are from the 2009 performances of *Les recluses* directed by Denis Mpunga at the Grand Varia Théâtre in Brussels which was in co-production with le Théâtre des Bambous (Ile de la Réunion) and MFB (Maison des Femmes au Burundi) and originally created in Burundi with women who were rape survivors. http://www.varia.be/fr/les-spectacles/les-recluses4/extra/. Accessed 14 September 2011.

50. Hesford and Kozol, *Just Advocacy*, 8–9.

51. Ibid.

52. Grossman, "A Question of Silence: The Rape of German Women by Occupation Soldiers,"55.

53. Sontag, *Regarding the Pain*, 69.

54. Sontag, *Regarding the Pain*, 70.

55. Sontag, *Regarding the Pain*, 71.

56. Borkgren, *Forever Changed: Berrlyze's Story*. http://grant.shootq.com/past_winners/.

57. Spivak, "Can the Subaltern Speak?" 69.

58. Borkgren, *Forever Changed: Berrlyze's Story*.

59. Sontag, *Regarding the Pain*, 80.

60. Hesford, *Spectacular Rhetorics*, 151.

61. Hesford, *Spectacular Rhetorics*, 153.

62. Hesford, *Spectacular Rhetorics*, 156.

63. Lauren Berlant, cited in Wanzo, 90.

64. Sontag, *Regarding the Pain*, 81.

65. Sontag, *Regarding the Pain*, 89.

66. Sontag, *Regarding the Pain*, 101.

67. Ahmed, *The Cultural Politics of Emotion*, 20.

68. Hesford and Kozol, *Just Advocacy*, 13.

69. See for example, Wendy Hesford, *Spectacular Rhetorics: Human Rights Visions, Recognitions, Feminisms* (Durham, NC: Duke University Press, 2011).

70. Chiwengo "When Wounds and Corpses Fail to Speak: Narratives of Violence and Rape in Congo (DRC)," 81.

71. Minoui, "Congo's Anti-Rape Crusader" *The Daily Beast* 28 June 2010. http://www.thedailybeast.com/blogs-and-stories/2010-06-28/chouchou-namegabe-and-the-rape-crisis-in-congo/?cid=tag:a112#.

72. Minoui, "Congo's Anti-Rape Crusader."

73. Mullins, "Exposing the Brutality of Sexual Violence in the Congo."

74. http://africanwomenincinema.blogspot.com/2011/08/shana-mongwanga-for-common-cause.html. Accessed 4 November 2016.

Epilogue

1. Sivac cited in Hesford, *Spectacular Rhetorics*, 114.

2. According to Haitian journalist Ansel Ernst, the video was accidentally exchanged when one of the members of the MINUSTAH was exchanging music with another young man in the town who was a friend of Joseph.

3. The rape of Jean was not an isolated event—MINUSTAH soldiers from various countries have been involved in several different rapes. In January 2012 a few months after Jean's case came to light, there was also the case of Jean Roudy in the northern Artibonite region. In 2012 there was a trial based in the city of Gonaives where two Pakistani soldiers accused of rape were found guilty, dismissed from the Pakistani army, sentenced to a year imprisonment and hard work.

4. Hesford, *Spectacular Rhetorics*, 58.

5. Ibid.

6. The human rights report by Poto Fanm + Fi *Beyond Shock* confirms and challenges prior findings on GBV and rape in Haiti by critically interrogating how we understand the "post-earthquake rape crisis." Among the significant findings of the report were that most post-earthquake rapes are committed by people known to the victim, few reported rapes were by perpetrators "in uniform," and that the earthquake has increased advocacy against sexual violence especially at the local and grassroots level.

7. Alexander, "Not Just (Any) Body can Be a Citizen," 7.

8. Hesford and Kozol, *Just Advocacy*, 15.

9. In light of the sex abuse scandal in the Catholic Church, and the conviction of Jerry Sandusky following the years of cover-up and sexual abuse at Penn State in the United States, the male face of sexual violence has been mostly associated with young boys.

10. Hekman, "Truth and Method," 344.

11. Rose and Robertson, *Representing Rape in Medieval and Early Modern Literature*, 4.

12. Adams, "Another blow to UN in Haiti with claims of sex attack by peacekeepers: Mobile phone video claiming to show rape stokes anger at agency's mission." *The Independent*. Accessed 6 August 2013. http://www.independent.co.uk/news/world/americas/another-blow-to-un-in-haiti-with-claims-of-sex-attack-by-peacekeepers-2349798.html.

13. Adams, "Another blow."

14. Bureau de Communication de la Présidence, "La Présidence condamne l'acte de viol perpétré sur un jeune haïtien à Port-Salut," 5 septembre 2011.

15. Ibid.

16. Hesford, *Spectacular Rhetorics*, 65.

17. Nolan, "Haiti, Violated," 96.

18. Nolan, "Haiti, Violated," 97.

19. Oliver, *Witnessing Beyond Recognition*, 10.

20. Lionnet, *Postcolonial Representations*, 1.

21. Wallstrom, "Women, Peace, and Security," 8.

22. Michel, "Unequal Distribution," 158–62.

23. Buchwald et al., preamble.

BIBLIOGRAPHY

Abbott, Elizabeth. *Haiti: The Duvaliers and Their Legacy*. New York: McGraw Hill Book Company, 1988.
Abdur-Rahman, Aliyyah. *Against the Closet: Black Political Longing and Sexual Figurations*. Durham: Duke University Press, 2012.
Adams, Guy. "Another blow to UN in *Haiti* with claims of sex attack by peacekeepers." The independent independent.co.uk. http://www.independent.co.uk/news/world/americas/another-blow-to-un-in-haiti-with-claims-of-sex-attack-by-peacekeepers-2349798.html.
Adesanmi, Pius. "Of Postcolonial Entanglement and Durée: Reflections on the Francophone African Novel." *Comparative Literature* 56.3 (2004): 227–242.
Adichie, Chimamanda Ngozi. "African Authenticity and the Biafran Experience" *Transition* Issue 99 (2008): 42–53.
"African Women in Cinema." http://africanwomenincinema.blogspot.com/2011/08/shana-mongwanga-for-common-cause.html.
Ahmed, Sara. *The Cultural Politics of Emotion*. London: Routledge, 2004.
Aimar, Mariane. "Rencontre avec Gisèle Pineau," *TVREGARD* (Numéro 7 17–23 octobre 1998): 17–19.
Allen, Beverly. *Rape Warfare: The Hidden Genocide in Bosnia-Herzegovina and Croatia*. London & Minneapolis: University of Minnesota Press, 1996.
Alexander, Jacqui. *Pedagogies of Crossing: Meditations on Feminisms, Sexual Politics Memory and the Sacred*. Durham: Duke University Press, 2005.
———. "Not Just (Any) Body can Be a Citizen: The Politics of Law, Sexuality and Postcoloniality in Trinidad and Tobago and the Bahamas. *Feminist Review* 48 "The New Politics of Sex and the State" (Autumn, 1994): 5–23.
Alexandre, Sandy. "From the Same Tree: Gender and Iconography in Representations of Violence in Morisson's *Beloved*." *SIGNS: A Journal of Women in Culture and Society* 36.4 (Summer 2011): 915–940.
Amnesty International. "Aftershocks: Women Speak Out Against Sexual Violence in Haiti's Camps" 6 January 2011.
Andrade, Susan. "The Nigger of the Narcissist: History, Sexuality, and Intertextuality in Maryse Condé's *Hérémakhonon*." *Callaloo* 16. 1 (Winter, 1993): 213–226.

―――. *The Nation Writ Small: African Fictions and Feminisms 1958–1988*. Durham: Duke University Press, 2012.
Arblaster, Anthony. "Violence" *The Blackwell Dictionary of Modern Social Thought*. Edited by William Outhwaite. Blackwell Publishing, 2002.
Arendt, Hannah. *On Violence*. New York: Harcourt, 1969.
Armstrong, Nancy and Leonard Tennenhouse. *The Violence of Representation: Literature and the History of Violence*. New York: Routledge, 1989.
Avelar, Idelber. *The Letter of Violence: Essays on Narrative, Ethics, and Politics*. New York: Palgrave McMillan, 2004.
Barnes, Elizabeth. *Incest and the Literary Imagination*. Gainesville: University of Florida Press, 2002.
Bell, Beverly. *Walking on Fire: Haitian Women's Stories of Survival and Resistance*. Ithaca, NY: Cornell University Press, 2001.
Belugue, Geneviève. "Gisèle Pineau entretien avec." *Notre Librairie* 127 (juillet–septembre 1996): 84–90.
Benítez-Rojo, Antonio. *The Repeating Island: The Caribbean from a Postmodern Perspective*. Durham, NC: Duke University Press, 1996.
Beti, Mongo. *Main basse sur le Cameroun: Autopsie d'une décolonisation*. Paris: Maspero, 1972.
Beyala, Calixthe. *Tu t'appelleras Tanga*. Paris, 1988.
―――. *Your Name Shall Be Tanga*. Translated by Marjolin de Jager. Heinneman, 1994.
Boni, Tanella. "Violences familières dans les littératures francophones du sud." *Notre Librairie* 148 (juillet–septembre 2002): 110–15.
Bonnet, Véronique. "Villes africaines et écritures de la violence." *Notre Librairie* 148 (juillet–septembre 2002), 20–25.
Borkgren, Sherrlyn. *Forever Changed: Berrlyze's Story*. http://grant.shootq.com/past_winners/.
Braidotti, Rosi. *Nomadic Subjects: Embodiment and Sexual Difference in Contemporary Feminist Theory*. New York: Columbia University Press, 1994.
Britton, Celia. "In Memory of Edouard Glissant." *Callaloo* (2011): 668–70.
Brody, Jennifer DeVere. *Punctuation: Art, Politics and Play*. Durham: Duke University Press, 2008.
Brooks, Daphne. *Bodies in Dissent: Spectacular Performances of Race and Freedom 1850–1910*. Durham: Duke University Press, 2007.
Brutus, Timoléon. *L'homme d'airain: Étude monographique sur Jean-Jacques Dessalines, fondateur de la nation haïtienne*. Port-au-Prince: Imprimérie N. A. Théodore, 1946–7.
Buchwald, Emilie, Pamela Fletcher and Martha Roth. *Transforming a Rape Culture*. Minneapolis, MN: Milkweed Editions, 1993.
Burt, Al and Bernard Dietrich. *Papa Dac et les Tontons macoutes*. New York: Librairie de France, 1971.
Busia, Abena. "This Gift of Metaphor: Symbolic Strategies and the Triumph of Survival in Simone Schwarz-Bart's *The Bridge of Beyond*." In *Out of Kumbla: Caribbean Women and Literature*. Edited by Carole Boyce Davies and Elaine Savory Fido. Trenton: Africa World Press, 1990.
―――, ed. *Theorizing Black Feminisms: The Visionary Pragmatism of Black Women*. London and New York: Routledge, 1993.
Butler, Judith. *Bodies that Matter: On the Discursive Limits of Sex*. New York: Routledge, 1993.
Cahill, Ann J. *Rethinking Rape*. Ithaca, NY: Cornell University Press, 2001.
Canneval, Jacques. "Viol à Domicile: les enfants en danger!" *Sept Magazine* n° 592 25 (Octobre 1990): 41–43.
Caruth, Cathy. *Unclaimed Experience: Trauma, Narrative, and History*. Baltimore: Johns Hopkins University Press, 1996.
Cazenave, Odile. *Femmes rebelles: Naissance d'un nouveau roman africain au féminin*. Paris: L'Harmattan, 1996.
―――. "Writing the Child, Youth, and Violence into the Francophone Novel from Sub-Saharan Africa: The Impact of Age and Gender." *Research in African Literatures* 36.2 (Summer 2005): 59–72.
―――. "Francophone Caribbean Women Writers." In *Sex and the Citizen: Interrogating the Caribbean*. Edited by Faith Smith, 87–100. Charlottesville: University of Virginia Press, 2011.

———, and Patricia Célérier. *Contemporary Francophone African Writers and the Burden of Commitment*. Charlottesville: University of Virginia Press, 2011.
Césaire, Aimé. *Le discours sur le colonialisme*. Paris: Présence africaine, 1989.
Chaacha, Mwita."Writing to Remember Genocide." *Sunday Nation*, 25 June 2000. 13.
Chancy, Myriam J. A. *Framing Silence: Revolutionary Novels by Haitian Women*. New Brunswick: Rutgers University Press, 1997.
———. "There are No Giraffes in Haiti: Haitian Women and State Terror." In *Écrire en pays assiégé: Haiti, Writing under Siege*. Edited by Marie-Agnès Sourieau and Kathleen Balutansky, 303–21. Amsterdam and New York: Rodopi, 2004.
Charles, Carolle. "Gender and Politics in Contemporary Haiti: the Duvalierist State, Transnationalism, and the Emergence of a New Feminism (1980–1990)." *Feminist Studies* 21.1 (Spring 1995): 135–64.
Chemain-Degrange, Arlette. "Violence destructrice, violence régénératrice: originalité de la littérature africaine subsaharienne." In *Figures et fantasmes de violence dans les littératures de l'Afrique subsaharienne et des Antilles*. Vol. 1, 13–32. Edited by Franca Marcato Falzoni. Bologna: Cooperativa Libraria Universitaria Editrice, 1991.
Clancy Nolan, "Haiti, Violated." *World Policy Journal* (Spring 2011): 93–102.
Clinton, Catherine. "'With a Whip in His Hand': Rape, Memory, and African-American Women." In *History and Memory in African American Culture*. Edited by Geneviève Fabre and Robert O'Meally, 205–18. New York: Oxford University Press, 1994.
Collins, Patricia Hill. "The Social Construction of Black Feminist Thought." *SIGNS: A Journal of Women in History and Culture* 14.4, Common Grounds and Crossroads: Race, Ethnicity, and Class in Women's Lives (Summer 1989): 745–773.
———. *Black Feminist Thought: Knowledge, Consciousness, and the Politics of Empowerment*. New York: Routledge, 2000.
Condé, Maryse. *Moi, Tituba Sorcière noire de Salem*, Paris: Mercure de France,1988.
———. *I, Tituba, Black Witch of Salem*. Translated by Richard Philcox. Charlottesville: University of Virginia Press, 1992.
———. "The Stealers of Fire: The French-Speaking Writers of the Caribbean and their Strategies of Liberation." *Journal of Black Studies* 35.2 (November 2004): 154–164.
Confiant, Raphaël. *Bassin des ouragans*. Paris: Mille et une nuits, 1994.
Conteh-Morgan, John with Dominic Thomas. *New Francophone African and Caribbean Theatres*. Bloomington: Indiana University Press, 2010.
Copelon, Rhonda. "Women's Rights, Human Rights: International Feminist Perspectives." In *Women's Rights, Human Rights: International Feminist Perspectives*. Edited by Julie Stone Peters and Andrea Wolper. London and New York: Routledge, 1994.
Cotta, Sergio. *Why Violence?* Gainesville: University of Florida Press, 1985.
Crenshaw, Kimberlé. "Mapping the Margins: Intersectionality, Identity Politics, and Violence Against Women." *Stanford Law Review* 43.6 (1991): 1241–1299.
Cubilié, Anne. *Women Witnessing Terror: Testimony and the Cultural Politics of Human Rights*. New York: Fordham University Press, 2005.
d'Adesky, Anne-christine with Poto Fanm +Fi Coalition. *Beyond Shock: Charting the Landscape of Sexual Violence in Post-Earthquake Haiti*. Santa Barbara, CA: UCSB Center for Black Studies Research, 2013.
Danticat, Edwidge. *Breath, Eyes, Memory*. New York: Soho, 1994.
———. "We Are Ugly But We Re Here." *The Caribbean Writer* Volume 10 (1996).
———. "The Dangerous Job of Edwidge Danticat." Interview with Renee H. Shea in *Callaloo* 19.2 (1996): 382–389.
———. *The Dew Breaker*. New York: Knopf, 2004.
———. *Anacaona: Golden Flower, Haiti, 1490*. New York: Scholastic, 2005.
———. "Introduction." *Love, Anger, Madness*. Translated by Rose-Myriam Réjouis and Val Vinkour. vii–xiii. New York : Random House, 2009.
Dash, Michael. Review, "*Ecrire en pays assiégé: Haiti, Writing Under Siege*." *Research in African Literatures* 37.1 (Spring 2006): 163–65.
———. "Vital Signs in the Body Politic: Eroticism and Exile in Maryse Condé and Dany Laferrière." *Romanic Review* 94, no. 3–4 (2003): 309–317.

Dauge-Roth, Alexandre. *Writing and Filming the Genocide of the Tutsis in Rwanda, Dismembering and Remembering Traumatic History.* Lanham, MD: Lexington Books, 2010.

Davies, Carole Boyce. *Black Women, Writing and Identity: Migrations of the Subject.* New York and London: Routledge, 1994.

Davis, Angela Yvonne. "Rape, Racism, and the Myth of the Black Male Rapist." *Women, Race and Class,* 172–201. New York: Vintage Books, 1981.

Dayan, Joan. *Haiti, History and the Gods.* Berkeley, CA: University of California Press, 1998.

———. "Erzulie: A Woman's History of Haiti." Research in African Literatures, 25.2, Special Issue: Caribbean Literature (Summer 1994): 5–31.

de Lauretis, Teresa. "The Violence of Rhetoric: Considerations on Representation and Gender." In *The Violence of Representation: Literature and the History of Violence.* Edited by Nancy Armstrong and Leonard Tennenhouse, 239–255. London and New York: Routledge, 1989.

den Toonder, Jeanette. "Un dimanche à la piscine à Kigali: Writing the Rwandan genocide. In Lorna Milne. In *Postcolonial Violence, Culture, and Identity in Francophone Africa and the Antilles.* Edited by Lorna Milne. 103–22. Oxford and New York: Peter Lang, 2007.

Dietrich, Bernard and Al Burt. *Papa Doc et les Tontons macoutes.* New York: Librairie de France, 1971.

Diop, Boubacar Boris. "Avertissement ivoirien à la Françafrique." *Le monde diplomatique* mars 2005, http://www.monde-diplomatique.fr/2005/03/DIOP/12014.

———. *Murambi: Le Livre des ossements.* Paris: Stock, 2000.

———. *Murambi: Book of Bones.* Trans. Fiona McLaughlin. Bloomington and Indianapolis: Indiana University Press, 2000.

———."Entretien avec Boubacar Boris Diop." *Africultures* 30, "Rwanda 2000: mémoires d'avenir," Paris: L'Harmattan, 2000 (septembre 2000): 15–16.

———. *L'Afrique, au-delà du miroir.* Paris: Philippe Rey, 2007.

Dmitracova, Olesya. "Post-quake chaos fuels . . . " Reuters, 6 January 2011.

Donadey, Anne. "Francophone Women Writers and Postcolonial Theory." In *Francophone Postcolonial Studies: A Critical Introduction.* Edited by Charles Forsdick and David Murphy, 202–10. New York: Oxford University Press, 2003.

Dugger, Celia W. "Clinton Makes up for Lost Time in Battling AIDS." *The New York Times* 29 August 2006. Accessed on 11 August 2013. http://www.nytimes.com/2006/08/29/health/29clinton.html?pagewanted=all&_r=0.

Duvivier, Sandra. "My Body is a Piece of Land: Female Sexuality, Family and Capital in Caribbean Texts." *Callaloo* 31.4 (2008): 1104–21.

Elba, Idris. "Interview with Idris Elba." *Honey Magazine,* March 2005.

Enloe, Cynthia. *Maneuvers: The International Politics of Militarizing Women's Lives.* Berkeley: University of California Press, 2000.

Fabrice, A. "L'inceste: Une réalité dans nos îles," *Sept Magazine* 592 (25 octobre 1990): 13–17.

Fanon, Frantz. *Les damnés de la terre.* Paris: S.A.R.L, 1961.

———. *The Wretched of the Earth.* Translated by Constance Farrington. New York: Grove Press, 1963.

———. *L'an V de la Révolution Algérienne.* Paris: Maspero, 1960.

———. *A Dying Colonialism.* Translated by Haakon Chevalier. New York: Grove Press, 1965.

Felman, Shoshana. "Education and Crisis, or the Vicissitudes of Teaching." In *Trauma: Explorations in Memory.* Edited by Cathy Caruth, 13–60. Baltimore: Johns Hopkins University Press, 1995.

Ferly, Odile. *A Poetics of Relation.* New York: Palgrave, 2012.

Forsdick, Charles. *Francophone Postcolonial Studies: A Critical Introduction.* New York: Routledge, 2003.

Foucault, Michel. *Discipline and Punish: The Birth of the Prison.* Translated by Alan Sheridan. New York: Vintage, 1977.

———. *Technologies of the Self: A Seminar with Michel Foucault.* Edited by Luther H. Martin, Huck Gutman and Patrick H. Hutton. Cambridge: University of Massachusetts Press, 1988.

Francis, Donette. *Fictions of Feminine Citizenship: Sexuality and Nation in Contemporary Caribbean Literature.* New York: Palgrave MacMillan, 2010.

———. "Silences Too Horrific to Disturb: Writing Sexual Histories in Edwidge Danticat's *Breath, Eyes, Memory.*" Research in African Literatures 35.2 (2004): 75–90.

Fratta, Carla. Avant-Propos. In *Figures et fantasmes de violence dans les littératures de l'Afrique sub-saharienne et des Antilles Vol. 2.* Edited by Carla Fratta, 7–12. Bologna: Cooperativa Libraria Universitaria Editrice, 1991.

Froula, Christine. "The Daughter's Seduction: Sexual Violence and Literary History." *SIGNS: A Journal of Women in History and Culture* 11.4 (1986): 621–644.

Garraway, Doris. *The Libertine Colony: Creolization in the Early French Caribbean.* Durham: Duke University Press, 2005.

Githrie, Njeri. "Horizons Adrift: Women in Exile, at Home, and Abroad in Gisèle Pineau's Works." *Research in African Literatures* 36.1 (2005): 74–90.

Glissant, Edouard. *Le discours antillais.* Paris: Folio, 1997 [1982].

———. *La case du commandeur.* Paris: Cadre Rouge, 1981.

Glover, Kaiama. "The Ambivalent Transnationalism of a Literature-World-in French." *Small Axe* 33 (November 2010): 99–110.

Goldberg, Elizabeth. *Beyond Terror: Gender, Narrative, Human Rights.* Rutgers University Press, 2007.

Goodwin, Jan. "Silence=Rape." *The Nation* (8 March 2004). Accessed on 9 March 2004. http://www.thenation.com/article/silencerape#axzz2bDWtRVEU.

Graham, Lucy. *State of Peril: Race and Rape in South African Fiction.* New York: Oxford University Press, 2012.

Grossman, Atina. "A Question of Silence: The Rape of German Women by Occupation Soldiers." *October Magazine* no. 72 (Spring 1995): 42–63.

Grosz, Elizabeth. *Volatile Bodies: Towards a Corporeal Feminism.* Bloomington, Indiana University Press, 1994.

Gunne, Sorcha and Zoë Brigley, eds. *Feminism, Literature, and Rape Narratives.* Oxford: Oxford University Press, 2010.

Haigh, Sam. *Mapping a Tradition: Francophone Women's Writing from Guadeloupe.* London: Maney Publishing, 2000.

Harrow, Kenneth W. "'Ancient Tribal Warfare': Foundational Fantasies of Ethnicity and History." *Research in African Literatures* 36.2 (2005): 34–45.

———. "Un train peut en cacher un autre: Narrating the Rwandan Genocide and Hotel Rwanda." *Research in African Literatures* 36.4 (2005): 223–232.

Hartman, Saidiya. *Scenes of Subjection: Terror, Slavery, and Self-Making in Nineteenth Century America.* New York: Oxford University Press, 1997.

Hekman, Susan. "Truth and Method: Feminist Standpoint Theory Revisited." *SIGNS: A Journal of Women in History and Culture* 22.2 (Winter, 1997): 341–65.

Hesford, Wendy and Wendy Kozol. *Just Advocacy?: Women's Human Rights, Transnational Feminisms, and the Politics of Representation.* New Brunswick: Rutgers University Press, 2005.

———. *Spectacular Rhetorics: Human Right Violations, Recognitions, Feminisms.* Durham: Duke University Press, 2011.

Higgins, Lynn A. and Brenda R. Silver. *Rape and Representation.* New York: Columbia University Press: New York, 1991.

Hitchcott, Nicki. "Writing on Bones: Commemorating Genocide in Boubacar Boris Diop's *Murambi*." *Research in African Literatures* 40.3 (2009): 48–61.

———. "A Global African Commemoration: Rwanda, Écrire par devoir de mémoire." *Forum for Modern Language Studies* 45.2 (2009): 151–60.

Horeck, Tanya. *Public Rape: Representing Violation in Fiction and Film.* London and New York: Routledge, 2004.

Hunt, Krista and Kim Rygiel. *(En)Gendering the War on Terror: War Stories and Camouflaged Politics.* Burlington, VT: Ashgate Publishing, 2007.

International Institute for Justice and Democracy in Haiti et al. *Our Bodies Are Still Trembling: Haitian Women's Fight Against Rape.* May 2010.

Ippolito, Emilia. *Caribbean Women Writers: Identity and Gender.* Rochester, NY: Camden House, 2000.

Jackson, Lisa. *The Greatest Silence: Rape in the Congo.* Jackson Films Inc., 2007.

Jackson, Shona. "Subjection and Resistance in the Transformation of Guyana's Mytho-Colonial

Landscape." In *Caribbean Literature and the Environment: between Nature and Culture*. Edited by Elizabeth M. DeLoughrey et al., 85–98. Charlottesville: University of Virginia Press, 2005.
Jenson, Deborah. "Francophone World Literature (*Littérature-monde*), Cosmopolitanism and Decadence: 'Citizen of the World without the Citizen?" In *Transnational French Studies: Postcolonialism and Littérature-monde*. Edited by Alec G. Hargreaves, Charles Forsdick, and David Murphy, 15–35. Liverpool: Liverpool University Press, 2010.
Jones, Adam. "Gender and Genocide in Rwanda." *Journal of Genocide Research* 4.1 (2002): 65–94.
———. "Gendercide and Genocide." *Journal of Genocide Research* 2.2 (June 2000): 185–211.
Julien, Eileen. "Rape, Repression and Narrative Form in *Le devoir de violence* and *La vie et demie*." In *Rape and Representation*. Edited by Lynn A. Higgins and Brenda Silver, 161–78. New York: Columbia University Press, 1991.
Kalisa, Marie Chantal. *Violence in Francophone African and Caribbean Women's Literature*. Lincoln: University of Nebraska Press, 2009.
Kaplan, Caren and Inderpal Grewal. "Transnational Feminist Cultural Studies: Beyond the Marxism/Poststructuralism/Feminism Divides." In *Between Women and Nation*. Edited by Caren Kaplan, Norma Alarcón, and Minoo Moallem, 349–64. Durham: Duke University Press, 1999.
Kaufman, Joyce P., and Kristen P. Williams. *Women and War: Gender Identity and Activism in Times of Conflict*. Sterling, VA: Kumarian Press, 2010.
Kemedjio, Cilas. "Rape of Bodies, Rape of Souls: From the Surgeon to the Psychiatrist, From the Slave Trade to the Slavery of Comfort in the Work of Edouard Glissant." *Research in African Literatures* 25.2 (Summer 1994): 51–79.
Kempadoo, Kamala. *Sexing the Caribbean: Gender, Race, and Sexual Labor*. New York and London: Routledge, 2004.
Koné, Amadou. "Violence du pouvoir et pouvoir de la violence dans *Monnè, outrages et défis* de Ahmadou Kourouma." In *Figures et fantasmes de violence dans les littératures francophones de l'Afrique subsaharienne et des Antilles*. Vol. 1. Edited by Franca Marcato-Falzoni, 163–82. Bologna: Cooperativa Libraria Universitaria Editrice Bologna, 1991.
Kourouma, Ahmadou. *Les soleils des indépendances*. Paris: Seuil, 1970.
———. *The Suns of Independence*. Translated by Adrian Adams. London: Heinemann, 1981.
———. Interview. *Chat* sur RFI 5/9/2001. http://aviquesnel.free.fr/Direlire/kourouma-le-soleil-des-independances.htm.
Kristof, Nicholas, and Sheryl WuDunn. *Half the Sky: Turning Oppression into Opportunity for Women Worldwide* New York: Random House, 2009.
Larrier, Renée Brenda. *Francophone Women Writers of Africa and the Caribbean*. Gainesville, FL: University of Florida Press, 2000.
———. *Autofiction and Advocacy in the Francophone Caribbean*. Gainesville, FL: University of Florida Press, 2006.
Lashgiri, Deirdre, ed. *Violence, Silence, and Anger: Women's Writing As Transgression*. Charlottesville: University of Virginia Press, 1995.
Laub, Dori and Shoshana Felman. *Testimony: Crises of Witnessing in Literature, Psychoanalysis, and History*. New York: Routledge, 1991.
Lawrence, Bruce and Aisha Karim, ed. *On Violence: A Reader*. Durham: Duke University Press, 2007.
Lebon, Cécile. "Véronique Tadjo: Voyages en tous genres littéraires." *Notre Librairie* 146 (décembre 2001): 50–52.
Le Bris, Michel Jean Rouaud, Eva Almassy, et al., eds. *Pour une littérature-monde en français*. Paris: Gallimard, 2007.
Leyburn, James. *The Haitian People*. New Haven: Yale University Press, 1966.
Lionnet, Françoise. *Postcolonial Representations: Women, Literature, Identity*. Ithaca and London: Cornell University Press, 1995.
———. "Geographies of Pain: Captive Bodies and Violent Acts in the Fictions of Myriam Warner-Vieyra, Gayl Jones, and Bessie Head." *Callaloo* 16, no. 1 (1993): 132–52.
———. "A Politics of the 'We'?: Autobiography, Race, and Nation." *American Literary History* 13.2 (2001): 376–92.

Loinsigh, Aedín, Ní. "Lying to Tell the Truth: Fiction and the Rwandan Genocide in Véronique Tadjo's *L'ombre d'Imana*." In *Postcolonial Violence, Culture, and Identity in Francophone Africa and the Antilles.* Edited by Lorna Milne, 83–102. Oxford and New York: Peter Lang, 2007.

Lorde, Audre. "The Uses of the Erotic: The Erotic as Power" *Sister Outsider.* Freedom, CA: Crossing Press, 1984. 53–59.

Loomba, Ania. *Colonialism/Postcolonialism: The New Critical Idiom.* 2nd ed. London and New York: Routledge, 2005.

MacCannell, Dean and Juliet Flower MacCannell. "Violence, Power and Pleasure: A Revisionist Reading of Foucault from the Victim Perspective." In *Up against Foucault: Some Tensions Between Foucault and Feminism.* Edited by Caroline Ramazanoglu, 203–238. London: Routledge, 1993.

MacKinnon, Catharine. "Rape, Genocide, and Women's Human Rights." In *Violence against Women: Philosophical Perspectives.* Edited by Stanley French et al. Ithaca: Cornell University Press, 1998.

Making Sometimes in April. HBO Films Documentary Short, 2005.Makward, Christiane. *Mayotte Capécia ou l'aliénation selon Fanon.* Paris: Karthala. 1999.

Mama, Amina. "Sheroes and Villains: Conceptualizing Colonial and Contemporary Violence against Women in Africa." In *Feminist Genealogies, Colonial Legacies, Democratic Futures.* Edited by M. Jacqui Alexander and Chandra Talpade Mohanty, 251–68. New York: Routledge, 1996.

Mamdani, Mahmood. *When Victims Become Killers: Colonialism, Nativism, and the Genocide in Rwanda.* Princeton, NJ: Princeton University Press, 2001.

Maison de mémoire. "Manifeste," http://www.africultures.com/partenaires/evenements/rwanda94/aimgr.htm.

Mardorossian, Carine. "Towards a New Feminist Theory of Rape." *SIGNS: A Journal of Women in Culture and Society* 27.3 (Spring 2002): 743–777.

Mars, Kettly. *Saisons Sauvages.* Arles: Serpent à Plumes, 2010.

Martelly, Michel. Bureau de Communication de la Présidence, "La Présidence condamne l'acte de viol perpétré sur un jeune haïtien à Port-Salut." 5 septembre 2011.

Matthews, Graham and Sam Goodman, eds. *Violence and the Limits of Representation.* Hampshire: Palgrave Macmillan, 2013.

Mbembe, Achille. *On the Postcolony.* Berkeley: University of California Press, 2001.

McClintock, Anne. *Imperial Leather: Race, Gender and Sexuality in the Colonial Contest.* New York: Routledge, 1995.

Mehta, Brinda. *Notions of Identity, Diaspora and Gender in Caribbean Women's Writing.* New York: Palgrave MacMillan, 2009.

Melvern, Linda. *Conspiracy to Murder: The Rwanda Genocide and the International Community.* Verso: London, 2004.

Michel, Claudine. "Unequal Distribution and Other Poems." *Meridians* 11:1 (2011): 158–62.

Milne, Lorna. *Postcolonial Violence, Culture, and Identity in Francophone Africa and the Antilles.* Oxford and New York: Peter Lang, 2007.

Minoui, Delphine. "Congo's Anti-Rape Crusader." *The Daily Beast* 28 June 2010. http://www.thedailybeast.com/blogs-and-stories/2010-06-28/chouchou-namegabe-and-the-rape-crisis-in-congo/?cid=tag:a112#.

Mohanty, Chandra Talpade. *Feminism without Borders: Decolonizing Theory, Practicing Solidarity.* Durham: Duke University Press, 2003.

———."Cartographies of Struggle." *Third World Women and the Politics of Feminism.* Edited by Chandra Talpade Mohanty, Ann Russo, and Lourdes Torres. Bloomington, IN: Indiana University Press, 1991.

———. "Under Western Eyes: Feminist Scholarship and Colonial Discourses," *Third World Women and the Politics of Feminism.* Edited by Chandra Mohanty, Ann Russo, and Lourdes Torres, 51–80. Bloomington: Indiana University Press, 1991.

Mondoloni, Dominique. "Comprendre." *Notre Librairie* 148 (juillet–septembre 2002): 3–4.

Mongwanga, Shana (director). *Congo: A Common Cause from London to Bukavu.* Africa Lives! Production: London, 2011.

Morris, Rosalind, ed. *Can the Subaltern Speak?: Reflections on the History of an Idea*. Columbia University Press, 2010.
Mouralis, Bernard. "Les disparus et les survivants." *Notre Librairie* 148 (juillet–septembre 2002): 12-18.
Mukagasana, Yolande. *Les blessures du silence: Témoignages du génocide au Rwanda*. Arles: Actes sud, 2001.
———. *N'aie pas peur de savoir*. Paris: R. Laffont, 1999.
———. *La mort ne veut pas de moi*. Paris: Fixot, 1997.
Mullins, Lisa. "Exposing the Brutality of Sexual Violence in the Congo." *PRI, The World*, 23 September 2011. Accessed on 6 August 2013. http://www.theworld.org/2011/09/namegabe-rape-sexual-violence-congo/.
Munro, Martin. *Exile and Post 1946 Haitian Literature: Alexis, Dépestre, Ollivier Laferrière, Danticat*. Liverpool: University of Liverpool Press, 2007.
National Coalition for Haitian Refugees. "Rape in Haiti: A Weapon of Terror." 1994. http://www.haitisolidarity.net/downloads/rape_in_haiti_1994.pdf.
Naudillon, Françoise. "Le continent noir du corps: représentation du corps féminin chez Marie-Célie Agnant et Gisèle Pineau." *Études françaises* 41.2 (2005): 75–82.
Ngalasso, Mwatha Musanji. "Langage et violence dans la littérature africaine écrite en français." *Notre Librairie* 148 (juillet–septembre 2002): 72–79.
Ngue, Julie Nack. *Critical Conditions: Illness and Disability in Francophone African and Caribbean Women's Writing*. Lanham: Lexington Books, 2012.
Ngwarsungo Chiwengo, "When Wounds and Corpses Fail to Speak: Narratives of Violence and Rape in the Congo (DRC)." *Comparative Studies of South Asia, Africa and the Middle East* 28, no. 1 (2008): 78–92.
Nkrumah, Kwame. *I Speak of Freedom: A Statement of African Ideology*. New York: Frederick A. Praeger, 1961.
Nnaemeka, Obioma. *The Politics of (M)Othering: Womanhood, Identity and Resistance in African Literature*. New York: Routledge, 1997.
Noakes, Beverly Ormerod. "The Representation of Women in Caribbean Fiction." In *An Introduction to Caribbean Francophone Writing: Guadeloupe and Martinique*. Edited by Sam Haigh, 101–17. Oxford & New York: Berg, 1999.
Nolan, Clancy. "Haiti, Violated." *World Policy Journal* (Spring 2011): 94–101.
Nora, Pierre. *Les lieux de mémoire I*. Paris: Gallimard, 1984.
———. "Between Memory and History: *Les lieux de mémoire*." Translated by Marc Roudebush. In *History and Memory in African American Culture*. Edited by Geneviève Fabre and Robert O'Meally, 284–300. New York: Oxford University Press, 1994.
Nottage, Lynn. *Ruined*. New York: Theatre Communications Group, 2009.
———. Lynn Nottage and Kate Whoriskey interview with Charlie Rose. 2009. Accessed on 2 February 2010. http://geffenplayhouse.com/show_video_listing.php?show_id=9&video_id=4.
Nowrojee, Binaifer. "Shattered Lives: Sexual Violence during the Rwandan Genocide and Its Aftermath." United States' *Human Rights Watch* (September 1996): 12–40.
———. *Your Justice is Too Slow: Will the ICTR Fail Rwanda's Rape Victims?* Geneva, Switzerland: United Nations Research Institute for Social Development, November 2005. www.unrisd.org/publications/opgp10.
N'Zengou-Tayo, Marie-José. "'Fanm Se Poto-Mitan': Haitian Woman, the Pillar of Society." *Feminist Review* 59 (Summer 1998): 118–42.
Oliver, Kelly. *Witnessing Beyond Recognition*. Minneapolis: University of Minnesota Press, 2001.
Orlando, Valerie. *Of Suffocating Hearts and Tortured Souls: Seeking Subjecthood through Madness in Francophone Women's Writing from Africa and the Caribbean*. Lanham, MD: Lexington Books, 2003.
Ouologuem, Yambo. *Le devoir de violence*. Paris: Éditions du Seuil, 1968.
———. *Bound to Violence*. Trans. Ralph Manheim. London: Heinemann, 1971.
———. *The Yambo Ouologuem Reader: The Duty of Violence, a Black Ghostwriter's Letter to France, and the Thousand and One Bibles of Sex*. Translated and edited by Christopher Wise. Trenton, NJ: Africa World Press, 2008.

Ousmane, Sembene. *Ô pays mon beau peuple!* Paris: Presse Pocket, 1957.
Oyewùmí, Onyèrónké. *The Invention of Women: Making African Sense of Western Gender Discourses.* Minneapolis: University of Minnesota Press, 1997.
———. ed. *Gender Epistemologies in Africa: Gendering Traditions, Spaces, Social Institutions, and Identities.* New York: Palgrave Macmillan, 2010.
Paravisini-Gebert, Lizabeth. "Women Against the Grain: Pitfalls of Theorizing Caribbean Women's Writing." *Winds of Change: The Transforming Voices of Caribbean Women Writers and Scholars.* Edited by Adele S. Newson and Linda Strong-Leek. New York: Peter Lang, 1998. 161–68.
Peck, Raoul (director). 2005. *Sometimes in April.* HBO Films.
Peterson, Michel. "Angoisse, corps et pouvoir dans *Amour* de Marie Chauvet." *Elles écrivent des Antilles.* Edited by Suzanne Rinne and Joelle Vitiello. Paris: L'Harmattan, 1997. 39–49.
Pineau, Gisèle. *L'espérance-macadam.* Paris: Stock, 1995.
———. *L'âme prêtée aux oiseaux.* Paris: Stock, 1998.
———, and Marie Abraham, *Femmes des Antilles: Traces et voix, cent cinquante ans après l'abolition de l'esclavage.* Paris: Stock, 1998.
———. *Chair Piment.* Paris: Mércure de France, 2002.
———. *Macadam Dreams.* Trans C. Dickson. Bison Books, 2003.
Placide, Jaira. *Fresh Girl.* New York: Random House, 2002.
Power, Samantha. *A Problem from Hell: America in the Age of Genocide.* New York: Perennial, 2002.
Prunier, Gérard. "Élements pour une histoire du Front Patriotique rwandais." *Politique africaine* 51 (octobre 1993): 121–38.
Rajan, Rajeswari Sunder. *Real and Imagined Women: Gender, Culture and Postcolonialism.* London: Routledge, 1993.
Reed, Cyrus. "Exile, Reform, and the Rise of the Rwandan Patriotic Front." *The Journal of Modern African Studies*, 34.3 (1996): 479-501.
Rentschler, Carrie."Witnessing: U.S. Citizenship and the Vicarious Experience of Suffering." *Media, Culture, and Society* 26.2 (2004): 296–304.
Rice-Maximin, Micheline. *Karukéra: Présence littéraire de la Guadeloupe.* New York: Peter Lang Publishing, 1998.
Rinne, Susanne and Joelle Vitiello, eds. *Elles écrivent des Antilles: Haiti, Guadeloupe, Martinique.* Paris: Harmattan, 1997.
Robertson, Elizabeth and Christine M. Rose, eds. *Representing Rape in Medieval and Early Modern Literature.* New York: Palgrave, 2001.
Romany, Celina. Keynote Address: "Human Rights and the Interaction of Race, Gender and Ethnicity: A View from the Americas." Advance on the Web.
Rooney, Ellen. "Criticism and the Subject of Sexual Violence". *MLN* 98.5 (December 1983): 1269–78.
Rosello, Mireille. *Littérature et identité créole aux Antilles.* Paris: Karthala, 1992.
Ross, Marlon B. "Race, Rape, Castration: Feminist Theories of Sexual Violence and Masculine Strategies of Black Protest." *Masculinity Studies and Feminist Theory.* Edited by Judith Kegan Gardiner, 305–43. Columbia University Press, 2002.
Roumain, Jacques. *Gouverneurs de la rosée.* Pantin, France: Les temps des cerises, 2000.
Rurangwa, Jean-Marie. "Why I Write, What I Write, How I Write It." *Africultures* 30, "Rwanda 2000: mémoires d'avenir." Paris: L'Harmattan, 2000.
"Rwandan Genocide." *BBC News Watch* 28 May 1994. www.bbc.co.uk.
Scarry, Elaine. *The Body in Pain: The Making and Unmaking of the World.* Oxford: Oxford University Press, 1987.
Scharfman, Ronnie. "Mirroring and Mothering in Simone Schwarz-Bart's *Pluie et vent sur Télumée Miracle* and Jean Rhys' *Wide Sargasso Sea.*" *Yale French Studies* 62 (1981): 88–106.
———. "Theorizing Terror: The Discourse of Violence in Marie Chauvet's *Amour, Colère, Folie.*" In *Postcolonial Subjects: Francophone Women Writers.* Edited by Mary Jean Green, Karen Gould, Micheline Rice-Maximin, Keith Walker, and Jack A. Yeager, 229–45. Minneapolis: University of Minnesota Press, 1996.
Schwarz-Bart, Simone. *Pluie et vent sur Télumée Miracle.* Paris: Éditions du seuil, 1972.
———.Translated by Barbara Bray. *The Bridge of Beyond.* London and Kingston: Heineman, 1982.

Scott, Joan Wallach. *Gender and the Politics of History.* New York: Columbia University Press, 1988.
Sharpe, Jenny. *Allegories of Empire: The Figure of Woman in the Colonial Text.* Minneapolis, University of Minnesota Press, 1993.
Sharpe, Christina. *Monstrous Intimacies: Making Post-Slavery Subjects.* Durham: Duke University Press, 2010.
Sharpley-Whiting, T. Denean. "When A Black Woman Cries Rape: Discourses of Unrapeability, Intraracial Sexual Violence, and the State of Indiana vs. Michael Gerard Tyson." In *Spoils of War: Women of Color, Cultures and Revolutions.* Edited by T. Denean Sharpley-Whiting and Renée White. Lanham, MD: Rowman and Littlefield Publishers, 1997.
———. *Frantz Fanon: Conflicts and Feminisms.* New York: Brown and Littlefield, 1998.
———. *Negritude Women.* Minneapolis: University of Minnesota Press, 2002.
Sheftall, Beverly Guy. *The Root Interview.* http://www.theroot.com/views/root-interview-beverly-guy-sheftall. 24 November 2010.
Sheller, Mimi. *Citizenship from Below: Erotic Agency and Caribbean Freedom.* Durham: Duke University Press, 2012.
Siebers, Tobin. "Language, Violence, and the Sacred: A Polemical Survey of Critical Theories." In *To Honor René Girard: Presented at the Occasion of his 60th Birthday by Colleagues, Students, Friends.* Saratoga, CA: Anma Libri, 1986. 210–11.
Sielke, Sabine. *Reading Rape: The Rhetoric of Sexual Violence in American Literature and Culture.* Princeton, NJ: Princeton University Press, 2002.
Skloot, Robert. "Old Concerns and New Plays in the Theater of Genocide.'" *Genocide Studies and Prevention* 5.1 (April 2010): 114–20.
Smith, Faith, ed. *Sex and the Citizen: Interrogating the Caribbean.* Charlottesville: University of Virginia Press, 2011.
Sontag, Susan. *Regarding the Pain of Others.* New York: Picador, 2004.
Spivak, Gayatri Chakravorty. "Can the Subaltern Speak?" In *Marxism and the Interpretation of Culture.* Edited by Cary Nelson and Lawrence Grossberg, 271–313. Urbana, IL: University of Illinois Press, 1988.
———. *In Other Worlds: Essays in Cultural Politics.* New York: Routledge, 1987.
Stockton, Sharon. *The Economics of Fantasy: Rape in Twentieth Century Literature.* Columbus: The Ohio State University Press, 2006.
Suarez, Lucia. "What Happens When Memory Hurts?: The Haunting of Rape." In *The Tears of Hispaniola: Haitian and Dominican Cultural Memory,* 61–90. Gainesville: University Press of Florida, 2006.
Tadjo, Véronique. *L'ombre d'Imana: Voyages jusqu'au bout du Rwanda.* Arles: Acte Sud, 2001.
———. *The Shadow of Imana: Travels in the Heart of Rwanda.* Trans. Veronica Wakerley. Johannesburg: Heinemann, 2002.
Tal, Kali. *Worlds of Hurt: Reading the Literatures of Trauma.* New York: Cambridge University Press, 1996.
Tanner, Laura E. *Intimate Violence: Reading Rape, Reading Torture in Twentieth Century Fiction.* Bloomington: University of Indiana Press, 1994.
Tansi, Sony Labou. *La vie et demie.* Paris: Seuil, 1979.
———. *Half Life.* Trans. Dominic Thomas and Allison Dundy. Bloomington : Indiana University Press, 2011.
Thomas, Dominic. *Nation-Building, Propaganda, and Literature in Francophone Africa.* Bloomington, IN: Indiana University Press, 2002.
Thomas, Deborah. *Exceptional Violence: Embodied Citizenship in Transnational Jamaica.* Durham: Duke University Press, 2011.
Thomas, Greg. *The Sexual Demon of Colonial Power: African Embodiment and the Erotic Schemes of Empire.* Bloomington: Indiana University Press, 2007.
Tinsley, Omise'eke Natasha. *Thiefing Sugar: Eroticism between Women in Caribbean Literature.* Durham: Duke University Press, 2010.
———. "Black Atlantic, Queer Atlantic Queer Imaginings of the Middle Passage" *GLQ: A Journal of Lesbian and Gay Studies* 14, nos. 2–3 (2008): 191–215.
Traoré, Aminata. *Le viol de l'imaginaire* Paris: Fayard, 2002.

Trouillot, Evelyne. *Rosalie l'Infâme*. Paris: Dapper, 2003.
Trouillot, Michel-Rolph. *Haiti, State Against Nation: The Origins and Legacy of Duvalierism*. New York: Monthly Review Press, 1990.
United Nations Population Fund (UNFPA) 25 November 2005. http://www.haiti info.com/article.php3?id_article=4073 http://www.haitisupport.gn.apc.org/Rape2005.htm.
Ulysse, Gina. Introduction. "Pawol fanm sou douz janvye" *Meridians* 11:1 (2011): 91–97.
Vieux-Chauvet, Marie. *Amour, colère et folie*. Paris: Soley, 2006.
———. *Love, Anger, Madness*. Translated by Rose-Myriam Réjouis and Val Vinkour. New York: Random House, 2009.
Volet, Jean-Marie. "Francophone Women Writing in 1998–99 and Beyond: A Literary Feast in a Violent World," *Research in African Literatures* 32.4 (2001): 187–200.
Walcott-Hackshaw, Elizabeth. "My Love is Like a Rose: Terror, Territoire and the Poetics of Marie Chauvet." *Small Axe* 18 (September 2005): 40–51.
Waller, Nicole. *Contradictory Violence: Revolution and Subversion in Caribbean Fiction*. American Studies: A Monograph Series. Heidelberg: Universitatverlag, 2005.
Wallstrom, Margot. *Women, Peace and Security*. UN Special Representative of the Secretary-General on Sexual Violence Council Report. February 2012.
Wanzo, Rebecca. *The Suffering Will Not Be Televised : African American Women and Sentimental Political Storytelling*. Albany: SUNY Press, 2009.
White, Aaronnette. "Talking Feminist, Talking Black: Micromobilization Processes in a Collective Protest Rape." *Gender and Society* 13.1 (February 1999): 77–100.
Wilkinson, Nancy. "Rape flourishes . . . " *Los Angeles Times*, 4 February 2011.
Willey, Ann Elizabeth. "Pornography or the Politics of Misbehaving? A Feminist Reading of the Voices of Yambo Oulouguem." In *Yambo Ouologuem: Postcolonial Writer, Islamic Militant*. Edited by Christopher Wise, 139–51. Boulder, CO: Lynne Rienner Publishers, 1999.
Wise, Christopher, ed. *Yambo Ouologuem: Postcolonial Writer, Islamic Militant*. Boulder, CO: Lynne Rienner Publishers, 1999.
Young, Hershini Bhana. *Haunting Capital: Memory, Text and the Black Diasporic Body*. Hanover and London: University Press of New England, 2006.
Zarifis, Ismène. "Haitian Women Speak Out against Violence." *Haiti Insight* 8, no. 1 (2008). Accessed 15 January 2012. http://www.nchr.org/nchr/insight/speakout.htm.
Zimra, Clarisse. "What's in a Name: Elective Genealogy in Schwarz-Bart's Early Novels." *Studies in 20th Century Literature* 17.1 (1993): 97–118.
Zobel, Joseph. *La rue Cases-Nègres*. Paris: Présence Africaine, 1974.
———. *Black Shack Alley*. Trans. Keith Q. Warner. London: Heinemann, 1980.

INDEX

abuse: childhood sexual, 138–39; civil rights, 66; domestic, 37, 39; human rights, 63, 66, 181, 193, 219, 236, 262–63; and murder of women, 102; sexual, 60, 266; violence and forms of, 44

activism, 3; anti-rape, 2, 5, 264; boundary between local and global, 258; of Congolese women, 258–60; women's, genealogy of engagement, 259

affect: audience, 205–60; photography and production of, 181

Africa: atrocities other than Rwandan genocide in, 161; conflict waged in, 9; discursive dynamics and politics of rape representation in, 6; francophone, 19, 33, 35, 48; as locus of violence and atrocity, 180; postcolonial independence, 3, 32; postcolonial subjects from, 3; prevalence of violence in, 154; problematics of images of war in, 220; prominence of articulations of violence in, 10; scripts of subject erasure in, 16; sexual violence in, 8; and stakes of genocidal representations, 154–56; war and representation in, 219, 251; "World War" in, 5, 206, 251.

Africans: as abject and deviant, 148; stereotypical pathologizing of, 147; subject/object dichotomy in visual representations of, 185

African women: as advocates, survivors, and agitators, 5; black bodies of, 255; bodies of, quotidian violation of, 23; as eternally oppressed, subjugated and victims of patriarchy, 217; intimate violations of, and global discourses of gender, power, and human rights, 152; positioning of as suffering object, 212; subjugation of, 5

agency, 3, 113, 126, 174–80, 192; boundary between victimization and, 94; compromising of, 120; of Congolese women, 258–60; erasure of, 259; futility of, 198; in studies of the subaltern, 260; subaltern, recording traumatic testimony as form of, 191

Ahmed, Sarah: *The Cultural Politics of Emotion*, 231, 253

Akayesu, Jean-Paul, 177, 197, 199

Alexander, Jacqui, 7; "Not Just (Any) Body Can Be a Citizen," 264

Algeria, war for liberation in, 20, 79, 276n24, 280n91

Amour, colère, folie (*Love, Anger, Madness*) (Vieux-Chavet), 14, 58–61, 88–89, 94–95, 98–100, 103; as capturing fear and brutality of era, 70; character perspective in, 76; critique of patriarchy in, 77; as critique of politics of sexual violence in Haiti, 59; Danticat's role in republication and translation of, 83; daring use of sexuality in, 71; as earliest "dictator novel," 59; and feminist lens, 76; intertextual relationship with

307

Saisons sauvages, 89, 99; looking as theme of, 75; narrative logic of, 72; narrative voice in, 76; occlusion of critical discussion of, 71; paratextual aspects of, 71, 72; repetition and revision of tradition in, 72; repoliticization of rape in, 72; resistance and refusal in, 74; scandal surrounding, 71; sexual violence in, 59–61, 71–74; temporality in, 76; and violence, 59, 70–83

Anacaona, 26, 86–87

anticolonialism, 18; as imbued with violence, 20; violence, 14, 280n92

anti-rape activism, 2, 5; not restricted to one gender, 264

Arendt, Hannah: *On Violence*, 43

Aristide, Jean-Bertrand: overthrow of, 27, 62, 66, 87, 263; restoration to power of, 27

Arusha: International Criminal Tribunals, 151, 176, 177, 178, 203; Peace Accords, 145–46

Association Internationale pour la mémoire du génocide au Rwanda, 158–59

Bell, Beverly, 66, 68, 277n31, 282n20

Benítez-Rojo, Antonio, 35, 118; *The Repeating Island*, 15, 106–10

Beti, Mongo, 19, 22–23; *Main basse sur le Cameroun*, 22–23

Beyala, Calixthe, 36, 39–40, 42, 53; *Amours sauvages*, 39; *Assèze l'africaine*, 39; *C'est le soleil qui m'a brûlée*, 39; *Femme nue, femme noire*, 39; *Le roman de Pauline*, 39; *Tu t'appelleras Tanga*, 39

Beyond Shock, 61, 67, 69–70

black bodies: of African and African diasporic women, 255; configuration and objectification of, 3; female, production of, 3; in pain, 11; ritualized violence against, 23; sexual and gender dynamics for, 16; suffering, and human rights discourses, 267

black feminism, 11, 13, 257, 275n31, 275n38, 280n93; antiviolent, rape representation and, 16; global iterations of, 3; optic of both/and, 252; standpoint theory, 7–8

black male rapist, myth of, 211, 277n37, 286n48, 293n15

black sentience, 10, 43

black women: collective experience of, 132; empathy and sympathy in suffering of, 212; as hypersexual, 109; legibility and audibility of suffering of, 207; obscuring of stories of, 211; oppression of, 37; as Other, 273n8; *Pluie et vent* as condemnation of violence against, 36; points of view based on multiple locations, 8; rape of as legal right, 47; and relations with white men as sign of alienation, 47; removal of capacity of desire of, 47; sexual violence as way of elucidating personhood of, 39; as unrapeable, 109; visibility of, 207

blame, 81, 94, 234

Les blessures du silence: Témoignages du génocide au Rwanda (Mukagasana), 15, 147–48, 150, 152, 179, 180–202, 203–4, 214, 258–59; dialogic structure of, 183–91, 193; and Diop, 291n70, 291n71; funding of, 184; layering of photographs, interviews, and paratext, 182, 183–84; metatextuality in, 183–84, 193, 201; use of silence in, 184, 187; testimonies and witnessing in, 191, 192–93, 241; and visual production of genocidal rape, 180–82; as worldwide exhibit, 181

bodies, women's: allegorization of, 48, 104; in atmosphere of violence, 19; attentiveness to, 104; black, 3; circulating in global political economy, 73, 88–89; effects of sexual violence on, 102; as enduring spoils, 2; enlisting of as prostitutes, 221; foregrounding of, 15; gendered, 109; impact of conflict on, 219; inscription of violence upon, 83; land and, 14–15, 48, 82, 110, 111–17; metaphoric or symbolic role of in rape representation, 48; militarization of, 230; as militarized zone, 219, 239; and national oppression, 109; and objectification, 118; rape of vs. rape of land, 103; as site of embodied memory, 170; spectacularization of, 254; as symbolic site, 109; as territories of colonial conquest, 27; transformation of into battlegrounds, 5; violation and pillaging of, 6; and violence, 3, 99

body/bodies: allegorization of, 48; chained to violence, 18, 112; as emptied of subjectivity, 220; as established site for mapping of histories of violence, 6; feminist theorists of, 103–4; material, and subjectivity, 103; metonymic use of, 220; as object to amass interest and sympathy, 220; as operational material and psychological sites of conflict, 9; as provocative site, 13; representation of in political rapes, 99–100; as sites of oppression, 44; shifting focus from conflict to, 254; subjugated, meaning assigned by, 3; surrender of to Duvalier regime, 71; transformation of from subjects into sights, 220

Boni, Tanella, 17, 53–54

Borkgren, Sherrlyn: *Forever Changed: Berrlyze's Story*, 206, 246–54, 255

Breath, Eyes, Memory (Danticat), 60, 83–84, 99, 284n51

Brutus, Timoléon, 26, 57

Bugul, Ken, 36; intertextual link with Kourouma, 40; *La folie et la mort*, 40; *Le baobab fou*, 40
Butler, Judith, 103, 285n12

Cahill, Ann J., 103, 131, 137, 170; *Rethinking Rape*, 103
Cameroon, 22–23
Capécia, Mayotte: *Je suis Martiniquaise*, 35, 47
Caribbean: collectivity, 25; cultural production, 25; evolution of discourses, 106; francophone, 19, 25, 35, 44; gender relations in, 85; imaginary, 106, 107–11, 126; intersections of race, class, sexuality and gender in, 113; landscape as feminized space in, 15, 102, 104–11, 114, 143–44; literature, 26, 36, 38, 44, 54–55, 104, 108, 114, 117; postcolonial discourses of, 14–15; race in, 107; as raped woman, 108; and sexual violence, 8, 108; tradition, folklore, and cultural practices in, 107–8
La case du commandeur (Glissant), 15, 24–25, 110–11
Cazenave, Odile, 36, 93
Céline, Louis-Ferdinand: debate surrounding work of, 290n49; *Voyage au bout de la nuit*, 168
Chancy, Myriam, 57, 60, 70, 282n12, 282n17
Charles, Carolle, 42, 65, 66
children: bodies of impacted by conflict, 219; born of rape, 198–99, 214; images of in human rights advocacy, 251; rhetorical agency of, 251; as spectacular objects, 251; as static noncitizen subjects, 252; survivors of sexual assault, 88, 138
Chiwengo, Ngwarsungu, 209, 255
citizenship, 64, 112, 261–71
class, 36–37, 86, 113, 255; stratification, 28–29
Clinton, Catherine, 17, 172
Clinton Global Initiative, 202
colonialism, 9–11, 13, 52, 280n93; allied brutalities of slavery and, 25; Belgian, 176, 215; epistemic violence of, 9; functioning of rape in context of, 21; independence from, 25; legacy of, 45; movements against, 5; residual effects of, 25; revenge for injustice of, 47; and site of gendered body, 50; structural and institutional marks of, 220; violence meted out by powers of, 22; and violence, 8, 9, 18, 20–22, 26, 32, 38, 43, 45, 49, 55
Commission of Women Victims for Victims (KOFAVIV), 267, 282n23
Condé, Maryse, 6, 36, 38–39, 42, 114; *Célanire cou-coupé*, 38; *Hérémakhonon*, 35, 38; *His-*

toire de la femme cannibale, 38; *Moi, Tituba, Sorcière*, 38
conflict zone, 6, 9, 219, 267
Congolese women, 1, 3; absence of, 212; as acting subjects, 5; activism and agency of, 258–60; concealed presence of, 253; demonstrating against rape warfare, 267; disidentification of, 212; marginalization of, 257; othering of, 212, 273n8; pain of, 205–60; protesting, 6, 11; reliance on Western liberal framework for discussing rights of, 217; as objects, 212, 231; situated knowledge of, 246; subject positions of, 206–7, 241, 255, 260; victimization of by war, 225; voices of, 213, 258
Conteh-Morgan, John, 232, 234
coups d'état, 26, 27, 62
Créolité movement, 113, 286n42
cultural production, 10, 13, 15, 21, 55, 61, 108, 112, 148, 154, 253, 255, 268, 271; African and Caribbean, violence as preeminent theme in, 25; failure of to convey rape, 51; francophone, 9, 45; Haitian women's 269; history of landscape and body in, 104; narrative strategy of, 29; postcolonial, 106; responding to and remembering Rwandan genocide through, 147, 155, 203–4; and violence, 44, 149
cyclone metaphor. *See* hurricane

Les damnés de la terre (*The Wretched of the Earth*) (Fanon), 18, 20–21, 47, 79, 275n30, 280n91
Danticat, Edwidge, 14, 83, 283n41; *Anacaona: Golden Flower*, 26, 276n27; *Breath, Eyes, Memory*, 60, 83–84, 99, 284n51; *The Dew Breaker*, 61, 83–86; "We Are Ugly, But We Are Here," 86–87
Darfur, genocide in, 52, 203, 290n66
Dash, Michael, 28, 38
Davis, Angela, 274n9, 286n48
decolonization, 18, 20, 22, 47
de Lauretis, Teresa, 14, 16
Democratic Republic of the Congo (DRC), 2, 9, 15, 151, 161; anti-rape movement in, 5, 208; colonial legacy of, 215–16; conflict in, 256; geopolitical space of, 209; history of, 215, 221; international community lack of awareness of rape in, 209; land and violence in, 215–16; landscape of, 215–16; pain of women in, 205–60; patriarchal culture of, 214; as "rape capital of world," 211; rape in, 1–6, 12, 208, 211, 218–19, 258; repercussions of Rwandan genocide in, 148, 203, 209; sexual violence against

women in, 154; subaltern subject in, 206; war in, 52, 206, 209, 218–19, 234, 256. *See also* Congolese women
The Dew Breaker (Danticat), 61, 83–86
dictator novel genre, 95, 281n6
dictatorship, 9, 13, 26, 34, 62; and site of gendered body, 50; unfurling of, 33
Diop, Boubacar Boris, 160, 162, 179, 281n110, 289n30, 289n40; *L'Afrique au-delà du miroir*, 161; and *Les blessures*, 291n70, 291n71; *Murambi*, 15, 147–48, 150–51, 156–66, 203–4
disembodiment, 48, 172
disempowerment, 172, 227
distance, 141, 169, 172, 174, 217, 234
Djedamoun, Nocky, 156, 157, 289n30
domestic abuse and violence, 37, 39
Duvalier regime, 14, 27, 59–62, 64, 66, 83, 85; effects of on women's lives and bodies, 71; extraction of rape from context of, 99; political context of, 72; sexual dynamics of, 89, 99; sexual politics of, 61; terror and fear of, 71; and violence, 70, 82, 95

embodiment, female, 31, 70
emotion, 207, 220, 244, 253
empathy: audience, 217; in *The Greatest Silence*, 212–13, 217; and obscuring of subject of drama or documentary, 206; and personhood, 205–6, 256; as point of departure, 255; representation of wartime rape beyond, 254–60; rhetorical significance of, 206; in *Ruined*, 231; and sentimentalism or romance, 255; and sexual violence, 205; theater and creation of, 205; vs. sympathy, 212
empowerment, 34, 225; of victims, 44
epistemic violence, 9–11, 35, 46
L'espérance-macadam (*Macadam Dreams*) (Pineau), 15, 102–44; "beasts" in, 119–21, 122, 128, 131, 135, 137, 142; burning in, 123, 125; catalogue of emotions in, 127–28; cyclone metaphor in, 104, 118, 120, 125, 129–31, 137, 144; gaze in, 126; graphic violence in, 113–14; identity in, 120–21; incest in, 118, 122, 127, 132, 134, 136–40, 143; intersection of natural and sexual violence in, 102, 117–22, 122–23, 129, 130–31; landscape poetics of, 119; metatextuality in, 129; minor characters of, 132–36; penetrating in, 123–24; ripping apart in, 123–24; silence and voice in, 122; superficial reading of, 103; textual fragmentation in, 119; third-person narrative in, 126; vicarious trauma in, 132–36

ethnicity, 7, 86

Fanon, Frantz, 14, 19, 20–22, 46–47, 53, 79, 279n80, 280nn91–93; *L'an V de la Révolution Algérienne*, 21; *Les damnés de la terre*, 18, 20–21, 47, 79, 275n30, 280n91; *Peau noire, masques blancs*, 47
fear, 70, 126–27; culture of, 71, 86
Felman, Shoshana, 151, 192
feminism: Anglophone, 7; black, 3, 7–8, 11, 13, 257, 275n31, 275n38, 280n93; black francophone, 42; global, 210, 217; in Haiti, 65, 268–69; mainstream analysis of Global South, 210; postmodern, 275n31; reading through lens of, 76; second-wave, 8; Third World, 275n39; transnational global, 2, 7–8, 12, 149, 210, 217, 267; truth claims of, 8
feminist politics, 275n39; of rape representation, 141–44
feminization of land, 30, 48–49, 102, 104, 108, 143. *See also* rape-of-the-land metaphor
la femme ligotée, 168–71, 179
la femme violée, 48
Ferly, Odile, 44–45, 103
Fest'Africa, 156–62, 176, 289n30, 289n40
Fitzpatrick, Lisa: "Signifying Rape," 228
Fondation de France, 159, 184
Forever Changed: Berrlyze's Story (Borkgren), 206, 246–53, 255
Foucault, Michel, 279n84, 280n85
France: attitude of European colonizers in, 29; collusion of in government injustice in African states, 23; complicity of in Rwandan genocide, 159–60
Francis, Donnette, 57, 64, 65
francophone studies, 2, 6–7; history of rape trope in, 17–56; and legacy of slavery, 25; representing rape in, 9, 13, 26–42, 107
francophone women's writing, 35–42
freedom, 2, 3–5, 16, 271
French language, 32, 53, 160
Fresh Girl (Placide), 60–61, 83, 87–88, 100
Front Patriotique Rwandais (FPR), 146, 287n3

gender, 7, 14, 152, 255; accounting for dynamics of sex and, 16; difference, 46, 109; and duty to violence, 19; dynamics, 10, 40, 196, 232; in Haiti, 85–86; intersection of with human rights, 219; intersection of with class and race, 36–37, 113; as location of identity, 86; oppression, 69, 71; politics, 19, 37, 42, 72; relations, 85, 107; and sexuality, 34; and sexual violence, 264; and slavery, 40; transcending of, 264

gender-based violence (GBV), 21, 27, 38, 66, 68, 211
gender violence, 12, 27–28, 30, 37–38, 53, 56, 66, 102, 111; cultural silence in response to, 12; and women's postcolonial condition, 39; and Duvalier regime, 95; Foucault and, 279n84; in francophone literature, 79; and history and land, 115; as human rights violation, 12; as layered, 149; normalization of, 49; nuanced depiction of, 143; and politics, 60; and power, 43; as social phenomenon, 60; as tool to mitigate other forms of, 71; voices and experiences of, 150–51; women writers' exploration and unveiling of, 21
genocidal rape, 155, 162, 174–80; definition of, 275n34; gang rape as, 195; narratives of, 201; rescripting of, 148–52; visual production of, 180–82
genocide, 9, 13, 26, 34, 196, 204; in Darfur, 52, 290n66; dialogic encounter with, 183–91; difficulty of relating testimonies of with fidelity, 202; and display of abject, 193; and essentialism and fixity, 147; interstices of, 171; spheres of influence of, 171; mythologies of, 204; problematic of representing, 151; question of naming, 147, 158; rape as act of, 177; rape body exposed as metonymy for, 179; rendering of, 179; and sexual violence, 165, 202; Rwandan, 15, 52, 145–204; and site of gendered body, 50; in Sudan, 203, 290n66; vs. violence, 146–47; translation of trauma of into art, 151; utility of testimonial narratives in aftermath of, 165–66. *See also* Rwandan genocide
Gide, André, 168, 290n50
Glissant, Edouard, 3, 6, 14, 19, 23–25, 94, 110; *La case du commandeur*, 15, 24–25, 110–11; *Le discours antillais*, 24–25, 110; *Le quatrième siècle*, 24
globalization, 2, 22, 45; contemporary cultures of, 220
global political economy, women's bodies circulating in, 73, 88–89
Global South, 22, 52, 68, 274n25; problems encountered by feminists concerning, 210; and sexual violence, 154; subaltern women as victims of "backward" regimes of, 219
The Greatest Silence: Rape in the Congo (Jackson), 16, 206, 207–18, 220, 234, 236; empathy and sympathy as central to, 212–13, 217–18; gaze in, 215; Jackson's positionality in, 208, 211–12, 216; landscape in, 215–16; power relations in, 213; self-reflective nature of, 211; sentimentality of, 217; title of, 209–10; subjectivity in, 255; use of to unveil human rights atrocities, 217; victim-blaming trope in, 242
Grewal, Inderpal, 7, 288n16
Grosz, Elizabeth, 103, 285n12
Guadeloupe, 2, 36, 101, 287n61; sexual violence in, 15, 117, 139; slavery in, 55
guilt, 32, 90, 92, 97, 126, 164, 189, 202, 237

Haiti, 2, 9, 12, 14, 26–28, 63, 66–67, 87, 154, 263, 266; Caco rebellions, 27, 276n28; contemporary novels, repoliticizing rape in, 83–100; *dechoukaj* period in, 62, 66, 282n20; displacement tent cities in, 28, 67–69, 154, 269; Duvalier dictatorship in, 14, 27, 59–62, 64, 66, 70–72, 82, 83, 85, 89, 95, 99; feminism in, 268–69; gender and class oppression in, 85; gender-based violence in, 27–28; gender issues in, 65, 85; Institute for Justice in Democracy, 61; Johnny Jean rape in, 261–68; *la terreur* in, 59, 70, 98–99; *Ligue féminine d'action sociale*, 64, 65; operation *machin enfènal*, 27, 66, 282n20; politics of rape/sexual violence in, 59, 62–70; post-earthquake, 67–69; post-earthquake rape myths, 61; rape in, 62, 64, 69, 270, 295n6; rape origin story in, 26, 57–58; Revolution in, 26–27; Revolutionary Front for the Progress of Haiti (FRAPH), 27, 66; sexual economies in, 113; slavery in, 55, 62; sovereignty of, 265; Tontons Macoutes in, 64, 71, 83–84, 283n38; UN Stabilization Mission (MINUSTAH), 12, 67, 261–63, 265–67; U. S. occupation of, 27, 62, 63, 276n28; women contributing to liberation in, 68; women's activism in, 269
Hakim-Rimpel, Yvonne, 64–66, 95
Harrow, Kenneth, 145, 148, 155, 180, 188
Hartman, Saidiya, 10, 11, 14, 43; *Scenes of Subjection*, 35
haunting, 198, 253
healing, 87, 117, 119, 121, 142–43, 208, 214, 231, 235, 237, 258
Hesford, Wendy, 191, 251, 262, 266, 288n16; *Spectacular Rhetorics*, 192–93, 202, 207
Higgins, Helen, 50, 52
Hitchcott, Nicki, 148, 159–60, 180
Hotel Rwanda, 175
human rights, 2, 3, 12, 16, 69, 149, 152, 177–78, 202, 210, 219, 236, 256; advocacy, 210, 253, 256, 258, 261–71; centrality of conflict zones to, 267; challenging rhetoric of, 187; critique of logics of, 207; discourses of, 12, 16, 187, 201–2, 210, 236, 241, 251, 253, 260,

263, 267; images of children in advocacy for, 251; limitations of project of, 206; logics of frameworks of, 189; and need for resolution, 232; public engagement with, 267; and sexual violence, 95, 267; shortcomings of, 254; and spectatorship and recognition, 191; testimonies of, 192–95, 220, 252; use of documentary to unveil atrocities, 217; violations of, 23, 151–52, 185, 219, 253, 262–63, 265, 267; vocabulary of frameworks of, 267
Human Rights Watch, 146, 288n7; *Shattered Lives*, 153
hurricane, metaphor of, 102, 120, 129–31, 137, 144; as material manifestation of several aspects of rape, 125; problematization of, 118; as vehicle for metaphorizing sexual violence, 102
Hurricane Hugo, 101–2, 117, 119, 140, 142
Hutus, 146, 153, 173, 194, 288n22

identity, 120–21; Caribbean, formation of, 111; formation of, 132; linguistic models of, 114; multiple locations of, 37, 86, 149, 246; national, 27, 48, 264; trauma, catastrophe and, 111; women's, 39
Ilboudo, Monique, 40, 54
imperialism, 7, 25, 43, 52
incest, 102–3, 122, 132, 134, 136–41, 143, 173; mothers' reactions to, 287n61; silence around, 117; symbolic meanings of, 103; trauma of, 103
independence: from colonialism and slavery, 25; colonial struggles for, 18; futility of, 3; 1960s struggles for, 31
Interahamwe (militant Hutus), 146, 199, 288n22
island: as female, 111; rape analogy, 45, 117, 124

Jackson, Lisa: 212, 215; *The Greatest Silence*, 16, 206, 207–18, 220, 234, 236, 242, 255; overidentification of with women she interviews, 213; positionality of, 210–12, 215–17; self-critical nature of, 210; use of personal experience of rape by, 208, 211–12, 216
Jean, Johnny, 261–68; citizenship rights of, 263–64; as symbolizing violation of nation, 263–64
Julien, Eileen, 46, 280n88

Kalisa, Marie Chantal, 36, 105, 274n28

Kazinierakis, Alain, 181, 184, 185–86, 189, 191, 192–94, 291n76
Kempadoo, Kamala, 73, 94
knowledge: individual situated, 258; production of , 69, 147situated, 8, 47, 89, 94; specifically African, 155; subjective and bodily, ignoring of, 46; subjugated, 254–57
Kourouma, Ahmadou: *Les soleils des indépendances*, 32–33; intertextual link with Bugul, 40; *Monnè, outrages et défis*, 278n48
Kwahulé, Koffi, 6; *Les recluses*, 16, 206, 231–46, 253–54, 255–56, 260; interrogation of form and position as playwright, 237; and role of theater, 237; use of gender and performance by, 232; violence in works of, 232

land: emphasis on value of, 82; and female body, 102–3, 105–17; feminization of, 30, 48, 111–17; functions of in Caribbean imaginary, 106; fusion/confusion of with women's bodies, 110; and history and gendered violence, 115; and slavery, 110; and violence in DRC, 215–16. *See also* rape-of-the-land metaphor
landscape: Conradian, 18; feminized, 49, 102, 104; gendering of, 113–14; metaphors of, 111; postcolonial Caribbean, 15, 105; rape and, 149–50; violated poetics of, 117, 119; and violence, 106–11
la langue violée, 32, 48, 53
language: disruptive use of, 32; failure of, 147; insufficiency of, 161; and trauma, 110
Larrier, Renée, 7, 137
Léry, Jean de, 168, 290n50
liberation: absence of men as form of, 232; African, 3; of Haitian women, 68–69; national, 3, 79; violence as, 20; violence as means for, 279n80
Ligue féminine d'action sociale (League of Feminine Social Action, Haiti), 64–65
Lionnet, Françoise, 7, 48, 148–49, 268
locations, multiple, 3, 8, 82, 86, 149, 173, 254, 268
Loinsigh, Aedín Ní, 155, 167

MacKinnon, Catharine, 103, 152
Mamdani, Mahmood, 146, 188, 287n4; *When Victims Become Killers*, 288n10
Mardorossian, Carine, 11, 95; "Towards a New Feminist Criticism of Rape," 49
Mars, Kettly, 14; *Saisons sauvages*, 60–61, 83, 88–99, 100, 103
Martelly, Michel, 263–66
Martinique, 28–29, 55

masks, use of, 232, 234, 244
material violence, 34, 51; failure of language to capture, 147
matrilineal genealogies, 36, 37, 41
Mbembe, Achille, 19, 21–22; *On the Postcolony*, 21–22, 45
McClintock, Anne, 28, 280n95
Mehta, Brinda, 35, 61, 104–5, 286n42
memory: development of into duty and obligation, 156; dismemberment of, 120; gaping wounds of, 190; generational transmission of, 121; literal embodiment of, 170; power of remembered rape as site of, 171; problematics of, 203; wounds of, 156
memory, traumatic, 24, 83–84, 170–71, 194
men: as colonized, 19; rape of, 262, 264; as victims of sexual violence, 281n113
Metellus, Jean: *Anacaona, Fleur d'Or*, 26
Michel, Claudine, 261; "Unequal Distribution," 268–71
MINUSTAH (United Nations Stabilization Mission in Haiti). See under Haiti
Mohanty, Chandra Talpade, 275n39, 288nn15–16; "Under Western Eyes," 210, 217
Mongwanga, Shana, 205, 257; *The Road to Bukavu*, 206, 207, 258–60
Moukoury, Thérèse Kuoh: *Rencontres essentielles*, 35
Mukagasana, Yolande, 145, 152, 180, *183*, 184, 187, 201, 203; *La mort ne veut pas moi*, 152; *Les blessures du silence*, 15, 147–48, 150, 152, 179, 180–202, 203–4, 214, 241, 258–59, 291n70, 291n71; *N'aie pas peur de savoir—Rwanda: une rescapée tutsi raconte*, 152; positionality of, 192–95; preface to *Blessures* by, 184, 187–88; as survivor, 184, 193
multiplicity, aesthetic of, 166–74, 206
Murambi: Le livre des ossements (*Murambi: Book of Bones*) (Diop), 15, 147–48, 150–51, 161–63, 166, 203–4, 291n76; sites of genocide and seeing rape in, 156–66
murder, 34, 102, 146, 165

Namegabe, Chouchou, 205, 223, 257–58, 260
narrative closure, 205–60
nation, 7; and disembodiment and objectification of women, 48–49; identifications that traverse, 255; trope of rape of, 265; violation of, 263; woman as signifier for, 109
national identity: role of rape in creation of, 26–27, 58; women as symbols and icons for, 48
nationalist discourse, 265; masculinization of, 30; and rape, spectatorship, and spectacular, 266

nationalist project: and allegorization of female body, 48, 104; and colonial violence, 26; gender, sexuality, and, 34; keeping women in submission to, 66; sexual violence and, 64, 100
natural disasters, 28, 68, 102
natural violence, 102, 140, 285n3; and sexual violence, 117–22, 122–23, 129, 130–31
neo-imperialism, 16, 44, 234, 271; destructive advance of, 265; domination and exploitation, 263; and *francophone* term, 6; movements against, 5; problems of, 263
Nora, Pierre: *lieu de mémoire*, 170
Nottage, Lynn: *Ruined*, 15–16, 206, 218–31, 232, 234, 236, 240, 242, 245, 254–55
Numa, Saint Arnaud: *Anacaona, Reine martyre*, 26, 276n27
N'Zengou-Tayo, Marie-José, 77, 82

objectification, 102, 260; disavowal of, 252–53; images of genocide and, 188; of intended subject, 231; land as vehicle for, 106; photographs and refusal to engage in, 193; subjectivity in place of, 142; of women, 118
Okeechobee hurricane, 119, 123, 136–37, 140
L'ombre d'Imana: Voyages jusqu'au bout du Rwanda (*The Shadow of Imana: Travels in the Heart of Rwanda*) (Tadjo), 15, 147–48, 150–51, 178, 203–4, 206; aesthetic of multiplicity in, 166–74, 206; *la femme ligotée* in, 168–71, 179
oppression: black women's, 37; class, 85; female, and political power, 276n13; gender, 71; national, 109; of plantocracy, 115; rape as gender-specific form of, 115; rape as tool of, 25; of Rwandese women, 149; sexed and gendered bodies as sites of, 44; from slavery, 104; and violent treatment of women, 82; women and confrontation by multiple forms of, 36; women as objects of, 47
Ouologuem, Yambo, 45, 46, 280n88; *Le devoir de violence*, 18, 23, 31–33, 46, 49, 156
Our Bodies Are Still Trembling (Institute for Justice and Democracy in Haiti), 61, 67–70

pain: black bodies in, 11; collision of with sex, female embodiment, and violence, 31; of Congolese women, 205–60; dialectics of healing, trauma and, 117; geography of, 148–52; incommunicability of, 11, 180; as political and personal, 46; and representation, 180; role of, 10; and subject forma-

tion, 11–12; and Tutsi women, 153; and violence, 43
passivity: and blame, 94; of raped women, 21
patriarchy, 109, 214, 225; critique of, 77; cultures of violence, 218; power operations of, 112
Peck, Raoul, 174, 184; *L'homme sur les quais*, 27; *Sometimes in April*, 15, 147–48, 150–51, 174–80, 199, 203–4
personhood, 187, 254; challenges posed to by conflict, 236; complex, 42; construction of, 206; and empathic connection, 205–6; and empathy, 256; female, negation of, 143; foreclosure of possibility of, 252; and politics of visibility and recognition, 189; rape, consent, and, 14; rape representations and, 40; self-actualization and, 122; undermining of, 210, 256; and victimhood, 259
photography, 193, 246; and affect, 181; and catastrophic events, 189; combination of testimony and, 152; and communication of incommunicable, 188; and communication of pain, 180; and emotion, 181; as form of rape representation, 181, 191; and genocide, 185; and politics of spectatorship, 181; and positioning, 186–87; as site of memory, 188; war, 253; wartime, avoidance of typical tropes of, 251
physical violence, 20, 34, 35; failure of language to capture, 147
Pineau, Gisèle, 6, 101–2, 114–16; *Chair Piment*, 114, 116–17; as female writer within Créolité movement, 113; *Femmes des Antilles: traces et voix*, 115; *L'âme pretée aux oiseaux*, 116; *L'espérance-macadam (Macadam Dreams)*, 15, 102–44; *L'exil selon Julia*, 116
Placide, Jaira, 14; *Fresh Girl*, 60–61, 83, 87–88, 100
pleasure, 93–94
Pluie et vent sur Télumée Miracle (Schwarz-Bart), 35–38, 143
political instability, sexual violence and, 62, 87
political rape, 14; boundaries entrenching, 94; rethinking, 57–100; as specifically gendered, 98; transcending to foreground politics of rape, 100
political violence, 40; and increase in sexual violence, 62
postcolonialism: development of state in, 21–22; epistemic violence of, 9; landscape of as feminized space, 15; regimes of, 23, 34; violence, 10, 21–22
postcolony, 22, 45
posttraumatic stress disorder (PTSD), 171, 280n91

power, 8, 43–44; construction of new circuits of, 5–6, 73–74; dynamics of, 90, 210, 255; Foucauldian understanding of, 44; global discourses of, 152; globalized, 263; machinations of sex, desire, victimization and, 92; negative nexus of, 36–37; patriarchal operations of, 112; politics of, 70, 264, 276n13; relations of, 11, 24, 33, 36, 213, 234; and slave system, 24, 25, 40; sexual dynamics of, 92–94, 98; spectacle, performance, and, 43; victims and destruction of, 43; and violence, 32, 43–44, 70, 93–94
prostitution, 221, 266, 284n54
protection, 63, 81, 230, 248

race/racism, 7, 23, 28–29, 107; identifications that traverse, 255; intersections of, 36–37, 113; as location of identity, 86; and slave system, 24, 40
Rajan, Rajeswari Sunder, 76, 288n14
rape: acceptance of, 47, 72; as bodily experience, 144, 170; and centrality of male subject, 35, 48–49; children born of, 198–99, 214; collective, 263, 265; collective failure to name, 71, 83, 86, 118, 240; during conflict and peacetime, 88, 154, 173, 203, 239; as crime against humanity, 203, 292n93; as crime of property, 109; and criminality, 62; cultural significance of, 10, 15, 19; culture of impunity in which no one is punished for, 250; as deviant behaviour, 98–99; dismantling of myths of, 69; as distilling possibility for dialogue about violence, 12–13; divergent multiple meanings of, 203; effects of on psyche, 179; elided, allegorized, or denied, 50, 231; erotic pleasure and desire as controversial topics in, 94; as ethnic cleansing, 292n93; as example of endemic violence of postcolonial regimes, 34; frequency of in world, 12, 240; gendered, sexed, and politicized context of, 2, 43; as gender-specific form of oppression, 115, 151; as global epidemic, 239; and human rights advocacy in twenty-first century, 261–71; as genocidal strategy, 152–54; as ignoring female subjectivity, 109; as impervious to sustained analysis, 47; as important cultural signifier for oppressor, 52; inaction and ignorance toward, 209; incorporation of into international human rights discourses, 12; as injury to masculinity, 150; insanity linked to violence of, 24; as institutionalized practice, 70; as integral to decolonization, 47; interracial vs. intraracial in U. S., 211; as keeping women

in submission to national project, 66; lack of media attention to, 219; lack of understanding of, 195; of land, metaphors of, 101–44, 149–50; marginalization of traumatic impact of, 48; as mark of disease or trauma, 133; of men or boys, 262, 264; men's reaction to, 239; as metaphor, 23, 29, 48, 58, 102–4, 112, 126; as metonymy, 22–23, 46, 48, 87, 91; as military strategy, 208; as more than sign or symbol, 39–40, 100; myths of, 136–41, 239, 286n56; narratives of, 86–87, 107; normalizing, denying, and analogizing, 42–49, 68; as obscured and ignored by other forms of violence, 72; pleasure and, 94; political, 11, 14, 57–100; and political conflict, 66–67, 69; politics of in postgenocide Rwanda, 202–4; psychological effects of, 213; public perception of vs. statistics on frequency of, 286n56; as punishment, 29, 64; rate of in Haiti, 27–28; reach of, 132–36; relativization and denial of subjective experience of, 49; remaking of subject in aftermath of, 86–87; repoliticization of, 61, 63, 70, 72, 83–100; rhetoric of, 42–43; and Rwandan genocide, 15, 145–204; sexual politics of, 63; sexual relations standing in for, 112; and slavery, 23–25, 114–15; social script for, 77, 98–99; societal and cultural responses to, 59, 208; as stench, stain and pestilent, 129; stigma of, 237; symbology of, 27, 42, 46, 49, 109; as tool of war, 205–60; underreporting of, 68; universality of, 241; unspoken nature of, 86; visibility, legibility and audibility of, 267; during war, 149, 152–54, 205–60; as war tactic, 211; as weapon, 1, 10, 70, 208; *See also* genocidal rape
Rape and Representation (Higgins and Silver), 50, 143
rape crisis advocacy, 8–9, 11, 236
rape cultural criticism, 2, 8–9, 11, 43, 49–52, 62
rape culture, 51, 68, 77, 88, 100, 216, 268, 292n6; discursive functioning of, 271; as global phenomenon, 52, 203; of silence, 51, 59, 62, 72, 82, 86, 87–88
rape discourses, global politics of, 1–16
rape-of-the-land metaphors, 101–44
rape representation, 6–10, 13, 16, 19, 35, 38, 45, 52, 59, 125, 154, 180, 268, 270; as alternative way of "thinking" Rwandan genocide, 148; and antiviolent black feminist politics, 16; and black women, 52; and colonial domination, 117; critical silence surrounding, 11; difficulties posed by, 36; in DRC as urtext for spectacle of sexual violence, 211; beyond empathy and sympathy, 254–60; feminist politics of, 141–44; genocidal, strategies of, 152–54; how vs. what of, 165; mapping critical tensions of, 131; metaphoric or symbolic role of female body in, 48; modalities of speech and voice in, 267; and new circuits of power and discourse, 73–74; other modes for in context of war, 254; and personhood, 40; photography as form of, 181; politics of, 69, 147; and reproduction of scripts of violence, 259; rhetorical and thematic tropes of, 235; social and cultural representations of, 50; tensions embedded in, 143; testimony and photography as modes of, 191; usefulness of documentary genre in, 207; wartime, avoidance of typical tropes of, 251; as way to engage trauma, 126; witnessing as new challenge for, 191

rape scripts, socially acceptable, 98–99
rape trauma syndrome, 10, 15, 60, 92–94, 97, 127, 129, 171, 179
Les recluses (Kwahulé), 16, 206, 231–46, 253–54, 255–56; as all-female production, 232; as avant-garde theatrical piece, 232, 246; Brussels performances of (2009), 294n49; enunciation as central to, 236–37; as feminist work, 231; fictitious vs. autobiographical nature of, 236; and Greek chorus, 232; and heterogeneity of women, 236; identity as multiply configured in, 246; male absence from, 232; masks in, 232, 234, 244; as multimedia performance, 241; music in, 245; projected images of testimonials in, 232, 236, 238, 241–42, 243; role of dialogue in, 232, 236, 244; role of staging in, 232; stigma of rape in, 237; struggle with genre of, 237; technology in, 232; as typical of Kwahulé's work, 234; as undermining spectator/spectacle dynamic, 234; *viol* not used in, 240
recognition: dynamics of, 209; politics of, 182, 185–86, 191, 192, 202, 254; spectatorship and, 191, 252
reconciliation, 167, 177–78, 232; truth and, 188; unwieldy project of, 181
remembering: as alternative to violence, 156; dialectics between forgetting and, 236
The Repeating Island (Benítez-Rojo), 15, 106–10
resilience: and black women's oppression, 37; tropes of, 28
resistance, 29, 74, 126, 174–80, 198; and black women's oppression, 37; and female slaves, 41; incomplete, 3; violations of women as instigation for, 47
revictimization, 11, 180, 263

Ruined (Nottage), 15–16, 206, 218–31, 232, 234, 236, 245, 254–55; conclusion of, 218, 230; critique and social commentary in, 219, 220; design and technical elements of, 220, 221; empathy and sympathy in, 231; feminism politics in, 224, 230; focus on female characters in, 218, 220; Huntington Theater Boston premiere of, 293n40; music in, 221; narrative strategy of, 218, 225; physical space of, 226; rape not explicitly staged in, 228, 240; and reception, 228; "speaking the unspeakable" in, 218, 223–24; undercutting of subjectivities in, 218, 231; use of word "ruined" in, 223–24; war as subtext of, 220–21

Rurangwa, Jean-Marie, 156, 160

Rwanda, 2, 157, 218; African writers from outside, 157; altering of image of in global imaginary, 146; children born of rape in, 198–99; collective memory in, 182; languages spoken in, 192; "mystification" of, 148; post-genocide, 195; violence in history of, 203; writing version of history for, 159

Rwanda: Écrire par devoir de mémoire, 156–61, 168; criticism of, 160–61; funding of, 159–60; list of contributors to, 289n32; manipulation of generic conventions by, 160; polyphonic structure of, 160; temporal shifts in, 160

Rwandan genocide, 15, 52, 145–204; and aesthetic of multiplicity, 166–74; African stakes of representations of, 154–56; dearth of commentary on and analysis of, 156; dialogic encounter with, 183–91; eclipsing of surrounding conflicts by, 209; as example of layered violence, 149, 191; as example of violence par excellence, 146; function of arts in global imagination after, 157; international guilt and anxiety about ignoring of, 202; international response to, 156; misconceptions and misrepresentations of, 157; as multilayered event, 182; multiple cinematic and literary representations of, 203, 291n91; mythologies of, 288n10; number of deaths in, 146; in photography, 180–202; politics of rape after, 202–4; prevalence of rape during, 152–53; rape as strategy during, 152–54; repercussions of, 148; rescripting of rape during, 148–52; and resistance, agency, and rape, 174–80; responding to and remembering through cultural production, 147, 155; role of non-Rwandese in communicating images of, 151, 157; silence surrounding, 150, 155, 191, 288n10; sites of, and seeing rape, 156–66; trivialization of experience of survivors of, 203–4; visual images of that err on side of objectification, 188; and visual production, 180–82; vocabulary of savagery in discourses of, 154–55

Rwandan Patriotic Front (RPF). *See* Front Patriotique Rwandais

Saisons sauvages (Mars), 60–61, 83, 88–99, 100, 103; as dictator novel, 95; interior monologue in, 89–90; intertextual relationship with *Amour, colère, folie*, 89, 99; poetics of erotic desire in, 89; political rape and victim-survivor's situated knowledge in, 89; power dynamics in, 90; rape trauma syndrome in, 92–93; as revision of *Colère*, 88

Scarry, Elaine, 11–12, 76; *The Body in Pain*, 288n14

Schwarz-Bart, Simone: *Pluie et vent sur Télumée Miracle*, 35–38, 42, 143

self-actualization, 103, 122, 126

self-recognition, 129, 215

Sembene, Ousmane, 29–31, 45; *Black Docker*, 277n37; *Faat Kiné*, 31; *Le camp de Thiaroye*, 29; *Les bouts de bois de Dieu*, 277n44; *Moolaadé*, 31; *Ô pays mon bon peuple!*, 29–30

Senghor, Léopold Sédar, 29, 31

sentimentality, 217, 255; emotion and in relation to black women's suffering, 207

sex, 10, 12, 16, 24, 19, 31, 40, 89, 92

sexual abuse, 60, 266; language of, 81

sexual dynamics, 45, 63, 89, 91, 94, 97–99, 109, 114, 131

sexuality, 7, 94; gender and, 34; intersections of, 93–94, 113; under slavery, 25

sexual politics, 42, 63, 64

sexual trauma, 93, 113, 143–44; healing from, 142; profundity of, 102

sexual violence: archival studies of, 15, 59–61; children and, 88; as complicating and enhancing female subjectivity, 150; as compromising humanity and human rights, 95; Condé and, 38; conflation of with political violence, 40; as constitutive element of subject formation, 116; construction of narratives of, 191; culture of silence surrounding, 131; denial of, 14; dynamics of, 44, 82; effects of on colonized men, 280n93; effects of on women's bodies, 102; emotional aftermath of, 171; expository act of writing, 122–31; extended to men or boys, 264; as facet of gender oppression, 69; francophone women writers and tropes of, 35–42; genealogies of in Haiti, 57–100; global incidence of, 9, 12; incidents of violence revolving around scene of, 12, 50; and increase in political violence, 62; as indicator of power relations of gender and sexuality, 36; as indistinguishable from other manifestations of violence, 46; interpreting and reacting to, 136–41; as issue of exchange among black and white men, 109–10; as justification for retaliatory violence, 48; lack of analysis surrounding, 49; as less painful and better alternative to other forms of violence, 71; material, physical, psychological, and social aspects of, 10, 60; material effects of, 126, 154; men as victims of, 281n113, 295n9; and natural violence, 117–22, 122–23, 129, 130–31; normalization of proliferation of, 46; obscured by nationalist narrative, 64; persistence of trauma of, 251; political instability and, 62–63; politics, power, and, 70; power and sexual dynamics of, 114; power relations structuring, 24, 33; as product and distraction from genocide, 165; psychological toll of, 154; reification of cultural silences surrounding, 63; re-imagining, re-theorizing, and prioritizing, 59, 82; re-veiling, through revealing violence, 108; revictimization of those who report, 263; rhetorical similarity of to genocide, 202; "ruined" as euphemism for, 224; slavery and, 23–25; social context of, 77, 80; socially informed silences surrounding, 98; stereotypes of, 210, 216; as taboo subject, 49; as tangential sign of deviance, 32; and terrorism, 2–3; as weapon of war, 267

shame, 32, 90, 92–93, 97, 126, 132, 153, 163, 213, 234, 237

Sharpley-Whiting, Tracey, 7, 18, 276n6, 277n37, 280n93

Sielke, Sabine, 47, 51, 279n76

silence: breaking of, 235; cultural, in response to gender violence, 12, 63; culture of preexisting, 71; in Danticat, 83; discursive, 107; as discursive practice for anti-rape advocacy, 208; around incest, 117; as index of pain, 224; interpretation of, 208–9; productive, 25, 184, 187, 224; of rape as pleonasm, 53; rape culture of, 51, 59, 62, 72, 82, 86, 131; structural presence and narrative significance of, 209; surrounding rape representation, 11, 68; around Rwandan genocide, 150, 155, 191; and subaltern identity, 273n 8; surrounding sexual violence, 208; of survivor, 33, 208; survivors forced into, 208; traumatic, 12; tropes of, 11; and voice, 62, 122; and women's experiences of violence, 82

Silver, Brenda, 1, 50

Skloot, Robert, 205, 219, 237

slavery, 9–11, 13, 23–25, 28–29, 42–45, 52, 55, 62, 110–11; gendered oppression of, 25; gender violence as wrath against, 49; heritage of, 24, 45; race, gender, sex, and power at work in, 40–41; rape and, 23–25, 29, 114–15, 204; and site of gendered body, 50; woman as land trope in context of, 114; women as worst victims of, 24

Sometimes in April (Peck), 15, 147–48, 150–51, 174–80, 199, 203–4

Sontag, Susan, 189, 220; *Regarding the Pain of Others*, 207, 246, 252

Sor Rose, 26, 57–60, 65

spectacularity, 211, 260, 266

spectacularization, of women's bodies, 254, 260

spectatorship: and human rights advocacy, 253; and national discourses, 266; politics of, 181, 185; positioning of, 234, 253; and recognition, 191, 252; and spectacle, 234, 252; sympathetic, 231; and testimony, 192; undoing traditional relations of, 201; and viewed subjects, 201

Spivak, Gayatri, 213, 273n8

standpoint theory, 7–8, 275n31

state terror: sexual dynamics of, 97–98; women subjugated to, 95

"subaltern speaking," 2, 5, 207–18, 254; directly to West, 209–10

subaltern subject: misrepresentation and affective denial of, 206, 254; speaking to West, 209–10; and visibility, vocality, and agency, 260

subaltern survivor: ability of to feel, 254; silence of, 254–55

subaltern women, as victims of "backward" regimes of Global South, 219

subject: dissolution of, 236; embodied, 137; erasure, 16, 234; formation of, 10–12, 116, 132, 237, 256; individuated, 251; positioning, 35–36, 48, 179, 253–54; subaltern, 206

subjecthood, 285n8; erasing of when subjection occurs, 43

subjective experience, 43; passed over in favour of discourse of sexual violence, 46

subjectivity/subjectivities, 3, 36, 44, 86, 113, 150, 178–80, 192, 217, 220, 247, 254, 267; affirmation of women's, 102, 254; black female, 280n93; compromising of, 120; disavowal of, 43; female, 30–31, 39, 54, 109, 117, 126, 143–44, 150; location of within portrayal of violence, 148–49; material body and, 103; of narratives, 171; power and bodily implications of, 103; power dynamics infringing upon, 255; privileging of embodied, 9; reality of victim's, 44; tenuous nature of, 43; textured elaborations of, 267; undercutting production of, 218, 231; of victim-survivors, 137, 174, 206, 208; and violence, 21, 43; vs. objectification, 142

subjugation: of African women, 5, 217; of knowledge, 254–56, 257, 264

submission, 43, 66, 106, 127

suffering, 37, 206, 220, 223, 263; of black women, 207, 212, 262, 267; of Congolese women, 231, 256–58; documentation of, 246; exoticization of, 246; fetishized and commodified signs of, 253; spectacle of, 172, 180, 192–95, 253; use of spectacle to relay, 251–52; visual iconography of, 247

survival: burden of, 189; difficulty of, 232; female, 230; tropes of, 28

survivors: teleological construction of victims and, 5; upsetting of static relationship between victims and, 94; violence and effects on, 72. *See also* victim-survivors

sympathy: children and generation of, 251; exploitation of gendering of, 217; in *The Greatest Silence*, 212, 218; representation of wartime rape beyond, 254–60; rhetorical significance of, 206; in *Ruined*, 231; spectator, 212; vs. empathy, 212

Tadjo, Véronique , 156, 167–68, 172, 176, 177, 184, 195, 259; *L'ombre d'imana*, 15, 147–48, 150–51, 166–74, 178, 203–4, 206

Tansi, Sony Labou, 33–34; *La vie et demie*, 34, 45; *Les sept solitudes de Lorsa Lopez*, 278n57

la terre violée, 15, 48, 102, 104

testimony/testimonials, 151–52, 153, 162, 165–66, 177, 191, 212, 236, 238, 241–42, 257; as acceptable purveyors of "real," 192; combination of photography and, 152; dialectics of, 166; human rights, 177–78; instability of genre of, 236; and logic of humanity, 192; as mode of rape representation, 191; rethinking genre of, 193; role of in representations of suffering, 192; as socially constructed and constituted, 191; transactional nature of, 164; traumatic, 191; and truth telling, 187–88

theater: and creation of empathy, 205; as medium for relating stories of war, 219; role of in addressing atrocity, 237; and possibility of healing and understanding, 237

Third World women: positionalities 3; construction of in opposition to white western women, 210; distance between rape victim-survivors and Western counterparts, 217; neocolonial scripts about First World women as fundamental to liberation of, 210

Thomas, Dominic, 34, 232, 234

Tinsley, Omi'seke Natasha, 7, 94, 104, 110, 111, 113, 137

Tontons Macoutes, 64, 71, 83–84, 283n38

torture, 34, 44; intricacies of war and, 12; rape as form of, 12

tradition: vs. modernity, 29; and violence, 32, 107

transnational global feminism, 2, 7–8, 12, 149, 210, 217, 267

trauma: accompanying layers of violence, 171; and confrontation with history, 110–11; dialectics of pain, healing and, 117; discourses of, 25; healing from, 142; history and language as fundamental products of, 110; important role of in fictive and historic texts, 61–62; of incest, 103, 134–35; as ineradicable mark, 134, 140; language of, 81; lasting ability of, 134–35; legacy of, 110; and memory, 83, 203; problematics of, 203; secondary, 133, 192; sexual, 87–88, 93, 102, 134, 142–44; sexual violence illuminating life of, 38; silence as response to, 209; speaking for personal history of, 159; studies, 13, 151; translation of into text, 158; translation of through multifaceted techniques, 168; vicarious, 132–36, 143; and violence, 14. *See also* rape trauma syndrome

trauma studies, 13, 151

Trouillot, Evelyne, 36; *Rosalie l'infâme*, 25, 40–42, 60

Trouillot, Michel-Rolph, 64, 65; *Haiti: State against Nation*, 64

truth: claims of feminism, 8; construction of, 155; contested nature of, 161; and reconciliation, 188; unstable quality of in testimony, 187–88, 192

Tutsis, 146, 153, 173, 194, 199

Ulysse, Gina, 68, 269

United Nations peacekeeping. *See* MINUSTAH

United States: call for end to violence in Rwanda by, 146; frequency of rape in, 12; inaction of in Rwanda, 202; interracial vs. intraracial rape incidence in, 211; occupation of Haiti, 27, 62, 63, 276n28; troops' responsibility for war crimes against women, 282n12

victimhood: discursive framing of, 263; personhood and, 259
victimization: boundary between agency and, 94; childhood, narratives of, 252; double, 188; gendered, 263; machinations of power, desire, sex and, 92; narratives of, 51; narratives of rape focusing on, 93; shift of focus from, 247
victims: and destruction of power, 43; domination of, 44; effects of violence upon, 44; empowerment of, 44; teleological construction of survivors and, 5; upsetting of static relationship between survivors and, 94; and victimizers, 193
victim-survivors: ability of to speak of rape, 241; as citizen-subjects, 264; collective vision for rehabilitation of, 198; difficulty of relating testimonies of with fidelity, 202; and disassociation, 126; distance between Third World and Western, 217; double victimization of, 188; embodied and subjective experiences of, 61; as female subjects, 35; as focus of violence, 6, 59; foregrounding perspectives of, 102; identity and rights of, 263; justice sought by, 68; opposition of, 208; as part of reconciliation process, 177; potential of for subjectivity, 137; and rape trauma syndrome, 92–93, 129–30; refusal to objectify, 193, 260; refusal to spectacularize, 260; revictimization of, 203; situated knowledge of, 89, 94; social script for treatment of, 77; specificity of rape experiences of, 143; strategies of for moving beyond rape, 69; subjective experience of, 43; subjectivity of, 8, 150, 174, 178–79, 206, 208; testimonies of, 102; voices of, 236
Victor, Gary: *Le diable dans un thé à la citronnelle*, 60, 284n51
Vieux-Chauvet, Marie: *Amour, colère, folie*, 14, 58–61, 70–83, 88–89, 94–95, 98–100, 103; as antecedent to Danticat, 83; daring use of sexuality by, 71; exile of, 71; *Fille d'Haïti*, 283n34; legacy of, 59
violated body, 45–46
violation: acts of as gendered and structured according to power relations, 11; as atrocity of slavery, 28; as deliberately disturbing culture of silence obscuring rape, 59; as gender specific form of punishment, 34; and informing elaboration of female subject, 38; and political conflict, 87; reinscription of patriarchal systems of, 19
le viol dans la violence, 19, 26, 55–56; etymology of, 56; masculine and feminine as encoding understanding of, 56; neutering of, 281n113
violence, 20, 31; by Africans unto other Africans, 32; as African theme, 159; African traditions and power founded on, 31; anticolonial, 14, 20; and autocratic governments, 43; being bound to, 18–26, 46; bodies chained to, 18, 112; challenges in cultural production of, 149; challenging hegemony of discourses of, 99–100; colonial, 8, 18, 22, 26, 32, 38, 43, 45, 46, 104, 107; endemic, 34; epistemic, 9–11, 14, 35, 46; epistemologies of, 99, 147; "exterior" mode of, 44–45; familiar, 54; focus on men's reactions to, 32, 47; focus on perpetrator of, 43, 47; as glorified and romanticized, 26; and government corruption, 40; in Haitian politics, 27; and historical struggle in Cameroon, 22; history and culture intertwined with, 55, 108; ideological subtext of, 42–44, 46; human and natural, 143; and imperial authority, 43; institutionalization of through codified practices, 85; as integral to Caribbean francophone literature, 55; "interior" mode of, 44–45; and land in DRC, 215–16; and landscape in postcolonial Caribbean discourses, 106–11; linguistic, 34; material, 34, 51, 147; native, 20, 46; natural and sexual, 102, 117–22, 122–23, 129, 130–31; neo-colonial, 23, 104; and neo-imperialism, 44; nexus of power, sexuality, pleasure and, 93–94; physical, 20, 34, 35, 147; postcolonial, 8, 18, 38, 104; in postcolonial context, 9, 10, 22–23, 32; precolonial origins of, 31–32, 46; private, 262; psychological, 20, 34, 79; rape as core form of, 11; rape as effective way of understanding, 11; rape as paradigmatic form of, 52; rape in theorizations of, 22; representation of, 33, 35, 147, 167, 268; rescripting and re-inscription of, 108; retaliatory forms of motivated by violations, 47; slavery and, 44–45; state-sponsored, 33; structural, 28–29, 34; subjective experience of, 21, 35, 43–44; symbolic use of against women, 28; as technology of power, 44; "universal," 36; vocabularies of, 42–48; vs. genocide, 146–47. *See also* gender violence; sexual violence

visibility: optics of, 254; politics of, 191, 192; in studies of the subaltern, 260; voice and, 189

Walcott, Derek, 107; *Drums and Colours*, 107
Walcott-Hackshaw, Elizabeth, 70, 106
Wanzo, Rebecca: *The Suffering Will Not Be Televised: African American Women and Sentimental Political Story Telling*, 207, 212, 217
white men: domination of over feminized landscape, 49; power dynamics between black men and, 110; relations with as sign of alienation, 47; as sources of violence, 36
Whoriskey, Kate, 219, 237
witnessing, 151–52, 153, 157, 186, 191, 192, 209; affective politics of, 209; dialectics of, 166; and secondary trauma, 192; voyeuristic, 238
Wittig, Monique: *Les guerillères*, 294n47
women: as acting subjects vs. raped objects, 5; activist engagement of, 259, 269; end of violence against as essential to freedom, 3; feminist renderings of as land, 111–17; as hapless victims of war, 230; as legal property of slave owners, 109; as most common targets of violence, 102; pain of in DRC, 205–60; physically disabled, 218; psychological undoing of, 82; rape of in DRC, 1–5, 205–60; role of as perpetrators of war crimes, 196; sex trafficking and destruction of mobility of, 267; as signifier for nation, 109; silence as obscuring and ignoring violence against, 71, 82; social exclusion of raped, 236; "subaltern," as victims of "backward" regimes of Global South, 219; subjective experiences of rape, 72; and subject positioning, 36, 48, 179, 254; as subjects in charge of own sexuality, 112–13; subjugated to state terror, 95; symbolic use of violence against, 28; as symbols and icons for national identity, 48; as targets of rape warfare, 150; Third World vs. First World, 210; treatment of under slavery, 25; as violated or raped land, 104; violence against as institutionalized through codified practices, 85; violence against by other women, 19; as worst victims of slavery, 24. *See also* bodies, women's; black women
Women and War: Gender Identity and Activism in Times of Conflict, 149
women's rights: in Haiti, 269; as human rights, 3

Zobel, Joseph, 45; *La rue Cases-Nègres*, 28–29, 104, 115

TRANSOCEANIC STUDIES
Ileana Rodríguez, Series Editor

The Transoceanic Studies series rests on the assumption of a one-world system. This system—simultaneously modern and colonial and now postmodern and postcolonial (global)—profoundly restructured the world, displaced the Mediterranean *mare nostrum* as a center of power and knowledge, and constructed dis-centered, transoceanic, waterways that reached across the world. The vast imaginary undergirding this system was Eurocentric in nature and intent. Europe was viewed as the sole culture-producing center. But Eurocentrism, theorized as the "coloniality of power" and "of knowledge," was contested from its inception, generating a rich, enormous, alternate corpus. In disputing Eurocentrism, books in this series will acknowledge above all the contributions coming from other areas of the world, colonial and postcolonial, without which neither the aspirations to universalism put forth by the Enlightenment nor those of globalization promoted by postmodernism will be fulfilled.

National Consciousness and Literary Cosmopolitics: Postcolonial Literature in a Global Moment
    WEIHSIN GUI

Writing AIDS: (Re)Conceptualizing the Individual and Social Body in Spanish American Literature
    JODIE PARYS

Learning to Unlearn: Decolonial Reflections from Eurasia and the Americas
    MADINA V. TLOSTANOVA AND WALTER D. MIGNOLO

Oriental Shadows: The Presence of the East in Early American Literature
    JIM EGAN

www.ingramcontent.com/pod-product-compliance
Lightning Source LLC
Chambersburg PA
CBHW030909040526
R18240000001B/R182400PG44116CBX00010B/9